# Islam in Modern Asia

# Islam in Modern Asia

by

I.K. Khan

MD Publications Pvt Ltd
New Delhi

*Published by*

**MD Publications Pvt Ltd**
B/231-E, Greater Kailash - I
New Delhi-110048.
E-mail : contact@mdppl.com
Website : www.mdppl.com

*Showroom*

"MD House"
11, Darya Ganj
New Delhi-110002
Tel. : +91-11-23268645, 23271378
Fax : +91-11-29235450

ISBN 81-7533-094-5



*Printed by*

Times Press
910, Jatwara Street, Darya Ganj
New Delhi-110002.

# Contents

# Preface

A religion, founded by Muhammad, whose members worship the one God of Jews and Christians and follow the teachings of the Koran. *Islam* means "submission to the will of God"; adherents of Islam are called Muslims. The fundamental belief of Islam is "There is only one God, and Muhammad is his prophet." Muslims are obliged to pray five times a day, to fast in the daytime during the holy month of Ramadan, to abstain from pork and alcohol, and to make gifts to the poor. All of them are expected to make a pilgrimage to Mecca, Muhammad's birthplace. at least once in their lives.

There are more than 1 billion Muslims worldwide, fewer than one fifth of whom are Arab. Islam is the principal religion of much of Asia, including Indonesia (which has the world's largest Muslim population), Malaysia, Pakistan, Bangladesh, Afghanistan, Azerbaijan, Turkmenistan, Uzbekistan, Tajikistan, Kyrgyzstan, Kazakhstan, Iran, Iraq, Syria, Jordan, the Arabian Peninsula states, and Turkey. India also has one of the world's largest Muslim populations, although Islam is not the principal religion there. In Africa, Islam is the principal religion in Egypt, Algeria, Tunisia, Djibouti, Gambia, Guinea, Libya, Mali, Mauritania, Morocco, Niger, Senegal, Somalia, and Sudan, with sizable populations also in Chad, Eritrea, Ethiopia, Ghana, Tanzania (where the island of Zanzibar is predominantly Muslim), and Nigeria.

The ethos of Islam is in its attitude toward Allah: to His will Muslims submit; Him they praise and glorify; and in Him alone they hope. However, in popular or folk forms of Islam, Muslims ask intercession of the saints, prophets, and angels, while preserving the distinction between Creator and creature. Islam views the Message of Muhammad as the continuation and the fulfillment of a lineage of Prophecy that includes figures from the Hebrew Scriptures and the New Testament, notably Adam, Noah, Abraham, Moses, David, and Jesus. Islamic law reserves a communal entity status for the *ahl al-kitab,* People of the Book, i.e., those with revealed religions, including Jews and Christians. Islam also recognizes a number of extra-biblical prophets, such as Hud, Salih, Shuayb, and others of more obscure origin. The chief angels are Gabriel and Michael; devils are the evil jinn.

Other Islamic obligations include the duty to "commend good and reprimand evil," injunctions against usury and gambling, and prohibitions of alcohol and pork. Meat is permitted if the animal was ritually slaughtered; it is then called *halal. Jihad,* the exertion of efforts for the cause of God, is a duty satisfied at the communal and the individual level. At the individual level, it denotes the personal struggle to be righteous and follow the path ordained by God. Communally, it involves both encouraging what is good and correcting what is not and waging war against enemies of Islam.

In Islam, religion and social membership are inseparable: the ruler of the community has both a religious and a political status. The unitary nature of Islam, as a system governing relations between a person and God, and a person and society, has contributed to the appeal and success of Islam.

# 1

# Islam in Asia: An Introduction

## Overview

The most obvious causes of this world-changing transformation were the collapse of communism in Eastern Europe and the end of the cold war. In the aftermath of these events, the Western media were full of commentaries attempting to explain the causes and consequences of what had taken place. Some observers saw the events as evidence of an unprecedented shift in world politics, a veritable "end to history" as we know it. The defining feature of this development, at least as described by Francis Fukuyama, was an end to the ideological struggles that had marked the late modern era and a new international consensus on the virtues of democratic governance and market-oriented development.

Unfortunately for this prognosis, world events quickly proved that, however much it might have marked the close of one era, this end of history was really just the beginning of another, animated by its own passions and polarities. The communist collapse was accompanied by growing ethnic, religious, and national conflict in the countries of the former Eastern Bloc as well as in much of the developing world. The genocide in Ruanda, the brutalization of Bosnia, religious and ethnic struggles in the Caucuses, interreligious strife in India — these and other conflicts served as painful reminders that, contrary to some optimistic ruminations, politics in much of the world had not yet reached a consensus on the means and ends of the modern age.

The intensity of international conflict eventually led other Western commentators to pull back from the optimistic forecasts of the immediate post-cold war era. Where before there was talk of a triumphant end to history, one now heard ominous predictions of a coming "clash of civilizations." In a widely read article published in Foreign Affairs in the summer of 1993, for example, the senior political scientist and State Department advisor Samuel Huntington suggested that international politics in the postcold war era would be shaped not by modern ideology or economic interests, but by deeply irreconcilable "civilizational identities." "The fault lines between civilizations," Huntington observed, "are replacing the political and ideological boundaries of the Cold War as the flash points for crisis and bloodshed". Among the most likely trouble spots on the horizon, Huntington advised, was the Muslim world. "Conflict along the fault line between Western and Islamic civilizations has been going on for 1,300 years," he warned, citing the briefest of evidence to buttress this astounding claim, and in the future this "military interaction between the West and Islam is unlikely to decline".

Against this backdrop of international ferment, in general, and Western anxiety as to the political future of the Muslim world, in particular, the authors of these essays came together to discuss Islam and nation building in the Southeast Asian nations of Indonesia, Malaysia, and the Philippines. In simple geographic terms insular Southeast Asia lies far from the Middle Eastern terrains conventionally associated in Westerners' minds with Islam. Indeed, many Middle Eastern Muslims are unfamiliar with Southeast Asia or uncertain as to the precise character of their fellow believers' faith. Notwithstanding this unfamiliarity, Southeast Asia is home to the most populous majority-Muslim country in the world and contains an aggregate Muslim population greater than the Arab Middle East. The study of Islam in Southeast Asia thus presents an opportunity to deepen our understanding of the Muslim world's diversity and to challenge unitary characterizations of Islam's civilizational identity. Equally important, given the tenor of our times, this exercise allows us to disengage Muslim politics from histories and circumstances that owe more to the peculiarities of the Middle East than to Islam itself. All this is to say that Muslim Southeast Asia provides us with a much-needed opportunity to reevaluate the varied political potentialities of Islam in the modern era.

For the contributors to this volume, the more immediate benefit of such an intellectual inquiry is that it allows us to deepen our understanding of Islam in Southeast Asia in its own right. The nations in which Muslim Southeast Asians reside are characterized by extraordinary cultural and linguistic variety. Stretching across Indonesia, Malaysia, Singapore, southern Thailand, Brunei, and the southern Philippines, this region contains hundreds of ethnic groups, a similar variety of languages, representatives from most of the world's historic religions, and numerous tribal and localized traditions. Perhaps because of this dizzying diversity, Western scholars have until recently paid relatively little attention to Islam in Southeast Asia. Several years ago William Roff may have been guilty of hyperbole when he wrote that "there seems to have been an extraordinary desire on the part of Western social science observers to diminish, conceptually, the place and role of the religion and culture of Islam...in Southeast Asian societies". But Roff's remark accurately conveys the conviction among many observers, Western and Southeast Asian, that Islam's influence on Southeast Asian society has been severely underestimated.

Recent developments in this region have made clear that such a neglect can no longer be justified. The economies of the two largest majority – Muslim countries in Southeast Asia, Malaysia and Indonesia, are today among the most rapidly growing in the world. Their economic dynamism has given both nations a heightened prominence in international affairs. Equally important, it has earned them the respect of Muslim leaders elsewhere in the world, many of whom have begun to wonder whether Southeast Asia might provide clues on how to manage market economies and cultural pluralism.

More significantly for the authors in this book, Islam in Southeast Asia can no longer be overlooked because since the late 1970s this region has experienced an unprecedented religious resurgence. Mosques have proliferated in towns and villages; religious schools and devotional programs have expanded; a vast market in Islamic books, magazines, and newspapers has developed; and, very important, a well-educated Muslim middle class has begun to raise questions about characteristically modern concerns, including the role and rights of women, the challenge of pluralism, the merits of market economies, and, most generally, the proper relationship of religion to state.

There have been many influences on this religious resurgence. Internationally, such developments as the Iranian revolution, the growth of Middle Eastern economic power since the 1970s, and the recent disenchantment in much of the Muslim world with secular nationalism have all played a role. However, at the center of all developments affecting Southeast Asian Islam looms one key institution: the modern nation-state. However rich its precedents, varied its influences, and diverse its motivations, the Islamic resurgence in Southeast Asia bears the imprint of this distinctly modern institution, with its projects for economic development and a state-shaped citizenry.

Though its policies and programs vary widely across national boundaries, the state in Southeast Asia, as in much of the modern world, has an "infrastructural reach" far greater than the traditional states that once predominated throughout this region. Its capacity to shape public affairs and intervene in the most intimate domains of private life has presented Southeast Asian Muslims with a historically unprecedented challenge. It has reduced the territorial fragmentation long characteristic of this region, undercut the autonomy of Muslim social organizations, and, at times, deployed its forces to hunt down and eliminate Muslim rebels. For many political Muslims, however, there is also a romantic allure to this modern institution. Whatever its current uses, the state appears to offer the means for realizing long cherished dreams of religious and social transformation on a societywide scale. The idea of the nation has thus captured the Islamic imagination and intensified debate on what Muslim society should become.

The resurgence also bears the imprint of something more uniquely Islamic: the emergence of a new style of religious activism that supplants or marginalizes the classically educated scholars of traditional Islam in favor of, as Dale E Eickelman has described it, "religious and political activists who seek open religious discussion and whose authority is based upon persuasion and the interpretation of accessible texts". Though its precise influences vary from nation to nation, the ascent of these "new Muslim intellectuals" with their untraditional training and unconventional concerns is everywhere related to urbanization, mass education, new print and electronic media, and the growth of a Muslim middle class. These new movements build, of course, on the struggles of an earlier generation of Muslim reformers, who sought to open the door of religious interpretation (ijtihad) and make Islam responsive to the demands of the modern world, including the threat posed by the West. A century after the appearance of reformist Islam, however, developments in majority – Muslim nationstates have worked to create a new kind of Muslim discourse and a new kind of renewalist dynamic. The new discourse of renewal is oriented to the needs of a broad, mass-educated public rather than a narrow circle of religious adepts. In place of esoteric doctrine, the spokespersons for this reformation conceive of Islam in modern, quasi-ideological terms, as a source of practical and systematic knowledge "that can be differentiated from others and consciously reworked". This shift in religious rhetoric and its relevances is one more symptom of an Islam reinterpreted in the altered circumstances of the nation-state, national "publics," and the media that sustain both.

Though some Western and even Muslim observers speak as if they were a unitary phenomenon, these new Muslim groups do not speak with a single voice. On the contrary, one of the most striking features of the contemporary revival here in Southeast Asia is the diversity of its adherents and the vitality of its debate. Admittedly, the region has its radical militants and others who seem to conform to Western stereotypes of Islamic "fundamentalism." And, more generally, as in many other parts of the Muslim world, the resurgence has been characterized by intense "competition and contest over both the interpretation of symbols and control of the institutions...that produce and sustain them". However, here in Southeast Asia, the dominant discourse to emerge from this contest has been marked not by theological totalism or strident authoritarianism, but by a remarkable combination of pluralism, intellectual dynamism, and openness to dialogue with non-Muslim actors and institutions.

However varied their emphases, most of these new Muslim intellectuals agree in their commitment to a developmental or activist understanding of their faith. Most show little enthusiasm for an Islam that is just a matter of pietistic study, personal morality, and ritual celebrations. Such conventional indices of religiosity remain important. But for new Muslim intellectuals and their followers, Islam must entail more than personal piety and public devotion. It must offer an alternative model of politics. It should provide moral discipline in the face of the anarchy and hedonism of the market. It can run schools, operate banks, and organize farmers' cooperatives. It may even provide an alternative, some say, to secular nationalism as the moral basis of the national community.

Unsympathetic observers might dismiss all this as the mere ideologization of religion. What is occurring, these critics might suggest, is the subordination of religion to the political needs of the moment or, worse yet, the ambitions of an unscrupulous leadership. Certainly there is such contestation and intrigue, as is the case whenever ethical ideas are drawn into the public sphere. But in Southeast Asia events have forced Muslims to confront a host of new questions and, in at least some instances, formulate new answers. Can Islam contribute to economic development? What posture should it adopt toward business and the market? And what of the status of women? The rights of non-Muslims? Is Islam compatible with pluralism and representative democracy? These questions emerge not from timeless theological doctrines, but from the efforts of Muslims to respond to the challenge of the nation-state and its associated projects for political and moral reconstruction.

Though Southeast Asian Muslims engage these issues with many of the scriptural, exegetical, and legal resources found elsewhere in the Muslim world, they do so within a social and historical horizon quite different from that of the Middle East. Their responses thereby reflect the creative tension everywhere characteristic of Islam (and, it should be said, all world religions) between the transcendent imperatives of the religion, as locally understood, and local histories, cultures, and identities. The latter heritage predisposes Muslims to selectively highlight certain elements of that heritage while neglecting others. Such a creative tension is reflected in the essays in this volume. To understand its politics and meanings, we have to look into the history of Islam in this region and examine our own understandings or, as the case may be, misunderstandings of that history.

## Dual Marginalization

One of the most serious impediments to the development of a systematic understanding of Islam in Southeast Asia is the fact that the topic has long been marginalized in the fields of Islamic and Southeast Asian studies. In Islamic studies Western and Middle Eastern scholars alike have tended to place Southeast Asia at the intellectual periphery of the Islamic world. Still today in some overviews of Islamic history and civilization, Southeast Asian Muslims are mentioned briefly if at all. Though Southeast Asian Islam has almost two hundred million believers, it is not uncommon for observers, even learned specialists, to identify Islam with the Middle East and to regard Southeast Asia as, at best, intellectually and institutionally derivative of Middle Eastern Islam.

There is a larger and, in one sense, understandable logic to this neglect. By comparison to Persia and the Arabian heartland, in insular Southeast Asia Islam became a civilizational force relatively late in Islamic history. Though Arab-Muslim traders traveled through island Southeast Asia as early as the seventh and eighth centuries, there was little settlement until the late thirteenth, when a Muslim town, inhabited in part by Arab-speaking foreigners, was established in the Pasai region of north Sumatra, an entrepôt for the trade with Muslim India and Arabia. Shortly thereafter, a Muslim presence appears to have been established in port towns along Java's north coast, territories still then under the control of the Hindu-Buddhist kingdom of Majapahit. Ruling elites in the Malay peninsula were converted in the fifteenth and sixteenth centuries, and those in coastal Sulawesi and much of the southern Philippines were won to the faith in the seventeenth and eighteenth centuries.

The primary impetus for this wave of conversion was not conquest or religious warfare, as had been the case in Islam's early expansion in Arabia and North Africa, but trade and interethnic intercourse. Certainly, as Anthony Reid has noted, Muslim potentates (like their Theravada Buddhist counterparts in mainland Southeast Asia) regarded forcible conversion of neighbors as "an honourable motive for conquest", and Muslim rulers periodically engaged in warfare with their Hindu-Buddhist, animist, or, in later times, Christian neighbors. However, as Thomas McKenna's essay in this volume illustrates, the causes of these conflicts were as much commercial and dynastic as they were religious.

More decisively, the rapid and relatively uniform spread of Islam to the insular world's maritime centers was related to broader historical developments, especially the growth of international commerce from the fifteenth to seventeenth centuries and the movement of large numbers of people out of localized societies into a multiethnic and interregional macrocosm. Most of the map of modern Muslim Southeast Asia was laid out during this "age of commerce," as Anthony Reid has so aptly described it. A few remote corners of Southeast Asia have been converted to Islam in this century, some even in the last decades. In general, however, the dynamism of Islam in contemporary times has had less to do with a new wave of conversion than with the reform and rationalization of religion among established Muslim populations.

By itself, the comparatively late arrival of Islam in Southeast Asia neither explains nor justifies this region's marginalization within the field of Islamic studies. Given the genesis of what has come to be regarded as "classical" Islamic civilization within the Arabic- and Persian-speaking world, however, there was a tendency on the part of early Western Islamicists to devote their attention to regions where the classical tradition was first composed. This emphasis was reinforced by the focus of this early scholarship on Islamic "culture," not in the modern, social-historical or anthropological sense of this term, but in its great-traditional sense, as in written literature, philosophy, art and architecture, and law. With several notable exceptions, the Orientalist commentaries that introduced Islamic civilization to a Western readership in the late nineteenth and early twentieth centuries were concerned with high culture, not the everyday meaning of Islam for ordinary Muslims. The focus of this writing was leading thinkers and civilizationwide achievements, especially those preserved for time in the printed word.

As a result of this textual emphasis, Southeast Asia — and other areas marginalized in the Orientalist understanding of the Muslim world, such as Central Asia, Bengal, and West Africa — was accorded only a minor role in early accounts of Islamic civilization. In some subfields of Islamic studies, such as jurisprudence (fiqh), this perception of Southeast Asia as a latecomer and bit player in

Islamic civilization seemed justified. As Hooker has noted, from the sixteenth century onward Muslim scholars in Southeast Asia were familiar with the standard works of Shafii law (one of the four schools of Sunni Muslim jurisprudence and the one most commonly applied in Southeast Asia). But local jurists confined their activities to the translation and interpretation of legal traditions codified in the Middle East; they never made an independent, distinctly Southeast Asian contribution to Islamic law. Equally important, the Shafii works familiar to Southeast Asian jurists were never used as the sole basis for legal deliberations in Southeast Asia's sultanates. Local potentates used a variety of legal systems, as was consistent with the cultural pluralism of their subjects.

This lack of originality in legal scholarship (if not legal practice), however, still tells us little about the ways in which Islam became part of the culture and lifeways of Southeast Asian Muslims. To understand this process requires that we distance ourselves from the legalistic, "shariahcentered" understanding of Islam that predominates in classical scholarship, Western and Muslim, and examine Islam in its local and regional context. From this perspective the diffusion of Islam into Southeast Asia looks more richly distinctive.

The first centuries of the Islamic expansion into Southeast Asia coincided with an era of great Sufi influence in Mecca, Medina, and northern India. Not coincidentally, then, mystic literature and practices were conspicuous among the items first appropriated into popular Islamic culture in Southeast Asia. As Anthony Johns has noted, the Sufi role in early Southeast Asian Islam was facilitated by the religious traditions already established in the region, which had an elective affinity with certain aspects of Sufism. Most notable among these affinities was the monist disposition of many of this region's existing religious traditions, with their idea that rather than standing apart from this world, divinity infuses it.

The Southeast Asian response to Islamic mysticism was not passive or derivative, but complex and creative. In the works of such learned mystics as Hamzah Fansuri and Abd. al-Rauf, Southeast Asian Muslims developed a literary and intellectualized variant of Islamic mysticism among the richest in the world. The impact of this thought reached far beyond esoteric circles, providing popular devotion with a nonlegalistic disposition and influencing the practice and meanings of kingship. In court-based variants of this Southeast Asian Muslim tradition, the ruler, rather than independent religious scholars (ulama), came to be seen as the mystical anchor of the religious community. He was the defender of the faith, the shadow of Allah on earth, and a mystically powerful "perfect man." By virtue of his spiritual preeminence, he, not the ulama, was responsible for the transmission and implementation of Islamic law. This prerogative provided rulers with discretionary leeway in deciding how strictly they wished to apply Islamic law. Though at times in early modern history (from the fifteenth to eighteenth centuries) ulama attempted to assert their authority against that of the court, sometimes in alliance with merchants hoping to limit the absolutist claims of rulers, the more general pattern resembled that Milner has described for Malay sultanates: "The Raja, not the Malay race or the Islamic ummat (community), was the primary object of loyalty". And the raja himself was usually concerned with worldly interests more varied than the unitary conduct of worship and law.

Here, then, is at least one clue to the way in which the univeralist injunctions of Islam were accommodated to Southeast Asian culture. In modern times, however, our appreciation of this tradition's distinctiveness in Islamic civilization has been hampered by the obscurity of its literary sources and the embarrassment of some modern Muslims in the face of religious traditions regarded (much too simplistically) as undemocratic or heretical. For these and other reasons, it was all too easy for students of Islamic great traditions to perceive Muslim civilization in Southeast Asia as derivative or, worse yet, as the curious product of peoples who, somehow, weren't quite "real Muslims."

## Islam in Southeast Asian Studies

The other marginalization to which the study of Islam in Southeast Asia has long been subjected unwittingly reinforced this neglect. This marginalization occurred within the field of Southeast Asian studies, particularly the form that took shape in the United States in the aftermath of World War II. In this emerging academic field, it was not uncommon for Islam to be portrayed as an intrusive cultural force or, as another widely used metaphor would have it, a late-deposited cultural "layer." The real Southeast Asia lay deeper and was somehow less Islamic.

This perspective on Islam in Southeast Asia had deep historical and, more specifically, colonial precedents. In colonial time, particularly in the Dutch East Indies, this notion of Islam as a "thin veneer" appealed to those who wished to justify the suppression of Islam on the grounds that it was a threat to colonial power. In Java, for example, nineteenth-century colonial administrators developed a "structure of not seeing", overlooking Islamic influences in Javanese tradition, while exaggerating and essentializing the influence of non-Islamic ideals. In the aftermath of the brutal Java War, colonial scholars worked to create a canon of Javanese literature that romanticized pre-Islamic literature as a golden age and portrayed the coming of Islam as a civilizational disaster. These Dutch Orientalists conveniently overlooked the fact that the proportion of Islamic-oriented literature in modern court collections was vastly greater than the so-called renaissance literature (preIslamic classics rendered in modern Javanese verse) that colonial scholars portrayed as the essence of things Javanese.

Colonial law effected a similar essentialization. Under the direction of Cornelis van Vollenhoven, the "adat (customary) law school" worked under state directive to develop what amounted to a system of legal apartheid. A classic example of the colonial "invention of tradition", European experts divided the native peoples of the Indies into nineteen distinct legal communities. Islamic law was acknowledged in each community's legal traditions only to the extent that colonial scholars determined that local custom (adat) explicitly acknowledged Islamic law. In this manner, colonial authorities reified the distinction between customary adat and Islam. As James Siegel's study of Aceh and Taufik Abdullah's of Minangkabau both demonstrate, however, this distinction between endogenous "custom" and exogenous "Islam" imposed an artificial polarity on a relationship that had always been dynamic. In fact, in the decades preceding the European conquest, legal traditions in places like Malaya and Minangkabau (west Sumatra) had already begun to accord a greater role to textually based Islamic norms. It was precisely this growing Islamic influence that prompted anxious Dutch authorities to implement their adatrecht policy.

British legal policies in Malaya differed from those of the Dutch. Drawing on their experience with Muslims in India, the British at first regarded Malay Muslims as "unheretical members of some idealized and uniform civilization". By treating adat as "custom that has no legal consequences" and allowing the Malay sultans a measure of jural authority, the British allowed the formation of institutional structures in which Islamic law had a substantial albeit circumscribed role. Nonetheless, lacking a framework for integrating the study of local traditions and Islam, British scholars of the colonial era fell into an "anecdotal empiricism" that failed to grasp the dynamics of religious change in Malay society as a whole.

Though there was a tradition of Islamic studies in colonial Southeast Asia, then, it suffered from the subordination of scholarship to the needs of the colonial political order. In the early postwar era, a new and more contextual framework for the study of Islam in Southeast Asia came on the scene. Harry J. Benda's 1958 studies of the Muslim role in the struggle for Indonesian independence provided rich insights into the relationship of Islam to Indonesian nationalism and the social bases for the fierce rivalries that pitted secular nationalists and communists against Muslims in the early independence era. Benda relied too uncritically on colonial historical scholarship in characterizing popular Javanese religion as "rooted in ageold pre-Hindu mysticism with accretions from later, including Muslim, religious elements". Nonetheless, his research into Islam and nationalism provided a critical foundation for the reassessment of political Islam in the postcolonial era. A few years later, William R. Roff's analyses of Islam and Malay nationalism guaranteed that, in Malay historical studies at the very least, Islam would never again be assigned a peripheral role. In Islamic literary studies, finally, the pioneering scholarship of G. W. J Drewes and Anthony Johns revealed the depth of mystical writing in Southeast Asian Islam and its intimate relationship to South Asian and Middle Eastern sources.

However divergent their concerns, the works of Benda, Roff, Drewes, and Johns together laid the foundation for the revitalization of the study of Islam in Southeast Asia. In the end, however, their influence in the broader field of Southeast Asian studies was limited, in part because other scholars working in the region saw little need to devote further attention to Islamic matters and in part because all four men were soon overshadowed by the most famous American anthropologist and Indonesianist of the early postwar era, Clifford Geertz. At least in the United States, it was Clifford

Geertz who set the agenda for the study of Islam in Southeast Asia from the 1960s until the mid-1980s. Later generations of Southeast Asianists would have to position themselves within and against Geertz' awesome legacy.

## Geertz and Islam

Clifford Geertz' perspective on Islam is a complex and fascinating one, and, contrary to the claims of some of his critics, does not allow for easy dismissal. Geertz' early writings on Islam and Indonesian society combine brilliant ethnographic insight with somewhat less careful historical generalization. Many of these works — particularly those written before the late 1960s, after which he distanced himself from the structural-functionalist methodologies in which he had earlier been trained — were strongly influenced by a sociological version of modernization theory adapted from the work of his mentors, Talcott Parsons and Edward Shils. Whatever their shortcomings in light of today's preoccupations, Geertz' works were unparalleled in their ability to combine subtle ethnnography with provocative theoretical reflection.

Although one of his most widely read books compares Islam in Indo- Indo- with that in Morocco, Geertz was generally impatient with the historical and literary scholarship long at the heart of Islamic studies. In retrospect, there can be little question that some of Geertz' skepticism was justified; whatever its logic, it allowed him to set off in new directions and make strikingly original contributions to the comparative study of Islam. In particular, by using an ethnographic approach and sensitizing Islam scholars to the issues it could illuminate, Geertz was better able than textually oriented Islamicists to explore the practice and meanings of Islam among ordinary Muslims. This concern with "everyday" or "practical Islam" — the activities and meanings through which ordinary Muslims experience their religion — has been a central and eminently welcome feature of Islamic studies since Geertz' work in the 1970s.

In another respect, however, Geertz' estrangement from Islamicist scholarship had less fortunate, if largely unintended, consequences. Whatever its high-cultural biases, Orientalist scholarship had amply detailed the variety of religious styles and world views within Islamic civilization. By failing to take note of this "burden of complexity," as William Roff has described it, Geertz tended at times to draw on what was, in fact, a narrow standard for distinguishing what is and what is not Islam. This shortcoming is especially ironic in light of Geertz' stated concern with looking at Islam from an ethnographic point of view; however, it illustrates the dangers of any approach to Islam that erects too great a divide between ethnographic and textual study. The fact is that proper ethnographic characterizations of local Islam require familiarity with Islam's textual and normative sources.

Ironically, Geertz may have been influenced on this point not merely by his own disciplinary predilections, but by the biases of his modernist informants in Java, where he worked in the early 1950s. Many of these religious reformers were only too willing to describe the religious practices of their less orthodox Javanist rivals, the so-called abangan, as un-Islamic or "Hindu," since this allowed them to discredit those activities more thoroughly. Whatever the precise influences on his ethnographic vision, Geertz identified an array of devotional practices in Indonesia as non-Islamic because they were inconsistent with the modernist practice of Islam. Rather than talking of pluralism and subalterity within Islamic tradition, then, he tended to see the Javanese Muslim community as split between those whom he effectively regarded as true Muslims, the so-called santri, and those whom he thought only nominally Islamized, the abangan (lit. "red"). Abangan religious culture, Geertz felt, owed more to animism and HinduBuddhism than to Islam.

Inasmuch as it worked at all in Muslim Southeast Asia, Geertz' model really applied only to Javanese society. In a few areas of the Indo-Malaysian archipelago such as Lombok, there existed religious divisions of equivalent severity to those found in Java. Until recently, however, throughout most of the region the more common religious opposition has been that John Bowen describes in his chapter in this book, between "old group" (kaum tua) traditionalists and "new group" (kaum muda) modernists. The modernists were strongly influenced by ideas of Islamic reform emanating from the Middle East, emphasizing the self-sufficiency of scripture and decrying what were regarded as unacceptable innovations (bid'a) in matters of worship. They were also critical of traditionalist religious jurists (ulama). The modernists felt that these caretakers of tradition had compromised their scholarship by relying too heavily on the scriptural and legal commentaries of previous scholars, especially as codified in the madhab, the recognized legal traditions of Sunni Islam. The modernists also felt that traditional ulama had been too tolerant of popular ritual practices that the modernists regarded as unacceptable innovations or, worse yet, polytheistic deviations (shirk) from true Islam.

In light of more recent research, however, it is clear that Geertz' categorizations exaggerated Hindu-Buddhist influences and oversimplified Islamic ones. For example, he described premodern Javanese Islam in terms of what he called a "classical religious style," which he felt had predominated in Java from the sixteenth to mid-nineteenth centuries. Its characteristics, he said, were a quietistic mysticism, rather than legalism, and a decided nonchalance as regards Islamic ritual obligations. In a loose sense this characterization is consistent with the raja-centered Islam that, indeed, had once held true across Southeast Asia. However, the distinction overlooks the fact that even in Java there was from early on a vigorous legalistic tradition, associated most especially with the pasisir culture of Java's north and northeastern coasts. While Geertz' account of one of the early apostles of Islam in Java, Sunan Kalijaga, emphasizes the aestheticized quietism of his conversion experience, other accounts of this saint (wali) emphasize his military and commercial prowess and his concern with the law. As Roff has observed, building in part on Pigeaud, the "classical style" of Javanese Islam had always been more richly differentiated and included a more significant legal-normative component than Geertz' rendering of the Kalijaga myth implies.

These shortcomings in Geertz' analysis were summarized by the renowned Islamicist Marshall Hodgson: "Influenced by the polemics of a certain school of modern Shari'ah-minded Muslims, Geertz identifies 'Islam' only with what that school of modernists happens to approve, and ascribes everything else to an aboriginal or Hindu-Buddhist background, gratuitously labelling much of the Muslim religious life in Java 'Hindu.' He identifies a long series of phenomena, virtually universal to Islam and sometimes found even in the Qur'an itself, as un-Islamic; and hence his interpretations of the Islamic past as well as of some recent anti-Islamic reactions is highly misleading". Among other things, Hodgson is referring here to Geertz' tendency to see numerous aspects of Malayo-Indonesian mysticism, with its Sufi-derived topography of self and divinity, as "Hindu-Buddhist"; his identification of trafficking with local spirits as animist, even though such beliefs have been accommodated within Islam since the time of Muhammad (as the Qur'an itself makes clear); and his repeated identification of ritual festival meals (slametan) as animist or Hindu-Buddhist, even though similar rites (complete with incense) are common in other parts of the Muslim world. More recently, Mark R. Woodward has extended this line of criticism, revealing strongly Islamic elements within, most notably, the Javanese tradition of kingship, ritual, architecture, and the arts. In identifying mysticism, slametan feasts, the veneration of ancestors, and trafficking with tutelary spirits as invariably "animist" or "Hindu-Buddhist," Geertz may have conveyed a view of Islam consistent with that of his reform-minded informants. In doing so, however, he unwittingly diminished the civilizational pluralism of historic Islam.

If, in the end, Geertz' categorization of things Islamic was too tightly drawn, this criticism is true in spades of Southeast Asianist scholars who followed in his wake, particularly in America-based Indonesian studies. By unwittingly sanctioning a restrictive view of Islam, Geertz seemed to confirm the suspicions of less careful scholars that Islam was of marginal or segmental importance to the study of Southeast Asian culture. In the Indonesian case, this impression seemed justified by the fact that the severe politicization of religion and politics in Java during the 1950s and the 1960s eventually led some nominal Muslims to repudiate Islam outright.

Not surprisingly, then, during the 1960s and 1970s some of the most influential essays on politics, personhood, and culture in Muslim Southeast Asia, especially in Indonesia, were written without serious exploration of Islamic influences. For example, Benedict Anderson's widely cited and otherwise remarkable essay, "The Idea of Power in Javanese Culture", drew extensively on Javanese literary and ritual traditions to develop a model of indigenous ideas of power in Java. In "A Note on Islam," which appears toward the end of the essay, Anderson cites Clifford Geertz to back up his claim that "the penetration of Islam scarcely changed the composition and recruitment of the Javanese political elite or affected the basic intellectual framework of traditional political thought". This observation raises complex and important issues. Its full assessment, however, would require at least some reference to Sufi notions of kingship, popular Islamic concepts of sainthood, and folk Islamic views of sacrifice and spiritual power, all of which exercise palpable influences on Javanese traditions.

In a later and equally influential book on the origin and spread of nationalism, Anderson displays a similar blind spot. His comments on early Indonesian nationalism abound with insightful references to the "creole functionaries" who were recruited by the colonial state into institutions of modern learning and resocialized in the ways of European administration. These "functionary journeys," Anderson argues, nurtured a sense of solidarity across linguistic and ethnic barriers that had previously segmented indigenous society, and thus created the links required for this group's leadership of the Indonesian nationalist movement. In this otherwise subtle account, however, we once again hear nothing about Muslim pilgrimages across ethnic and linguistic boundaries. In places like North Sumatra, Java, and South Sulawesi, these movements also shaped an anticolonial imagination. Though, like their non-Islamic counterparts, many of these Muslim pilgrims at first enunciated political visions premised on only pre- or protonationalist ideals, their religious pilgrimage and political struggles still worked to create a commitment to transethnic solidarities. Eventually, like their counterparts in most of the Muslim world, Muslim leaders elaborated their own versions of the nationalist ideal. These were not secondhand derivatives of secular nationalism, but fullblown alternatives to the version created by Anderson's European-schooled, "creole nationalists." In religious centers in Aceh and eastern Java, among others, Muslim thinkers elaborated a vision of the nation premised on shared religion, not merely common ethnic culture. They linked its meanings to Islam's ancient glories and the distant rumblings of Turkish, Persian, and Arab nationalism.

In this and other examples, a generation of scholars went much further than Geertz had ever intended in marginalizing Islam in Southeast Asian studies. Slowly, however, the cumulative effect of scholarship by such pioneers as Benda, Roff, Drewes, and Johns led to a deeper appreciation of Islam in contemporary life. Renewed interest in Islam was not merely the result of accumulating scholarly wisdom, however. More significant was the impact of Islamic resurgence itself, which swept across Muslim South- South- in the 1970s and 1980s. The evidence of those decades made all too clear that Islam was not a declining cultural force but an ascendant one.

## Nationalism and the Secularist Juggernaut

Another reason Islam poses such problems for students of modern politics has to do with the conviction once widespread among Western political theorists that religion is, at best, a declining historical force, destined to give way to the twin forces of economic modernization and nation-state formation. One of the more remarkable facts of late-nineteenth- and twentieth-century Western political theory was the near universality of this belief. On the left and on the right, among Marxists and Weberians, and among modernization theorists and their postmodern critics, the view that modernity is inherently secularizing — or, at the very least, so thoroughly destabilizing of religious certitudes as to demand the privatization of religion within a realm of personal belief — has dominated all the important schools of modern Western social thought.

Outside of Marxism, which had its own version, the most sustained expression of the secularization thesis was associated with the modernization theory of the 1950s and 1960s. Drawing on the works of émile Durkheim and Max Weber, modernization theory asserted that modern political-economic development involves, above all else, the increasing differentiation and specialization of social and economic structures. Commerce and, later, industrialization bring about a growing division of labor, and this in turn promotes the differentiation of society into the pluralistic entities characteristic of much of the world today. It is the cultural consequence of this change that is the primary concern of secularization theorists. Where previously there was a "sacred canopy" stabilizing life experience and providing shared meanings, in modern times the canopy is rent and the collective bases of morality and identity are diminished or destroyed.

Given the severity of its forecasts, it is not surprising that from early on observers began to express doubts regarding the relevance of secularization theory for the Muslim world. Some theorists, such as the Turkish-born sociologist Bassam Tibi, continued to insist that secularization is intrinsic to modernization, and the Islamic world is no exception. How then to explain the Islamic revival occurring in the Muslim world today? Citing the experience of Christianity in Western Europe, Tibi notes that Protestantism, too, once had grandiose political aspirations, but it was eventually "domiciled within the sphere of interiority". Islam, he predicts, will develop in a "parallel direction" because this is what modern development requires. It would seem that only inasmuch as the Islamic world is commandeered by antimodernizing reactionaries can it evade this privatization.

Other observers of the Muslim world, however, appeared less certain of this prognosis. In his Islam Observed (a work that still shows the influence of his earlier training in modernization theory, which he subsequently rejected), Clifford Geertz argued that the "secularization of thought" is characteristic of the modern world. He attributed this trend to the "growth of science" and its destabilizing influence on revealed truths. Geertz qualified this generalization, however, by noting that "the loss of power of classical religious symbols to sustain a properly religious faith" can provoke the "ideologization of religion," as the bearers of revealed truths mobilize against secularist assault. While thus embracing a variant of the secularization thesis, Geertz recognized the possibility of antisecularizing movements. Contrary to what he might argue today, however, he also implied that these were by their very nature countermodernizations, rather than alternative modernities.

Some observers, such as the philosopher and anthropologist Ernest Gellner, have been even more adamant in rejecting the relevance of the secularization thesis for the Muslim world. Unlike Tibi or Geertz, Gellner attributes this exceptionalism not to Islam's antimodernizing dispositions, but to its uniqueness in adapting to the modern nation-state. The key, Gellner argues, is that Islam has been able to play a role in the nation-state functionally (but not substantively) equivalent to that of nationalism in the West. In the West, nineteenth- and early-twentieth-century nationalists revived and idealized popular ethnic culture, using it as an instrument of nation building. This change in political culture was facilitated by the social dislocation reshaping Europe, as the vertical allegiances of the feudal era were undermined and replaced by new lateral ones. Nationalism seized on the realities of vernacular language, folk customs, and myths of national origin to respond to this crisis and forge a new basis for the political order, one founded on the sovereignty of a "people" defined by common culture. In this manner, nationalism displaced Christianity as the key idiom of European political identity and, along the way, accelerated the secularization of modern European politics.

Gellner points out that a similar detraditionalization has altered social ties in the Muslim world. However, he argues that for several reasons Islam has been able to respond to the change while avoiding the secularist juggernaut. Islam, Gellner notes, had long been divided between an elite and a popular variant. The high tradition was associated with the transethnic and transregional clerisy, the ulama, who were responsible first and foremost for preserving and implementing the law, the master institution in Islamic tradition. By contrast, the low or folk tradition in Islam was grounded on tribal organizations, kinship politics, and the veneration of living Muslim saints. While paying homage to the high tradition of scholarship and law, popular Islam had an only intermittent interest, at best, in its casuistic detail. Throughout history the two traditions flowed into and influenced each other. Periodically, however, they also erupted into conflict, when reformers "revived the alleged pristine zeal of the high culture, and united tribesmen in the interests of purification and of their own enrichment and political advancement" (ibid.). For a while thereafter, a purified Islam would dominate the political scene, but eventually it too would succumb to the twin corruptions of urban decadence and tribal parochialism.

With its industries, education, and, above all, powerful state, the modern era has irreversibly altered this "flux and reflux" in the life of Islam, shifting the historical advantage to the supporters of the clerisy-sustained high tradition. Modernizing reformists have blamed folk Islam for the Muslim world's backwardness. In reformers' eyes, the twin challenges of modernization and Western dominance demand that this backward tradition be replaced once and for all with a purified, high Islam. Only through such a total-cultural revolution can the Muslim world restore its lost glory and propel itself into the modern era. With the machinery of the modern state at their disposal, Gellner suggests, Muslim reformists can for the first time implement their programs of total-cultural revolution on a societywide scale. For Gellner, Islam is unique among the world's historic religions in being able to pull off this feat, using "a pre-industrial great tradition of a clerisy as the national, socially pervasive idiom and belief of a new style community".

There are several problems with Gellner's analysis. While emphasizing the vitality of religion in the modern Muslim world, Gellner preserves a too-Weberian understanding of religion's decline elsewhere. He thereby exaggerates the degree to which the non-Muslim world has been secularized, at least in the dual meaning of secularization as privatization and decline. Recently a number of scholars have commented on the inadequacy of this portion of the secularization argument for characterizing religious developments in the West, not least of all in the United States, where religious institutions have shown great resilience. This resilience is not just another example of American exceptionalism. Throughout large portions of Latin America, Africa, and eastern Europe, Christianity has demonstrated an ability to project itself into the public arena with a vigor and expansiveness quite contrary to post-Enlightenment understandings of religion as essentially a matter of "private" belief or as a declining historical force.

It is not just at the margins of the Christian world that one sees problems with secularist models of nation building and modernity. Recently India has witnessed the rise of a virulently anti-Muslim but broadly popular Hindu nationalism. In Sri Lanka Theravada Buddhists have been at the vanguard of Sinhala nationalist efforts against the Tamil minority. Even in Thailand, Burma, and Laos, Buddhism has been forcefully drawn into nation building. All this leads to an obvious but important conclusion. Whereas in the 1950s and 1960s the marginalization of religion from northern European nation building was seen as the prototype for modern development, nation building now appears consistent with a wider array of moral-ideological regimens, including some in which religion plays an important public role.

In half-century retrospect, then, it is clear that the secular nationalism of the postwar era was not the harbinger of a worldwide evolution, but the peculiar product of a particular historical epoch. Today, secularist modernism is being challenged in many parts of the world. A general theory of religion and modernity must begin with this fact and with the more contextsensitive approach to religion it requires. It is just such a contextualized understanding of the politics and meanings of nation building — and the plural nature of the project of modernity itself — that underlies the essays in this volume.

## Islam and Nation

Each of the nations discussed in this volume is markedly different with regard to the role of Islam in the nation and in the public sphere more generally. As is the case throughout the Muslim world, the ideals and activities of the new Islamic resurgence reflect not the irremediable influence of inalterable ideological forms, but country-specific patterns of civil and state organization. More specifically, most show the strong impact of state-society interactions that have evolved over the course of several decades of national independence.

In Indonesia, Muslim organizations played a pivotal role in anticolonial resistance from the very beginning of the nationalist movement; eventually, however, they had to resign themselves to a less central role in the institutions of government. At the beginning of the independence war in 1945, the Muslim leadership was itself divided on the question of an Islamic state. Some leaders advocated it; others merely wanted the government to enforce religious obligations among that portion of the population who professed Islam; and still others advocated a plural and liberal-constitutional democracy. In the face of bitter opposition from Christians and secular nationalists, the leadership opted for a compromise formulation, whereby there would be no unitary establishment of religion within the Indonesian state. Unlike a secular European state, however, the Indonesian constitution would require all its citizens to profess a state-recognized world religion, and it would otherwise promote religion through schools and other public institutions. Though the precise nature of the state's support for religion was left vague at the time of independence, this principle of state support for religion provided Muslims with grounds for argument against secular nationalists in years to come.

During the 1950s, the nonsectarian compromise struck in 1945 was again the subject of intense debate. Some in the Muslim leadership felt that the spirit of the 1945 compromise violated

Islamic doctrine and should therefore be repudiated in favor of a new drive for an explicitly Islamic state. Other Muslim leaders, however, strongly disagreed with this view. In the nation as a whole, as discussed in the essays by Feillard and Hefner below, the nationalist and communist parties eventually came to exercise greater influence than their Muslim rivals, at least until the cataclysmic violence of 1965-1966. The destruction of the powerful Indonesian Communist Party at that time set a new political dynamic in motion and once again raised questions regarding the proper role of religion in national life.

The military-dominated government that emerged after 1965-1966 came to power with the support of Muslim organizations, many of which actively participated in the physical liquidation of the Communist Party. But the new regime soon marginalized its erstwhile allies by adopting policies designed to undercut the political capacities of the Muslim community as well as anyone else who might aspire to independent political organization. While suppressing political Islam, however, the regime was more tolerant of what it regarded as a depoliticized "cultural Islam" — especially those Muslim organizations that accepted the government's ideological principles of Pancasila pluralism, thereby renouncing the goal of establishing an Islamic state.

The latitude for civil (as opposed to explicitly political) organization provided by the government inadvertently worked to favor the efforts of those Muslims unhappy with the party-based rivalries of the 1950s. These advocates of nonpolitical activism wanted the Muslim community to concentrate its energies on education, social welfare, and the deepening of religious piety. Twenty years later, it is clear that this strategy of working in the system and promoting a moderate Islam has, for the moment, proved a success from the government's point of view, as well as for most of the Muslim community. Contrary to the hopes of some in the ruling elite, however, this government support for nonpolitical Islam helped to fuel an Islamic revival of unprecedented proportions. Moreover, as in other Muslim countries where the government has sponsored Islamic proselytization, it is by no means clear that the long-term consequences of this development will coincide with government strategists' intentions.

In Indonesia the consequences of these changes for state and society are as yet unclear. The New Order regime has consistently adopted a policy toward nonstate organizations that is centralizing, hierarchical, and corporatistic. In a pattern of heavy-handed cooptation that goes back to the Sukarno era, political, professional, labor, religious, and other civil associations are subjected to extensive state controls, including tests for ideological correctness and strong pressures to choose leaders amenable to government directives. In such circumstances, it is difficult for any civic organization to operate independently of strict state supervision. Indeed, as Indonesia's private business sector has grown in recent years, the government has sought to force even business associations to play by these corporatist rules.

Such a hierarchical authoritarianism creates a political atmosphere in which it is all too easy for rival claimants to power to conclude that the only rational way to engage in politics is to work behind the scenes, forging alliances with ascendant factions in the ruling elite and taking care not to push for broader political participation. It is important to emphasize that this corporatist policy is in fact quite contrary to the Muslim community's own organizational history. Prior to the patrimonial politics of the independence era, Muslim organizations had a long history of pluralism and extragovernmental independence. In precolonial and colonial times, most of the Islamic community stood apart from the state, in village schools and networks of trade, learning, and pilgrimage. Though the state had its hired clerics, often recruited from the ranks of the lesser aristocracy, most Islamic scholars kept a careful distance from state bureaucrats. In the face of Old Order patrimony and New Order controls, some Muslim organizations have had difficulty maintaining their independence. Nonetheless, in recent years such organizations as Nahdlatul Ulama and the Muhammadiyah have preserved a vital nonstate organization and have been among the most consistent advocates of social and political reform.

Under the government's corporatist controls, however, it is understandable that some in the political arena, Muslim and non-Muslim alike, may be tempted to opt for a state-centered strategy aimed at capturing control of government, keeping the system closed, and using the state to suppress rival claimants to power. Were a vigorously Islamic leadership to move into a governing coalition and opt for such a strategy, it would destroy the Muslim community's historic role as a promoter of civil association and extragovernmental freedom. The Muslim world would have lost one of its brightest prospects for a democratic and pluralist Islam.

There is considerably less of a historic precedent for Muslim civil autonomy in Malaysia, though even here the situation is complex. Influenced by their longer experience with Muslims in India, from early on in the colonial era the British formally acknowledged the role of Islam among the Malay population. Primary responsibility for the management of Islamic affairs was left in the hands of the native elite, especially the sultans, under the watchful eye of British supervisors. From an organizational perspective, then, Malay Islam in colonial times remained a more state-centered entity than was the case in Indonesia. In part as a result of this precedent, Malaysian Islam has tended until recently to display a more socially conservative, establishmentarian face than Islam in Indonesia.

This tendency to work through government rather than through civil institutions was reinforced in the late colonial era. At the end of the Second World War, Malayan society was shaken by events known as the "Emergency," a combination of ethnic and political disturbances provoked in the first instance by a Chinese-led communist insurgency against British occupation. In its first months, this struggle was marked by gruesome episodes of violence between Chinese and Malays. The Chinese had suffered under the Japanese occupation, and many among them resented what they regarded as Malay collaboration with Japanese authorities against the Chinese. The communist rebellion was suppressed by the British authorities after a long antiguerrilla campaign. In its aftermath, as Malaysia prepared for independence, the British instituted political and constitutional measures that effectively guaranteed Malay dominance in the government. (Malays make up just over 60 percent of the country's population, Chinese 30 percent). Equally important, they perpetuated the tradition of direct government involvement in the management of Islamic affairs. The three-sided dialogue seen in Indonesia between nationalism, state organization, and independent religious association was here replaced by a more unitary pattern of (limited) religious establishment and Malay political dominance.

It is important to note, however, that the British introduced legal institutions and constitutional balances into the Malaysian political system of a far more extensive sort than those developed by the Dutch in the East Indies. Indeed, the Dutch bequeathed a legal tradition that preserved large portions of the colonial system's police-state controls. However shaken they have been by recent developments, Malaysia's legal and political structures provide a significant counterweight to the establishmentarianism of the political order and have insured a greater measure of political and associational freedom than seen in Indonesia during the New Order. Nonetheless, the identification of Islam with Malayness and Malayness with political dominance has guaranteed that, unlike in Indonesia, there has been a strong tendency to coordinate Islam through state bureaus rather than through independent social organizations. As Peletz' essay in this volume indicates, many of Malaysia's new Muslim movements have focused not on building extrastate associations, but on challenging the government's Islamic credentials and calling for greater state involvement in religious affairs.

Some Malay religious organizations have responded to this situation by withdrawing from the political arena in favor of the purity and privacy of cult organization. However, as Malay politics in the Mahathir era has moved out of the hands of aristocrats and into those of new administrative elites, government Islam itself has been opened to people from a wider range of social backgrounds, even if its basic structures have remained unchanged. The situation of Malaysian Muslims thus reflects two contrary influences. On one hand, Muslim interests have been premised on Malay political dominance and pursued in the corridors of state power rather than through civil association. On the other, Malaysia's remarkable economic boom and the growth of a more confident Malay middle class have served to mute demands for a more radical establishment of religion in the state. How much these latter qualities – and Malaysian democracy in general are dependent upon the country's continuing economic growth remains unclear.

In the third Muslim community represented in this volume, the Philippines, the relationship of Muslims to the nation-state has been different yet. If, in Malaysia, the state has been an official promoter of Islam and, in Indonesia, Muslims have struggled to guard their independence and project their influence into an otherwise nonsectarian state, in the Philippines the Muslim community has had to balance dominance within their own territories against marginalization within the institutions of the nation-state as a whole. In recent years, as a result of an influx of Christian Filipino migrants from the north, Muslim dominance even in regions of historic Muslim settlement has been severely threatened. As McKenna shows in his essay in this volume, this combination of regionalist vigor and national marginalization has given rise to armed movements for political secession. Yet, even here, the Muslim leadership has not been willing or able to agree on a unitary formula for Islam and state. As the essays by Horvatich and McKenna indicate, the Muslim community does not comprise a nation united around common religion and regionalism. On the contrary, it is cross-cut by competing affiliations, most notably those of ethnicity. These ties work to push segments of the Muslim community into alliance with non-Muslims. Even among those who joined the secessionist Moro National Liberation Front at the height of its armed struggle in the 1980s, there was strong disagreement as to whether the goal of their movement was the establishment of an Islamic state or a regionally encapsulated, nonsectarian state. Given the vulnerable position of Muslims in Philippine society as a whole, this contest of views among Philippine Muslims will be as much influenced by state actions as it will by ideological dispositions in the Muslim community itself.

## Conclusion: Islam and the Public Sphere

These three examples should make us wary of talking about a single "Islamic politics" or, worse yet, "civilizational identity" in Southeast Asia. Islamic politics there is, but it spans a range of ideologies and organizations. Not insignificantly, it includes in its ranks a good number of ardent democrats and liberal-constitutionalists. "Civilizational identity" there is too in Muslim Southeast Asia. While providing for certain commonalities of worship, law, and custom, however, this identity is not the sort of thing that engenders commitment to a shared or totalizing political ideology.

These Southeast Asian examples also provide several more generalizable lessons on Islam in an era of nation-states. First and most basically, this region's diverse history demonstrates that the nation-state and nationalism have been as decisive an influence on Muslim politics as have any timeless principles of Muslim governance. It is important to stress this point, not to diminish the moral and transcendental truth of Islam, but to check the essentializing claims of those analysts, Western and Muslim, who would see Islam as an unchanging and all-encompassing blueprint for political order. Such a simplification does violence to the historical diversity of Islamic politics; more basically, it ignores that most Muslims in modern times have embraced the idea of the nation-state and incorporated its cen tral ideological assumptions into their political world view. Equally important, such a simplification overlooks the way in which the great majority of Muslim intellectuals in this region have embraced the ideals of popular sovereignty and citizenry participation.

Just how Muslims should work to implement these ideals in the real world, however, is another, more complicated, matter. On this point there are great differences of opinion. Even as Muslim leaders have embraced principles of popular sovereignty, they disagree on what institutional structures might best realize that ideal. Even as they agree on the importance of respecting other religions, they disagree on how those religions should be accommodated within the nation.

In general terms, and leaving aside a few marginal groupings, one can distinguish two general views on these matters. The one – and in Southeast Asia it is held by a minority – would insist that anything short of a total Muslim state regulated by divine law (shari'ah) is a betrayal of Islam's promise. Islam, it is often said, is a "total way of life." The way in which this principle should be implemented, these advocates insist, is to subordinate all institutions to Islamic law (shari'ah) and to bring the full weight of the state to bear on its implementation. Hence, the argument goes, Muslims must seek to win control of the state and, once captured, reorganize its institutions in line with this total social plan. In absolute terms, government is not subject to the sovereignty of the people, but only to that of God.

Though advocates of this position insist that it is premised on the oldest of Muslim values, its manner of articulation here is distinctly modern. Often it is linked to the principle of God's oneness (tauhid), an ideal that is, indeed, at the very core of Islamic belief. In the context of Muslim political theory, however, the concept of tauhid is applied by these conservative Islamists to an issue with which historically it has not been associated: the idea that society itself must reflect the unity and lordship of God through its subordination to a single body of divine principles supervised by the state. Interpreted in this way, tauhid becomes an argument against modern social differentiation and against, in particular, the open expression of divergent interests sanctioned under constitutional democracy. No social divisions should be allowed to destroy the unity of the Muslim community and nation. Both are subject to divine law, the supervision of which is the responsibility of modern government with all its intrusive power.

Many people in the second group of new Muslim intellectuals also respect the idea that Islam is a total way of life; and they embrace the principle of God's oneness. But they interpret these principles quite differently from the first group of conservative Islamists. For these civic modernists, the ideal of tauhid requires precisely the opposite of the pluralism-denying unitarianism advocated by conservatives. God's oneness is such, it is said, that under no circumstance can it be profaned through its confusion with things nonsacral. On this point, these intellectuals are in general agreement with the great Egyptian reformer Muhammad Abduh, who insisted that Islam does distinguish between the religious and the secular, and who allowed great latitude for human reasoning in the organization of the latter – including, in this instance, the organization of modern government. According to this liberal interpretation of tauhidic truth, then, it is imperative not to confuse the urgent reality of God's oneness with any particular state structure, political establishment, or, least of all, powerholder. Though God has provided guidelines, their interpretation is often difficult; pluralism and tolerance are thus imperative. Though Islamic tradition provides precedents regarding how specific principles should be interpreted, the precedents themselves demonstrate that Muslim thinkers must be responsive to historical context and their conceptual reformulation.

The law demands freedom and pluralism, not an inalterable list of rules.

Most who advocate this latter position would reject the Western secularist argument that the way to resolve problems of religion and state is by erecting a high wall between the two and declaring religion a "private" matter, barring it from the public stage. But Western observers must remember that this rejection is by no means peculiar to Muslim modernists. In fact, on this point, these modernists sound a good deal like the Christian advocates of a post-Enlightenment "civil politics" described by Jose Casanova in his recent book on Christianity and civil society in the West. Like these Christian critical theorists, these civic Muslims insist that to restrict religion to the private domain is to deprive it of its vital ethical role in public discourse and activity. Such a privatization of religion only cedes the moral high ground to the opportunistic instrumentalities of market forces and political entrepreneurs. Neomodernist Christians and Muslims thus agree in seeing virtue as vital to political life. Hence, as a source of moral guidance, religion is never just a matter of personal belief, but the most vital of public concerns.

These Southeast Asian Muslims and their Western counterparts also agree in insisting that religion's public role is best served by maintaining a careful distance from any particular government or political faction. Religion's goals must not be profaned through their identification with efforts to seize state power. Religion must be anchored in the religious community and civil society, not in state bureaucracies, and from there it should work to inform public policy and discourse. For this Muslim variant of civic republicanism, then, the very principle of God's oneness (tauhid) mandates what is, in effect, a kind of secularization. But this secularization is not the same as that espoused by laicist secularists, with their privatization of religion and abandonment of the public domain. On the contrary, religion remains a vital element in public life, through its elevation above party politics and state structures into a more abstract moral ethos that pervades the whole of society.

It would be an exaggeration to claim that this latter view is now or will necessarily become dominant in Southeast Asian Islam. At the moment, the sense of political (not to mention military) crisis in the Muslim Philippines leaves little room for the luxury of such careful reflection. Similarly, for historical reasons noted above, such civic views tend to be more popular in Indonesia than in Malaysia. Nonetheless, it is remarkable that this view is as widespread as it is throughout the region. Could this pluralist Islam predominate in the long run? It is much too early to answer this question. At least in Malaysia and Indonesia, the Muslim community is just now emerging from a period of extraordinary and, in many ways, unexpected revival. Confident that it has secured a solid social base, it is only now beginning to grapple with the difficult questions posed by its increased influence.

At the very least, however, those of us with a sympathetic interest in the region would do well to acknowledge the significance of what has already been achieved in Muslim Southeast Asia. Though Western scholars once thought that the most distinctive feature of Southeast Asian Islam was the strength of so-called pre-Islamic survivals (some of which, we now realize, were actually subaltern variants of Islam), from a political perspective the more unusual feature of Islam in this region is its long-established tradition of intellectual and organizational pluralism. Even in an earlier era when virtually all Javanese, Malays, or Minangkabau called themselves Muslims, neither the courts nor the ulamo exercised an effective monopoly of power over the Muslim community's moral and intellectual life. There were varied religious views even in premodern times and diverse ways of being a good Muslim. This pluralism was perhaps more pronounced in Indonesia than it was in Malaysia, and, as several chapters in this volume illustrate, certain forms of authoritarian cooptation threaten its vitality today. Nonetheless, it is remarkable to see how throughout this region the Muslim community has maintained its diversity and eschewed totalizing political formulae.

Though a few Muslim leaders occasionally lament this pluralism, seeing it as a fatal political weakness, from a democratic perspective, this pluralism is really a blessing in disguise. Much as with post-Reformation Christianity in Western Europe, this situation has led some Muslim leaders to the realization that the aspiration for monopolistic unity must be renounced in favor of pluralism, tolerance, and the abstraction of Islam into a deeply pervasive civic influence. There are other influences on this tradition of Islamic tolerance as well. In Indonesia, for example, the experience of Muslims since independence has impressed upon many the dangers of politicizing religion too directly. It was, after all, during the Old Order (pre1966) period, when religious issues were politicized to an extreme, that one heard the loudest cries among some in the Javanist community for a turning away from Islam. Similarly, it was in the aftermath of the bloodshed of 1965-1966 that one saw some Muslims flee Islam for Hinduism and Christianity. Conversely, there has been an unprecedented deepening of Islamic piety since the 1980s, a period during which political Islam has been far less influential than a civic-minded, cultural Islam. It is clear that for some Indonesians this dampening of political-religious passions, which is to say, the "desacralization" of certain kinds of party politics, has allowed for the realization of deeper Islamic ideals.

Though historical lessons of this sort may seem a fragile basis on which to build a consensus for democratic pluralism and tolerance, it is this same kind of heritage that promoted, and promotes, pluralist ideologies in the West. Conversely, where such a pluralist precedent is lacking, a modern society can easily slip into bitter civic discord. As Nazi Germany, contemporary Bosnia, and today's debates over the Muslim minority in France and Britain all illustrate, the struggle for pluralism is not something the West resolved once and for all in the nineteenth century; as in the Muslim world, it remains a living challenge. Where precedents for civic tolerance exist -and especially where their principles have been abstracted from public culture and reinforced in legal-political charters – they are among the most vital of resources for civil accommodation. As in the early modern West, religious pluralism can also serve as a school in which young nations learn the habit of political tolerance.

At the same time, Southeast Asia has other political precedents – most of them owing little to Islam – that look unfavorably at social autonomy and are little inclined to respect pluralism. We know, however, that, in the economic sphere, this heritage of a hierarchical and corporatist "bureaucratic polity" has proved itself less of an impediment to market dynamism than observers a generation ago would ever have thought possible. Unfortunately, on the evidence of recent world history, it seems that the formulae required to manage religious and ethnic pluralism are considerably less certain than those required to manage capital and labor markets. Even today religious and ethnic absolutism has reappeared to ravage otherwise prosperous societies, including European ones.

The challenge for Southeast Asian Muslims is thus to build on and extend their tradition of pluralism and autonomy. The tradition can serve as a vital ingredient in any effort to devise a modern and democratic politics. Muslim success in this effort is no more guaranteed in Southeast Asia than that of Christians and Jews in the West. As in the West, however, the prospects for long-term success depend less on the timeless momentum of "civilizational identities" than on the fault lines of modern contests and, it is to be hoped, the creative efforts of willing men and women to make good on their religion's promise of universality and justice.

# 2

# Islamization and Democratization in Asian Countries

## Introduction

Many foreign specialists of Indonesia were convinced that the Suharto government was a resolute defender of abanganJavanese values, deeply opposed to anything that might expand Muslim influence in Indonesian politics and society. Yet it was President Suharto himself who on December 6, 1990, authorized the formation of Indonesia's newest and most controversial Muslim social organization, the Association of Indonesian Muslim Intellectuals. Though the action caught many Western observers by surprise, most Muslim Indonesians were aware that the president's act was merely the latest in a series of overtures directed at the Muslim community. Nonetheless, for many non-Muslim and secular Indonesians, the president's actions seemed a dangerous departure from the nonsectarian principles of the New Order. After all, they noted, ICMI was not merely a politically neutral cultural organization. Many of its members declared quite openly that the organization's primary purpose is to promote the Islamization of Indonesian state and society.

Many ICMI critics at first reassured themselves that the president's actions were part of an only momentary effort to court Muslim support in advance of the 1992 national elections; once the elections were over, they forecast, the organization would disappear. When, in the months following the elections, it became clear that ICMI was not only going to survive but would play an expanded role in the president's new cabinet, these observers realized that ICMI must be part of a longer-term presidential strategy. They correctly noted that, since the late 1980s, President Suharto had faced growing challenge from segments of a military who up to that time had provided his most important base of support. As military and civilian opposition to his rule grew, it was argued, the president chose to "play the Muslim card." In so doing, he fell back on his often-used strategy of alternately coopting and dividing his opposition. In this instance, it was said, the president's courtship of Muslims was intended to deflect challenges from his military opposition, while simultaneously splitting Muslim democrats from their Christian and secular allies.

The ICMI leaders with whom I spoke over summers from 1991 to 1995 had varied opinions on the president's motives. Most insisted, however, that the president's intentions were of much less importance than the benefits ICMI might provide for individuals, the Muslim community, and the nation. Even on these issues, however, there was a sharp range of opinion among the ICMI membership. Many of the government officials who rushed to join the organization after 1993 confessed privately that they did so because membership had come to be seen as obligatory for upwardly mobile Muslim officials. Though some officials of nominal or abangan Muslim persuasion resisted the trend, all were aware that a sea change in bureaucratic attitudes toward ICMI had taken place after the installation of the sixth development cabinet in March 1993 (notable for its large number of ICMI sympathisizers). Concerned about the risks of aligning oneself with the wrong government faction, many prior to 1993 had still hesitated to join the Muslim organization. By the end of 1995, however, all such hesitation had ended: ICMI had come to be seen as the dominant civilian faction within the bureaucracy, and Muslim government officials not otherwise allied with the military or nonsectarian nationalists felt great pressures to join.

However significant its government faction, ICMI'S membership does not comprise career bureaucrats alone. From the very beginning, many independent-minded Muslims also joined the organization, both from the ranks of government and from independent social organizations. Their motives for doing so were varied but, in general, fell into one of three groupings. The first group, which we might call "cultural Islam," consisted of pious individuals strongly opposed to any effort to drag Islam into poli- lb /> tics. Citing the disastrous consequences of the politicization of religion during the 1950s and early 1960s, supporters of cultural Islam wanted ICMI (and Muslims in general) to remain outside and above politics, acting as a moral rather than political influence on society. For them, ICMI was but one more instrument in this effort to promote social decency, political moderation, and piety.

Drawn primarily from the ranks of the modernist Muslim community, a second group within the independent Muslim community agreed with this emphasis on Islam as a source of ethical guidance, but also spoke of the need to address long-term political concerns. They were troubled by the arbitrary and undemocratic nature of the presidential regime. However, marginalized from Indonesian politics since 1960 (see below), these modernist supporters of ICMI had concluded that, over the long run, the most important measure for the long-term transformation of Indonesian politics was a deeper Islamization of society. They felt that, if this ethical change could be achieved, a more just and democratic political system would inevitably follow. Muslims should therefore take advantage of the resources and political protection provided by the president's actions, whatever his motives, and work to promote a deeper Islamization of Indonesian society.

A third group among the independent ICMI membership, the smallest, consisted of prodemocracy activists convinced the organization could play a vital role in the demilitarization of the Indonesian state. These people agreed with the ethical concerns of the first two groups and also recognized that the president's administration was rampant with corruption. However, they emphasized, Suharto's rule is inevitably limited. Over the long run, then, the most serious obstacle to Indonesian democratization is less the person of the president than it is military dominance of the political system as a whole. Inasmuch as this is the case, they argued, it is important to take advantage of the resources provided by the president's actions, whatever his motives, so as to consolidate nonmilitary influence within the government. Only by taking advantage of the cracks in the system in this way could one hope to lay the grounds for a reduction of the military's role in state and society.

In what follows, I examine the issues raised by these varied perspectives on Islamization and democratization in contemporary Indonesia by considering the circumstances of ICMI'S founding and its first years of operation. At its most basic level, the example provides insight into the changing nature of elite attitudes on Islam in the New Order era and counsels against the long-familiar view that the Suharto regime is in some way irrevocably committed to abangan values. ICMI'S ascent suggests that the political elite is much less committed to Javanist values than it is to preservation of its own political and economic interests. More generally, and of far greater relevance for the comparative study of Islam, the ICMI example also sheds light on the dilemmas faced by Muslim reformers where the cause of Islamization is embraced by an authoritarian regime. In such circumstances, ruling elites can easily play the interests of Muslim reformers off against those of secular democrats. As in Indonesia, such manipulation inevitably unleashes a difficult debate among Muslims about the relative importance of democracy to Islamization and the proper means to achieve both.

## Javanism and Islam in the Early New Order

For many years it was a truism of Indonesian studies in the West that the military-dominated, New Order government that has ruled Indonesia since 1966 was essentially hostile to Islam. "Suharto and the generals on whom he relies were brought up in a Hindu-Javanized milieu that made them more nominal (abangan) than practicing (santri) Muslims". The putative opposition of the ruling elite to "orthodox" Islam is thought to have shaped government initiatives in the late 1960s intended to undercut the influence of Muslim political parties. Confounding Muslim expectations, for example, the government in 1968 refused to recognize the Jakarta Charter as the preamble to the national constitution, thereby dashing Muslim hopes that (as the charter specifies) the state (negara) would be obliged to "carry out" (menjalankan) Islamic law (shari'ah) among the Muslim portion of the populace.

Not long after this incident, the government again frustrated Muslim hopes by refusing to rehabilitate Masyumi, the party of Muslim modernists suppressed by the late President Sukarno in 1960 for its alleged involvement in regional rebellions. Adopting an even harder line, the government then barred Masyumi leaders from participating in the newly formed Partai Muslimin Indonesia (PMI), an organization intended by its sponsors to be the electoral voice of modernist Muslims. In the two years following the 1971 elections, finally, the government moved once more against Muslim power by consolidating the nine political parties still operating in the political arena into two, one of which was supposed to represent the interests of Muslims. Both of the newly reorganized parties were subject to extensive government controls. In the face of these restrictions, Muslim party activists – who at the beginning of the New Order had dreamed of greatly expanded influence, since they had played so central a role in the crushing of the Indonesian Communist Party during 1965-1966 – could only conclude that the ruling elite was determined to prevent Muslims from ever again becoming an independent political force.

Faced with these and other measures, many in the Muslim community came to the additional conclusion that the New Order government had been hijacked by an anti-Muslim alliance of Chinese Catholics, former PSI socialists, and army officers. Most fingers pointed to Major General Ali Murtopo as the mastermind behind these policies. The head of the powerful OPSUS, a special operations intelligence bureau linked to the Army Strategic Reserve Command (Kostrad), Murtopo was one of President Suharto's two closest aides during the first years of the New Order. General Murtopo was known to have Chinese Catholics among his most trusted advisors, several of whom went on in 1971 to establish the influential Center for Strategic and International Studies (CSIS). Murtopo and his aides are also credited with having developed the strategies behind the 1971 elections, the formation of Golkar (the government party), and the application of draconian restrictions on Muslim and other political parties in 1973.

Subsequent events in these first years of the New Order only deepened this sense of disappointment among Muslims. In 1973 the People's Consultative Assembly (Majelis Permusyawaratan Rakyat or MPR) seemed poised to rebuke Muslims by proposing to elevate mystical belief (kepercayaan) to the same status as "religion" (agama), that is, to a position of equality with the scripturally based monotheistic religions officially recognized by the Indonesian state. This legislation caused deep concern among Muslim leaders, since many regarded the mystical Javanism that was to benefit from this elevation as a heterodox threat to Islam. During the same legislative session, the Assembly moved to "unify" laws on marriage and divorce by greatly limiting the jurisdiction of Islamic courts. Though the force of the Muslim response to both of these measures eventually made the government back down, many Muslim observers were convinced that these initiatives were proof of an ominous new turn in New Order policy, designed not merely to limit Muslim political power, but to restrict Islam's influence in Indonesian civil life as well.

## Islamic Renewal and the Politics of "Cultural" Islam

There were always Muslim intellectuals who took a less pessimistic view of the New Order government. They insisted that restrictions on "political Islam" – that is, on the Islamic parties that aimed to capture the reins of government – should not be equated with government opposition to "cultural" or "civil" Islam, which is to say, an Islam whose primary role in the life of the nation is to serve as a source of ethical and cultural guidance.

One group of young Muslims among whom this view was popular consisted of development-oriented economists and technocrats who emerged from the student groups known as the "generation-of-'66." The generationof-'66 were student activists who, in the months following the failed leftwing officers' coup of September 30, 1965, joined forces with reform factions of the military in a successful campaign to outlaw the Communist Party and topple President Sukarno. Though generation-of-'66 activists came from many different religious backgrounds (and even included a number of Chinese Catholics), the single largest grouping in their ranks consisted of students from Muslim organizations. The two most important among these were the university-based Islamic Students Association (HMI) and the high-school based Indonesian Islam Students (PII). Though modernist in theological orientation, some among the HMI and PII activists were known to be sympathetic to the liberal ideals of the Indonesian Socialist Party (PSI). Over the years the PSI had become more social democratic and developmentalist than socialist in orientation and had attracted many Western-oriented modernizers to its ranks. A fierce critic of President Sukarno's authoritarianism, the PSI had been banned by Sukarno in 1960. When, in 1966-1967, the Suharto regime turned to Western-trained economists to devise policies to extricate Indonesia's economy from its woes, many among the high-ranking economists it recruited were specialists with known ties to the Socialist Party. These men in turn provided the opportunity for a small number of Muslim technocrats from the HMI and the PII to secure employment in New Order planning agencies in the mid1960s. In years to come, these government Muslims would act as quiet but persistent advocates of an accommodating, development-oriented Islam.

From very early on, then, there were Muslim activists who chose to cooperate with the New Order regime and work for change from within the system. Besides the technocrats, however, there was a second group of young Muslims from the ranks of the generation-of-'66 who were also sanguine about the prospects for a long-term accommodation with the government. Though the most influential of these individuals also came from the ranks of the HMI and the PII, they were neither technocrats nor economists. Most worked with Muslim social associations and nongovernmental organizations (NGOS) rather than in government, serving as activist-intellectuals in the liberal wing of the Muslim community. Precisely because of their independence from government and their prominence as writers and activists, over the long run they would exercise a more decisive influence on Muslim political attitudes than the Muslim technocrats.

In the late 1960s this second grouping included such young Muslim intellectuals as Usep Fathudin and Utomo Danadjaja from the PII, Ahmad Wahib, Dawam Rahardjo, and Djohan Effendi from the "Limited Group" discussion circle in Yogya, and Nurcholish Madjid from the Jakarta headquarters of the Himpunan Mahasiswa Islam, or HMI. Though most came from modernist theological backgrounds and had had at least indirect ties to Masyumi leaders in the late 1950s and early 1960s, their polical situation was quite different from that of the senior Masyumi leadership. During the first years of the New Order, senior Masyumi chiefs had staked their political reputations on the unsuccessful campaign to rehabilitate the party. As the depth of their failure became more apparent, which is to say as the New Order regime made clearer its determination to prevent the reemergence of any independent Muslim party, their frustration with the new government deepened. At the same time, their leadership positions were threatened by hardline critics in their own ranks, who had always been skeptical of the leaders' commitment to Western-oriented principles of constitutional government and a separation of powers. The hardliners wanted a more uncompromising commitment to Islamist political ideals. With nothing to show for their long years of dedication to the ideals of constitutional democracy, the senior Masyumi leaders were obliged in the aftermath of their defeat to denounce the regime and adopt some of the rhetorical idioms of radical Islamism. They withdrew from politics to dedicate themselves to religious proselytization (dakwah). They did so, however, with the explicit recognition that Islamization was itself a form of politics. Barring a change of national leadership, it was only the latter, they felt, that could bring about the cultural change required to restore political Islam to its proper place.

The young Muslim activists from the generation-of- '66 were familiar with the plight of their elders. During the first two years of the New Order, most had participated, if often halfheartedly, in the effort to rehabilitate Masyumi. However, when it became apparent that this strategy had failed, these young activists were unwilling to follow the senior leadership into opposition. They felt there was still sufficient room to work within the system for changes beneficial to Muslim Indonesians.

There was a larger reason that these young activists were less enthusiastic about the struggle to revive the party system or directly oppose the government. Many were convinced that the mass politics of the late 1950s had only wrecked the economy, politicized religion, and driven many nominal Muslims into the arms of the Communist Party. Like their colleagues in the youth groups of the Socialist Party, many of these young Muslim intellectuals had grown deeply disenchanted with populist politics. Not having invested all their energies in party organization, they found it easier than their elders to contemplate a national politics based on forms of participation other than electoral politics alone.

Equally important, many of these same young modernist Muslims had, like some PSI socialists, concluded that collaboration with the military was not necessarily an evil thing. During the lean years from 1960 to 1965, when the Masyumi and the PSI were banned and the Communist Party became the nation's most powerful party, military officers in many parts of the country had secretly provided resources and protection for Masyumi and PSI youth. This support was particularly vital for youth from the Islamic Students Association (HMI), since, in the aftermath of Sukarno's ban on the PSI and Masyumi, the Communist Party launched a ferocious campaign to have the HMI banned. The rewards of this behind-the-scene collaboration seemed confirmed after the failed left-wing officers' coup of September 30, 1965. Having blamed the communists for the coup attempt, the military turned to Muslim social organizations and student activist groups (Christian and Muslim) to help in its campaign against the Indonesian Communist Party (PKI). In the course of this struggle, the military provided the anticommunist students with extensive financial and material resources, and left them with the impression that they could play a significant role in national politics.

For all these reasons, many Muslims in the generation-of-'66 had concluded that the military could be a force for progress. Hence, in the face of continuing government restrictions on political parties in the late 1960s, they found it easy to distance themselves from mass politics in favor of a new strategy of Islamic revitalization. At its heart lay the conviction that only a long-term, "cultural" approach to revitalization could neutralize military suspicions while slowly deepening the roots of Islam in the nation as a whole.

The young intellectuals responsible for developing this strategy at first did so in several separate discussion groups in Jakarta, Bandung, and Yogyakarta. However, the man whose name has come to be most widely associated with this strategy is Nurcholish Madjid, the former leader (1966-1971) of the Islamic Students Association. In a series of public presentations in the late 1960s and early 1970s, Madjid asserted that the Muslim community itself bore much of the responsibility for its failure to achieve political influence under the New Order. The party organizations that Muslim politicians were attempting to revive, Madjid argued, had in the 1950s already demonstrated their inability to capture the hearts and minds of the majority of Indonesians. Rather than perpetuating this failure, the Muslim community should develop new organizations capable of winning the allegiances of all Indonesian Muslims. Only through such a revolution in values, Madjid claimed, could Indonesia escape the debilitating cycle of polarization whereby party-based Islam inveighed against a government and military deeply suspicious of political Islam.

As in his writings still today, Madjid's style of argument in these presentations was a complex mix of theology, political analysis, and academically informed historical sociology. The novelty of this unconventional blend was especially evident in Madjid's remarks on what Western observers might have thought an academic issue, the phenomenon of secularization. Madjid accused his fellow Muslims of having "sacralized" profane institutions, such as, most notably, Islamic political parties and an Islamic state (negara Islam). Noting, quite correctly, that there is no Qur'anic injunction mandating an Islamic state, Madjid criticized Indonesian Muslims for sanctifying an idea that was in fact a human fabrication. Muslims, Madjid concluded, should "secularize" this commitment while preserving Islam's lasting values.

According to Madjid, this effort at desacralization or "secularization" is necessitated by the most central of Muslim doctrines, tauhid, belief in the uncompromised oneness of God. "Islam itself, if examined truthfully," Madjid wrote, "was begun with a process of secularization. Indeed the principle of Tauhid represents the starting point for a much larger secularization". This commitment to tauhid requires a vigilant and never-ending effort to distinguish what is divine from what is merely human in Islamic tradition. By this requirement, Madjid argued, tauhid also implies a commitment to reason, knowledge, and science, all of which can be understood as acts of devotion to a Creator whose majesty is immanent in the natural laws of the world. "Thus modernity resides in a process, a process of discovery of which truths are relative, leading to the discovery of that Truth Which Is Absolute, that is Allah".

From a theological perspective, Madjid's comments on tauhid lay well within the tradition of Islamic modernism and neomodernism, with their emphasis on the unity of God and the compatibility of science and progress with Islamic revelation.

Where Madjid disagreed with his Indonesian modernist elders, however, lay in his insistence that, while paying lip service to these ideals, Muslim leaders had done little to insure their practical implementation. Rather than taking steps to bring about intellectual and economic renewal, Madjid implied, Indonesia's Muslim leaders had wasted their time on ideological bickering and frivolous political adventures. By prioritizing political concerns in this manner, Madjid asserted, Muslims had failed to develop the "psychological strike force" needed to meet the challenge of the new era. The quest for state power, Madjid wrote, led to a fetishism of the Muslim community's "quantity" rather than a nurturing of its educational, social, and economic "quality".

The cumulative result of this failed strategy, Madjid argued, was that Muslims were left unprepared to compete with more modernized groups in Indonesian society. Surveying the New Order scene, Madjid took note of the preponderance of Chinese, Christians, and Western-oriented technocrats in private and public enterprise. Rather than condemning this disparity as evidence of a government bias against Muslims, Madjid implied that it was in part the result of the Muslim community's own blunders. If Muslims continued to invest all their energies in bankrupt political initiatives, they would only further marginalize themselves from centers of influence in New Order society.

Enunciated as it was in the face of the government's continuing suppression of Muslim political activity, some observers, including many senior Muslim leaders, concluded that Madjid's stance was little more than an effort to court government favor. But Madjid's long involvement in the religious community (ummat) and his reputation as a thoughtful, principled, and pious activist suggested that he was genuinely concerned about Muslims' long-term prospects in a fast-changing Indonesia. Often described in the Muslim media in the late 1960s as the youthful heir to the modernist leader Muhammad Natsir (the former chairman of the Islamic political party Masyumi), Madjid was well aware that confronting the Muslim establishment might imperil his political career. Yet he felt that the Muslim community was reacting in a self-defeating manner to the challenges of the New Order; what was needed, therefore, were bold words to shock the leadership into new ways.

In the months following his well-publicized broadsides, the risks implicit in his initiative seemed confirmed. Madjid was denounced by such formidable modernist leaders as H.M. Rasyidi, Hamka, and Muhammad Natsir. Several supporters of Madjid in other youth organizations, such as Utomo Danadjaja and Usep Fathudin from the PII, were also expelled from their organizations. Many observers concluded that Madjid's career as an Islamic leader was finished, and he and his associates would play no future leadership role in Indonesian Islam.

As is often the case in Islamic debates, the theological, not just the political, elements in Madjid's argument excited some of the most furious criticism. Madjid and the "renewal" (pembaruan) group's support for secularization provoked especially bitter controversy. Critics argued that this idea amounted to a Westernized interpretation of Islam. By understanding tauhid as the desacralization of all but God's oneness, it was said, Madjid and his friends ignored Islamic Sunnah, the tradition of the community as sacralized by the example of the Prophet. The Sunnah, critics said, provides clear normative precedent for how society should be organized. As one Malaysian critic of the renewal movement asserted to deny this precedent is to rid Islam of its sociological wholeness, transforming it into a mere "spiritual personalist ethical system" akin to what Christianity has become in the West. This may be conveniently accommodating to New Order interests, these critics said, but it is deeply contrary to Islam's claim to being an integrated way of life.

In fact, much of the detail of Madjid's argument was lost in the sound and the fury of the subsequent debate. Though he and his colleagues were accused of being secularists, they consistently distinguished secularization, described as the desacralization of domains wrongly valorized as sacred, from secularism, a Western ideology advocating a rigorous separation of religion from social life. They condemned the latter, while insisting that the former was required by the spirit of Islamic monotheism. In the aftermath of the controversy, however, Madjid himself expressed some misgivings at his choice of terms, commenting publicly that his reference to "secularization" had invited misinterpretation.

Much as his critics suggested, Madjid's understanding of secularization did show Western influences, at least in the sense that it cited the work of such liberal theorists as the American sociologist Robert Bellah and the Protestant theologian Harvey Cox. But rather than expressing uncritical enthusiasm for the West, Madjid's appeal to these authors was illustrative of the way in which he and his colleagues felt that Muslims should not hesitate to draw on scientific and religious literature from outside Islam, both to broaden their own understanding and to demonstrate Islam's universality. This affirmation of an inclusive and universal Islam has remained a key theme in Madjid's writings to this day and underlies much of his popularity among liberal members of the educated middle class. In the early 1970s, however, the subtlety of such a message was lost amidst a debate that seemed to equate secularization with secularism and secularism with the relegation of Islam to a position of political impotence.

Though conceding, then, that his choice of terms had caused some confusion, Madjid never drew back from his broader position on the attitude the Muslim community should take toward the New Order government and toward Islamic renewal generally. Though his influence temporarily waned in the mid-1970s, Madjid is important because he provided intellectual grounds for justifying something much larger than his own views. In effect, he reassured Muslim members of the generation-of-'66 that their disenchantment with party politics did not amount to a betrayal of Islam, and piety did not require that they work for the establishment of an Islamic state. In this sense, the initiatives of what had come to be known as "renewal" (pernbaruan) Islam legitimated the efforts of a larger community of nonparty activists seeking to develop new Islamic initiatives, especially in the fields of education, the economy, and social welfare.

Equally important, the efforts of the renewal group also served to provide moral sanction for the growing numbers of educated Muslims who, beginning in the mid-1970s, saw fit to take up government service. The 1960s' trickle of Muslims moving into the bureaucracy had, by the 1980s, turned into a flood. Many of these officials labored behind the scenes to promote Muslim interests, while awaiting a softening of attitude on the part of a government determined to prevent any reinvigoration of massbased party politics.

## Fruits of Rene wal

This effort at "new thinking" (pemikiran baru) was but one of several related developments in the Muslim community at this time, the importance of which lies less in their specific detail or associated personalities than in their sanctioning of a shift of Muslim energies out of formal politics and into social and educational activities. Commenting on Madjid's impact on younger activists, Fachry Ali and Bahtiar Effendy – Muslim scholars and activists themselves – make the point that Madjid's understanding of Islamic renewal encouraged a more "empirical" attitude toward Islam. Rather than quibbling over doctrine or ideological details, Muslims were enjoined to recognize the reality of the New Order and undertake initiatives that could enhance their influence within its institutions.

The political consequences of this change in Muslim attitudes were quite real. Although there were a handful of uncompromising Islamist movements in Indonesia during the 1980s, the really notable feature of the period was the patient effort of moderate Muslims to build institutions for Islamic education and socioeconomic advance. Indeed, on this point, Indonesia was unusual among Muslim societies during the tumultuous decade stretching from 1978 to 1988. The country witnessed a general decline in the influence of Muslim political parties but saw a great leap forward in the social and intellectual vitality of the community.

It is important to emphasize, however, that Muslim civil associations were not the only agencies involved in these renewal initiatives. The New Order state also supported a number of cultural-Islamic programs, usually under the auspices of its enormous Ministry of Religion. At first sight, the state's role in the strengthening of Islamic institutions and piety may appear surprising in light of the government's reputation among Western scholars as a bastion of abanganism and, more significantly, in light of its very real restrictions on political Islam. In the opinion of Muslim intellectuals, however, the expansion of state support was related to a gradual change in government attitudes that first became noticeable in the mid-1970s, in part as the result of a curious synergy between "renewal" leaders and moderate Muslim officials in the Ministry of Religion.

The first hints of this change were seen in 1972-1973, when the government intervened to tone down MPR initiatives on Javanist "belief" (kepercayaan) and marriage laws, reversing legislation that devout Muslims had regarded as deeply hostile to their interests. By most accounts this reversal was little more than a strategic and limited concession in the face of overwhelming Muslim protest. Indeed, the government seems at first to have been divided on how forcefully to push for the new regulations. In the case of the marriage law, for example, the legislators in the ruling party (Golkar) who sponsored the legislation were initially confident they had the full support of the government in their efforts to limit polygamy and restrict the role of Islamic courts in marriage and divorce. As the scale of the Muslim unrest became apparent, however, high-ranking military officials-with the clear encouragement of Suharto advisors – intervened, pushing aside the legislators and negotiating a compromise solution with Muslim politicians on their own.

If these early government concessions looked like little more than strategic retreats, the Ministry of Religion's Decision No. 70 in 1978 seemed to reflect a more deliberate opening to Muslim interests. The decision banned missionizing by the members of any one religion (Christians being the main target) among citizens who already professed, however nominally, another government-recognized religion. Christians protested that many Javanese are Muslim in name only and thus should not be subject to the stricture. But the government brushed these objections aside. Indeed in 1979 the ministries of Religion and Home Affairs joined forces to strengthen the restrictions with their Joint Decision No. 1 of that year. As Bambang Pranowo has observed, "The Islamic groups enthusiastically welcomed these decisions, for they were directed especially toward the Christian missionaries actively carrying out religious propagation amongst the Muslim community". Conversely, Indonesian Christian missionaries whom I interviewed in East Java in the late 1970s, 1985, and 1991 acknowledged these restrictions had a disastrous impact on their missions to Javanists.

The significance of these new policies is readily apparent if one remembers that, just ten years earlier, the same ministries of Religion and Home Affairs had joined forces to implement a program of ideological "construction" (pembinaan) that openly encouraged access by Christian missionaries to villages identified as former strongholds of the Indonesian Communist Party (PKI). Missionaries were also given access to PKI prison camps. Still today Muslim commentators, including some among the ICMI leadership, regard this unrestricted access of Christian missions to nominal Muslims as a clear indication that Christians and secular modernizers wielded disproportionate influence in the early New Order. Conversely, reversal of the policy in 1978-1979 is seen as an indication that, despite controls on political Islam, segments of the ruling elite were beginning to recognize the need for a more sympathetic accommodation with Muslims, especially those willing to work within the framework of Pancasila politics.

The other program to which Muslim leaders today point as evidence of a basic change in attitude on the part of the government was the Ministry of Religion's efforts to expand the institutional resources for Islamic education and dakwah (religious predication; see Feillard, this volume). One important feature of this effort was the enormous expansion in State Islamic Institute Colleges (IAIN), which began in the 1960s and which, during the 1970s and 1980s, produced large numbers of graduates trained in Islamic theology, law, arts, and pedagogy. As in the Middle East ( Eickelman 1992), mass education of this sort contributed significantly to the Islamic renewal.

These efforts in higher education were accompanied by an equally impressive program of infrastructural development sponsored by the Ministry of Religion, focusing on the construction of mosques, prayer halls (musholla), and Islamic schools (madrasah), especially in areas regarded as weakly committed to Islam. The construction of mosques in East and Central Java shows the clear and unrelenting progress of this program. In East Java, the number of mosques increased from 15,574 in 1973 to 17,750 in 1979, 20,648 in 1984, and 25,655 in 1990. By comparison, over the same seventeen-year period, the number of Catholic churches increased from 206 to 324. Protestant churches (including many small, evangelical meeting halls) increased from 1,330 in 1973 to 2,308 in 1984, but then declined again to 1,376 in 1990. There was a similarly effective program of mosque construction in Central Java, where, between 1980 and 1992, the number of mosques almost doubled, from 15,685 to 28,748. In addition to ministry programs, there was a smaller but more conspicuous program sponsored by President Suharto himself, under the auspices of a presidential foundation for the support of Islamic initiatives, the Amal Bakti Muslimin Pancasila. The Amal Bakti program sponsored the construction of four hundred mosques and provided support to one thousand Muslim proselytizers (dai), posted to areas of Indonesia that were deemed devotionally weak, including many on the island of Java. In all this, proponents of cultural Islam felt that they saw visible confirmation of the wisdom of their strategy of working within the system.

The progress of cultural Islam was not matched in the official political arena. Indeed, in the early 1980s the government escalated its efforts to force all social and political organizations to acknowledge the national ideology (the "Five Principles" or Pancasila) as their "sole foundation" (asastunggal). The government's effort caused deep resentment among Muslims and even some Christians. In the Muslim case, however, the policy had an especially devastating impact. It splintered an already fractured Muslim leadership, as fierce disputes erupted over the proper response to the government policy. In the electoral arena, these developments reinforced the domination of Golkar, the government-supported party. Despite the occasional defection of supporters during the 1980s, Golkar generally improved its share of the Muslim vote at the expense of the putatively Muslim party, the Partai Persatuan dan Pembangunan or Party of Unity and Development (PPP). Election observers decried what was widely regarded as governmental manipulation of the leadership of the opposition parties. But the result, in any case, was the continuing atrophy of Muslim electoral muscle.

Some observers have described these government actions as reminiscent of the earlier Dutch colonial policy of tolerating Islamic religion but ruthlessly repressing all forms of political Islam. There is a measure of truth to the analogy. It obscures, however, a fact that the renewal leaders and other moderate Muslims seem to have understood: though they tolerated Islamic devotion, the Dutch never provided the massive infrastructural support to Islamic piety that the New Order has. Despite political setbacks, then, Muslim leaders today look back on the 1980s as a decisive turning point for Islam and at least a partial vindication of the accommodative group's attitude toward the government.

Indeed, the great majority of Muslim intellectuals today believe that their acceptance of the asas tunggal policy had an important unintended consequence. Once Islam was no longer associated with any single party and once politicians recognized that the nation was experiencing an Islamic resurgence, all of the political parties began to advertise their commitment to Islam. This "greening" (penghijauan, green being a symbol of Islam) of the campaign process was most dramatically evident during the 1992 electoral campaigns and received widespread comment in the national media. Lukman Harun, a Muhammadiyah leader and director of the Center for Islamic Studies at Jakarta's National University, summarized what is perhaps the most general view among Muslim intellectuals on this change: "Yes, we compromised in accepting the Pancasila, and there were many people who disagreed. But at first we didn't really understand what the consequence of this would be. Before there was one party identified with Islam. But look at what has happened. After being depoliticized, suddenly Islam is no longer confined to any one party but promoted by all of them".

There was another, perhaps deeper dimension to the cultural changes of the 1980s. In Java, where the nominally Islamic Javanist community had long posed a serious obstacle to Islamic reform, media and academic reports in the 1980s took note that many former strongholds of Javanist Islam were beginning to take on a santri (pious Muslim) face. The type of Islam being promoted in most such cases, it should be emphasized, owed more to the politically neutral, "neo-santri" Islam supported by the government than it did to the party-based Islam of the 1950s or the decentralized, fiercely independent Islam of colonial times. Nonetheless, the growth of Islamic devotionalism in areas previously renowned for their Javanist heterodoxy was welcomed by Muslim leaders. Indeed, for many, this change in religious culture is a far more meaningful achievement than anything that might be accomplished in the electoral arena.

On all these points, the contrast with the first ten years of the New Order government is striking. While those early years had been marked by a small but controversial movement of Javanese from Islam to Hinduism and Christianity, by the 1980s there was clear evidence of Islamic revival and Javanist decline. Indeed, reports since the late 1980s have suggested that some of the earlier converts to Christianity and, especially, Hinduism were returning to Islam, as the Islamic revival reached into the very heartlands of Javanism. The impact of "cultural" Islam was thus reaching into civil society; unbeknownst to many, it was also preparing the ground for an important shift in Indonesian politics.

## The Quest for the Middle Class

It was in the booming metropolitan regions of Indonesia, however, that the most spectacular evidence of cultural Islam's advance was visible. In Indonesia's large cities, a new middle class was taking shape, even as the gap between rich and poor increased. Not surprisingly, universities were at the forefront of this trend. Earlier, in the 1950s and early 1960s, Indonesia's national universities had been centers of secular nationalism, in which the santri community, though represented, was typically among the weaker of the factions in the student body. The 1970s, however, saw the rapid growth of the so-called Salman movement (gerakan Salman) and related Muslim initiatives on state university campuses. Salman students rejected the scholastic arguments of traditionalist Islam and the exclusivism of modernism. In order to Islamize the secular university, they adopted relaxed, democratic forms of dress and amusement, while encouraging strict adherence to Muslim devotional acts (ibadah), including daily prayers, the fast, and payment of alms (zakat) to the poor.

The model for this campuswide devotional movement was developed at the Salman Mosque, located at the Bandung Technological Institute, under the guidance of M. Imaduddin Abdulrahim, a charismatic intellectual who, years later, would play a central role in the establishment of ICMI. Conducting an extensive campaign of religious outreach, the Salman Mosque Committee invited pop bands to play at the mosque, sponsored seminars on religion and development, published a small journal of culture and economic affairs, and developed a variety of educational and economic programs for poor residents living near the university.

By the early 1980s Salman-inspired religious activities had become a conspicuous feature of campus life at virtually every major university in Java and Sumatra. The movement also led to the formation of discussion groups that sought to formulate Muslim political and economic policies. A few of these smaller groupings provided the nucleus for the more radical Islamic movements that attracted attention, if not significant public support, in the 1980s and 1990s.

The mainstream movement for Islamic revival, however, eventually reached far beyond the university and touched the lives of the urban poor and the middle class. A decade earlier, in the 1970s, few Indonesians could have predicted such a development. Those years had witnessed a rapid expansion in urban wealth and an infusion of Western and East Asian consumer styles into elite and middle-class circles. Night clubs proliferated, alcohol became widely available, and rebellious youths affected permissive lifestyles that their elders, even non-santri, found shocking. Urban society was widely regarded as becoming more "monied," and many people took offense at the callous disregard of elite youth for traditional mores and etiquette.

Benedict Anderson's analysis of cartoons and media images from this period captures the widespread ambivalence toward these changes in certain urban circles. Anderson's discussion focuses on the unease felt by elite Javanese officials in the face of their own privileged children abandoning the reassuring, if hierarchical, etiquette learned by their parents in smalltown Java. Ripped from their earlier social background and unable to fall back on the assertive nationalism of the 1950s, the senior generation's neotraditionalism seemed quaintly obsolete to a generation of privileged offspring. Anderson describes the anxiety this caused among the Jakartan elite: "Such events suggest to Indonesia's rulers that the future threatens to elude them, and so the past is summoned to their aid. Most of them are deeply aware of the far journey they have made in their lives from the rural townships of late colonial Java to the metropolitan pomp of the 'cosmopolitan' Jakarta they now enjoy.... Their past has also not prepared them morally for the lives they now lead. Most of them grew up in the sphere of provincial Javanese society, and the norms and values of that society have left powerful residues at the core of their consciousness".

It was against a less privileged but otherwise similar background that many middle-class Muslims came to feel uncomfortable with what they regarded as a narrowing or "privatization" (pribadisasi) of moral concerns during the 1970s.

Unlike the Javanese officials whom Anderson describes, however, Muslim urbanites tend to carry a less amorphous experiential "residue" from their early years. Rather than diffuse existential anxiety and appeals to an invented Javanese "tradition," they typically respond to the anomie and hedonism of urban life with precise ethical prescriptions and calls for a deepening of faith. For them, Islam seems better suited to the challenges of urban existence than Javanist traditions, which they see as incapable of responding to the social and economic needs of ordinary Indonesians. Unlike the elite's ersatz Javanism, they point out, Islam – especially the neatly modularized and eminently educable variant associated with Islamic modernism and neomodernism – is both modern and transethnic. Even in the absence of the tranquil communities of yesteryear, it can work to instill ethical discipline and restraint. Yet Islam is also thoroughly Indonesian. Its roots reach back to precolonial society and into most, if not all, of the ethnic communities of the archipelago. Equally important, however much certain Western observers have identified Islam as an opponent to Indonesian nationalism, Muslim intellectuals know that they too can rightly claim the mantle of Indonesian nationalism, albeit a nonsecularist version.

One need only compare Anderson's portrait with that of Kuntowijoyo in the epilogue to his Paradigma Islam: Interpretasi Untuk Aksi to discern that, however much they shared a similar sense of moral anxiety, Muslim intellectuals were not plagued by the existential vagueness afflicting the Javanist elite. A Yale-educated historian from Gadjah Mada University, Kuntowijoyo describes the moral crisis among urban youth in terms strikingly similar to those of Anderson and attributes its origins to similar causes. "Apparently social changes since 1965 have given birth to a new social class, a middle class, one that is almost without roots in any prior historical period". But Kuntowijoyo's analysis goes on to suggest that there is a complex dialectic to the crisis, one not apparent in Anderson's descriptions of the Javanist elite. Alongside the self-indulgent hedonism of privileged youth, Kuntowijoyo observes, there is an emergent counterculture of high moral idealism and principled criticism. This critical culture is not based on traditional Javanese notions of power; indeed, Kuntowijoyo claims (referring to Anderson's work on ideas of power in traditional Java), it self-consciously rejects these in favor of an unhierarchical tradition that, for Kuntowijoyo, originates in modern Islam.

When the New Order government brought this new middle class into existence, Kuntowijoyo writes, it expected it to be "faithful" (mempunyai kesetiaan) to its policies. But among those making the pilgrimage from village to city, there were some who brought an Islamic ideology contemptuous of the elitist values of government bureaucracy. Thus, in Kuntowijoyo's view, this neo-santri tradition acts as an antihegemonic subculture, quietly subverting elite culture from within: "The process of decolonizing and detraditionalizing consciousness has already gone so far that the bureaucracy cannot assume [popular acceptance of] a concept of power like that of a magical source radiating invulnerability.... The social and moral basis of the authoritarian bureaucracy is finished".

This theme of santri subversion of Javanist elitism was common in the critical Islamic literature of the 1980s. The confidently assertive attitude of Kuntowijoyo's commentary is equally characteristic of this writing, distinguishing it from the more tentative tone of the 1970s renewal literature. Like many in this new generation of scholar-activists, Kuntowijoyo shows little of the self-doubt of the earlier period. Muslims have joined the ranks of government and business, he notes, and they are prepared to Islamize not only the peasantry, but large segments of the middle class and ruling elite.

Not surprisingly, a now-middle-aged Nurcholish Madjid has himself been at the forefront of this newly robust cultural Islam, with its eyes set on government officials and the middle class. In 1986, Madjid established an association for urban proselytization known as Paramadina (from the Spanish para, "for," and the Arabian city of Madinah). Zifirdaus Adnan has wryly observed that, though the Paramadina officials "explained that the target of the dakwah (missionary activity) was the middle class people who have not received sufficient understanding of Islam," the presence of the ministers for religion, education and culture, environment, and youth affairs at the organization's inaugural celebration indicates that "the target is not only the middle class but also the elite class". The organization counted no fewer than eight cabinet members on its first advisorial board. In interviews during 1992 and 1993, Cak Nur, as he is affectionately known, openly acknowledged this desire to deepen the faith of the urban elite. He pointed to the expansion of mosques and prayer halls in businesses, hotels, government offices, and Jakarta's affluent southern suburbs as dramatic evidence of success.

An additional feature of the Islamic advance into the middle class has been the emergence of a new kind of revivalist proselytizer (dai). Many of these pop revivalists come from backgrounds in film, music, literature, and other mass media rather than from Muslim schools. They use deeply emotional accounts of their conversion experience rather than complicated exegesis of doctrine to move people to a deeper faith. Their prominence testifies to a dispersion of religious authority beyond the ranks of traditionally trained Islamic scholars, a trademark of the Muslim revival in other Muslim countries as well.

Despite setbacks in the formal political arena, then, by the late 1980s Muslim activists and intellectuals showed a new confidence about their long-term prospects under the New Order. It is this air of confidence that is so powerfully evident in Kuntowijoyo's article, with its open contempt for ersatz Javanism. By itself, the critical tone of this article is, again, not unusual, as it was a regular feature of Muslim criticism in the 1980s. More distinctive than the message of Kuntowijoyo's broadside, however, was its medium. The paper was first presented at ICMI'S inaugural meeting in Malang, East Java, in December 1990. It was then reprinted in the published proceedings of the conference, alongside more cautious articles by government intellectuals.

The example is telling. Inaugurated to the beat of the president's drum, some of the ICMI membership showed a marked inclination to march to a different drummer. From the start, however, there was a tension in the organization between those who wished to work closely with the government and those who hoped to see ICMI act more independently. This tension would become increasingly apparent in the months following ICMI'S founding.

## State and Society in ICMI's Founding

Media reports on ICMI's genesis often portray it as the spontaneous creation of five students from the Universitas

Brawijaya in Malang, East Java. The five students, the story goes, were devout but otherwise unexceptional Muslim youth who yearned to bring Muslim intellectuals together to talk about the future of the nation and the ummat. To do so, they proposed a meeting to which leaders from all of Indonesia's major Islamic associations as well as from government and the media would be invited. Having come up with the idea in early 1990, the students then proposed the plan to the rectors of the state-run Brawijaya University and Malang's Muhammadiyah University. The rectors responded favorably but hesitated in face of the expense and political sensitivity of such a symposium. Undeterred, the five youths set out at their own expense to visit centers of Islamic education in Java, to promote their idea with leading intellectuals and to raise funds for the conference. In the course of their travels, they met with prominent Muslim intellectuals, including, most notably, Dr. M. Imaduddin Abdulrahim and Drs. M. Dawam Rahardjo, who jointly suggested that the students move beyond the idea of a mere symposium and promote the formation of a national association of Muslim intellectuals.

Sensing the importance of government sponsors if the organization was to survive, Imaduddin proposed that the students invite the minister of the environment, Emil Salim, and the minister of research and technology, Dr. B. J. Habibie to act as chairmen of the national organization. Emil Salim was one of the architects of the New Order's early economic policies. A kindly, mild-mannered gentleman, he was among the technocrats who had sponsored the admission of development-minded Muslims into government planning bureaus in the late 1960s and 1970s; he had long been known as a gentile proponent of better government-Muslim relations. Imaduddin and the students were not personally acquainted with Dr. Habibie. Quite unlike Salim, Habibie was best known for his passionate commitment to technology; indeed, though a mutual friend, he was indirectly critical of the policies technocrats like Salim had helped to craft. He favored governmentsupported high-technology industries rather than labor-intensive export industries. Though less well known for his piety, Habibie had recently been featured in several television interviews and a story in the popular Muslim magazine Kiblat, where he spoke warmly of his devotion to Islam.

In subsequent meetings, Emil Salim agreed to attend the national symposium but declined to play a leadership role in any organization, insisting that he was "too old" and that Habibie would be more energetic and effective. The students thus turned to Habibie to lead the proposed organization, which, at Nurcholish Madjid's suggestion, had tentatively acquired the title of ISMI – Ikatan Sarjana Muslim Indonesia. Contacted through letters and by telephone, Habibie at first declined to meet with the students. According to the reports of his aides, Habibie said privately that, though his devotion to Islam was real enough, he was not sufficiently well versed in Islamic doctrine to play such a leadership role. "How can I do it? I am an engineer and a builder of airplanes, not an Islamic scholar!" More important, no doubt, he is also reported to have expressed fears that by agreeing to lead the organization he might contradict the wishes of President Suharto.

It was only after Habibie was contacted by the former minister of religion and Suharto confidant (retired) General Alamsyah Ratu Perwiranegara that he agreed to meet with the students. It was Imaduddin who urged the students to overcome Habibie's reluctance by working through Alamsyah. Though the retired general was well known for his unswerving devotion to the president, he had over the course of his career maintained open lines of communications with Muslims. In any case, Imaduddin's suggestion proved effective; the students and their supporters were granted a meeting with Habibie.

On August 23, 1990, the students, accompanied by Imaduddin, Dawam Rahardjo, and M. Syafi'i Anwar (a close associate of Rahardjo and a former reporter for the Muslim newsweekly Panji Masyarakat), traveled to Dr. Habibie's office on Jalan Thamrin to present their formal request to the minister. The group had been granted one half hour from Habibie's busy schedule. The students and their supporters presented their ideas directly, in what one of the participants later described as a long and slightly anxious monologue. Afterwards, Habibie commented positively on the idea of the association, but again protested that he was not the most appropriate figure for the role, saying, as before, that he was not sufficiently learned in Islamic matters. But he did not turn down the students' request outright. Instead, he asked that a petition be drawn up and circulated among prominent Muslim intellectuals to express support for his leadership of such an organization, so as to impress upon the president (and, no doubt, the Indonesian public) that their appeal had broad support in the Muslim community. In addition, he asked for an outline of the association's organization and goals, which he would then present to the president. "I am a servant of the president," he said (according to the reports of some present at the meeting), "so I must go to him to request permission to work with you."

Over the next week, Imaduddin, Dawam Rahardjo, and Nurcholish Madjid drew up a document outlining the organization's goals and expressing support for Dr. Habibie's chairmanship. The document was circulated among prominent Muslim intellectuals in Jakarta, Bogor, Bandung, and Yogyakarta; eventually forty-nine individuals signed it. In the meantime, too, Habibie talked with several of his colleagues in the cabinet, soliciting their advice on the wisdom of his joining the organization. Most, I was told, urged him to decline the invitation. One, Dr. Saleh Afiff advised him not to turn down the request but to seek President Suharto's counsel directly. Habibie agreed and arranged an appointment with the president, sending him the petition and the outline of the association's goals.

Only Habibie and Suharto were present during their meeting, but a more or less uniform account of their exchange has become common knowledge among cabinet officials and ICMI officials whom I interviewed. According to this report, Habibie began the meeting by repeating his disclaimer that he is an engineer, a maker of airplanes, and unqualified to lead an association of Islamic intellectuals. Then, more quietly, he is reported to have turned to the president and said, "Also, if I lead this organization, maybe I will be separated (terpisah) from Bapak (father, sir). Perhaps my and Bapak's understanding of Islam differ?" Throughout his public life, Habibie has made a point of demonstrating his unswerving loyalty to the president. His close relationship has been an especially crucial political resource for Habibie because, until ICMI'S founding, he has had no significant political base outside the bureaucracy. So Habibie's question struck to the heart of his own political future.

President Suharto is reported to have responded without hesitation to Habibie's query, saying, "This is good; you can do it."

Then, in a demonstration of his own mastery of Islamic knowledge, the president told Habibie to take a pen, open his notebook, and record what follows. The nowmythic account of this meeting recounts that, over the next two hours, the president "dictated" (mendikte) a long discussion of the basic principles of Islam, including the meaning of the Sunnah, obligatory prayer (sholat) and passages from the Qur'an. At the end, the president said, "Now you understand what I know." From this demonstration Habibie was to appreciate that the president's knowledge of normative Islàm was great and consistent with his own. The whole meeting lasted six hours, and, from it, Habibie emerged with a clear presidential mandate to lend his hand to the Islamic association.

After this, Habibie invited several ministers to his home, where he described ICMI and invited them to join in its establishment. Those present included the minister of internal affairs, Rudini; Fuad Hasan, the minister of education and culture; Azwar Anas, the minister of transportation; Emil Salim, minister of the environment; Nasruddin Sumintapura, vice-minister for finance; Saleh Afiff, state minister for national development planning and chairman of the National Development Planning Agency (Bappenas); and H. Munawir Sjadzali, minister of religion. Also present were two people without ministerial ties: Nurcholish Madjid and Professor Dr. Insinyur Ahmad Baiguni, an advisor to Habibie from the Agency for the Assessment and Application of Technology (BPPT). Of those present, Minister Rudini, who was a military man known for his Javanist sympathies, initially expressed reservations about the organization. However, on learning of the president's support for ICMI, he quickly agreed to join.

Now with presidential and cabinet support, on September 27 Habibie again met with the students and their supporters, informing them that the plan had the president's blessing. As a condition of his becoming chairman, however, Habibie requested that he be allowed to bring some of his administrative staff from BPPT to work in ICMI. Among those assistants was Dr. Wardiman Djojonegoro, an engineer and close assistant to Habibie at the BPPT, later to become Habibie's right-hand man within ICMI. A Madurese of aristocratic (priyayi) background, Wardiman had a reputation for having decidedly "nationalist" views on Islam. Some Western observers thus saw in Wardiman's appointment an effort to "abanganize" ICMI. Those familiar with Wardiman, however, note that he is better known for his loyalty to Habibie and his reputation as a cool-headed administrator than as an ideologue. Whatever his background, he quickly demonstrated his loyalty to the Islamic cause. Among other things, during the first year of ICMI's existence, Wardiman was a bold but even-handed critic of Christian dominance in education and the media.

In this case, as in many of his subsequent appointments, Habibie revealed his preference for a loyal and controlled managerial team, like that which he had built at the national technology institute, the BPPT. His appointment of trusted BPPT staff to ICMI steering committees also reflected his determination in the face of continuing military suspicion to demonstrate that the organization was not political, but technoscientific and educational. At this same meeting, Habibie suggested that the term sarjana ("scholar") in the organization's title be changed to cendekiawan ("intellectual"), so as to avoid the impression that the organization was only open to people with academic degrees. He also suggested that the organization's first national symposium be held at the beginning of December. All those present agreed, and three teams were set up to coordinate preparations for the symposium, which was to take place on the campus of Brawijaya Unversity in Malang, East Java.

With presidential blessing, preparations for the December meeting proceeded apace. What had begun as an extragovernmental initiative launched by a few Muslim intellectuals – some of whom had once had a less than cordial relationship with the regime had now evolved into a top-heavy, if still unsteady, coalition of government and extragovernment Muslims. Officials from the state-sponsored Council of Islamic Clerics (Majelis Ulama Indonesia) were drawn into planning meetings during October and November, as were the minister of religion, H. Munawir Sjadzali (a political moderate and a theological liberal), and his staff. A close supporter of the president and a Habibie ally, Harmoko, minister of information, was also active in the planning meetings.

Far more interesting than the government officials recruited to the planning committees were the nongovernmental Muslims drawn in. They continued to play a central, if somewhat less visible, role in meeting preparations. The appointees to the main planning committee, for example, included Dawam Rahardjo, Sri Bintang Pamungkas, and Muslimin Nasution. Nasution was head of the Bureau of Research and Development in the government's Department of Cooperatives and thus (despite otherwise impressive credentials as a Muslim intellectual and an ideological liberal) could be regarded as a "government" Muslim. Dawam and Bintang, however, were known for their outspokenness and prodemocracy views. Dawam was a well-known social and theological progressive, linked in the 1980s to the NGO community and the struggle for equitable development.

Bintang was, in theological terms, a more conventional modernist than Dawam; however the strength of his public commitment to democratization and clean government often placed him at the edge of allowable discourse in Indonesia. Educated at the Bandung Technological Institute and then at Iowa State University, Sri Bintang in 1990 was employed in the Department of Economics at the Universitas Indonesia. In the late 1980s he acquired a reputation among Muslim and NGO activists as a courageous and principled critic of government policies. His denunciations of corruption in government were regularly featured in the national press. Moreover, having refused in 1988 to join Golkar, the government-sponsored party that most public employees are required to support, Sri Bintang went on to run for and win a seat in the the National Assembly (DPR) under the banner of the opposition Muslim party, the PPP. His campaign during 1992 was, by all measures, remarkable for its blunt criticisms of corruption, economic inequality, and the continuing involvement of the military in national politics. The appointment of two such public figures to key planning posts for the new organization surprised many skeptics and was taken as a sign that, whatever the president's intentions, Habibie was intent on building a broad coalition reaching beyond the halls of government.

Imaduddin Abdulrahim was another, equally remarkable appointment to the various steering committees for the December meeting. Up to that year Imaduddin had had a troubled relationship with the government security agencies. A founder and leader of the Salman movement at the Bandung Technological Institute,

Imaduddin had been detained by security forces on several occasions in the early 1970s, denounced as "fundamentalist and anti-Catholic," and arrested and held without charges during fourteen months of 1978-1979. Eventually he was barred from state employment. After his detention, he traveled to the United States to take a Ph.D. in management at Iowa State University, hoping that upon return to Indonesia the employment ban would be lifted. On completing his degree in 1984, however, he learned that the ban still applied. He thus taught for two years in the United States, returning to Indonesia only in 1986. Still unable to get state employment, he eventually formed his own management company, where he has enjoyed considerable financial success.

Not all Muslim critics were won to the ICMI cause. Deliar Noer, for example, a distinguished intellectual of the senior (pre-Madjid) generation, refused to join on two grounds: first, that Habibie himself had previously demonstrated no deep commitment to Islam and, second, that ICMI was not a truly representative organization, but was designed to promote President Suharto's reelection. Others with ties to the NGO community, such as M. Billah, preferred to remain outside the organization for fear that membership might compromise their ability to act independently. Still others, like the respected historian Taufik Abdullah, declined to join despite repeated invitations, on the ground that ICMI was too closely controlled by the bureaucracy. Like many other independent intellectuals, however, Abdullah has also refrained from publicly criticizing ICMI. In private, he acknowledges that the organization has done some real good, such as sponsoring public discussion of human rights.

Others, however, have not hesitated to criticize ICMI on the grounds that it encourages exclusivistic and sectarian attitudes at a time when what is needed is interreligious tolerance and a nonreligious nationalism. For example, Djohan Effendi, a Muslim liberal associated with Madjid and Rahardjo during the earlier movement for Islamic renewal and now employed in the Ministry of Religion (and, as of April 1993, a special assistant for religious and social affairs to State Secretary Drs. Moerdiono, an outspoken ICMI critic), has quietly but repeatedly warned that ICMI is once again politicizing Islam. In doing so, he has said, ICMI risks undermining the hard-won accomplishments of cultural Islam and indeed may eventually provoke the military to move against those who use Islam for political ends.

The outspoken chairman of Nahdlatul Ulama, Abdurrahman Wahid, also accused ICMI of sectarianism. Despite a personal appeal by Habibie, who visited Wahid when he was hospitalized in February of 1991, Wahid has refused to join ICMI, saying its focus is "exclusivistic" and elitist rather than pan-Indonesian. Ridwan Saidi, chairman of HMI from 1974 to 1977 and a former PPP activist who had joined Golkar (only in 1995 to try to form a new Islamic party), criticized ICMI on similar grounds, claiming that ICMI reflects a peculiarly bureaucratic vision of Islam.

Wahid's comments have been widely featured in the media. He argues that at this juncture in history the struggle for democracy and justice must take precedence over less inclusive concerns, including those of the Muslim community. He phrases this argument in unusually blunt terms, shocking even some of his own supporters in the Muslim community. "I am for an Indonesian society, not just an Islamic one," he has said in several public assemblies. Islam, he argues, should not be idealized so that it is regarded as the only ground for democracy, law, or economic justice. Rather, Islam should serve as an "inspirational base for a national framework of a democratic society". In interviews Wahid expressed his additional concern that, with the support of some government officials, ICMI might be used to promote a rigidly exclusivistic Islam contrary to Indonesian Islam's long history of tolerance. It is significant that, despite his criticisms, Wahid did not forbid Nahdlatul Ulama members to join ICMI, and several prominent figures did join.

In April 1991, however, Wahid made his own position all the clearer, with his participation in the founding of a nongovernmental and nondenominational coalition known as the Forum Demokrasi. Some of Wahid's sternest critics launched a vicious rumor campaign, implying this effort was related to a putative "alliance" with Christians in general and the minister of defense and security, Benny Murdani, in particular. Wahid's defenders vigorously deny these charges of a political alliance with Murdani. Though the Democratic Forum was not banned, the government made clear its displeasure with Wahid's initiative. Among other things, it refused to reappoint him to the MPR on October 1, 1992. Conversely, the new MPR had a large number of Muslim leaders with ties to Minister Habibie and ICMI.

It is striking that, during this first phase of ICMI'S formation, even as aides to Minister Habibie came to exercise growing influence in its administration, ICMI managed to mobilize a diverse array of Muslim intellectuals. They included what Wardiman Djojonegoro, the general secretary of ICMI and one of Habibie's closest aides, referred to in interview with me as the "right and left wings" of the Muslim opposition. This diversity reinforced the sense of spirited exchange so evident during the first ICMI congress, from December 6 to 8, 1990. Most of the speeches presented were scholarly, cautious, and even dryly academic in tone; the published versions of several came with long bibliographies. The substance of the papers, however, was more varied. Most respectfully echoed President Suharto's speech, endorsing the government's goals for twenty-first-century development. This emphasis was consistent with the title of the symposium, "To Build a Twenty-First-Century Indonesian Society," equally notable for its developmentalist emphasis and its lack of reference to Islam. The papers presented by Habibie's associates stressed this same theme, underscoring the importance of science and technology in the next phase of Indonesia's industrialization and urging Muslims to assure themselves a greater role in national development by mastering new information and technologies.

As Kuntowijoyo's above article indicates, however, much of the discussion was considerably less technodevelopmentalist in tone. Several discussants raised pointed questions about economic justice and echoed Kuntowijoyo in criticizing the bureaucratic values of the Javanist elite. Rather than simply endorsing the government's developmentalist goals, these independent scholars emphasized the need to use Muslims' political and intellectual influence to democratize Indonesian society.

## Politics of Cultural Breakthrough

The effort to unite Muslim intellectuals under a single, all-embracing organizational banner has historic precedent. Previously the most notable initiative was the formation of Persami, the Union of Muslim Scholars (Persatuan Sarjana Muslim Indonesia). Founded in 1964 to combat the growing influence of the Communist Party,

Persami played an active role in supporting then-GeneralSuharto in his rise to power during 1966-1967. It declined after 1968, however, as the result of leadership disputes and the regime's interest in limiting social organizations that might prove inclined to criticize its programs.

ICMI'S umbrellalike organization also replicates a pattern of corporatist control that, as Benedict Anderson and David Reeve have emphasized, is a long-standing characteristic of Indonesian politics, elaborated to its most effective degree under the New Order. However, if bureaucratic control was an intent, its imposition nonetheless had unintended effects. One was that Muslim activists previously regarded as enemies of the state and thus subject to political controls suddenly had unprecedented freedom of movement and access to the press. In the months following the first ICMI congress, the media gave prominent attention to Islamic discussions of politics and development, discussions that, just a few years earlier, would have been regarded as dangerously sectarian.

Here again, Imaduddin Abdulrahim's experience provides a telling illustration of the depths of this change. In interviews in August 1992 and June 1993, Dr. Imaduddin commented that before ICMI'S founding he had great difficulty giving public lectures. Wherever he went, his sponsors were required to obtain permits from the national police, and these were often denied. Since his association with ICMI, he noted, all this has changed. Now he travels freely around the country, "from Aceh to Java," as he put it, and not once has he had to secure police permits.

Dr. Imaduddin's testimony is all the more striking inasmuch as, by his own and others' accounts, before 1990 he had made several unsuccessful attempts to establish an association of Muslim intellectuals. The most recent of these occurred in January 1989, when Imaduddin and Dawam Rahardjo invited fifty intellectuals to the town of Kaliurang, near Yogya- , to discuss establishing such an organization. Forty of the fifty invitees showed up. On the second day, however, police arrived too and closed down the meeting, insisting that it had not received prior clearance and was thus illegal. Participants in the conference blamed the action on Benny Murdani, the Catholic-Javanese minister of defense and security.

Another effort to create an association of Muslim intellectuals had been made considerably earlier, in 1984, at a meeting in Ciawi, Bogor. The meeting had been organized through the joint efforts of the governmentsponsored Majelis Ulama Indonesia (Council of Indonesian Ulama) and Dawam Rahardjo's respected (and theologically liberal) Institute for Religious and Philosophical Studies. At the meeting, Rahardjo expressed the view that the time seemed right for such an organization. Representatives from the MUI and the Ministry of Religion balked, however, fearing government disapproval, and the plan was eventually shelved. A similar effort was made in 1987. This time the activists behind the effort reached even higher into the upper echelons of the New Order elite, hoping that with General Alamsyah Ratu Perwiranegara (the Suharto confidant) as one of its official sponsors, the organization would secure government approval. Once again, however, the initiative was stopped when security officials expressed their concerns that the organization might give rise to "sectarian" influences.

From this brief historical account, it can be seen that press reports on the role of the five Brawijaya students in ICMI'S founding hid what was, in fact, a more complex history. From the start, prominent Muslim intellectuals were deeply involved in the effort to establish an ICMI-like organization. For political reasons, however, they chose to distance themselves from the publicity surrounding ICMI'S founding. Indeed, the initial Malang meeting in early 1990 at which the five Brawijaya students were supposed to have come up with the proposal for an ICMI-like organization was not simply a private campus event. It occurred in the context of a visit to the campus by none other than Dr. Imaduddin. Not coincidentally, the rector who had approved Dr. Imaduddin's visit to the campus of Brawijaya University— at a time when Imaduddin was still barred from most campuses — was an alumni of the Association of Muslim Students (HMI), of which Nurcholish Madjid had been chairman and Imaduddin himself a member in the late 1960S. After the talk, Dr. Imaduddin urged the students to approach the dean with the idea for a national symposium, saying that they would be remembered in history for such a pathbreaking initiative.

The media story of the students' role correctly underscores that the effort to establish an association of Muslim intellectuals, at least in the first instance, originated within the independent Muslim community. However much it was to be drawn into bureaucratic intrigues, the original idea for ICMI was not simply a matter of government political engineering, but the product of a state-society interaction with a longer and more contested history. Rather than being the brainchild of five anonymous students from a provincial university, however, the original plan for the association originated with well-placed but independent Muslim intellectuals. Some of those intellectuals had a reputation with the security forces that might have compromised efforts to establish the organization, had their names been given too much prominence. An activist like Imaduddin openly acknowledges this fact, noting that it was his idea to look to Minister Habibie for support, since he feared that his own reputation in security circles might jeopardize the organization's prospects.

The question that remains is, what had changed between 1988 and late 1990 so that the government, and the president in particular, felt compelled to support an organization that just eighteen months earlier security forces had sought to suppress? Surprisingly, on this point both supporters and critics of ICMI share similar views. Both groups acknowledge that the president's rivalry with segments of the military, in particular Benny Murdani and his allies, intensified in 1989 and 1990, in anticipation of the 1992 elections. As several interviewees commented, one had to look all the way back to the early 1960S, to the conflict between President Sukarno and the military, to find a breech between government and the military of similar proportions.

It is noteworthy in this regard that numerous high-ranking military officers are reported to have advised against government legalization of the organization. In the days before the president's approval of ICMI'S formation, Vice-President Try Sutrisno is said to have urged the president to reject the proposal. Eventually, as it became clearer that ICMI had the support of the president, the military stopped its public sniping, and Try Sutrisno himself attended the Malang meeting. Despite this apparent accommodation, military criticism of ICMI continued. Rather than attacking the organization as a whole, however, military critics over the next months warned of factions within ICMI who want to use it and Islam itself for their own political ends. In a widely publicized speech presented on June 18, 1993, Vice-President Try Sutrisno warned, without mentioning names, that there were signs that some people were using Islam as an "instrument of legitimation." In April 1993 – one month after the installation of a new cabinet heavy with ICMI sympathizers – the vice-president participated in an even bolder challenge to ICMI, giving his blessing to the formation of an "Association of Nusantara Intellectuals" (ICNU). This was a nondenominational organization of intellectuals intended to fight "sectarianism" and other challenges to Indonesia's "five principles" of government. Despite the vice- president's blessing, however, ICNU failed to take off. However, there were two additional efforts to launch nonsectarian, militaronationalist alternatives to ICMI in 1994 and 1995.

Many independent Muslims have also continued to criticize ICMI. Critics such as Deliar Noer and Ridwan Saidi have cited the president's role in ICMI'S founding to buttress their claim that ICMI was little more than a vehicle for the mobilization of presidential support. Other critics have complained that Habibie has used ICMI for his own political ends, including what some people regard as his failed effort to win nomination to the vicepresidency in March of 1993. In retrospect, it seems unlikely that Habibie ever seriously thought he could win the vice-presidency in 1993. But there clearly were political advantages to his involvement with ICMI. In particular, before his appointment to the ICMI chairmanship, Habibie enjoyed the confidence of President Suharto but lacked ties to any national organiza- tion that might provide a mass base. ICMI has provided him with that.

Over the years since the organization's founding, ICMI'S activities have continued to expand. As Imaduddin commented above, ICMI'S prominence has allowed previously marginalized Muslim intellectuals to air their views in public settings. It has also provided Muslims with the resources and political latitude to undertake initiatives that were heretofore unthinkable. These have included the establishment of an Islamic Bank, the Bank Muamalat, and of a respected national newspaper, Republika; a national Islamic Center is also being planned. Whatever ICMI'S long-term fate, these initiatives have allowed an important institutional consolidation of the new Muslim middle class.

It should be noted, finally, that there is a broader, economic dimension to Habibie's appeal. Many Indonesians see Habibie as one of the few government leaders speaking to the problem of the continuing marginalization of Muslims in Indonesian enterprise. The economic liberalization of the late 1980S has unleashed a new entrepreneurial dynamic, but Muslims and pribumi (indigenous, non-Chinese) Indonesians remain, with a few exceptions, but secondary players in it. Though his economic ideas have been criticized as elitist, wasteful, and, ultimately, self-defeating, Habibie's impassioned discourses on technology and "value-added" industry appeal to many middle-class Indonesians who fear that the low-wage, export-oriented industrialization favored by economic technocrats may provide low-paying employment for the poor but very little for the indigenous middle class. From this perspective, Habibie has sought to present himself as but one in a long line of Indonesian bureaucratic nationalists who would bend the rules of the market to allow state intervention to improve the position of Indonesia's indigenous majority. Ironically, the great majority of his enterprises, such as airplanes and shipbuilding, are capital-intensive and labor-poor. They offer few employment opportunities and do little to provide the native community with the business skills with which they might compete with Sino-Indonesians.

Despite all these controversies, Habibie's national influence has continued to grow. So too have the questions surrounding his commitment to openness and liberalization. In his role as director of the state airplane manufacture industry (IPTN), Habibie has consistently supported large and unaccounted state subsidies to his own enterprises. Critics of his enterprises suggest that the strategic industries under Habibie's direction receive subsidies totaling more than a billion dollars each year. In April 1994 Minister Habibie was also strongly criticized in the press for secretly "borrowing" 300 million dollars from funds designated for reforestation to plough into his capital-hungry state firms. These and other incidents, discussed below, have shaken public confidence in Habibie's commitment to governmental reform and led even some of his supporters to wonder whether he can avoid being compromised by the culture of corporatist cronyism.

## Developmental Tensions

However extraordinary ICMI'S ascent, several incidents in the months following its founding illustrated its vulnerabilities to elite control. The examples also suggest that, though ICMI may succeed in winning concessions from the government, the long-term impact of the organization will depend entirely on broader political developments, including the president's willingness to make concessions to those demanding greater political participation and Muslim leaders' interest in promoting those demands.

From the beginning certain incidents revealed serious tensions within ICMI over the organization's proper structure and political posture. For example, as Habibie and his aides laid out ICMI'S organizational structure in early 1991, it became clear that they were under pressure from above to limit the organization's autonomy by bringing ICMI under tight executive control. Up to that time, the print media had almost uniformly speculated that Dawam Rahardjo was the top candidate for the important post of general secretary. Unlike other independent Muslims, Dawam had never been regarded by security forces as an extremist or an antigovernment activist. He has strong ties to the NGO community and for years has managed to walk a fine line between criticism of specific government policies and support for the general goals of national development. Like Imaduddin, however, Dawam also had a long history of involvement in efforts to establish a national association of Muslim intellectuals. He also had impeccable credentials as a devout Muslim, an accomplished scholar, and someone who, though occasionally cooperating with the government on development projects, maintained a careful distance from the bureaucracy. Over the years, finally, Dawam had also distinguished himself as development theorist (his academic training was in economics), a credential well suited to the kind of pragmatic role Habibie hoped ICMI would play. For all these reasons, Dawam's election to general secretary appealed to independent Muslims and seemed acceptable, it was thought, to the government.

In the first weeks of January 1991, Habibie supporters leaked hints to the press of the eventual organization of ICMI. Claiming that it would have a state-of-the-art "matrix" structure like that common in Western high-tech enterprises, Habibie's assistants indicated that ICMI would not have a general secretary, because none was needed under a matrix system. While independent intellectuals would figure prominently within each matrix sector, the crucial managerial positions at the top of the organization were to be recruited from Habibie's Agency for the Development and Application of Technology.

Independent prodemocracy intellectuals, including Sri Bintang Pamungkas and Dawam Rahardjo, were quick to criticize Habibie's plan. In public statements they complained that the proposed structure was undemocratic and denied independent Muslims their right to positions of influence in the organization. Speaking in unusually blunt terms, Dawam accused Habibie of allowing ICMI to be taken over by bureaucrats. Over the next three weeks there was great tension; many observers thought the fledgling organization was about to collapse. The criticism seemed to seal Dawam's fate, guaranteeing that he would not be accorded a truly influential leadership position in the organization. The most important leadership position in the organization thus went not to Dawam, but to Habibie's trusted advisor (and the future minister of education) Wardiman Djojonegoro.

To the surprise of many observers, however, ICMI survived, indeed with relations among Habibie, Dawam, and others still intact. Rahardjo was given a prestigious if somewhat symbolic position in the ICMI leadership. More significant, his journal, Ulumul Qur'an — a well-respected mouthpiece of liberal Islam, which to this day continues to serve as a forum for democratic and theologically liberal ideals — was provided with some ICMI subsidies. At the same time, Habibie took great pains to insist that, in obvious contrast with others in the president's inner circle, he welcomed criticism and debate. Despite criticisms over his choice of officials in ICMI, leading figures associated with the prodemocracy wing of ICMI thus relented and continued to give Habibie their public, if somewhat shaken, support.

Two subsequent incidents highlighted once again tensions between reform-minded independents and Habibie aides. In May of 1991 Emha Ainun Najib, a popular Javanese playwright, social critic, and director of the "Cultural Discussion" bureau within ICMI, sought to have ICMI sponsor a small conference on the Kedung Ombo dam project in West Java, a highly controversial development project that has displaced thousands of rural dwellers from their lands. Before the conference could take place, Najib received a notice from an ICMI higher-up, warning that ICMI could not properly sponsor such an event. Behind the scenes, other independents were reminded that this kind of activity was foolish, embarrassing Habibie and needlessly squandering ICMI'S political capital on an initiative doomed from the start. Eventually, Emha Najib resigned from ICMI.

On May 2, 1992, another incident revealed much the same tension between independent reformers and government officials. In the seminar room of the ICMI Secretariat on Jalan Thamrin in Jakartra, several dozen people gathered to discuss human rights in Indonesia. Among them were independent ICMI members; prominent and, from the government's perspective, controversial human rights advocates such as Mulya Lubis, Aswab Mahasin, and H. J. C. Princen; and longtime critics of the Suharto government, such as Chris Siner. As the event's opening address was coming to an end, ten uniformed officers appeared and requested to see the conference permit. The ICMI members explained that no such permit was needed because the seminar was an internal ICMI affair, like others that had taken place at the headquarters. The police insisted that all meetings of more than five people required a permit, and they politely but firmly insisted that the meeting stop. The organizers relented and the meeting ended without further incident.

Events such as these have prompted a handful of individuals to quit ICMI so as to maintain their independence from the bureaucracy. However, through early 1994, most reform-minded independents remained optimistic about the organization, believing that it could work to enhance democracy and economic equity simultaneously. To justify their hopes, they pointed to examples like an ICMI-related research center's sponsorship of a controversial seminar on human rights. The research center, known as CIDES, the Center for Information and Development Studies, had on its steering committees such outspoken Muslim liberals as Adi Sasono and Dewi Fortuna Anwar. Shortly after its founding in September 1992, Adi Sasono took what was, in light of the previous failure in May of 1992, the rather bold step of announcing that CIDES would sponsor a one-day seminar on human rights after ICMI'S annual national meeting in December. The fact that this was the first national event to be sponsored by CIDES prompted some observers to wonder whether the meeting would be allowed. Despite rumors that it was to be banned by security officials, the meeting took place. Moreover, as with the attempted May meeting on human rights, this conference included presentations by prominent human rights activists from outside ICMI, such as T. Mulya Lubis.

This bold commitment of the CIDES leadership to human rights issues did not end there. CIDES publishes two newsletters and a journal, Afkar. When the first issue of Afkar appeared in February of 1993, it astounded even many ICMI members by reprinting the texts of six of the panelists at the December human rights meetings, several of which contained unusually blunt assessments of human rights in Indonesia. At first, Minister Habibie privately expressed concern that the pilot issue of a journal promoted as ICMI'S flagship publication should concentrate on such a controversial issue. Forced to decide whether he would go along with the journal's publication, however, Habibie affirmed his stance that CIDES should be independent and willing to take on timely issues. Although some observers had speculated that Adi Sasono's daring action might cost him his job, Habibie made a point of expressing his confidence in Sasono and his discussion of human rights.

These and other developments reassured many in the Muslim community that ICMI could continue to play an important role in the cause of democratization and justice. However, events over the course of 1994 shook the confidence of these democratic Muslims once again. In early 1994 there were a series of press stories questioning Habibie's role in the purchase of naval ships from Germany, the "borrowing" of reforestation funds from the Department of Forestry to finance Habibie's technology programs, and several other schemes. What these events had in common was their outspoken criticism of Habibie's behind-the-scenes maneuvering and his reluctance to provide a public accounting of expenditures. To many observers, including many independent Muslims, these incidents suggested that, rather than working to open up the system, Habibie was perpetuating a longstanding pattern of government mismanagement, corporatist cooptation, and bureaucratic cronyism.

A move that shocked even Habibie's closest supporters seemed to confirm the worst of these fears when, on June 27, 1994, the government, with clear presidential support, banned three of Indonesia's most respected news magazines, Tempo, Editor, and DeTik. All three had been in the forefront of efforts to raise questions about Habibie's offstage deals. Sources close to Habibie insist that he opposed the bans, preferring to challenge the press account through the courts. President Suharto, however, insisted that such a tedious legal procedure made no sense; he thus insisted on the immediate closing of all three news establishments.

In the aftermath of these shocking events, most ICMI leaders made no public comment on the bans. In private, most liberals were deeply embarrassed or even outraged. However, with an air of sad resignation, one liberal ICMI cadre explained in June of 1995 that the president's supporters in ICMI had viewed the press bannings as a litmus test of loyalty. Politics is politics, ICMI leaders were told, and they were obliged to give no hint of disloyalty to either Habibie or the president. One high-ranking official commented to me, "Look, you have to realize politics is not perfect; our option is either support Habibie or give up and let the military control the whole show." This calculated realpolitik had an understandable logic. However it provided little consolation to the many prodemocracy activists who had hoped that ICMI reformers would act as principled advocates of democracy and the rule of law.

There were important exceptions to the deafening silence from ICMI ranks. While avoiding direct criticisms of Habibie, Dawam Rahardjo and Nurcholish Madjid continued to speak intelligently and courageously of the need for tolerance, openness, and a renewed commitment to democratization. However, the majority of ICMI leaders remained silent, and a few even hinted at their support for the press closures. Most astounding among those in the latter group was Adi Sasono, the former student activist turned dependency theorist, NGO champion, and proponent of the demilitarization of government. In public comments that astonished people in the prodemocracy movement, Adi suggested that Muslims had to be cool-headed about the closings and clear about their priorities. None of the news magazines affected by the closure was Muslim, and thus Muslims were still free to promote their views in the media. These comments were seen by secular democrats as sad evidence that the regime's strategy of dividing the democratic opposition had borne bitter fruit indeed.

## Epilogue: Islam and Democratization

We are so accustomed to thinking...only of politicians using religion for political ends, that it is extremely hard for us to understand what politics might look like if we could see it through religious eyes, or in a religious perspective, and thus imagine the possibility of religious people using politics for religious ends.

Marginalized from real influence since the late Sukarno era, Indonesia's Muslims, especially the modernist community, are understandably relieved that they are finally being accorded a measure of influence in national policies and programs. Few have illusions about the degree to which real reform of the Indonesian political system is, at this point, possible. Many are troubled by their accommodation with the president and recognize that theirs is an alliance of unequals in the extreme. They can point nonetheless to genuine social, if not structuropolitical, achievements. The Ministry of Religion continues its programs for the construction of mosques and Islamic schools. Its support for dakwah proselytization stemmed the tide of Hindu and Christian conversion and reinforced a reverse process of Islamization that has had significant impact even in Javanist portions of the countryside. Governors and regency officials now regularly exchange Islamic greetings at public events and are prominently featured in television coverage celebrating Muslim holidays. In 1988 rules for religious education in the schools were reinforced. In 1989 the authority of the nation's Islamic courts was strengthened, over the strenuous objections of secular-nationalist members of parliament. In 1990, after months of stormy protest, the government allowed Muslim schoolgirls to wear jilbab (religious scarves) to classes. In 1991 an Islamic bank was established. Also in 1991, President Suharto became Haji Muhammad Suharto, after his celebrated pilgrimage to Mecca. Finally, in several sensational cases between 1990 to 1993, the government secured harsh prison terms against journalists and performers accused of slandering Islam.

Whatever the precise balance of forces in government, these developments provide clear evidence that Western scholars can no longer fall back on their familiar characterizations of government cultural policies as abangan or, worse yet, "secularist." It is doubtful that such monolithic characterizations were ever fair to the complexity of religious interests at work within the government.

Such pioneering figures as Djohan Effendi, Dawam Rahardjo, and Nurcholish Madjid seem to have sensed this from the start and maneuvered accordingly. Their strategy of Islamic renewal has borne fruits that, ten years ago, most Western Indonesianists would have thought unimaginable.

For the Muslim community itself, the growing influence of Muslim social styles has, as the human rights advocate Aswab Mahasin once explained to me, "made many people who were previously embarrassed about their faith, because it looked backward and unmodern, proud to act like Muslims." For Western scholars who see religion as no more than an instrument for achieving political-economic ends, such accomplishments may seem trivial because they are peripheral to the real flesh and blood of politics. However, many devout Muslims view the matter differently. Many see the state and politics not as ends in themselves, but as means for the creation of a greater good, the realization of Islamic ideals in society. For such people, the symbolism of Islamic devotionalism is not just symbolic, but the very basis for an ethical order.

Inevitably, however, recent Muslim successes have also raised questions. In a Western historical idiom, these questions have to do with the nature of the "civil" society toward which Indonesia may be moving, however haltingly. The idea of civil society refers to a sphere of action and interests between the level of the household and the institutions of the state, one that in certain circumstances can work to counterbalance the state's monopoly of ideological and coercive power. By itself such an intermediary domain guarantees neither democracy, justice, nor pluralist tolerance. It becomes a vital support for all three, however, if and when it serves to strengthen the presence of two other elusive social arrangements: extragovernmental associations that act as counterweights to the state's monopoly of power and a social pluralism that helps to legitimate the idea that people have a right to their own ideas and actions.

For a few Islamist purists the idea of a civil society is itself suspect because it is seen as a Western creation. It first emerged in European historical experience, after all, the product of a long social evolution whereby, in a few (and, at first, very few) corners of Western Europe, a complex social compromise emerged. Despite the best efforts of tyrants and the deepest hopes of clergy, no single estate, class, or religious community found itself strong enough to impose its will on the whole of society. Out of this happenstance stalemate, a "pluricentric" balance of social powers emerged. With it – though subject to unending challenge by its ideological rivals – there emerged an idiom of rights and freedoms that placed serious limitations on the authority of the state.

Given its Western genesis, it is not surprising that some Muslims regard the concept of civil society as an abnegation of one of their most cherished ideals: that religion can and should serve as the groundwork for the reformation of society as a whole. The concept of religion implicit in the idea of civil society is a deliberately uncomprehensive one. Rather than providing a master plan for the whole of society, religion under this model serves primarily as a moral compass for legal, economic, and political structures. "Civil" religion may be influential and informative, but it is not exhaustively determinative of state and societal institutions.

Most devout Muslims profess allegiance to the idea that Islam is a total way of life. But the implications of this truism for Muslim visions of modern society are varied, as different Muslims interpret its truth in profoundly different ways. For those for whom it means that Islam can and should impose an all-encompassing political system on society, the Western notion of civil society seems decidedly anemic. It suffers from the same deficiency that, in some Muslims' eyes, modern Christianity does: it places religion too much at the margins, making it appear as if religion lacks the capacity to reform the whole of social life.

Whatever ICMI'S fate, Muslim intellectuals in Indonesia will continue to confront this question of just how comprehensive a role Islam can and should play in societal reformation. With unusual insight into a process about which Western scholars had only vague ideas at the time, Abdurrahman Wahid, the renewal-oriented leader of Nahdlatul Ulama, anticipated this question in a modest paper presented at a conference at Monash University four and one-half years before ICMI's founding:

Different Muslim groups have responded [to this rising consciousness of Islam] by formulating two main strategies to achieve those objectives. The first is by idealizing Islam as the only feasible social system able to maintain true democracy, strict adherence to law and economic justice. The so-called "Islamization process" taking place in the life of the whole nation should be used to promote the idea of an "Islamic society" in Indonesia. This strategy of struggling for an Islamic society in Indonesia naturally collides with the other strategy. According to the so-called "soft" groups, Islam plays an important role in the life of the nation, if only for the reason that Muslims constitute the overwhelming majority of the population. But the role Islam should play is not derived from the idealization of itself as the only alternative to the existing situation, but rather as the inspirational base for a national framework of a democratic society. As such, Islam is not an alternative to other social systems, but a complementary factor among a wide spectrum of other factors in the nation's life. A bitter debate is therefore unavoidable between those opposing views. As of now, it is not clear where the support of the Muslim middle class will go to.

As this quote implies, Wahid is an outspoken proponent of the "national" rather than the "Islamic" society idea. In recent years, he has expressed concern over the way the government has courted conservatives in the Muslim community. He has cautioned that the government should make clear its opposition to fundamentalism and support Muslims, like himself, committed to the idea of Islam as a moral influence within a plural society. Having resisted pressures to affiliate with ICMI and having loudly proclaimed his support for the prodemocracy movement, Wahid has since 1994 been the subject of an intense government campaign to topple him from the Nahdlatul Ulama leadership and marginalize him in the Muslim community.

Other intellectuals, like Sugeng Sarjadi, a former Muslim student activist who, in 1992, shocked his Muslim friends by joining the nominally democratic-nationalist PDI (Indonesian Democratic Party) and running for the DPR, go even further than Wahid. Recently Sarjadi has publicly criticized his Islamic colleagues for, in his view, once again confusing incidental opportunities with Islam's deeper values. In an interview with me during July of 1992, he said that Muslims have been seduced by the government's embrace of Islamic symbolism. What is really needed, he claimed, are principles of justice and fair play that can be implemented for Indonesians of all faiths: "What's the meaning of this religion, Islam? If an abangan makes the pilgrimage and becomes a santri, what's the point? Is that Islam? Make the pilgrimage but add to it corruption, what do you get? Isn't Islam really about universal values of justice? Can you buy the symbolism of Islam without its ideals of justice?"

This is the crux of the matter. Observers of Islamic politics since the time of Ibn Khaldun have noted that Islamic values (like those of the other world religions) can be interpreted to support the most varied of political orders. The critical matter in determining which interpretation of Islamic values predominates in society depends on a process of "competition and contest over both the interpretation of [Islamic] symbols and control of the institutions, formal and informal, that produce and sustain them". It is just such a contest that is unfolding in Indonesia right now. The question is not just the simplistic matter of whether Muslim leaders will be accorded greater influence in the government's inner circle. The question is, how those leaders, once accorded influence, will interpret their responsibility to Islam and nation.

The two years that followed the 1994 press bannings saw discouraging developments in this regard. While Muslim leaders continued to be accorded prominent roles in regime affairs, the government moved to narrow the political opening that seemed to have begun in the late 1980s. The press bannings and the campaign against Abdurrahman Wahid were the first in these restrictive salvos. Then, in 1995, the government launched proceedings against another outspoken Muslim democrat (this one active in ICMI), Sri Bintang Pamungkas. Sri Bintang was accused of having slandered President Suharto in the course of speeches given during a visit to Germany. To its credit, the ICMI leadership resisted pressures to expel Sri Bintang from the organization. However, that leadership including some with close personal ties to Sri Bintang was forced to stand by in silence as the government made behind-the-scenes deals to arrange Sri Bintang's expulsion from the parliament and his conviction of the slander charges in a court of law. Though he has appealed his sentence, Sri Bintang's influence in national affairs, not to mention ICMI, has been drastically circumscribed. The government's effort to split accommodating Muslims from prodemocracy activists had taken another victim.

To their credit, several independent Muslims, such as Dawam Rahardjo and Nurcholish Madjid, have continued to make brave and principled statements on the need to tolerate opposition and effect a deeper democratization of Indonesian politics. Sadly, however, their comments have come to be treated by some realpolitik Muslims as the irrelevant musings of political idealists. Meanwhile, the government has escalated its campaign against more influential prodemocracy activists. At the time of this writing, it launched a fierce assault on the the leader of the Indonesian Democratic Party, Megawati Sukarnoputri. The daughter of Indonesia's first president, Sukarno, Megawati's increasingly bold calls for democracy and justice appear to have so alarmed the regime's inner circle that they arranged her ouster from the party leadership.

All this shows that Muslims in general and ICMI members in particular operate in a political environment that is constrained to an extreme by the authoritarian nature of Indonesia's leadership. Though certain Muslim individuals have been accorded greater influence, others those who raise more serious challenges to the structure of authority itself – have been systematically marginalized. The danger here is not merely that the mass of ordinary citizens, Muslim and non-Muslim, are being excluded from civic life. It is that, in addition, such corporatist centralization will smother what is most remarkable in Indonesian Islam, its rich tradition of independence, pluralism, and tolerance. By itself, the participation of Muslims in government says little about which Islamic principles will be implemented in policy and even less about how Islam might contribute to democratization.

The depoliticization of Islam under the New Order created challenges and opportunities for the Muslim community, a situation that favored the growth of a moderate, civil leadership. However, developments since mid1994 make all too apparent just how difficult it will be for civic-minded Muslims to realize their ideals in practice. In the face of growing Muslim influence in society, the government may respond with concessions to a few leaders while stifling criticism and independent civic organization. In such circumstances, Muslim leaders face a painful dilemma: how to balance the interests of the religious community (ummat) with those of the nation as a whole. This tension has been exploited by New Order strategists in their campaign to split Muslims from secular-democratic reformers. In years to come, Muslim efforts to respond to this tension will determine which vision of Islam predominates in the Muslim community and which vision of nation.

# 3

# Islamic Studies

## Introduction

A number of studies have been conducted on intellectual trends developed through scholarship in particular periods of Islamic history. However, never before has a study been done which examines the intellectual trends that grew out of the numerous 'ulama' who were linked to each other in loose scholarly networks such as those under discussion. They were different from one another not only in terms of their geographical backgrounds, which had their own 'little' Islamic traditions, but more importantly in their intellectual preferences, as reflected by their legal (madhhab) and tariqah affiliations.

Furthermore, leading scholars in the networks, before settling down in the Haramayn or elsewhere, had been peripatetic scholars, travelling from one centre of Islamic learning to another, studying with and learning from various teachers who had their own personal traditions of religious scholarship. Thus, scholars were influenced not by one single teacher but by many; they were exposed to and absorbed various lines of thought and intellectual tendencies. Because of this, describing the contents of teachings developed and transmitted by the scholarly networks is not easy. At this stage we will attempt to draw the broad outlines of the intellectual trends of the networks; this will perhaps help us comprehend the nature and characteristics of these scholarly networks.

In a certain sense the Haramayn was a ' melting pot', where various 'little' traditions of Islam melded to form a ' new synthesis'which was strongly in favour of the ' great' tradition. We have seen previously how scholars from the Indian subcontinent, for instance, carried their mystical traditions to the Haramayn, while those from Egypt and North Africa came with an inheritance of hadith scholarship. These traditions interacted with each other as well as with the tradition already established in the Haramayn itself.

It must be kept in mind at the outset that what we call a ' new synthesis' is not entirely a new development in the history of Islamic social and intellectual traditions. Even though it has some distinctive characteristics, compared with the previous tradition, in many respects it also contains elements of continuity with earlier traditions. The return to the Sunnl orthodoxy that gained momentum after the twelfth century appears to reach its culmination in the period under discussion. This can be seen not only in the intellectual contents of the networks but also in their ' organisational' aspects, or more precisely the linkages among scholars. Thus, the revivalist spirit that inspired the establishment of madrasahs everywhere in the Middle East after the founding of the Nizamiyyah madrasah in 459/1066 continued to flourish in a variety of ways.

The salient feature of the scholarly networks is that the rapprochement between the shari'ah-onented ' ulama' (more specifically, thefuqaha') and the sufis reached its climax. The long-standing conflict between these two groups of Muslim scholars appears to have greatly diminished; the rapprochement or reconciliation between them, which had been preached insistently by such scholars as al-Qushayri and al-Ghazall several centuries earlier, became a common goal among our scholars. Most of them were ahl al-shan'ah ifuqaha') and ahl al-haqlqah (sufis) at the same time; thus, they were learned not only in the intricacies of the shan'ah but also in the haqlqah (mystical or Divine Realities). However, we should be very careful not to conclude that they took this reconciliation for granted; instead, they continued to nurture it.

The rapprochement between the shan'ah and SUFIsm and the enrolment of the 'ulama' in the tariqah resulted in the rise of ' neo-

SUFIsm'. There has been considerable discussion on the meaning and use of the term ' neoSUFIsm', which was coined by the late Fazlur Rahman. According to Rahman, neo-SUFIsm is the reformed SUFIsm largely stripped of its ecstatic and metaphysical character and content, these being replaced by a content that was nothing other than the postulates of the orthodox religion. As he explained, this new ' type' of SUFIsm emphasises and renews the original moral factor and puritanical self-control in SUFIsm at the expense of the extravagant features of the popular unorthodox SUFIsm. Neo-SUFIsm brings to the centre of attention the moral reconstruction of Muslim society, as contrasted with the earlier SUFIsm, which had primarily stressed the individual and not society. As a consequence, Rahman concludes, the overall character of neo-SUFIsm is undoubtedly puritanical and activist. We will now see more clearly how neo-SUFIsm developed in the networks.

## Neo-sufism and Hadith Study

Fazlur Rahman maintains that the most important group of Muslim scholars responsible for helping to crystallise the rise of neo-SUFIsm were the ' people of tradition' (ahl al-hadith). He further argues that after the sufi movement captured much of the Muslim world emotionally, spiritually and intellectually during the sixth/ twelfth and seventh/ thirteenth centuries, the traditionists found it impossible to neglect the sufi forces entirely. Therefore, as Rahman puts it:

> *they tried, in their methodology, to incorporate as much of the sufi legacy as could be reconciled with orthodox Islam and could be made to yield a positive contribution towards it. First, the moral motive of SUFIsm was emphasised and some of its technique of .dhikr or muraqabah, 'spiritual concentration', adopted. But the object and the content of this concentration were identified with the orthodox doctrine and the goal redefined as the strengthening of faith in dogmatic tenets and the moral purity of the spirit. This type of neo-SUFIsm tended to regenerate orthodox activism and reinculcate a positive attitude to this world.*

The Haramayn, from the early years of Islam, had been known as the main centre of the hadith. This is not hard to understand, as the Prophet, the source of the hadith, lived and initiated Islam there. Furthermore, two of the four major schools of Islamic law, the Malikl and the Hanball, known as ahl al-hadith, had in fact initially developed and gained their stronghold in the Arabian Peninsula. It is true that the Malikl madhhab, introduced by Malik b. Anas in Medina, later became more dominant in North and West Africa and Upper Egypt, but the Hanballs also came to exercise a predominance in the Arabian Peninsula. Although the Hanballs are known for their strong reliance on hadith and their refusal of rational philosophy and speculative mysticism, many accepted SUFIsm as long as it was practised in accordance with the sharl'ah. There is no evidence that such prominent Hanball scholars as Ibn Taymiyyah and Ibn al-Qayyim al-Jawziyyah were opposed to all types of SUFIsm; what they fiercely attacked was unorthodox ecstatic and antinomian SUFIsm that is, SUFIsm which regards itself free from injuction of sharl'ah orfiqh. For this reason, Fazlur Rahman considers them pioneers of neo-SUFIsm.

There was also reluctance to accept SUFIsm among the ahl al-had:th of the Malikl madhhab in the North African region and Upper Egypt. The Maghribl Malikls in particular were more puritanical and, in some cases, also aggressive. It is well known that the early Egyptian (Nubian) sufi Dhu al-Nun al-Misri (d. 245/859) was persecuted by the Egyptian Malikl jurist 'Abd Allah b. 'Abd al-Hakam; al-Ghazali's books were condemned and banned by the Malikl fuqaha' of Spain, and one of the fiercest attacks on SUFIsm in Egypt, particularly of the extravagant type, came from Ibn al-Hajj al-'Abdari, a leading Malikl faqlh in the fourteenth century.

Again it is important to note that not all Malikl scholars were hostile to SUFIsm. Some of them were even zealous sufis. A good example of this is 'AH b. Maymun (854-917/1450-1511), a noted Moroccan Malikl, who was responsible for spreading a revivalist version of the Shadhiliyyah order in Syria. He regenerated the decadent Syrian SUFIsm by not allowing his disciples to isolate themselves in khalwah (seclusion) at the khanqah. It appears that when scholarly contacts and linkages between the Maghrib! Malikis and scholars of other madhhabs gained momentum after the sixteenth century, some began to soften their tone of opposition to SUFIsm and joined other scholars in preaching neo-SUFIsm.

Despite these exceptions among the Hanbali and Malik! muhadddiths, the majority did not make use of their expertise in hadith for accelerating the reform of SUFIsm on any larger scale.

These muhaddiths generally continued to concentrate their hadith studies on maintaining, reorganising and interpreting the six canonical books of the hadith in light of their madhhaUs point of view. However, they increasingly established contacts and connections with scholars of the intellectual traditions. In this way they were exposed to other little traditions' of Islam. At the same time they played an important role in connecting scholars living in various regions of the Middle East through their hadith scholarship.

This is particularly true among the leading Malik! muhaddiths, who lived mostly in Egypt and the North African region. As we will see shortly, they were among the scholars most responsible for transmitting hadiths, and thus for establishing crucial linkages between various traditions of hadith scholarship in the Middle East. The material shows that most isnads in the networks were transmitted through the major fifteenth and early sixteenth century muhaddiths in Egypt, namely Ibn Hajar al-'Asqalam (d. 853/1449), Jalal al-Din al-Suyup and Zakariyya al-Ansari, noted earlier. These prominent scholars in fact constituted a group of networks among themselves. They were considered the most superior hadith isnads, and therefore became the most sought-after isnads by later scholars in the networks.

As a result of this development, beginning in the late sixteenth century, connections among scholars in the Haramayn resulting from hadith scholarship increasingly widened in scope. In addition to the Egyptian isnads above, we find the isnads of North Africa coming into the picture. The North African isnads in many cases also had strong linkages with the Egyptian isnads. Being possessors of superior isnads, major muhaddiths from the two regions not only became crucial links among scholars but more importantly stimulated new intellectual trends in the networks. This is perhaps best illustrated by the experience of such prominent muhaddiths as 'Ala' al-Din al-Babili, 'Isa al-Maghribi and Sulayman al-Maghribi.

One of the most superior isnads these three brought to the Haramayn was that of Shams al-Din al-Ramli, the tenth century renewer of Islam, also known as the ' little ShafiT (al-Shafi'l al-Saghlr). As a superior isnad, Shams al-Din received hadiths from his father, Shihab al-Din al-Ramli (d. 957/1550), who in turn received them directly from his renowned teacher, Zakariyya al-Ansari. Although Shihab al-Din al-Ramli was not as famous as al-

Ansari, he was undoubtedly one of the prominent Shafi'I muhaddiths of his generation.

Even major scholars in the networks, who have been mainly identified as sufis, such as al-Qushashi, al-Kuram, al-Nakhli or 'Abd Allah al-Basri, had in fact extensive linkages with the Egyptian and North African traditions of hadith scholarship. There is no doubt that hadith studies constituted the most important subject in these scholars learning. Al-Kuranl, in his accounts of his isnads in various Islamic disciplines, devotes more than 40 pages to disclosing his hadith isnads before going on to those in fiqh, sharl'ah and tasawwuf. His hadith isnads mostly go back through al-Qushashi to al-Shinnawi and further to Egyptian isnads, or directly in ascending order from Shams al-Din al-Ramli to Shihab al-Ramli to Zakariyya al-Ansari to Ibn Hajar al-Asqalam and so forth to Malik.

But Ibrahim al-Kuram also possessed a hadith isnad, beginning with 'Abd Allah al-Lahuri (d. 1083/1672), who migrated from Lahore, India, to Medina. Al-Lahuri, by way of this isnad, connected him with Qutb al-Din al-Nahrawali. This isnad also includes Ibn Hajar at its apex, and has names not in the Egyptian and North African isndds. By way of this isnad, alKuram is directly connected to the Indian tradition of hadith studies.

It is interesting to note that al-Kuram has also an interesting hadith isnad, which runs through sufi shaykhs that connect him to Ibn 'Arabi. It went from al-Qushashi, who received it from al-Shinnawi, who took it from his father, 'All b. 'Abd al-Quddus 'Abbasi al-Shinnawi, who got it from his master, al-Sha'ram, who got it from Zakariyya al-Ansari, who got it from Abu al-Fath Muhammad al-Maraghi, who got it from Sharaf al-Din b. Ibrahim al-Jabarti al-Zabidi from Abu al-Hasan 'All al-Wani, who got it from the great master Ibn 'Arabi, who got it from 'Abd al-Wahhab b. 'AH al-Baghdadi, who got it from Abu al-Fath al-Karukhi, who got it from Abu Isma'il al-Ansari al-Harawi, who finally got it from 'Abd al-Jabbar al-Jarrahi. This isnad was inherited by al-Kurani's disciples, such as 'Abd Allah al-Basri. Al-Basri tells us in his Kitab al-Imdad hi Ma ' rifah ' Uluw al-Isndd that he studied al-Tirmidhi's Sunan and al-Nasa'i's Sunan with al-Kurani on the authority of this isnad.

The importance of stating Ibrahim al-Kurani's long isnad above is that it will enable us to see how chains of transmission can increasingly become orthodox and, by extension, how Ibn 'Arabi, often accused of being an 'unorthodox' sufi, was a source of authority to scholars who were mostly known as muhaddiths.

On the above list of names, three are perhaps most important: Ibn 'Arabi, Zakariyya al-Ansari, and 'Abd al-Wahhab al-Sha'rani. For some Muslims it may be a shock to learn that a major muhaddith such as al-Ansari possessed a hadith isnad that went back through Ibn 'Arabi, who had been condemned by many other muhaddiths. It is important to note that, although Zakariyya al-Ansari was widely known as a great muhaddith and chief qadi, he was in fact also a sufi. He studied with and received tasawwuf from, among others, Muhammad al-Ghamri. Al-Ansari also wrote several treatises on SUFIsm, including a commentary on al-Qushayri's Risdlat al-Tasawwuf, which is known for its insistence on the conformity of SUFIsm to the sharl'ah. Therefore, it is not a mere historical coincidence that al-Ansarl initiated the young al-Sha'ranl (d. 973/1565) into Islamic mysticism. The fruit of the masterdisciple relation of this type of scholar was the emergence of al-Sha'rani's 'neo-SUFIsm' or, as Trimingham calls it, the ' middle course', that is, a combination of tasawwuf and fiqh.

The connection between the leading Haramayn scholars and the neosufi al-Sha'rani was far from simply a chain in the transmission of particular hadiths or authority in studying hadith books. Instead, their linkages were crucial to the transmission of the doctrines of neo-SUFIsm. Ahmad al-Qushashl, for instance, traces his teachings on the obligation of disciples of the tariqah to move (hijrah) from negligence and ignorance to enlightenment, to wage jihad against inward and outward enemies, and to persevere in facing hardships, or on the permissibility of women to be initiated into the mystical ways, to al-Sha'ram. Al-Sha'ram taught them to 'All al-Shinnawi, who taught them to his son, Ahmad al-Shinnawi, who in turn taught them directly to al-Qushashi. But it is important to note that al-Sha'ram derived his teachings from the authority of alSuyuti. Al-Qushashl also attributes similar teachings to Zakariyya al-Ansarl through Ahmad al-Shinnawi, who got them from Shams al-Din al-Ramli, who received them by way of ' general ijazah (al-ijazah al'ammah) from al-Ansarl.

Similarly, Ibrahim al-Kurani had connections with al-Sha'ranl, which appear in more ways than simply by way of hadith isnad'.

He read al-Sha'ram's works with Ahmad al-Shinnawi, who received them from his father, 'AH al-Shinnawi, who acquired them directly from the author, al-Sha'ranl. Therefore, it is clear that al-Kurani was fully aware of al-Sha'ram's neo-SUFIsm.

Another example of the scholars in our networks who treated hadith scholarship with particular regard is Ahmad al-Nakhli. He presents his isnads in the search of exoteric (zahir) and esoteric (batiri) sciences in his Bughyat alTalibln li bayan al-Mashd'ikh al-Muhaqqiqln al-Mu'tamidln. He possessed, for instance, an Egyptian hadith isnad which began directly from 'Ala' al-Din al-Babili, who in turn connected him with Shams al-Din al-Ramli, Zakariyya al-Ansari and Ibn Hajar. He also acquired a North African and Egyptian isnad by way of 'Isa al-Maghribi as well as an Indian isnad that went back through Sibghat Allah to al-Ansarl. In addition to the ' Kutub al-Sittah', he studied numerous other hadith books, such as the al-Muwattd' of Malik b. Anas, alSunan al-Kubra of al-Bayhaqi and al-Jami' al-Saghlr of al-Suyup.

The particular importance placed by these scholars on hadith reflects their conscious attempts to make the way of the Prophet, besides the Qur'anic teachings, not only a source of law but also a boundless inspiration towards proper moral conduct. Therefore, as a rule, in their hadith studies they did not confine themselves to studying standard hadith books.

We have cited several books, outside the ' Kutub al-Sittah', studied by al-Nakhll. It is also clear from al-Kuram's accounts that the six canonical hadith books constituted only a small portion of his hadith studies. Many lesser-known hadith books, such as the Musnad al-Dariml, Musnad al-Bazar, Musnad al-Kisl and Musnad 'All al-Tamlml al-Mawsull, in fact constituted a substantial portion of his hadith scholarship. There were indeed serious efforts on the part of our scholars to go beyond the traditional study of the ' Kutub al-Sittah'.

Thus, these scholars did not view hadith studies in the traditional way that is, for the sake of the sharl'ah as such. HadITh studies were directed to achieving other, higher, pious purposes. Ahmad al-Nakhll, for example, believes that the hadith will lead to real intimacy with the Prophet, who was second only to God as the essence of faith. According to Ahmad al-Qushashi, the Prophet was the most important figure for the tariqah people, as he was the source of the sharl'ah after God himself. So attached were our scholars to the hadith that Ibrahim alKuram asserts, 'I have no doubt that it [hadith] will be everlasting on earth'.

Our scholars were also aware of the fact that there were scholars who fabricated hadith in order to pursue their own ends in the name of the Prophet. For that reason, in their hadith studies, they preferred what these scholars called the ' high isnads' or the superior isnads ('tuluw al-isnad or al-isnad al-'ali), namely, those consisting of scholars of renowned integrity. According to 'Abd Allah al-Basri, a superior isnad for a scholar is much like a sharper sword for a fighter: it is a more effective tool. He gives another illustration: a scholar without the superior isnad is like a wood gatherer who comes in the night into a forest that has venomous snakes without light.

Thus, a superior isnad is essential to scholars in the networks in order for them to be able to receive the true hadith?, not the fabricated ones. Al-Nakhll takes special note of those scholars who fabricated or advertently abused the hadith?, by citing a tradition of the Prophet which states that whoever says something the Prophet does not say, then his seat in the hereafter will be of fire. In a different tone, al-Kuram appeals to his fellow sufis to interpret the hadith only with sufficient knowledge and understanding of all teachings of Islam; to do otherwise would lead only to the elimination offana' ('tannihilation' or ' passing away' of physical consciousness), an important stage of the mystical journey.

There is no doubt that the special emphasis placed by these scholars on hadith studies had considerable impact not only in linking the scholars together, as well as the various Islamic ' little traditions', but also in bringing changes in their view of SUFIsm, especially in its relation to the sharl'ah.

## Neo-sufism and the Shari'ah

The emphasis on the study of hadith or the way of the Prophet, the second source of Islamic law, led our scholars to a greater appreciation of the significance of the sharl'ah in SUFIsm. It is interesting to take Ahmad al-Qushashl as an example in this respect. Al-Qushashl was initiated by Ahmad al-Shinnawi into the Shattariyyah order, often associated with Indian SUFIsm, which tended to transgress the rules of the sharl'ah at least in the earlier growth of this order.

Ahmad al-Qushashl played an important part in the reorientation of the Shattariyyah order by emphasising the importance of Islamic legal doctrines in the mystical way. In his opinion, both exoteric (legal/sharl'ah) and esoteric (mystical/haqlqah) aspects of Islam should be in harmony and not in conflict with each other. Citing the Mlzan [al-Kubra] of al-Sha'ram, he believes that there must be loyal adherence to the precepts of the shan'ah on which the doctrine and practice of the haqlqah would be built. Therefore, all mystical aspirants must practise the whole doctrine of the shan'ah before they can hope to gain God's trust.

Al-Qushashl recognises certain differences between the two 'ways' indeed ' way' or ' path' is among the meanings of both sharl'ah and tariqah. He maintains that they originated from the same sources namely, the Qur'an and the hadith. Basically, Muslims could attain certain stages of the haqlqah while ignoring doctrines of the sharl'ah laid down by the Qur'an and the hadith, but they could not ' feel' the real blessing of God. Therefore, the sufi needs to travel the mystical path with the guidance of the shan'ah. According to al-Hamawi, ' When he [al-Qushashl] speaks about the haqlqah, he always supports it with Qur'anic verses and the tradition of the Prophet'. Johns rightly concludes that, in contrast to a few other sufis who devoted most of their exegetical skill to the Qur'an, al-Qushashl always presented his views by citing both the Qur'an and the hadith.

With a clear vision of the proper relation between the sharl'ah and SUFIsm, it is not surprising that al-Qushashl was an ardent supporter of neo-SUFIsm. He holds that there would be no real maqam nor ahwal (stages of mystical progress) without having sufficient knowledge ('ilrri) and good deeds ('tamal) as taught by the Qur'an and the hadith. 'Ilm alone is not enough; there simply would be no real mystical progress for those who did not fulfill the obligatory 'ibadah, such as prayers, fasting or alms, and other recommended actions.

Al-Qushashl takes the Prophet Muhammad as the exemplary figure of the perfect man of SUFIsm. As a sufi, the Prophet did not alienate himself from society; he not only asked people to enjoin good and prohibit evil but also intermingled with their brethren, and performed his ' mundane' duties. Al-Qushashl, on the authority of the scholar and historian al-Sakhawi, refutes the belief held in certain sufi circles that the Prophet used to take from his companions what later became known among sufis as 'al-khirqat al-sufiyyah' (lit. 'stiffs rag'). He simply could not accept the inclusion of the Prophet in specific tariqahs, which would have supported the oftenheard claim that it was sanctioned by the Prophet himself.

Similarly, Ibrahim al-Kuram emphasises the paramount importance of the sharl'ah without necessarily putting aside his attachment to SUFIsm. He argues that stifls should not allow their views and actions to conflict with the sharl'ah and other religious duties. The ahl al-kashf, people of intuitive revelation, have their own understanding of the meanings of the Qur'an and the Prophetic hadith. He reminds them, however, that each verse of the Qur'an or main (text) of the hadith has not only esoteric (batiri) meanings as understood by the ahl al-kashf- but also exoteric (zahir) meanings. As a consequence, the stiffs must not put their understanding of the Qur'an in opposition to that of the ahl al-sharl'ah. He takes as an example the issue of fana' ('tannihilation') in the Qur'an (55: 25). He explains that, according to its exoteric meaning, fana' is clearly not natural death (al-mawt al-tabi'i), but esoterically it is a kind of ' death' (al-mawt al-ma'nawl).

It is clear that for al-Kuram the reconciliation between the sharl'sharl and SUFIsm is not to be taken lightly. In dealing with this matter, his argument is subtle and philosophical. This is not surprising because, as al-Hamawi tells us in detail, he was familiar with various kinds of intellectual discourses, ranging from Mu'Mu and Ash'ante kalam to Ibn 'Arabi'Arabi philosophical mysticism and the Greek philosophy of Plato and Aristotle. In this regard he was a scholar of distinctive stature in the networks. But it must be borne in mind that his tone was always conciliatory and all-embracing. Thus, in addition to emphasising total obedience to the sharl'sharl, he makes appeals for the recognition of the kashfas a valid path to understanding the inner meaning of the Qur'an and the hadith.

For common Muslims, the intricate realm of Islamic philosophical interpretation could lead them to confusion and even lead them astray. Many scholars in the networks realised this. They shared a sense of responsibility for preventing their fellows from being heretical through a misunderstanding of the mystical doctrines and practices of Islam. This concern is shown by some scholars in the networks not simply by issuing fatwas but more importantly by devoting special works to the subject.

There are several outstanding examples of this. Prominent among them is Ibrahim al-Kuram. He seems to have been very responsive to answering questions either directly or indirectly posed to him. At least nine out of his 49 works listed by al-Baghdadi were devoted to responding to a variety of difficult issues, ranging from the relation of SUFIsm to the sharl'sharl and the question of whether man will be able to see God, to the issue of taqlld (blind imitation). His most important work of this type is Ithdf al-Dhakl bi Shark al-Tuhfat al-Mursalah ila Ruh al-Nabl, which has been cited several times earlier. Johns claims that it was al-Kuram'Kuram most important single work.

Al-Kurani wrote the Ithaf al-Dhakl in response to Fadl Allah al-Burhanpuri'Burhanpuri al-Tuhfat al-Mursalah ila Ruh al-Nabl. As Johns concludes, in this succinct work, complemented by its short commentary, al-haqlqat al-Muwafiqah li al-Sharl'Sharl, al-Burhanpuri essentially attempts to restrain the extravagant type of SUFIsm by emphasising the essential elements of Islam, such as the absolute Being (Wujud) of God and the importance of the sharl'sharl. Apart from this, I would argue, the author'author basic concepts, such as the seven grades of being and his arguments to explain them, are absolutely philosophical. These in turn might or could obscure the real intention of the author, especially if the work was read by the awwam (common believers).

The Tuhfat al-Mursalah was written in 1000/1590, and in 1030/1619 or earlier it was already known in the Malay-Indonesian world. The effects of this book on Islam in the archipelago were recorded by al-Kuram and his disciple, al-Hamawi. The latter tells us that he first met and studied with al-Kuram in 1086/1675. The Ithaf al-Dhakl had obviously been completed before that year, for al-Hamawi read it together with other books, such as the Sahih al-Bukhdrl (and other ' Kutub al-Sittah'), the Jami' al-Saghir of al-Suyuti, the Ihya' ' Ulum al-Dln of al-Ghazali and the Futuhat al-Makkiyyah of Ibn 'Arab! In his account of Fadl Allah al-Burhanpuri, al-Hamawi relates that:

Our Shaykh al-Khatimat al-Muhaqqiqln Ibrahim al-KuranI told me, while we were reading the Tuhfat al-Mursalah with him, that some of our Jawl companions (ba ' d ashabina al-Jawiyylri) informed him that this treatise and matters it treats was popular and famous in their land and that it is read in their religious schools, and that youth study it as one of the minor treatises in their rudimentary studies.

Al-Kuram himself, in his introductory notes to the Ithaf al-Dhakl, provides further background to his writing of the commentary:

> *We have had reliable information from a group (jama'jama) of the Jawiyyln that there have spread among the population of the lands ofJawah some books on the haqlqah [Divine Realities] and gnostic knowledge ('ulum al-asrar) passed from hand to hand by those attributed with knowledge because of their study and the teaching of others, but who have no understanding of the 'Urn al-sharl'sharl of the Prophet [Muhammad], the Chosen, the Elect [by God], peace be upon him, nor the 'Urn al-haqa'haqa bestowed upon those who follow the path of God, the Exalted; those who are close to Him, those admirable ones, or those who have set their foot on any path of their paths founded on the Kitab [Qur'an] and the Sunnah [Tradition] through perfect obedience both outwardly (al-zahir) and inwardly (al-batin), as is done by the devout and pure. This is the reason for the deviation of many of them [the Jawiyyln] from the right path, for the rise of impure belief: in fact they have entered into the crooked camp of atheism (al-zandaqah) and heresy (al-ilhad).*

It is mentioned [by the Jawiyyin] to me that among the famous books was the compendium named al-Tuhfat al-Mursalah ila [Ruh] al-Nabi, peace be upon him, written by the adept by God'God help, Shaykh Muhammad ibn Shaykh Fadl Allah al-Burhanpuri, may God the Almighty render him of service. More than one of them have repeatedly asked my poor self (al-faqlr) to write a commentary on it to make clear of the questions [it discusses] to the principles of religion, confirmed by the Noble Book and the Sunnah of the Master of the apostles, peace be upon him.

While Drewes points out that al-Kurani wrote the work on the orders of al-Qushashi, the accounts of both al-Kuram and al-Hamawi provide no evidence to substantiate his view. If it is true, the work must have been conceived before the death of al-Qushashi in 1071/1660. Whether he wrote it after having been asked directly by his Jowl students or whether it was recommended by al-Qushashl, or both, what is important is that al-Kuram took the task very seriously. He made special prayers for guidance (istikharah) at the tomb of the Prophet in Medina, and he began the work only after he was sure that his prayers were answered and that it was appropriate for him to do the work. What follows in the Ithafal-Dhakl is a long presentation on the mystical interpretation of Islam based on the Qur'an and the hadith.

Ibrahim al-Kuram seems not to have been satisfied with writing only a single work on the 'al-Masa'Masa al-Jawiyyah (the questions of the Jawl people). He wrote another work entitled al-Jawabat al-Gharawiyyah 'An al-Masa'Masa al-Jawiyyat al-Jahriyyah, in which he once again attempted to clear the matter up. It is unfortunate that we can find no trace of it; we hardly have any concept of it beyond what its title indicates.

The religious problems of the Jawl evidently persisted for some time in al-Kuram'Kuram circle. 'Abd al-Shukur al-Shami, very likely one of his students, wrote a work called Ziyadah min 'Ibarat al-Mutaqaddimln min Ahl al-Jawl. This work, like the Tuhfat al-Mursalah, deals with the question of the Being and Unity of God. The name 'Abd al-Shukur occurs in one of al-Sinkili'Sinkili silsilahs of the Shattariyyah tariqah. al-Sinkili, according to this silsilah, received the tariqah from 'Abd al-Shukur, who took it from al-Kurani, who in turn received it from al-Qushashl. alKurani also wrote a work for 'Abd al-Shukur entitled Kashf al-Mastur fl Jawab As 'ilah 'Abd al-Shukur, which could indicate their close relationship.

Despite controversy around the Tuhfat al-Mursalah, it was used as an important reference by virtually all major Malay-Indonesian scholars throughout the seventeenth and eighteenth centuries. From Shams al-Din al-Samatram (d. 1039/1630), al-Raniri, al-Sinkili and al-Maqassari to al-Palimbam and Muhammad Nafls al-Banjari, all referred to the Tuhfat al-Mursalah in their writings.

Another prominent scholar who wrote a work of this nature in order to meet the special religious needs of the Jawl was Taj al-Din b. Ahmad, better known as Ibn Ya'Ya. He also devoted a special work to answering problems originating from the 'Bilad al-Jawah. The problem concerned the concept of the wahddniyyah (Unity of God). The title of the work is alJadat al-Qawlmah ila Tahqlq Mas'alat al-Wujud wa Ta'Ta al-Qudrat al-Qadlmah fi al-Jawab 'An al-As'As al-Waridah min [Bilad] Jawah. It is doubtful whether the work is available today, as I found no trace of this very important text on the intellectual relations between the MalayIndonesian world and the Middle East. It seems probable that it was al-Sinkill, who asked Ibn al-Ya'Ya to write this work, as he was included among the scholars coming into contact with him in Mecca.

The fact that at least three works are devoted by leading Haramayn 'ulama' in the seventeenth century to what our sources call 'al-Masa'Masa al-Jawiyyah indicates the nature of the relationships between the Jowl students and scholars in Mecca and Medina. As we will see later, in the second half of the eighteenth century Sulayman al-Kurdl, a leading Haramayn scholar who was also the teacher of a group of MalayIndonesian students, wrote a work of the same nature, entitled al-Durrat al-Bahiyyah flJawab al-As'As al-Jawiyyah. All of this indicates the existence of an intense intellectual discourse between Malay-Indonesian students and scholars in the centres of the Haramayn. It also shows us the concern among the Haramayn scholars about, and commitment to, intellectual reform among their fellow Muslims in the Malay-Indonesian world. They simply would not allow them to go astray because of any misunderstanding of the proper relationship between the shan'shan and SUFIsm.

Ibrahim al-Kuram was fully aware of this danger. He thus insists that those who aspire to follow the mystical path should prepare themselves for this journey by a correct understanding of the Qur'an and the hadith and by total attachment both outwardly and inwardly to shan'shan doctrines. To do otherwise, he believes, will only result in deviation from the right path and, worse still, to unbelief and heresy. Furthermore, as related by al-Hamawi, al-Kuram maintains that young students should initially be taught articles of faith, the exoteric meaning of the Qur'an and the hadith, and the teachings and practices of the righteous predecessors (al-Aslaf al-Salihln) before they are exposed to mystical doctrines by masters who are learned not only in SUFIsm but also in shan'shan.

Ahmad al-Qushashi' s daily practice also demonstrated his concern with common believers going astray because of their inability to comprehend the correct significance of the mystical way. Citing al-Kuram, al-Hamawi relates that al-Qushashi usually would not allow his friends to read and discuss with him certain difficult and problematic passages of Ibn 'Arabi'Arabi al-Futuhat al-Makkiyyah, except in a very restricted manner. He would discuss them only when uneducated people were not present, and then only in a special room with locked doors. al-Qushashi believed that great sufis, such as al-Junayd, never discussed anything about the haqa'haqa except with select (khawwas) friends or disciples. He then goes on to cite some examples from the Prophet Muhammad, who never said anything that could lead to confusion among his companions, and who indeed made distinctions between the common believers (al-'awwam) and the select (al-khawwas).

## Neo-sufism and Activism

Another striking intellectual tendency characteristic of the networks is the emphasis on the use of reason and, by extension, on the exercise of individual judgment (ijtihad) in religious matters. There is no evidence, however, that they actually employed the familiar slogan ' open the bab al-ijtihad ('tthe gate of individual judgment'), which has, since the early twentieth centry, been declared by modern Muslim scholars.

Ahmad al-Qushashl is reported to have urged Muslims who possessed sufficient 'Urn (knowledge) to understand both outward and inward meanings of the verses of the Qur'an and the hadith. He appealed to those who devoted themselves to religion (faqaha fi al-Dlri) to exercise ijtihad. He takes Ibn 'Arabl as an example of this. According to al-Qushashi, Ibn 'Arabl made use of hadith extensively in order to make his own ijtihad. Although many traditionists opposed Ibn 'Arabi'Arabi judgment, al-Qushashl believes that he had brought all his learning together in his attempts to produce his own ijtihad. Ibn 'Arabl'Arabl ijtihad essentially constituted a new interpretation of the mystical doctrine of Islam. Al-Qushashl then cites his own experience of having changed his madhhab from Malik! to Shafi'Shafi, after he exerted himself to produce his own ijtihad. As for those who have little knowledge, al-Qushashl considers it better for them to take others' ijtihads and simply become muqallids ('tfollowers').

Al-Qushashl places emphasis not only on the exercise of reason but also on activism. Time after time he urges Muslims to abandon their negligence and ignorance by searching for 'Urn, and by using their time to good purpose. He also insists that Muslims fully perform their worldly duties in order to support their lives by teaching, trading or farming. In his opinion, a real sufi is not one who alienates himself from society but one who enjoins good and prohibits evil, and lends his helping hand to the oppressed, the sick and the poor. Furthermore, a real sufi is one who can mutually cooperate (ta'ta) with other Muslims for the betterment of society. These are some examples given of good deeds that should be done by those who aspire to be perfect men (al-insan al-kamil) as ideally envisioned by SUFIsm.

In contrast to most sufis, who would simply emphasise the total emotional commitment to God without the interference of reason, Ibrahim al-Kuram, like Ahmad al-Qushashl, encourages Muslims to exercise their reason. Speaking in a more philosophical way, he promotes an intellectual understanding of God and His role as Creator and the relation of the Creator to creation. In bringing up the issue of reason here, he evokes the classic heated discussion between the mutakallimun ('ttheologians') and the ahl al-hadith ('ttraditionists'). It is beyond the scope of our discussion to dwell on the long analysis in his Ithaf al-Dhakl on such hotly debated topics as the Realities of God, the obscure meaning (mutashabihat) of some verses of the Qur'an and the nature of stages of mystical journeys. I do not feel, however, that by bringing back these issues he intends to reactivate controversies among scholars. Rather, as al-Hamawi tells us, all he wants to do is to promote mutual understanding among scholars by emphasising their points of agreement. After all, as al-Kuranl reminds the Muslims, by citing al-Shafi'Shafi, al-Ghazall and Ibn 'Arabl, the power of reason is not without limit.

It is worth noting, however, that not all scholars involved in the networks were ready to present long and complicated arguments to promote activism in their societies. An exception to this trend was Sulayman al-Maghribl, who was indeed a ' radical' scholar. Although he was a sufi himself, and founded the famous Ibn Sulayman ribat in Mecca, he was opposed to the extravagant type of SUFIsm which permitted drum-beating and dancing in the ribats, and to those siifts who alienated themselves from mainstream society. In his opinion, this type of SUFIsm was not sanctioned by the Qur'an and hadith. Taking the law into his own hands, he expelled the ashab al-khalawi (secluded people) who had carried on those practices from those ribats, affiliated with the madrasahs of Qayt Bey and Sharabiyyah in Mecca. In so doing, he made more room for resident students (al-mujawiruri), who, he believed, better deserved them. Sulayman al-Maghribl, who had endowed a number of madrasahs and ribats in the Haramayn, also challenged misappropriation of the waqf properties by the Sharifian family. These things brought him into open conflict with the Meccan Sharifs. After several failed attempts, they were finally able to expel him from Mecca in 1093/1682 with the reluctant help of the Ottoman authorities. A year later he died in Damascus.

The reformism of the networks, as we have seen thus far, is clearly centred on the social, moral and intellectual reconstruction of Muslim society. Although we find little evidence to indicate that specific discussion occurred among scholars about the regression of Muslim society, they apparently realised that society needed to be revitalised. The most logical way to achieve that end, it seemed to them, was by engendering a more balanced comprehension of each of the aspects of Islam itself: emphasising all its teachings in a unified fashion, such as legal and mystical, intellectual and practical, and social and individual. Thus, none of our scholars rejected SUFIsm or dismissed the importance of the shari'shari. Their stress is clearly reformist, purificationist and activist in tone. In short, they sought to bring about changes in their society by their own efforts rather than waiting for eschatological intervention. There is no evidence to suggest that there were any among the scholars who adhered to such ideas as millenarianism or Mahdism. In fact, they strongly rejected these views.

The best-known example of the rejection of millenarianism is the polemic concerning the claim among the Indian subcontinent scholars that Ahmad al-Sirhindi (971-1034/1564-1624) was the renewer of the second millennium (mujaddid-i alf-i thani) of Islam. The strongest refutation to such a claim came from the 'ulama' involved in the networks. The most prominent among them, Muhammad b. 'Abd al-Rasul al-Barzanji, devoted two works to the issue, entitled Qadh al-Zand wa Qadah fi Radd Jahalat Ahl al-Sirhindi, completed on 15 Rajab 1093/20 July 1682, wAal-Nashirat al-Ndjirah li al-Firqat al-Fujirah, completed on 7 Muharram 1095/26 December 1683. Hasan al-'Ajami wrote another work called al-'Asab alHind li Istisal Kufriyat Ahmad al-Sirhindi. It is reported that al-Kuram also wrote a treatise on the subject, but we cannot find any trace of it in various lists of his works. Meanwhile, al-Qushashi is said to have written a treatise after he engaged in a long discussion with Adam Banuri (d. 1053/1643), a leading follower of al-Sirhindi, who preached his master'master doctrine in the Haramayn.

Al-Sirhindi claimed that his age was full of darkness. A thousand years after the death of the Prophet Muhammad, Islam had regressed; at the same time, infidelity and bid'ah (unwarranted innovations) held sway among the Muslims. He believed that he himself was a scholar of perfect knowledge, who was capable of fulfilling the task of the steadfast prophet to renew and revive Islam. Friedmann shows us that eschatological speculations are in the background of al-Sirhindi'Sirhindi view of his times. His eschatology, however, does not anticipate the ultimate end of the world but rather the arrest of the process of decline at its nadir by means of tajdld '(renewal). By attributing the necessity of tajdld to the period of 1000 years, he evidently adheres to the concept of millenarianism.

The crux of the issue attacked by al-Barzanji was the very concept of and belief in the second millennium. He poses the following rhetorical questions:

> *What is the meaning of the Renewer of the Second Millennium? Does a second millennium remain from the time allotted to this community so that he [al-Sirhindi] can be its renewer? Did the 'ulama' not agree unanimously and did al-hafiz al-Suyutl not say in his epistle (called) al-Kashf['an Mujawazah Hadhihi al-Ummah al-Alf\ that not even five hundred years will elapse after the Millennium and that the Day of resurrection will take place four hundred old years after it.*

Unlike the concept and belief in the centennial renewal of Islam widely accepted by Muslim scholars, al-Sirhindi'Sirhindi views on the millennial renewal imply the abolition of Muhammad' Muhammad prophecy and of his law. This becomes clearer when he asserts that the Ka'bah is superior to the Prophet; that the Prophet reached perfection only 1000 years after his death, the time when the haqiqat-i muhammadi was changing to haqiqat-i ahmadi', and that he had a direct relationship with God without Muhammad' Muhammad prophetic mediation. With regard to these teachings, al-Barzanji, after mentioning alKurani, who discussed these issues in the light of the Qur'an and the hadith, concludes that al-Sirhindl was an infidel. It is not very clear whether al-Kuram, who was known for his conciliatory nature, really shares al-Barzanji'Barzanji conclusion. Al-Qushashl, however, supports alBarzanji when he points out that it was infidelity to state that the reality of the Ka'bah was superior to the reality of the Prophet Muhammad.

## Neo-sufism and Organisation of the Tariqahs

What was the impact of all the above doctrinal changes in SUFIsm on the organisational aspect of the tariqahsl In attempting to assess the organisation of the tariqahs, we will take a comparative perspective.

The most striking feature of the tariqahs in the period under discussion is that they appear to have been loosely organised; there were no clear cut boundaries between the numerous tariqahs in either their doctrines and practices (ritual and ceremonies) or their ' membership'. SUFI shaykhs and murlds (disciples) did not necessarily owe their loyalty to a single tariqah', they could become masters and disciples of a number of tariqahs. Furthermore, they could be affiliated not only with certain tariqahs originating from or mostly developing in one particular area of the Muslim world but also with those coming from other regions. This fact undoubtedly explains further the cosmopolitanism of our scholars in the networks.

Ahmad al-Qushashl is a good example to support this observation. As he tells us, he was affiliated with almost a dozen tariqahs: the Shattariyyah, Chishtiyyah, Firdawsiyyah, Kubrawiyyah all of which he received from Ahmad al-Shinnawi or directly from Sibghat Allah. He also took the Suhrawardiyyah order from Sibghat Allah, and from al-Shinnawi by way of a silsilah which included al-Sha'Sha. As for the Qadiriyyah tariqah, he took it from his father, and al-Shinnawi and Sibghat Allah. He was also affiliated with the orders of Tayfuriyyah, Awlsiyyah, Khalwatiyyah and Naqshbandiyyah, all of which he received from al-Shinnawi and Sibghat Allah. Then he took the Batiniyyah order through a silsilah which went back to Hasan al-Basri. Finally he received the Shadhiliyyah order and tariqah of Ibn 'Arabl from al-Shinnawi by a silsilah which included al-Sha'Sha.

Al-Qushashi'Qushashi isnads of these orders tell us how the Indian and North African traditions of SUFIsm had their meeting points initially in al-Shinnawi and later in al-Qushashi. They also indicate how Ibn 'Arabi'Arabi mystical tradition passed through generations down to the scholars in the networks. Similarly, al-Nakhli received several sufi orders from various traditions. He took the Naqshbandiyyah order from Taj al-Hindi and Mir Kilan, the Qadiriyyah order from Ni'mat Allah al-Qadiri, the Shadhiliyyah order from 'Ala' al-Din al-Babili, and the Khalwatiyyah order from Muhammad 'Isa b. Kinan al-Hanbali.

Although affiliation with numerous tariqahs was widely practised, once a disciple declared his allegiance (bay'ah) to a certain Shaykh he was required to obey his orders. As al-Qushashi maintains, allegiance to the shaykh would lead him to the real meaning of the mystical way. However, al-Qushashi appears to have opposed the teachings of most tariqahs in earlier periods, which required disciples to behave vis-a-vis their masters as 'a dead body in the hands of its washer'. He asked disciples to leave their masters and their tariqahs if they transgressed Islamic legal doctrines as laid down by the Qur'an and the hadith. This is because al-Qushashi believes that the essence of joining the tariqah is entering the shan'shan.

Thus, the rules of the shan'shan become the norms for disciples wishing to be initiated into the tariqahs. Among the most important requirements for the acceptance of disciples is maturity (bulugh), which makes them accountable for practising all the pillars of Islam; in short, a total obedience to the shan'shan both outwardly and inwardly. With such stringent requirements, the membership of the tariqah becomes quite restricted. These restrictions go even further in the adoption of such divisions among disciples as 'awwam (lay) and khawwas (elite). Both al-Qushashi and alKuram believed that only the khawwas disciples could be taught the real substance of the mystical ways. Exposing all secrets of the tariqah doctrines to the 'awwam would result only in religio-intellectual confusion and heresy. All these restrictions make it clear that the tariqah organisation was intended more as a vehicle for intensifying religious beliefs and devotional practices than for recruiting mass followings.

Although membership in the tariqahs was quite restricted, disciples in the Haramayn were far from homogeneous. In contrast to, for instance, the disciples of Muhammad al-Shinnawi a master of al-Sha'Sha who were mostly fellahs, the Haramayn sufis and disciples were heterogeneous in many respects. The Haramayn sufis geographically came from various parts of the Muslim world; religiously they adhered to different madhhabs; and socially they occupied various positions in society, from teachers and traders to rulers. The heterogeneity in the membership of the tariqahs in the Haramayn undoubtedly comes from the existence of cosmopolitanism in the area.

Partly also because of their cosmopolitanism, the succession in the Haramayn tariqahs is ascriptive rather than descriptive. There was a tendency among certain orders in Egypt in the fifteenth and sixteenth centuries to make the post of sufi shaykh a hereditary position. However, the Haramayn sufi shaykhs, as a rule, designated their best disciples to lead their tariqahs. We have numerous examples of this. Ahmad al-Shinnawi designated al-Qushashi his successor in several tariqahs. The latter, in turn, appointed al-Kurani to succeed him as the Shattariyyah shaykh. al-Qushashi also appointed al-Sinkili as his Shattariyyah khallfah for one of its branches in the Malay-Indonesian world. It is not very clear whether this pattern of succession in the Haramayn tariqahs was in one way or another influenced by al-Sha'Sha's opposition to the principle of automatic hereditary succession among his fellow Egyptian sufi shaykhs.

Furthermore, the Haramayn sufi shaykhs appear to have been free from the image of ' holy men' that we often find in the accounts of earlier tariqahs. The image of the wandering dervish is almost entirely absent in the accounts of the Haramayn sufis. This is related to the special emphasis put by scholars involved in the networks on the importance of the sharl'sharl in the tariqah practices and of following the example of the Prophet Muhammad. They generally believe that the real sufi is not the one who distinguishes himself from the rest of society by wearing distinctive clothes.

In this respect, according to al-Qushashi, the real sufi is the one who dresses well in accordance with the rules of the sharl'sharl. The clothes a sufi wears should be clean, for cleanliness reflects the purity of the soul. As for al-Kuram, al-Qannuji vividly narrates that despite his reputation as a great scholar and sufi, he wore only the clothes of ordinary people, disregarding the style of dress of certain 'ulama' who lengthened their sleeves and enlarged their turbans in order to command people'people respect, or of some sufis who wore dervish clothes to raise their aura of sanctity.

Another important organisational aspect of the tariqah?, concerns their centre of activities. If most tariqah?, in other parts of the Muslim world carried out their activities mainly in the ribats, khanqahs or zawiyahs, the Haramayn sufis were centred in the Holy Mosques, teachers' houses and ribats. However, the Haram Mosque in Mecca and the Nabawi Mosque were the most important centres of devotional and learning activities. Most of our sufi scholars studied and later taught as well as practised their SUFIstic rituals there. The accounts of Ahmad al-Nakhli, cited earlier, demonstrate this.

Furthermore, those scholars who had settled in the Haramayn had their own houses, which sometimes also had large libraries. Thus, the sufi shaykhs, in most cases, did not live in the ribats, but in their own houses, where they also held learning sessions. This significantly reduced the tendency among the sufi shaykhs to style themselves in a more dervish fashion if they lived in the ribats. The ribats were, of course, also important centres of learning and devotional activities for the Haramayn sufis. But they were occupied mainly by disciples, who stayed there temporarily until they returned to their homelands or travelled elsewhere. These ribats were usually led by an appointed head who was an administrator rather than a sufi shaykh.

## Continuity and Change

It is important to keep in mind that with the emergence of neo-SUFIsm the old paradigm of SUFIsm did not completely disappear. Extravagant SUFIsm was still practised by some people in Mecca, as we have seen in the experience of Sulayman al-Maghribl. In spite of this, there is no evidence that our scholars attempted to remove all aspects of the earlier tradition of the tariqahs. Therefore, it is appropriate to describe this phenomenon as one of continuity and change. While the scholars in the networks substantially reduced the extravagant and ecstatic features of earlier SUFIsm and emphasised loyal adherence to the sharl'sharl, at the same time they maintained their doctrinal links with, for instance, Ibn 'Arabl. However, in maintaining their connection with Ibn 'Arabl they tended to disengage themselves from some points of his controversial doctrines.

Johns has pointed out that Ibrahim al-Kuranl was one of the last great exponents of the school of Ibn 'Arabl, so far as his philosophical and theological ideas are concerned. But we should be careful not to conclude that his thought was dominated by Ibn 'Arabi'Arabi teachings. It is true that, in his Ithaf al-Dhakl, he often cites Ibn 'Arabl, but at the same time he puts forward his own arguments by citing al-Ghazali, al-Qushayri and even Ibn Taymiyyah. Furthermore, he studied not only Ibn 'Arabi'Arabi philosophical doctrines but also his legal teachings. As he tells us, he learned this often neglected aspect of Ibn ' Arabl'Arabl teachings not from a sufi but from a prominent Meccan scholar, Zayn al-'Abidm al-Tabari, who was known as a muhaddith.

The same is true of Ahmad al-Nakhli. In the same vein he expresses a great appreciation of al-Ghazall and Ibn 'Arabl. He tells us that he studied al-Ghazali'Ghazali Ihya' ' Ulum al-Dln with Sayyid Ahmad al-Husm al-Maghribl al-Maliki, better known as al-Mahjub, who later issued him an ijazah to teach al-Ghazali'Ghazali teachings. But from the same teacher he studied the rules of fasting in a chapter of Ibn 'Arabi'Arabi al-Futuhat al-Makkiyah. In another passage he relates that he studied the Ihya' ' Ulum al-Dln with al-Kuranl, who told him that this book was very popular in his homeland, Kurdistan. Interestingly enough, al-Nakhli also learned the Ihya' ' Ulum al-Dln from al-Qushashi, who studied it with Ahmad al-Shinnawi, who received it by way of an isnad which included al-Sha'Sha, Zakariyya al-Ansari and Ibn 'Arabl.

With this evidence it is clear that there was a conscious effort among scholars in the networks to reconcile different streams of thought that had often been seen as in conflict with each other by scholars before them. There seems to have been no bias against scholars who had been the subject of controversies, such as al-Ghazall or Ibn 'Arabl. On the contrary, scholars in the networks studied them in order to understand their teachings and later attempted to reconcile them. An example of this had been set earlier by the neo-sufi al-Sha'Sha, who sought to reconcile doctrines of the speculative theologians (ahl al-fikr) and the mystics (ahl al-kashf) by taking care not to associate himself entirely with Ibn 'Arabl, despite his admiration for him, and linking himself to famous fuqaha' and muhaddith.

Although such a scholar in the networks as Ibrahim al-Kuranl was by nature a conciliator, who preferred to reconcile two opposing points of view rather than choose one or the other of them, he was bitterly criticised by a number of scholars, such as the Algerian Ibn al-Tayyib and Yahya alShawi. Ibn al-Tayyib writes a short biography of al-Kurani in the Nashr al-Mathanl. In this work, Ibn al-Tayyib recognises al-Kuram'Kuram high reputation. Despite this, he attacks him on various issues: that he was in favour of the Qadariyyah interpretation of the ability of created power to be responsible for the acts of human beings; that he leaned to the Mu'Mu point of view by writing a treatise on the material character of non-being; that he accepted the historicity of the report that the Prophet Muhammad had uttered the so-called 'Satanic verses', allegedly interpolated into the Qur'an (53:21); and that he wrote a treatíse on the faith of Pharaoh according to Ibn 'Arabi'Arabi philosophical framework. Meanwhile al-Shawi (fl. 1096/1685), in his work entitled al-Nabl al-Raqlq ft Hulqum al-Sabb al-Zindlq, goes even further by accusing al-Kurani of atheism and demanding his death. Al-Shawi'Shawi accusation, in turn, was answered by al-Barzanji, in his work al- 'Iqab al-Hawi 'Ala al-Tha ' lab al- 'Awl wa al-Nushshab alKawl li al-A'A al-Ghawl wa al-Shihab al-Shawl li al-Ahwal al-Shawi.

The fact that Ibrahim al-Kurani was attacked on such a wide range of issues is, as Johns points out, an index of his learning. He had sufficient status in various Islamic disciplines to provoke disagreements. He was a master of various disciplines of Islam, and on the basis of his learning made his own ijtihads. Eclectic and original, he was the kind of scholar about whom others must have divided views and who thus exercises a creative role among his contemporaries. To sum up, these attacks on al-Kurani indicate the dynamics of intellectual discourse in the networks, which continued to gain momentum in the succeeding periods.

# 4

# Nation Formation and Islamic Revivalism in Asia

## Introduction

The editors observed that the complex relationship between religion and nation formation has often engendered what they called a "crisis of authority." In their words,

> *The process of creating modern nation states has...entailed two rather contradictory stances towards religion. While the modernizing stance leads to a deemphasis of ritual practices, the nation-building one leads to the promotion of selected practices and even the invention of new rites. Modernization emphasizes rational action; nation-building insists on a commitment of faith. The tension between these two stances as well as that between each of them and those of religious practices that derive their authority from other than the state have contributed to the crisis of authority.*

Building on this argument, I would add that the contradiction underlying the "crisis of authority" is often the result of a contestation of faiths, in particular, faith in the religion versus faith in the nation. We have ample evidence from world history that multitudes of people have died or are willing to die, rightly or wrongly, for the sake of the "nation" or "religion." In this essay, however, I examine an instance in which religion and nation have overlapped or fused, so that religious identity has become part and parcel of national identity; there seem to be similar cases in many countries around the world. An interesting feature of this process is that the concept of national identity itself is often a contested one, especially where the concept is developed in a multiethnic and secular society.

What interests me in such cases is how, in its effort to construct a national identity based on a particular religion, the state sometimes ends up confronting the very religious revival it had earlier sought to promote. Although, as in Malaysia, the challenge is often perceived by the state as an internal one, its transnational or global nature cannot be dismissed lightly. In the Malaysian case, the revival's impact on domestic interethnic relations has to be considered as well. In light of all these issues, the Malaysian experience provides a worthy case for examining the contestation between the state and Islamic revivalism.

Before I proceed with this analysis, let me make a few remarks on the analytical approach I adopt here. I contend that, like most social phenomena, identity construction and nation formation take place within two levels of social reality. The first is the official or "authority-defined" social reality, created by people who are part of the dominant power structure; the second is the "everyday-defined" social reality, experienced by the people in the course of their everyday lives ( Shamsul n.d.b). At any given time, these two social realities exist side by side. Although intricately linked and mutually influential, they are in fact rarely identical. Both are mediated through the social class position of those who experience and interpret social reality. Both are also embedded in relationships of social power.

In this chapter I wish therefore to locate the discourse, ruptures, and tensions that have characterized the contestation between the state and the Islamic revivalist (dakwah) movement in Malaysia over the past twenty-five years. Elsewhere I have dealt with microsociological aspects of this contest examining the lives of individual activists in an Islamic revivalist group; these individuals have largely escaped the attention of Malaysianists writing on the revivalist movement since the mid-1970s. Most analysts have focused on the movement as a group or organization, outlining its origin, leadership, and overall impact on society. My present contribution, a macrosociological one, is meant, first, to complement my recent microsociological study and, second, to frame the study of Islamic revivalism in Malaysia within the broader study of identity and nation formation.

## Ethnicity, Identity and Religion

The social categories of "race" and "nation" entered into the indigenous world view in Malaysia through European colonization. Their introduction had a humble and unnoticed beginning. What seemed to be harmless bureaucratic practices of census taking actually helped to introduce and consolidate the racial categories of Malay, Chinese, and Indian. The introduction of legislative measures such as the Malay Reservation Act, the establishment of a Department of Chinese Affairs, and the founding of government-approved toddy shops for Indians all further drove home the point. The racial categories of Malay, Indian, and Chinese came to be vital for anyone who wished to take advantage of the colonial bureaucracy or avoid its wrath.

The evolution and consolidation of these racial categories was further promoted through the vernacular education system. In such contexts racial categories developed into racially based understandings of nation. Ethnic difference came to be the defining mode of everyday social reality. The idea of Malayness and, eventually, the aspiration for a "Malay nation" were thus deeply affected by the circumstances of British rule. Although the British never established a unified Malay nation as such (instead endorsing a union of Malay principalities [kerajaan]), the concept of "Malayness" came to be accepted as an official feature of colonial and native politics.

"Malayness" came to be defined in terms of the three pillars of agama, bahasa dan raja, i.e., Muslim religion, Malay language, and the aristocratic government of the sultans. These pillars were then written into the constitution of postcolonial Malaysia. Thus, for example, the constitution requires that Malays be Muslims. In other words, by definition, Malays cannot but be Muslims in Malaysia. A Chinese or an Indian who marries a Malay has to agree to convert to Islam as a precondition of the marriage; in so doing he or she is assimilated into the Malay community, a process popularly known as masuk Melayu (lit. "become a Malay"). Their offspring are subsequently categorized as Malays.

Having one's identity officially designated as Malay is, of course, not a matter of free choice; nonetheless it has its benefits. For instance, as a Malay, one is entitled to numerous benefits under the terms of the the proMalay affirmative action policy known as the New Economic policy (NEP), launched in 1971 and completed in 1990. In fact, ethnic Malays enjoy other privileges under the terms of the national constitution. However, not every Malay succeeds in acquiring access to these benefits because policies like the NEP are based on, to borrow W. Wertheim's famous phrase "betting on the strong few and not on the weak many." Elsewhere I have examined this problem of access to official benefits in a rural community where I conducted research in the early 1980s, a decade after the NEP was implemented.

Both from the authority-defined as well as the everyday-defined perspective, to be Malay in Malaysia is to be Muslim. However, the relationship has by no means been a static or an uncontested one. It is constantly being redefined by new influences and events. This dynamic was keenly illustrated with the emergence in the 1970s of the Islamic revivalist movement, popularly known as the dakwah (lit. "to summon or call") movement. One consequence of the dakwah movement's development was that Islam came to be highlighted as the pillar of Malay identity. Through its ruling elite and political party UMNO, the state was forced to respond to this revivalist movement. This response led to the state's increased attention to Islam and its subsequent adoption of an Islamization strategy of its own.

Though Nagata perceives, rather simplistically, that the contestation between the state and the Islamic revivalism involves competing "models of development", I believe that the contest involves considerably more than that. Among other things, it involves the general effort to redefine Malayness in the aftermath of the May 1969 racial riots and to improve the generally unfavorable economic situation of Malays. As undertaken by the state, the effort to redefine Malayness led to the mainstreaming of Islam into all domains of Malaysian social life. If previously Islam was mainly expressed in symbolic terms, especially in relation to the institution of the royalty and popular Malay culture, the government's efforts drew Islam into the heart of all economic and noneconomic life. By implication, the government's effort also means that Muslim Malays have now entered the mainstream of the economy as full participants in the corporate world. This perception is neatly captured in the now popular phrase "Melayu baru". This notion implies that the Malay community has itself been thoroughly transformed, with a new identity, a high economic profile, and an increased sense of religiosity.

It should also be noted that the role of Islam as a pillar of Malay identity is today especially critical because the other two original pillars of Malayness, royalty and language, have come to be seen by the Malay elite as problematic. After independence, the Malay ruling elite came to view the native Malay royalty as serious competitors rather than as corulers. The situation of the royalty was further undermined by a series of scandals and corruption charges publicized in government-controlled dailies during 1992. A similar downgrading of importance in Malay identity, has occurred with the Malay language. While recognizing the political importance of the Malay language, the government elite has come to view the economic and technological utility of Malay as limited in an era of globalization. In 1994 the prime minister, Dr. Mahathir Mohamed, thus suggested that technical subjects be taught in English in Malaysia's colleges.

In the following pages, I shall present a description and an analysis of the government's mainstreaming effort, whereby it sought to respond to the revivalist movement by developing religious programs of its own. I shall divide the history into four stages over a twenty-five-year period. In doing so, I also want to examine the two major wings of the revivalist movement, namely the radicals and the moderates, paying particular attention to how each asserts its ideological positions and identity based on its particular way of claiming truth. The radicals, we shall see, demand a total and uncompromising response to the revivalist appeal, while the moderates are more tolerant of heterogeneity. I shall also examine the reasons for the government's preference for the moderate revivalist approach, with particular reference to the government's political goals and the global development of Islam.

## Phases of the Dakwah Movement

As the term is used throughout this essay, "revivalism" refers to the attempt to restructure the past in a form relevant to contemporary social interests. Terms used interchangeably with "revivalism" are "resurgence," "rediscovery," "rebirth," "reassertion," "renewal," and "reformulation," to name but a few. In my opinion, Islamic revivalism in Malaysia has been motivated by at least six major intentions, some of which have motivated revivalism elsewhere in Southeast Asia. Not in any order of importance, they are as follows: (1) to overcome the pressures of or construct a reply to modernization; (2) to express anti-imperialist or antihegemonical sentiments; (3) to promote spiritual renewal from within a given religion, such as the move to "re-Islamize knowledge"; (4) to counter the influences of societal rationalization; (5) to resolve how to live in a world of radical doubt through the reformulation of traditional symbols and systems of meaning; and (6) to reinvent and reconstruct tradition, thus allowing a redefinition or reassertion of ethnoreligious identities in a plural society.

In practice these intentions often overlap; rarely does any one of them dominate the dakwah movement at a given moment. The Malaysian dakwah movement was never a really homogenous one, even in its initial stages when it was dominated by university students. The best way to determine how these varied motives interact is to construct a periodization of the movement to date. I have identified four phases of Islamic revivalism in Malaysia over the past twenty-five years: the "reawakening period" ( 1969-1974), the "forward movement period" ( 1975-1979), the "mainstreaming period" ( 1980-1990), and the "dakwah and industrialized Malaysia period" ( 1991 onwards).

## Phase 1: The Reawakening Period (1969-1974)

A racial clash between Chinese and Malays took place in Kuala Lumpur, Malaysia's capital. It has been argued that Islamic revivalism in Malaysia emerged in the aftermath of this riot, a crisis that generated a sense of failure among young Malaysian Muslims, especially university students. From this perspective, the riot could be seen as a catalyst for the turn to Islam among Malay youths attempting to resolve how to live in a world of radical doubt. However, this was not the first or the biggest SinoMalay racial clash in Malaysian history. A bloodier and more extensive conflict occurred during the interregnum of 1945, in which religion and millenarianism were also central to the Malay response to the violent attack by Chinese. During the war, the Chinese had been abused politically by the Japanese; in several infamous incidents many Chinese were mercilessly massacred and buried in unmarked mass graves. Malay nationalists tended to support the Japanese during the occupation, however, since both groups shared certain nationalist ideals.

In the aftermath of the 1969 riot, there was a reemergence of Islamicoriented, millenarian-inclined, martial art (silat) cult groups. These groups traced their origins back to the armed Sabilillah movement that attacked rural Chinese settlements in revenge and self-defense during the Sino-Malay clashes in late 1945, almost immediately after the Japanese surrendered to the British. Most of these "reborn" groups were based in Malay settlements on the outskirts of the national capital, Kuala Lumpur, where most university students lived because of the Malay social environment and inexpensive housing. Many of these students were caught in the crisis mood of the time because of sheer proximity to centers of violence. Some went on to become members or supporters of silat cult groups. In an atmosphere of millenarian expectation, it was not suprising that their ethnic and religious consciousness was heightened to a level where they "awoke" to Islam and turned to mysticism and magic to resolve their spiritual and material problems.

The pivotal moment in the institutionalization of the revivalist movement took place in August of 1969 on the campus of the University of University of, the only university in Malaysia at the time, when the National Association of Muslim Students decided to establish a Muslim youth organization named Angkatan Belia Islam Malaysia (ABIM), or the Malaysian Muslim Youth Movement. Designed to operate off campus, ABIM was to serve as an organizational platform for young Muslim graduates to continue their dakwah activities in the broader public sphere after leaving the university.

ABIM was officially registered in 1971 and grew to a position of strength by the mid-1970s. The organization's motto was to strive "toward building a society that is based on the principles of Islam." It had an educational wing, the activities of which center around a private school, Yayasan Anda (lit. "Your Institute"). The school played multiple roles, providing cheap education for the poor, financing for ABIM, a recruitment office for new cadres, a publicity organization, a think tank for the forward movement, and a headquarters for the coordination of dakwah projects among various Muslim youth organizations.

The situation on the local campus also influenced the birth of the dakwah movement. It is not an exaggeration to describe the atmosphere at the University of Malaya in the 1960s and 1970s as an open, liberal, and exciting one, at least until the introduction of the Universities and the University College Act, 1971, which imposed draconian restrictions on student activities. University life remained intellectually vibrant, however, and by 1971 Malaysia had established three other universities, Universiti Kebangsaan Malaysia (UKM), Universiti Pertanian Malaysia (UPM), and Universiti Sains Malaysia (USM). The resulting expansion of the student population provided additional opportunities for the recruitment of dakwah supporters.

The sense of political crisis, doubts about their future after graduation, and the exhilarating freedom of campus life encouraged students to turn to Islam. In doing so, however, they quickly discovered that, beyond the daily rituals, they knew very little about intellectual aspects of Islam. Students thus awoke to their personal religious deficiency as they joined the appeal for "Muslims to be better Muslims."

There was another form of revivalism in Malaysian society that resulted from the 1969 race riot. Between May 1969 and February 1971, parliament was suspended and the country came under emergency rule. This became a period of serious rethinking, bargaining, reconstructing, and reconciliation at all levels of the society. New ideas, strategies, and institutions emerged; some were rediscovered, others were modifications of previous ones. All were related to attempts to recreate the racial harmony that had existed before the riots. The pro-Malay Muslim affirmative New Economic Policy (NEP) was one especially important creation of this rethinking process. The Islamic revivalist movement must be examined in this wider social context.

Most analyses of the revivalist movement overlook the importance of the link between the Malaysian dakwah activists and their Indonesian counterparts, especially Muslim student associations, during this formative stage from 1969 to 1972. As the movement's first influential international contact, the Indonesians provided an important stimulus to Islamic revivalism in Malaysia. This is perhaps not surprising, as it is a well-established tradition for Malaysian Muslims to look toward Indonesian Muslims for spiritual inspiration, intellectual guidance, and practical help. The two regions share many cultural and linguistics traits, and Indonesia was the main route through which Islam came to Malaysia some five centuries ago. By the mid-1970s, Indonesian contacts and influence had declined as the dakwah movement became more pluralistic and internationalized, owing to developments in the Middle East, Pakistan, and other parts of the Islamic world.

The single most important event that gave the dakwah movement, particularly ABIM, its much needed political credentials in the eyes of the Malaysian public took place in December 1974, when thousands of students demonstrated in the streets of Kuala Lumpur to protest against peasant hunger and poverty. The event was organized by dakwah leaders within the student organization. The government reacted to the demonstration by arresting 1,200 of the protesters and treating the protest as a student problem rather than an Islamic challenge to its legitimacy and authority. It would take the federal government another five years to recognize that the protest was motivated by Islamic objectives and to take appropriate counteraction. At the time the government was preoccupied with other matters, trying to settle a series of internal leadership crises, mainly in the Malay ruling party, UMNO. In the same year Partai Islam, a Malay-based opposition party, joined the ruling coalition, which until then had been dominated by UMNO. This created a political vacuum into which ABIM comfortably positioned itself, with considerable support and sympathy from disappointed supporters of Partai Islam.

Thus it could be said that in its first phase the dakwah movement moved from a limited concern with Muslim consciousness raising to a broader concern with controlling national politics through student activism. This transiton in just five years from the personal to the national-political was indeed a great achievement for the dakwah movement. It made Malaysia more Islamically inclined and enabled the movement to address Islamic issues more positively.

## Phase 2: The Forward Movement Period (1975-1979)

The second phase of Malaysian dakwah can be regarded as the "forward movement" phase in two senses. First, the movement had consolidated itself and found its niche in the Malaysian sociopolitical sphere. Hence it was ready to proceed with its religious agenda and political strategies. Second, during this period the government and the ruling coalition suffered from unprecedented internal strife, with bitter battles among the top leaders of UMNO. The fact that the battles were about "money politics" and the "siphoning of party election funds" – in a word, about corruption among top party leaders – helped to make ABIM, with its progressive approach, a credible political opposition. Part of ABIM'S appeal lay in the fact that it did not see Islam in black and white, as a choice between good and evil, or right and wrong, and did not believe in imposing Islam on nonMuslims.

From 1969 until about 1976 or 1977, ABIM and the National Association of Muslim Students were dominated by liberal arts students with only a small number of science students. The reason was simple: Most of the Malay Muslim students were in the arts faculties, and they had primary responsibility for running student organizations. Some time later, however, ABIM'S influence declined, at least on local campuses. The National Association of Muslim Students and student unions in local universities were taken over by a new dakwah student group, dominated this time not by the arts but by the science students. By this time the number of science students in Malaysian universities had increased dramatically with the expansion of Malaysia's science faculties. Despite the popularity of the new dakwah organization, most arts students continued to support the ABIM approach to dakwah.

The new dakwah group was known on campus as the IRC (Islamic Representative Council). It had originated overseas among Malay Muslim science undergraduates whose study was sponsored by the Malaysian government. Because this organization was born outside the Malaysian sociopolitical milieu and was informed mainly by sectarian Islamic groups based in the Middle East and South Asia, its focus was more religion for religion's sake rather than religion for society's sake. The IRC saw ABIM'S Islam as too spicy and impure (read: tolerant of heterogeneity), unlike theirs, which was more true to the original and pure (read: demanding total response).

The IRC and similar groups adopted a covert, guerrillalike style of organization. They established secret cells to spread their Islamic message and infiltrated existing organizations to try to initiate change from within. The group adopted the "education" approach or tarbiyah, through the formation and spread of small secret cells among the students. It denounced the Malaysian government as un-Islamic and accused it of upholding a secular and infidel system of rule.

Recruiting from among the science students, the IRC adopted what could be seen as a black and white approach to Islam. In their view, one either practices Islam in a complete way or is an infidel; one either fights for Islam or is irreligious; if a member of an Islamic group, one must be a fulltime dakwah activist, not merely a sympathizer. One incident drew the attention of the entire country to the new dakwah movement. One day the daughter of then-prime minister Hussein Onn arrived home veiled and announced that she had married a fellow student without her father's consent or knowledge. From this, it was obvious to everyone that Islamic revivalism had touched not only alienated overseas students, most of whom came from poor or ordinary rural families, but also children of the urban middle and upper class, brought up in a Westernized way.

Thus, by the end of the 1970s, the dakwah movement in Malaysia had been pluralized and radicalized. As a result, ABIM'S dominance was reduced substantially. On campuses, there was a sharp divide between ABIM and IRC supporters, who looked down on each other with a holier than thou attitude. By this time, too, the government had devised a response to the Islamic challenge. The option for the government was not so much to dismantle the dakwah movement – by then it was almost impossible to do so – but to coopt or mainstream it so that it could serve government interests. The 1980s were a period during which the government was preoccupied with just this struggle.

## Phase 3: The Mainstreaming Period (1979-1990)

A combination of international and domestic factors influenced the government's renewed focus on Islam. Government initiatives were notable in the late 1970s and increased to unprecedented levels in the 1980s with the appearance in 1981 of a new prime minister, Dr. Mahathir Mohamed. Mahathir had earlier been influential in the drafting and implementation of policies as the acting prime minister when Prime Minister Hussein Onn had fallen seriously ill in 1978. One of Mahathir's chief policy concerns was the position of Islam in Malaysia and Malaysia's position as an Islamic nation in the Muslim world.

At the international level, too, a number of events influenced internal Islamic affairs: the oil crisis of 1973 and the Arab-Israeli war in the same year; the rise of Middle Eastern Islamic states as "Islamic financiers"; the strengthening of the Organization of the Islamic Conference (OIC) as a basis for the formation of a so-called Muslim Bloc; the Palestinian issue and the PLO'S rise to prominence; the perceived Libyan dominance in the international politics of violence; the Russian occupation of Afghanistan; and, most important of all, the Islamic revolution in Iran. All these events not only transformed the perception and position of Islam in global politics but also heightened Islam's domestic role in Islamic countries like Malaysia.

During these years, there was a visible increase in Malaysian participation in the Muslim Bloc as a result of its pro-Muslim foreign policy. Malaysia's unqualified support for the PLO struggle, for instance, prompted Arafat to make the comment that "Malaysia is even closer to us than some of the Arab nations." Relations with Muslim countries provided excellent political capital for the government in its attempt to prove its Islamic credentials to Malaysian Muslim voters. Malaysia also profited substantially in its trade relations with the petro-dollar rich Islamic nations in the Middle East.

The most immediate challenge shaping the government's policies on Islam was the domestic dakwah movement. The movement not only had achieved a formidable position in the political sphere but also had transformed Malay thinking and culture. The most obvious illustration of this influence was the widespread use of mini-telekung, a head cloth that covers not only the neck and hair but the chest as well, now worn by growing numbers of Muslim women. The challenge to the government increased when Partai Islam left the ruling coalition and resumed its role as the Malay Muslim opposition. Its new leadership jettisoned its Malay nationalist orientation in favor of a more universalistic Islamic focus, similar to the one adopted by the me group of the student dakwah. In the government's estimation, the combination of the student-based dakwah movement and Partai Islam was politically explosive.

To defuse the situation, the government chose to adopt a "mainstreaming" rather than a confrontational approach to this perceived threat. First and foremost, the government had to accept the increased importance of Islam globally. It did this by approaching any Islamic issue in a positive manner, politically and economically. Domestically, the government attempted to coopt groups and offered its own version of dakwah, one more moderate, tolerant, and suitable to Malaysian society, with its multiple ethnic groups and almost equal proportion of Muslims and non-Muslims.

To demonstrate the sincerity of its Muslim-oriented foreign policy, the government introduced a series of policies designed to demonstrate its commitment to developing Islamic institutions among Malays, spending millions of dollars on these projects between 1979 and 1982. The projects included a pledge of MRY$26 million toward the establishment of the Southeast Asian Islamic Research Center, based in Malaysia; the introduction of Islamic religious knowledge as a subject in national education examinations; the official launching of the National Dakwah Month; the plan to remodel the Malaysian economic system into an Islamic one, beginning with the establishment of Islamic banks, pawnshops, insurance, and an Islamic Economic Foundation; the formation of Islamic think tanks, such as the Islamic Resources Group and a Special Islamic Enforcement Group; and the commitment to establish an International Islamic University in Kuala Lumpur.

These policies and programs were enough to convince Anwar Ibrahim, the internationally respected and locally popular ABIM leader, to join UMNO and the government in 1982. Soon thereafter he was appointed deputy minister of religious affairs in Mahathir's cabinet. Later he assumed full and more powerful ministerial positions. Other Islamic-oriented programs were introduced after Anwar Ibrahim joined UMNO, including the establishment of the Islamic Medical Center, the founding of International Islamic

University in 1983, and the upgrading of the Islamic Center as the nerve center of the government's Islamic bureaucracy.

Officially, Islam is the prerogative of the state governments within the Federation of Malaysia. In the face of these federal efforts, many states began to introduce their own Islamization programs, especially as regarded issues of public morality. Thus many states banned alcohol consumption by Muslims in public. In this manner, the momentum of dakwah ism at the federal level spread to state governments, affecting not only urban but rural areas, where Islam has been practiced for generations in a manner different from the overt and self-righteous "dakwah way." The overall impact was the heightening of Islamic consciousness nationwide. By the end of the 1980s, the once-urban phenomenon of dakwah had migrated to rural areas. The wearing of mini-telekung by women became a common sight in the countryside, largely as a result of government efforts.

By the end of the 1980s, more and more of the government policies became "ABIMized," in a fashion that paralleled Anwar Ibrahim's ascendancy from deputy minister (in charge of Islamic affairs) to minister ofagriculture and then education and finance. In early 1994 Anwar became Malaysia's deputy prime minister. In this context, dakwah groups that had not been mainstreamed became targets of government surveillance and dismantlement. The banning of Darul Arqam, a well-known economically oriented dakwah group, in 1994, was one such example. However, such efforts were not always successful, as evidenced in the government's limited success against the IRC in local universities. In general, university campuses resisted government mainstreaming and remained bastions of nongovernmental dakwah.

Nationally, however, the dakwah movement as a whole has demonstrated considerable ideological flexibility. The movement today is quite pluralized and appeals to a wider spectrum of Malays than it did in the late 1960s. This diversity allows the movement to accommodate political dissidents as well as those seeking spiritual salvation as an alternative to modernization.

The main attraction of the dakwah movement, however, was its ability, however limited, to combine theory and practice by attempting to implement the doctrinal precepts of fundamentalist Islamic ideology in the context of Malay Muslims living in a multiethnic country. The movement succeeded in exploiting numerous doctrinal and programmatic emphases: the sense of brotherhood in a community of believers, the relative autonomy of individual Muslims in practicing their religion and preserving their dignity, the encouragement of communally oriented social and welfare activities, and the "religious" obligation to be "political" so as to change a bad society into a good one consistent with the precepts of Islam.

In the public sphere, the impact of dakwah on the social fabric of Malaysian life is widespread and felt not only by Muslims but also by nonMuslims of Chinese and Indian descent. Consequently, relations between Muslims and non-Muslims (read: Malay and non-Malay) have become tense and awkward at times because of the influence of strict Islamic codes of behavior promoted by the dakwah movement. One example that demonstrates how the dakwah ethos has permeated every layer of society and affected everyday forms of social interaction at the grassroots level can be seen in Malay Muslim dietary rules or food taboos. Many Muslims now will not eat food brought by non-Muslim colleagues to social gatherings, be they at the workplace or at the homes of non-Muslim colleagues. In the past such food, as long as it was not pork, was eaten without fuss. Now, however, food taboos extend to anything cooked by non-Muslims, because they have not cleansed their cooking utensils in the Islamic way. Fast-food restaurants have to observe Muslim rules very strictly or their licenses can be revoked. Even in five-star hotels there are now separate Muslim and non-Muslim kitchens. Non-Muslims see this as evidence of increasing Muslim intolerance of non-Malays and non-Muslims.

## Phase 4: Dakwah and Industrialized Malaysia (1991 Onwards)

One must not forget the wider social context within which the dakwah movement in Malaysia has flourished, especially in terms of Malaysia's economic performance. The 1990s and the twenty-first century hold great promise for Malaysia's economic future, as the nation moves into a different phase of its existence. Without doubt the dakwah movement too will be affected by this transformation. In this context, one could ask, what is the future of the dakwah movement as a whole, and what actions will the government take in relation to the movement?

It is not difficult to find evidence that the government has responded successfully to the challenge of the dakwah movement. It has managed to keep the radical movements at bay while coopting moderate elements, avoiding serious confrontation over the past decade. It achieved this by introducing its own version of dakwah, one palatable both internationally and locally. The success of this effort can be attributed to several things, the most important being the government's willingness to embrace the cause for reasons neither purely religious nor political.

One must not underestimate the contribution of the mastermind himself, Malaysia's prime minister, Dr. Mahathir Mohamed, whose personal interest in matters relating to student politics and dakwah goes back to the days of the 1974 student uprising when he was the minister of education. With his intimate knowledge of student politics and the evolution of the dakwah movement, he was in the best position to observe what was going on in both domains. With the whole machinery of government at his disposal, he was also able to reshape aspects of the sociopolitical landscape of the country to the government's advantage in responding to the challenges of Islam in general and the dakwah movement in particular. Malaysia's spectacular economic success, achieving some of the highest growth rates in the world, has also made it possible for the government not only to finance its dakwah programs lavishly but also to initiate special Islamic-oriented policies in the economy. To observers in the industrialized nations, Malaysia is one of the "mini-tigers" in the making. To the developing world, Malaysia is a success story and a model of Third World development. To the Muslim Bloc, Malaysia is a successful Islamic nation and one that is rich and kind enough to assist other struggling Muslim nations.

The economic and political confidence that Malaysia has gained at home and abroad has made it more ambitious, though cautiously so. It is ambitious in that it aspires to be a developed industrial nation by 2020. It is cautious because it understands that realization of this vision is contingent upon the nation's ability to maintain not only economic growth but also, more importantly, political and social stability. Thus, in early 1991, Dr. Mahathir announced that Malaysia shall not follow the same route the West took in its journey to industrialization and modernization. He has said that Malaysia's path to 2020 shall be guided by spiritual, religious, and moral consciousness of the highest level. This is a tall order indeed. The issue here is what shall be the source of this guidance.

Such a pronouncement could be dismissed as merely rhetorical. But it is significant in the context of this essay that the propagation of such religious values and the confidence with which these values are now being proclaimed by the government can be attributed to the government's success in dealing with the Islamic and dakwah challenge. Because the whole issue of Islam and dakwah is so intricately linked to issues of ethnic identity and the political survival of the nation, it is no surprise that the government has taken the matter seriously. Seen from this perspective, dakwah has an important role in the government's vision of a developed and industrialized Malaysian nation.

At the international level, Malaysia's successful response to the dakwah challenge contributed tremendously toward enhancing Malaysia's image as a successful nation within the Muslim Bloc. This image has resulted in a manifold increase over the past five years in Malaysia's trade relations with oil-rich Islamic nations in the Middle East and even Central Asia. In the first half of 1993 alone, Malaysia has concluded business agreements worth more than U.S.$5 billion with Iran and another U.S.$2 billion with Kuwait, Uzbekistan, and Saudi Arabia. Only Japan has been able to make comparably sized deals with the Middle Eastern nations in the past. This is just the beginning of Malaysia's large-scale trade with other Muslim countries, which is projected to increase twofold in the next ten years.

It seems likely that in the next century we will see the development of a "two-tier" dakwah in Malaysia. On one level will be the government version of dakwah, with its wider network of subscribers involved in the everyday practice of governance and social interaction. Because the government has a large bureaucratic machine and almost unlimited funds at its disposal, its particular version of dakwah will be continuously maintained, supported, and propagated for domestic and international consumption.

On the second level will be the dakwah groups created outside the structure of government. The government will no doubt persist in its struggle to dismantle these groups, no matter how large their organization. Over the past two years this is exactly what the government has done to Darul Arqam, the best-known noncampus dakwah organization in Malaysia, which was established shortly after the May 1969 racial riot. Groups like the Darul Arqam are basically small-scale in terms of organization and funding, but compact and solid enough to resist being dismantled for a while by outsiders, including the government. But in 1994, Darul Arqam was disbanded after being banned by the government for its alleged "deviationist" activities. However, most of the non- ABIMdakwah organizations are found in the universities and are particularly strong in the natural sciences faculties. They are perceived by university authorities in Malaysia as "social irritants." They have survived in the universities, because forming an association or club in a university is much easier than establishing a nongovernmental organization outside the campus.

The dakwah movement is here to stay in Malaysia. It has now moved from a peripheral position, when it first appeared in 1969, to a central position in the social life of Malaysians. It has also spread from urban to rural areas and extended its influence from the middle class, where its founders were located, to both upper and lower classes. It has become ideologically pluralized, so that individuals drawn to the movement have the ability to choose extremist or moderate dakwah as they please. In daily interaction, to be "dakwah" can mean merely being relatively more strict in one's observance of Muslim codes or it can mean committed activism.

## Conclusion

It is difficult to separate the birth of the Malaysian dakwah movement from the aftermath of the race riots of 1969. The riots were a significant watershed in Malaysia's postcolonial politics, economy, and society. As with the bloodier racial clashes of 1946 after the Japanese surrender, religious elements, Islamic and non-Islamic, became the natural refuge with which Malays coped with intense disorientation and social turmoil. In 1946 the social context within which the religious elements appeared was dictated by the need to survive a violent and vengeful attack, mainly by the Chinese. In 1969 religious elements reappeared, but this time as a response to the pressures of modernization and the need to maintain the ethnic boundaries required for political hegemony. The Islamic revivalist movement emerged from these circumstances and, once established, began to function with its own logic, albeit not unrelated to the rise of Islamic influence globally.

Equally important, the movement's emergence also redefined Malay identity. Islam as a pillar of Malayness was pushed to center stage in politics and society. In its initial stages, the dakwah movement was inwardlooking and primarily concerned with reeducating the Muslim self. Its political attitude was moderate and integrated into Malaysian student politics, demanding social and economic justice for the weak in a multiethnic society. Its mission, however, was clearly Islamic, emphasizing the need for the Muslim-dominated government to return to the teachings of the Qur'an and to try to turn to Islam as a panacea for the ills besetting society. The orientation was clearly one of "Islamism," conceiving of Islam as a political ideology. It has been informed by the so-called Islamic political imagination, dominated by the paradigmatic ideal "of the first community of believers at the time of the Prophet and of the first four caliphs".

This Islamism was the main feature of the first phase (1969-1974) of Malaysia's dakwah movement, shaped by the students' experience in organizations in the arts faculty. This arts-based tradition of dakwah continues to this day. In the second phase (1975-1979), however, this moderate dakwah lost ground to a more radical version of dakwah, brought home from abroad by government-sponsored science graduates. As part of the same policy, the government also created a number of fully residential junior science colleges for Malay students selected on the basis of their excellent performance in national examinations. Radical dakwah found its way into these colleges as a result of the patient and dedicated campaigning of dakwah teachers who had trained abroad and then been posted to these colleges. Dakwah thus migrated from the university level to the secondary schools and was dominated in the science colleges by the radical group. In the ordinary secondary schools the moderate dakwah was also influential, but only among the arts-stream students.

Radical dakwah finally found its way into the campuses through students from the junior science colleges. The influence of radical dakwah grew as the number of science students in the universities increased. By the end of the 1970s, dakwah activists had a strong grip on national student politics, controlling all the student unions in the country. At the same time the government began to respond to the Islamic challenge. Previously it had been unable to do so because of internal leadership crises and its error in mistaking the dakwah movement for mere student politics.

The third phase of the dakwah movement (1979-1990) was dominated by the government's effort to mainstream dakwah groups by implementing Islamic-oriented programs, funding local and foreign Islamic organizations, establishing Islamic economic institutions, promulgating a pro-Muslim foreign policy, and becoming active in Muslim Bloc politics. It emphasized the need for a moderate approach toward Islam in a multiethnic society like Malaysia. These actions convinced arts-based dakwah groups like ABIM to join the government, thereby providing the bulk of the ideas and practical projects for the government's dakwah programs. While the machinery of government embraced a moderate dakwah approach, however, the student unions in government-funded universities did not. They remained in the hands of the radical dakwah from science faculties. University authorities were unable to dismantle this movement because of the weakness of university bureaucracies and the dakwah groups' resilience.

Events during these phases of Malaysian dakwah largely support Dale Eickelman's argument that mass education and mass communication facilitate awareness among the Muslim majority of a "plurality of traditions" within Islam; they thus expand "the style and scale of possible discourse, reconfigure the nature of religious thought and action, and encourage explicit debate over meaning".

In the early 1990s the government prepared the nation to move into the next century, guided by the vision that Malaysia should be an industrialized nation by the year 2020. The moderate dakwah emphasis on the spiritual and moral foundations required for such an effort became national policy. Meanwhile, the government's efforts to mainstream and moderate the dakwah movement continues. This attempt at "dakwah cleansing" will likely fail, however, because the government itself indirectly nurtures radical dakwah through its system of junior science colleges. Students at these colleges became dakwah at an early age through systematic tarbiyah (education) used by the radical dakwah group to recruit new members in secondary school. The positivistic scientific paradigms of the West have provided these students with the analytic tools for the reinterpretation of Islam in a narrow, legalistic way.

The arts students continue to propagate moderate dakwah and dominate the government's efforts to "Islamize" Malaysian society. The government's effort to dismantle radical dakwah, therefore, has been initiated by moderate dakwah elements in the government itself. In one sense, the contest seems like a continuation of the rivarly between science and arts students. As one of my arts informants remarked, "Being clever and brilliant like the science students is not good enough in this country. Being powerful is most important, and power is what the arts students have controlled in this country for so long".

In this sense, what we see in Malaysia today is the ongoing interaction of global knowledge, both Western and Islamic, and local knowledge, both indigenous and indigenized. The interaction hardly provides a fixed point of reference for the society, because it keeps on shifting as historical and other circumstances shape its form and content. Among the crucial questions being asked is "Is Western social knowledge the only source of social knowledge? What is the role of revealed knowledge?" The science students have reeducated themselves about Islam in a detailed and systematic manner not by using any method borrowed from famous Islamic Sufis or Ayatollah Khomeini, but according to the positivistic canons of the natural sciences. By using the approach that they know best, that is, the Western, rational, positivistic method, they have, in fact, adopted a narrowly legalistic, black-and-white, conservative position regarding Islam. They see "Islamic knowledge" or theology in terms of rules, formulae, and equations, a way of categorizing and perceiving the world they have learned from their study of the natural sciences.Sociologically speaking, this contest is a classic example of a struggle over the definition of tradition, particularly "authentic" tradition. The contest to define what is and what is not authentic inevitably takes on a confrontational form, as different versions of "tradition" compete with one another. One could thus argue that one of the most important elements in Islamic fundamentalism is precisely this struggle over the definition of what is an authentic Islamic tradition – a tradition with which the believers are to confront the forces of unbelief, corruption, and oppression. Malaysian dakwah has demonstrated the intensity and complexity of this struggle to define the authentic Islamic tradition. Seen from the perspective of a multiethnic and multireligious Malaysian society, this internal process involves a struggle to define and maintain an authentic Malay Muslim tradition and identity relative to non-Malays and non-Muslims, while also confronting the centrifugal pressures of a market economy, affluence, and growth of a middle class. However, the interesting twist to this search for authenticity is that during the process Malayness itself came to be redefined and reconstituted. This profound social transformation will continue to play a significant role in the shaping of Malaysia's future.

# 5

# Reshaping of Identities of Islamization

## Introduction

In today's Indonesia, however, this socioreligious diversity has to a certain degree been counteracted by an official ideology locating Muslim identity within the framework of national development and progress. For much of the New Order (post-1966) era, influential segments of the government and military elite have sought to separate the state's national and developmentalist ideals from Muslim identity. This political strategy has largely been based on government efforts to require all social and religious organizations to accept the state ideology known as the Pancasila, with its emphasis on the equality of the five government-recognized religions. In rural areas where Islam is the dominant religion, however, the population often perceives modern development and Muslim identity as intimately related; to be "modern" is to be Muslim. There are other local communities, however, where this identification of Muslim identity and developmentalist ideology is still in a very early or unfinished state. In these regions, Islam and ethnic or regional identity vie for the allegiance of the local population in an often unstable way. The study of religious change within these Muslim communities provides an opportunity to investigate the individual motivations and strategies of action that influence actors' commitments to one or another of these divergent, unfinished identities.

## Rise of Islam in Gowa: A Historical Sketch

Bontolowe, the village in which I conducted my research, is a community of Makassar wet-rice cultivators located about fifty miles east of Ujung Pandang in the highlands of the regency (Ind. kabupaten) of Gowa, within the Indonesian province of South Sulawesi. Bontolowe is a new village established in the 1960s after the original settlement, known as Bulo, was moved from the river valley up to a road on the top of a steep hill overlooking its previous site.

South Sulawesi – and in particular the kingdom of Gowa formerly located in this region – has long been regarded as one of the main centers of Islam in the Malay archipelago. The region has played a significant role in the history of Islam in Indonesia, both in earlier times and in the modern republican era.

The arrival of Islam on the peninsula is commonly dated as September 22, 1605, when the king of the empire of Tallo' converted to Islam. Since that time the Makassar people have been renowned for their strict adherence to Islamic faith. Only a few years after their king's conversion, in 1611, the Makassar are said to have spread Islam to other parts of South Sulawesi. The arrival of Islam coincided with a period of intense political turmoil on Sulawesi's southern peninsula. In addition to the long-standing conflicts between Makassar and Bugis kingdoms, in 1627 the local population came into conflict with the Dutch East Indies Company (voc). It is commonly assumed that Islam at first provided Makassar and Bugis with a sense of common (Muslim) identity in the face of the European enemy. Forty years later, however, when the war against the Dutch reached its final stage, Arung Palakka, leader of the Bugis, chose not to side with his Makassar fellow-believers but with the commander of the Dutch forces. He thereby took revenge for the compulsory Islamization his kingdom had experienced some decades earlier. In 1669, Gowa surrendered (see Pelras 1985; Andaya 1981).

From 1630 until the early twentieth century, Gowa's political leaders and Islamic functionaries were both recruited from the ranks of the nobility. The ruling nobles were explicitly concerned about preserving their power by filling Islamic offices with their own kinsfolk. Much later, in 1926, the Muhammadiyah, an influential Indonesian Islamic reform movement, was brought from Java to South Sulawesi. Its activities eventually led to the development of a marked social dichotomy between the nobility and preIslamic religion, on one hand, and commoners and Islam, on the other.

One of the primary practices targeted by the Muhammadiyah was the veneration of sacred heirlooms. Muslim reformists criticized the practice because they saw heirlooms as the pre-Islamic basis of the nobility's power and regarded the nobility as incompatible with Islam, which they saw as emphasizing equality among men. Conversely, the colonial government and its allies among the nobility regarded the Muslim reformists as a political threat. With the outbreak of the war for independence in 1945, the Muhammadiyah became one of the main forces struggling against the Dutch administration, which was still supported by influential nobles from Gowa and neighboring kingdoms. A few years later, the Darul Islam rebellion (1950-1965) broke out and, under the leadership of the charismatic Qahar Muzakkar, challenged the region's power structure even further. The rebellion was fueled by a complex array of ethnic, regional, and religious motives. Significantly, however, many of Qahar's followers were associated with the Muhammadiyah, which shared the rebels' anticolonialist and antifeudal attitudes. The cumulative effect of the struggle was that the Muhammadiyah and Islamic purification generally came to be regarded by many rural people as synonymous with the Darul Islam rebellion.

Though there have been numerous studies of Islam in lowland Makassar society, the role of Islam in the mountainous area east of Ujung Pandang has only recently become the focus of systematic study. Research has revealed that Islam in this region appears to differ profoundly from that commonly reported for South Sulawesi. This disparity may be explained by the fact that it was not until 1910 – immediately after Gowa's surrender to the Dutch – that Islam first gained influence in the highlands of South Sulawesi. The first imam, or leader of congregational prayer, in the region where I conducted research was Suleiman Daeng Bunding, a member of the high nobility of Gowa. He had been appointed by the Dutch colonial administration. In contrast to the situation in the western lowlands, the colonial government in this region wanted to weaken the influence of the rural nobility, whose political power was largely based on pre-Islamic religious institutions. The government and its native representatives did so by supporting the spread of Islam in these upland regions. Daeng Bunding was responsible for many conversions, using a mission strategy that, among other things, involved his marrying girls from the local nobility. He was successful in part because no Makassar family of commoner or lower noble status would refuse a man of high noble rank as their son-in-law. These families in turn converted to Islam because they considered it a distinguishing feature of the high nobility.

Daeng Bunding — whose children and grandchildren dominate local political life to this day — is reported to have used a variety of equally gentle methods in spreading Islam. Nonetheless, historical evidence indicates that by the late 1940s he was openly supportive of reformist Islam and the idea of the Republic of Indonesia, and opposed to the Dutch and their indigenous noble allies. In 1949, he was murdered by loyal followers of the district head of Kasepekang, who for years had been collaborating closely with the Dutch. A few months later, the Darul Islam rebels began to roam through the highland forests of Kasepekang. Many people who had derived advantage from collaborating with the Dutch were executed, including the district head. Darul Islam rebels also used this opportunity to eliminate many of the institutions and symbols of traditional belief. By the time the Muslim rebels left the area in the late 1950s, most of the sacred places and objects of pre-Islamic religion had been destroyed.

It is difficult to assess the attitude of the local population toward the rebellion during this period. Though in the 1930s and 1940s Daeng Bunding had built the first prayer houses in a few large highlands settlements, popular knowledge of Islam at that time appears to have remained limited. Few people understood the ideological principles motivating the Darul Islam rebellion. In 1984, an eighty-year-old man from Bontolowe described the stituation for me in the following way: "The only thing we saw was that these people in the name of Allah burned down our houses and killed our friends and family. These men were very dangerous. We did not understand. Some of us, including [name] went with them. I do not recall why they did so. Anyway, most people did not care." Another old man, a rebel partisan, described the events of that year in the following manner: "There was trouble everywhere. I went into the forest to join Muhammadiyah. We hid there during the daytime and by night entered the villages, burning down houses. The following day, those who had remained in the villages burned down their own houses so that we would not burn them down. Sometimes it was quite ridiculous." I asked him: Why did you do that? Did you do it for reasons of Islam? Did you become "Muhammadiyah"?

No, that's just how we called them. I don't remember much. Everything was just in a mess (kacau). We knew almost nothing about Islam or politics. How could we have known? There was no school, no one could read or write, no one could speak Indonesian. Few people had ever left the village for distant places such as Makassar. Sometimes if two men quarreled, on the following day one of them went off into the forest to join Muhammadiyah, while the other one stayed with his family. It was for whatever reason. I can't tell you why. It was disorder.

In the end, the rebellion had only a limited effect on the process of Islamization in the highlands. It was not long before the sacred spots destroyed by the Darul Islam were restored.

In the 1960s, however, other developments began to promote changes less compatible with indigenous ways. The first stone mosque was built in Kasepekang. This coincided with government efforts at administrative reform that transformed Kasepekang into an official administrative village (desa). For the first time too a man was installed as village imam. In addition, since 1970, the government's "head of spiritual affairs" has had a direct role in the regulation of local religious affairs. The holder of the office is commonly referred to as the Daeng Imang. For some fifteen years, the office has been held by Aziz Nawa, whose father and younger brother have played important roles in other developments, described below.

## Islam in a Highland Region

Suleiman Daeng Bunding, the primary missionary of Islam to Kasepekang, had earlier restricted his religious appeals to the families of the lower nobility. He only occasionally visited remote villages like Bulo, the site of my research. In the village itself, Bossong, the first man to study the art of Qur'anic recitation (Ind. mengaji), was the brother of a man who had earlier served as a priest (Mk. sanro ada') in traditional, non-Islamic ritual. Older villagers recall that there was never any conflict between these two brothers. Daeng Bunding eventually installed Bossong as the village's first religious teacher. This was not a formal office, however, and its precise purpose was not understood by villagers. Indeed, at first Bossong and the few men who joined him in Islamic study were regarded as members of some kind of religious brotherhood similar to the groups that practice black magic still today in some villages.

In 1941 Giling, a trained religious teacher from Makassar, was installed as Bunding's assistant imam in the administrative complex of Likopancing, which at that time also included the settlement of Bulo. Bossong felt slighted by this appointment and migrated to Makassar. Giling held his position until 1960, when the government decided that every larger settlement within the new desa Kasepekang should have its own imam. In 1945, Nawa, a peasant from Bulo, married Giling's daughter, and during the following years he learned much about Islam from his father-in-law. He was a diligent student, and, when in 1960 a village congregational leader (imam) was to be appointed, Nawa was chosen for the position since he was the only Bulo resident capable of reciting the Qur'an. He has held the post to this day.

Even though commoners occupied the offices of imam and head of spiritual affairs, the practice of Islam in the highlands during these years remained strongly identified with noble rank. According to local nobles, the reason had to do with familial obligations originating with Daeng Bunding's activities. The present subdistrict head of Kasepekang and the village chief of Bontolowe are Daeng Bunding's grandsons. Fatimah, a Bontolowe resident who has played a great role in local Islam, is one of his granddaughters. Finally, the head of the primary school in Bontolowe is married to Daeng Bunding's youngest daughter. All of these people share two characteristics that until recently distinguished them from most commoners: their education is far above average (many had finished secondary school or even attended colleges), and they explicitly identify Islam with progress and modernity.

When I began my fieldwork in 1984, Islam was a topic that, at least in the presence of the anthropologist, was discussed almost exclusively by nobles. One day I asked the head of the village school, who was originally from Ternate (Moluccas), about the population's general attitude toward Islam. He answered in the following manner:

You cannot compare the people here to those who live in the lowlands or in the city. The mountains provide no place for religious fanaticism (agama fanatik). The only thing these people consider important is cultivating their fields to make a living. Time and again there have been people from the city who settled in the villages and made propaganda for Muslim brotherhoods. These men, as a general rule, very soon returned to where they had come from. They were told by the villagers: "You guys may have the time to practice Islam, but not we. The soil is difficult in the mountains, and we must work very hard so that we can eat rice and stay alive." I am the son-in-law of Daeng Bunding, I am a Muslim, and I am educated. But I am not a man whose roots lie here. The people here are different. In my opinion, people in this and other villages have been living in their religious community for centuries, and they simply do not care if this is a Muslim community or one of the old belief. I find this quite understandable, and I have never bothered.

Such a view of local religion and society was typical among the elite in the mid-1980s. More remarkably, it is also broadly consistent with ordinary villagers' assessment of Islam. During my fieldwork I heard many people comment that the increasing influence of Islam, which is believed to stress the separation of the secular from the sacred, would transform religion into an individual rather than a communal affair. Furthermore, it was widely felt that Islam, in contrast to the indigenous belief system, would require that much time be set aside for prayers, fasting, and reflecting on God. Villagers say such conditions are consistent with city life, but not with the life of hard-working rice farmers. In other words, many people regard Islam as a religion whose basic principles are inconsistent with indigenous patterns of social and economic organization.

Besides religious officials in the village and subdistrict, one of the few individuals dissenting from this view was the head of Kasepekang. His views are illustrated by a comment that I recorded in my notebook on the occasion of the celebration of the Prophet's Birthday (Ar. maulid) in 1984: "As you know, maulid is a matter of religion (agama), isn't it? So there is a public declaration (penerangan) and a sermon (khutbah) in the mosque, and then the celebration is valid (sah). But the people in the villages haven't yet understood. They would still perform maulid rituals in their houses, burn incense and prepare special meals, and so on. This is not religion, this is just culture and custom (kebudayaan dan kebiasaan). We can only become a modern society if some day these peasants understand what religion means." In the eyes of the administration, the way to achieve this aim is religious education. Most of the local nobles, of course, have had some exposure to higher education. By contrast, the first primary school for ordinary villagers was built in Bontolowe only in the 1960s. Most of Daeng Bunding's older children had been educated at Dutch schools in Makassar before the war. Some among his descendants later went to secondary school and even college. Since, by comparison with other parts of Indonesia, the educational system in South Sulawesi was until recently poorly developed, higher education was limited to those of greater economic means. Only nobles, with their vast landholdings, government jobs, and trading enterprises, could afford the cost of education. In the village, there is only the most basic religious training in primary school. In addition, the imam regularly holds courses in Qur'anic recitation for children between six and ten years of age. However, neither the imam nor his pupils understand the literal meaning of the Arabic words they utter.

Before turning to a closer examination of pre-Islamic religion in highland Gowa, let me briefly explain how its relationship with Islam is now officially viewed. Such an assessment is complicated by the fact that there are no indigenous (Makassar) terms to characterize the conceptual opposition between traditional "belief" (Ind. kepercayaan) and Islam as a "religion" (Ind. agama). Throughout Indonesia, however, this contrast between belief and religion is expressed as a relationship between a (subordinate) kepercayaan and a (superior) agama. Thus everything that is not "religion" tends to be identified as mere "superstition" (takhayyul), "culture" (kebudayaan), or "custom" (kebiasaan). In other words, traditional culture as understood in the human sciences is in official Indonesian discourse likely to be viewed as mere folklore or, in other contexts, aestheticized as indigenous "art".

This manner of categorization is not only a problem for social research but also for — and, I hasten to stress, primarily for — local people. Imam Nawa one day explained:

> *I accept the old belief (kepercayaan), and I know how to perform the old rites. Actually it is also my belief, because I am of the same descent as all the other people here. We have common ancestors, and so we share the same belief. But I am the imam, and so I must be careful not to act in contradiction to agama. Once I asked a great imam how I should deal with the contrast between agama and kepercayaan. He was silent for a moment and then responded: "If they ask you for help, you may help those who do not act in accordance with Islam. But if they receive help by one of their kind, then leave them alone." I have always followed this advice, and therefore I don't have any enemies in the village.*

The imam's comments reveal the continuing importance of local identity and illustrate the ambivalence regarding the distinction between Islam and the old belief. Nawa's attitude contrasts with that of his son Nasir, who acts as a kind of deputy imam in the village. In 1984, when he was twenty-four years old, Nasir made the following observation: "The old belief is irreconcilable with true religion (agama). How can we village people ever become modern when even our leaders [i.e., the holders of traditional offices] practice the old belief? They make offerings to the ancestors so that the harvest be rich. No one can hear what the priest is saying during the offerings. Why is he whispering? In Islam, it is different. Our prayers are pronounced loudly and clearly, the words are Arabic, and they are taken from the holy Qur'an." As these comments indicate, when I first began my fieldwork in Bontolowe, religious life was still to a great extent governed by pre-Islamic ritual practices; but these practices were encountering growing opposition.

My primary concern here, however, is not with an elite-sponsored Islam, but with the social practices and experiences of "ordinary" people, especially the mostly illiterate peasants who until recently had no reason to distinguish "scripturalist Islam" from their own religious practice. These people's religious experiences differ significantly from those described, for example, in contemporary Java.

The divergent nature of individual and group experience within this local context, however, can shed light on aspects of Islam and Islamization elsewhere in Southeast Asia. It must be kept in mind at the outset that what we call a ' new synthesis' is not entirely a new development in the history of Islamic social and intellectual traditions. Even though it has some distinctive characteristics, compared with the previous tradition, in many respects it also contains elements of continuity with earlier traditions. The return to the Sunnl orthodoxy that gained momentum after the twelfth century appears to reach its culmination in the period under discussion. This can be seen not only in the intellectual contents of the networks but also in their ' organisational' aspects, or more precisely the linkages among scholars. Thus, the revivalist spirit that inspired the establishment of madrasahs everywhere in the Middle East after the founding of the Nizamiyyah madrasah in 459/1066 continued to flourish in a variety of ways.

The salient feature of the scholarly networks is that the rapprochement between the shari'ah-onented ' ulama' (more specifically, thefuqaha') and the sufis reached its climax. The long-standing conflict between these two groups of Muslim scholars appears to have greatly diminished; the rapprochement or reconciliation between them, which had been preached insistently by such scholars as al-Qushayri and al-Ghazall several centuries earlier, became a common goal among our scholars. Most of them were ahl al-shan'ah ifuqaha') and ahl al-haqlqah (s?f?s) at the same time; thus, they were learned not only in the intricacies of the shan'ah but also in the haqlqah (mystical or Divine Realities). However, we should be very careful not to conclude that they took this reconciliation for granted; instead, they continued to nurture it.

The rapprochement between the shan'ah and S?F?sm and the enrolment of the 'ulama' in the tar?q?h resulted in the rise of ' neo-SUFIsm'. There has been considerable discussion on the meaning and use of the term ' neoS?F?sm', which was coined by the late Fazlur Rahman. According to Rahman, neo-SUFIsm is the reformed S?F?sm largely stripped of its ecstatic and metaphysical character and content, these being replaced by a content that was nothing other than the postulates of the orthodox religion. As he explained, this new ' type' of S?F?sm emphasises and renews the original moral factor and puritanical self-control in S?F?sm at the expense of the extravagant features of the popular unorthodox S?F?sm. Neo-S?F?sm brings to the centre of attention the moral reconstruction of Muslim society, as contrasted with the earlier S?F?sm, which had primarily stressed the individual and not society. As a consequence, Rahman concludes, the overall character of neo-S?F?sm is undoubtedly puritanical and activist. We will now see more clearly how neo-S?F?sm developed in the networks.

## Neo-sufism and Hadith Study

Fazlur Rahman maintains that the most important group of Muslim scholars responsible for helping to crystallise the rise of neo-S?F?sm were the ' people of tradition' (ahl al-had?th). He further argues that after the s?f?.

## Identity, Religion, and Sociopolitical Organization

Like most Indonesians, the people in Bontolowe have a national identity card with the entry "Islam" under the heading "religion." There is no one who, when questioned about his or her religious affiliation, would not speak of himself or herself as Muslim. Yet at least some people living in this region say that the majority of the population is not Muslim at all. How can we reconcile the label of Islam with individual experience and cultural meaning?

Identity in highland Makassar communities was traditionally defined in terms of several inseparable components, the most important of which were territory, religion, and membership in kin groups. Each village is located within a territory (Mk. pa'rasangeng), the boundaries of which are regarded as fixed by customary law (Mk. adat), and inhabited by the localized core of a bilateral kin group (Mk. pammanakang). As a general rule, in precolonial times a cluster of several such village territories, such as Kasepekang, constituted an autonomous principality ruled by a karaeng. Some of the highland village territories, including Bulo/ Bontolowe, had been autonomous before they were incorporated (in most instances by force) into principalities or the kingdom of Gowa. According to oral tradition, this happened to Bulo in the sixteenth century. Oral traditions from Bontolowe as well as from

Kajang, which is located in the southeastern corner of South Sulawesi, suggest that in both regions elite domination, titles, and stratification emerged only after their subjugation by the kingdom of Gowa. Accordingly, many indigenous traditions today still reflect egalitarian ideals. Thus it is said that within the village territory, no difference between people must be displayed. Members of the high nobility from the court of Gowa must not be treated as superiors, and even the king himself will not be allowed to enter the village on horseback.

In the course of recent history, however, the precise meaning of most of these traditions was lost, and today social ranking in Kasepekang is as great a concern as in the western lowlands. The society as a whole is divided into nobility, commoners, and (former) slaves; each of these strata is in turn internally differentiated. In addition, evaluation of individual rank, also important among commoners, depends largely on membership in cognatic descent groups. Specific terms (Mk. pattola) are applied to those groups in which membership entitles one to traditional political offices, such as the community head (karaeng). Marriage is the primary avenue for upward mobility. Low descent rank can also be mitigated by bravery, education, wealth, occupation, or religious knowledge.

Although after the incorporation of the interior highlands into the kingdom of Gowa the translocal notion of "Makassarness" became an important concept, social identity was, and to a great degree still is, based on more localized groups. Still today anyone who does not own village land is regarded as an outsider (tu palili'). Even someone who marries a village resident and resides for decades in the village is regarded by the "people owning land" (tu pa'butta) as "a person living here, but not one of us." Beyond the framework of the village, no overarching criteria of identity are recognized. Even the historical territory of a principality lacks such a culturally acknowledged common identity. Below its ruler, there was not a centralized government but a council composed of (in the case of Kasepekang) the heads of the twelve most important villages. In two principalitywide rituals (now rarely performed), it was not common identity but the distinguishing identities of each village within this council that were highlighted. While all this might appear to be merely a matter of descent and territoriality, it also entailed a religious dimension, because descent and territoriality mark not only social divides but boundaries between religious microcosms. The influence exercised by ancestral souls, for example, was and is still today believed to be restricted to the territory inhabited by their descendants.

Despite such great historical changes as the expansion of the kingdom of Gowa, it appears that Makassar living in the central and eastern mountains remained distinct from those dwelling in the western and southern lowlands. This picture is strikingly similar to the relationship of the Tengger people of East Java to the lowland Javanese population. Thus, although it is difficult to explain the distinctiveness of the highland people by reference to any sociopolitical structure, there are important differences of language, material culture, and, above all, indigenous belief. Though there is no specific term for the latter as a body of religious belief, there is a word for the people who adhere to certain practices and beliefs. This term is patuntung, meaning "a person who strives to bring his or her behavior into conformity with tradition." According to oral traditions from Kajang, these norms and values above all relate to honesty and modesty. But being a patuntung also means adhering to a system of belief and practice that includes religious ideas, a world view, and norms for everyday behavior. "Being Patuntung" was the most important criterion of local identity before Islamization.

One among them, "Almighty Lord" ( Karaeng Kaminang Kammaya), is thought to live in an indefinite realm between the world and nothingness, exercising supreme control over the universe. From this it seems that there was traditionally a monolatric understanding of divinity. In present-day ritual it is sometimes difficult for the outside observer to determine whether this "Almighty Lord" or Allah is being addressed. Notions of Allah (Karaeng Alata'ala) have also entered traditional ritual texts, where the Islamic term has replaced Karaeng Kaminang Kammaya. Indeed, in general traditional rituals reveal widespread Islamic terminological influences, including such terms as malaeka' (Ar. mala'ika, "angel"), and jing (Ar. jinn, "spirit"). Yet locals do not consider most such usages an effect of Islamization, but merely as an aspect of "traditional" belief.

The presence of so many religious terms of Islamic origin clearly reflects the long-standing nature of Islamic influence, related, no doubt, to the long-established dominance of the kingdom of Gowa in this region. It is reported that, even in the early seventeenth century, the king of Gowa had officially integrated elements of Islamic rites of passage (including Islamic marriage, the nikah) into court custom. The annexation of formerly autonomous principalities in the following two hundred years resulted in the spread of these and other rituals, such as the practice of circumcision. The latter may be of pre-Islamic origin and was formerly accompanied by the filing of the upper incisors, a practice still important in some highland regions. According to Pénard, both rites were regarded as an initiation into the community of patuntung. Old people from Bontolowe remember that tooth filing was once practiced in Kasepekang. They were told about it when they were children, but none of them had ever seen the performance. Today, circumcision is regarded as a boy's initiation into the community of Muslim faithful (ummat).

From an indigenous standpoint it is not important whether the beings toward which local people direct their offerings bear Arabic or indigenous names, or whether certain spiritual beings addressed in ritual action are of Islamic or non-Islamic origin. All beliefs and rituals, even if they have long since been modified by Islamic ideas, are regarded as part of traditional heritage. The belief system shared by patuntung is seen as "pre-Islamic," regardless of whether it bears Islamic elements or not. The dichotomy in terms of "Islamic" versus "non-Islamic" emerged recently, only after Islamic modernists began to label certain unfamiliar practices as "nonIslamic" and the suppression of such rites became a matter of official policy.

Of particular importance for the political and religious life of the village, principality, and kingdom were sacred heirlooms (Mk. kalompoang). These objects were used by noble and commoner leaders alike to legitimate their authority, by providing a means for individuals to trace their descent back to regional founders. However, the traditional leadership was abolished as a result of the administrative reforms carried out around 1960, and from that point on any man could strive for political power. Descent became less important, and the office of the village chief turned into a stage for open competition, as some people saw an opportunity to improve their social position. Between 1960 and 1983 no fewer than seven men held the office in Bontolowe. In 1975, for the first time in history, an "outsider" (tu palili') of slave descent named Jumali became village chief.

These changes also worked to create tension between the formal office of the village chief and that of the traditional leader or karaeng. The last karaeng of Bontolowe was installed in 1961 but was forced by the national government to bear the Indonesian title of "village chief" (Ind. ketua rukun kampung) rather than the traditional title karaeng. Though soon replaced as village chief, this man is regarded as the karaeng to this day, and he still performs traditional rituals, including those centering on the sacred heirlooms. Despite the decline of this traditional leadership role, the official village chiefs who have held power since 1960 have not tended to work as direct agents of Islamization. However, the abolition of traditional political roles has led to a situation where, even if leaders adhere to the old belief rather than Islam, they no longer have any institutionalized authority in traditional religious matters. Village officials are thus in an ambiguous position, obliged to observe instructions from the district government but still involved in social networks linked to traditional beliefs and rituals.

Recently the situation has been further complicated by efforts at religious outreach undertaken by district — and provincial-level officials as well as students from the Islamic teaching colleges in Ujung Pandang. In 1990, for example, IAIN students visited a number of houses doing surveys on the potentially sensitive issues of villagers' habits of prayer and fasting, and the quality of their belief in Allah. After their interviews, the students found that no family invited them for coffee, let alone a warm meal. According to local custom, to treat guests — even those whom one dislikes — in such a way is not only extremely impolite but unthinkable. But local people protested the students' actions, asking, Why do such people say that we are not good Muslims? Am I a better human being if I pray five times daily, without any particular cause? Life is good when offerings are given to the Owners of the Earth or to others Who Are Powerful. They give us rice and children, and when we die some day, we will be with them. They cannot be bad beings, but these people say so. What more can Allah do than also give us rice and children?

These discussions raise complex questions about the changing role of Islam in individual and group identity. It is not a question of whether villagers profess formal adherence to Islam; clearly they do. What is at issue is instead the relationship of individual consciousness, experience, and interpretation to some wider, collective body of action or belief linking individuals and groups. In the case of the world religions, ultimately in question are abstract standards of action and belief the historical complexity of which is determined by much more than local actions and meanings.

Observing and interpreting these standards of action and belief in Islam is facilitated by the fact that the framework of religious action is formulated around Islam's famous "Five Pillars." These devotional obligations are intended to bring believers nearer to God and to help them fulfill their duties toward Him. The Pillars consist of testifying to the unity of God (Ar. shahâda), worshiping five times daily (Ar. salât), making the annual payment of the tithe (Ar. zakât), engaging in the the annual fast (Ar. saum), and making the pilgrimage (Ar. hajj). Throughout the Muslim world, these Five Pillars "are practised to widely differing extents, and the importance attached to each Pillar varies from one place to another". The way in which they are practiced in different Islamic contexts helps to illuminate the processes whereby Islamic identity is often divergently constructed. This can be clearly seen here in South Sulawesi in relation to two of the most important Islamic feasts, îd al-fitr (Ar.) and id al-qurbân or îd al-adhâ.

## Imam's Family and a Dispute over Prayer

In the summer of 1984, a few weeks after the end-of-the-fast celebration of îd al-fitr, a district military official delivered an address about nonreligious matters in the school building. Nasir, the young son of the village imam, then took the opportunity to accuse the villagers of too rarely joining the evening prayers. Jumali, the former village chief, was again drunk and vigorously supported him, shouting that the present village chief should prohibit primitive superstition and the veneration of "wood and stones." The meeting soon dissolved in total confusion because the official did not know how to reply. The result of the turmoil was that the mosque was locked for several days. Nasir, who controlled the key, was disappointed about his failure. Most of the village's residents, however, were deeply irritated by his behavior. How could he, a young man of low social rank, dare to make such a point in public, giving the district government probably more reason for further religious propaganda?

This event is typical of how public Islamic affairs are treated at the village level. It had only temporary consequences for evening prayers, and a few weeks later everything went back to normal. The incident revealed, however, an important point: that the social position of individuals is often a decisive influence in religious conflicts and, more specifically, that marginal individuals often have a vital interest in the promotion of reformist ideas.

To understand this point requires a closer look at the imam's family. Nawa's parents ran away to get married around 1918. Contrary to most other Indonesian societies, among Makassar marriage by flight is not just a symbolic act, but often results in bloodshed. After the young couple had hidden for several years in a small settlement deep in the forest (where Nawa was born), Nawa's father was still unable to pay the bride price to his parents-in-law. If they had hid any longer, all of them would have risked discovery and death. Thus, Nawa's mother went home to her father, giving him a dagger and asking him to kill her. Though it is said that no father had ever killed his daughter in such circumstances, this conventionalized act, called "running up to the blade" (allari matanna bassia) has severe social consequences. The young family settled down in Bulo, but from that day on, Nawa's mother was labeled a whore. The self-respect (Mk. siri') of all family members was destroyed. Neither Nawa nor his siblings found a spouse in Bulo or any of the neighboring villages. Since Nawa had to cultivate the fields of his father, he could not follow his brothers and sisters and migrate to some distant place. Several older people told me that the only chance Nawa ever had to improve his deplorable position as the son of a whore occurred in 1960, when the district government was looking to appoint someone to serve as a congregational leader (imam) for the community.

But this avenue to upward mobility had its own pitfalls. Acting as the first village imam served to further isolate Nawa, since in the early 1960s, as he repeatedly told me, spreading Islam in the village was a very difficult task. Appointment of the imam was regarded as an affront to village tradition (adat). In fact, to this day Nawa's family is in some sense isolated, despite the fact that Nasir's elder brother, Aziz, holds the highest Islamic role in the subdistrict (desa). Though by virtue of their offices, Nawa and Aziz exercise considerable authority within the community, the whole family is nonetheless regarded as "odd" by most villagers. "They hold governmental offices, but without these, they would count for nothing," I was once told. Because descent is the most important determinant of rank, Nasir and Nawa had no chance of improving their social position by using traditional mechanisms of status mobility such as taking a spouse from one of the adat descent groups. Excluded from such traditional status arrangements, Nawa has succeeded in achieving some respect in the village through the warmth of his personality and his involvement in Islamic affairs.

The situation is quite different with Jumali. He is an "outsider" of slave descent — a stigma that long after the official abolition of slavery under Dutch colonial rule is still of great social significance — and is widely regarded as a man of the worst character. Though he had repeatedly been accused of theft, insulting women, embezzlement, and acts of violence, he was installed as village chief in 1975. The reason was that at that time he already held a government job in the district capital, which provided him with useful political connections. Since he is also an eloquent man with an excellent knowledge of the Indonesian language (which in the 1970s was exceptional for the local people), he was seen as the best candidate for the post.

During the weeks before the meeting mentioned above, there had been constant quarreling between the village chief and Jumali. It was the dry season, and water was in short supply. Whenever he was drunk, Jumali raged outside his house, brandishing his sword and threatening to cut the whole water pipe network into pieces (which one day he did) if that "most stupid of all village chiefs" would not remedy things quickly. In the weeks and months after the meeting, he made Islam the main topic of his accusations. He was aware that the village chief, whose father had been karaeng in the late 1940s, was closely tied to traditional authority and rituals. In addition, the chief repeatedly refused to speak in the mosque when requested to do so because of his poor command of the Indonesian language. Thus Jumali frequently complained to district officials that under the chief's inept guidance Islam would never be established in Bontolowe.

Until very recently, opportunities for social and political mobility in these highland communities were limited, particularly for illiterate people without the chance of obtaining employment in some small government office, as Jumali had done. Now some individuals can advance their rank on bases other than traditional descent, including the manipulation of Islamic appeals, and these strategies at times are having a significant effect on social and religious life.

## Fast and the Alms: Support for the Imam

"Fasting is an armour with which one protects oneself," states a hadith (Ar.) put down by Bukhari. In villages in the Makassar highlands, only a few individuals actually carry out the fast for the whole of the fasting month (Ramadan), most giving it up after a few days. At another public meeting two weeks into Ramadan in 1984, a district religious official accused the population of ignoring Islam by not faithfully keeping the fast. From that day on the mosque was empty. Indeed, in general villagers tire of listening to lectures each night of the fasting month by officials or students from Islamic colleges in Ujung Pandang. Some men made a habit of walking two hours to a small prayer house up the road every day because officials never came there to deliver addresses. In 1991 further discontent was evoked by a new regulation that denied women access to the mosque of Bontolowe; they were instead to sit outside during the evening prayer. For many villagers, Ramadan has become a month of disharmony rather than purity and devotion.

Similar tensions are evident during the last days of the fasting month, when people are obliged to give alms in the form of zakât al-fitr (Ar.), the only zakât payment made here. According to a decree by the district government, every household is obliged to give zakât. In effect this regulation implies that there are no poor or needy people in the village. Therefore, the village chief and Imam Nawa are the only individuals who receive a portion of the alms. In 1991 every household was asked to give four liters of rice or 1,600 rupiah for each of its members; the figure had been 700 rupiah in 1984. Data from 1984 as well as from 1991 reveal that the alms had in fact only been rendered by about a third of the population. Many people who came with rice or money to Nawa's house asked him to keep it for himself and not to hand it over to the district officials. Although the money and proceeds from selling the rice are supposed to be used for public purposes such as repairing the school building, it is more often divided among district officials and high-status people, a fact not appreciated by most villagers.

The fasting month ends with the celebration of id al-fitr, which in the highlands is the greatest Islamic feast. Every household prepares cakes and sweets for visitors. The strategies people follow with regard to these visits correspond closely to social and economic position. Basically, there are only two categories of households during the feast: first, the high-status and better-off, whose members stay at home to receive guests, and, second, the low-status and poorer households, whose members spend the days of the feast moving from one house to the other. Social rank and relationships determine the selection of households to be visited.

## The First Haji

The fifth Pillar of Islam concerns the pilgrimage (hajj) to Mecca, considered obligatory for those who can afford the journey. The pilgrimage occupies an unusual position among the highland population, quite different from its role among wealthier lowlanders. In the highlands, the pilgrimage is regarded as something extraordinary and exceptional, something one can hardly afford without risking one's very existence. In 1984 a young man named Hasan became a sensation when he announced that he would perform the hajj as the one and only person from the whole district in that year and as the very first man from the village. This astonished most villagers, because until then only nobles were regarded as rich enough to perform the pilgrimage. Hasan, who was married to the daughter of Banci, a former traditional priest (Mk. sanro ada'), had sold all his possessions, including his house and all of his fields and cattle, in order to be registered as a pilgrim. This event caused great excitement, but it also divided the population. Some people simply shook their heads at such an "obscure adventure," while others regarded Hasan as a shining example of piety, whose willingness to sacrifice his existence for the sake of God would surely be rewarded some day. Nasir made the following observation in 1984: "All right, Hasan is a poor man now, as far as material wealth is concerned. But that will not last long. Once you are haji, you soon become rich. Allah will love you, and He will reward you. All haji are wealthy. And in a few months Hasan will be wealthier than ever before, believe me!" By 1991 it was clear that this prediction had not come true, and Haji Hasan was still earning his means by helping other people cultivate their ricefields.

As noted above, Hasan was the son-in-law of Banci, who had formerly held the office of priest in the traditional (non-Islamic) religion, commonly regarded as the very opposite of institutionalized Islam. After the ritual performed in 1984 on the occasion of Hasan's departure for Mecca, Imam Nawa said to me: "It; is good that soon we shall have a haji in the village, but don't you ever trust Banci! He is as old as I am, but he does not believe in God. He does not follow the words of the Prophet; instead he only communicates with the ancestors. This is probably because he had once been sanro! His way is not the right one."

Seven years later, in April 1991, I found myself again talking with the imam about Banci, but this time his words were different: "I don't want to have anything to do with Banci, no way. He is a very pious man, perhaps he is a better Muslim than I am, even though I am the imam. But Banci only believes in the new Islam (Mk. isilang beru), which is the religion of the pious townsfolk. You know, this is a kind of Islam that forbids almost everything. I feel that it is not good for us people here in the mountains. Banci always tells me: don't do this and that, this is not in accordance with the words of the Prophet, and so on. But I cannot agree, I don't want this sort of Islam." What had happened to Banci over these years? I soon began to understand when the funeral ritual of Banci's sister brought me together with him. My earlier research on funeral rites showed them to be only superficially influenced by Islam, stressing the incorporation of the deceased person's soul into the community of the ancestors. Yet at the funeral of Banci's sister recitations of the Qur'an on the third, seventh, and twentieth night were not accompanied by the traditional acts of sacrifice, incense burning, and purification.

Banci's sister had been a high-ranking woman in the most prestigious local descent group, membership in which entitles one to the office of karaeng. According to local tradition, then, her death should have been accompanied by a specific sequence of ritual acts. Yet all that happened each night was the recitation of the Qur'an. I presumed that this might be related to the presence of a certain haft at the services each night, a man I did not know. But later I came to understand the real reason. The unfamiliar haji was Banci's younger brother, who lived in a distant village. He had made the pilgrimage in 1989 and, immediately after returning from Mecca, had strictly prohibited the performance of any pre-Islamic ritual in his home village. I was told that he had made that place a center of "the new Islam," a term that villagers used to refer to a strict Islam associated with the Muhammadiyah in the lowlands. He had also strongly influenced his brother Banci. To not anger him or Banci, I was informed, the family at the funeral had agreed to avoid all of the traditional activities that might be seen as contrary to the "new Islam."

What was particularly striking about this situation – aside from Banci's changed attitude and the assertion of a "new Islam," a term that I had never encountered in previous years – was the fact that a single individual, who was not socially prominent even in his own village, could exercise such influence on ritual performance. However, by rejecting someone's advice to perform a "minimalist" funeral, people would have risked being stigmatized as enemies of Islam and progress. Government authorities regard minimalist funeral rites as representative of pure Islam. As Aziz Nawa once told me: "When someone is dead, why be fussy about him? He is dead and gone, and we put him under the ground, and then it's finished. There is no need to make offerings or to put flowers on his grave at the end of Ramadan. He can neither see nor smell them any more, can he?"

I soon learned, however, that very early in the morning, when Banci and his brother were visiting other households, the sequence of ritual acts required for their deceased sister's soul was secretly carried out by other members of the family, under the leadership of the deceased woman's father-in-law, a leading traditional functionary. The rites include offerings of rice and fowl, part of which is regarded as "daily food" for the deceased's soul. According to traditional belief, during the first moments after death, the soul is frail and not able to feed itself. The soul remains in this state until the death rites end, as marked by a ritual where one traditional functionary (baku') hands over a fowl to another functionary (gallarang). The fowl in this case symbolizes the soul, and, after the gallarang gives it back to be slaughtered, the soul is regarded as having been moved from the community of the living into the community of the ancestors. These rites need not be performed in public. What is most remarkable here is that they were performed at all.

## Hajj and Hierarchy

Because of the enormous funds required for such a journey, then, the pilgrimage is considered the ultimate attribute of Islam and the sign of a remarkable person. Some are convinced that such individuals are motivated to sacrifice all their possessions by their extraordinary devotion to God. Others, however, interpret the rite with reference to the Makassar proverb "naiki ri butta lannyinga, ammotereki ri butta tangkasa' ": "off he went to the holy land, home he came to a waste land." This proverb is applied to people who, with the aim of achieving the high prestige of the pilgrim, sell house and home — and after their return have nothing left, except for "the most expensive cap in the world," as another popular saying goes.

In any case, is it possible to judge by scientific standards what motivates such actions as the pilgrimage or to estimate what kind of religious change they bring about? Whatever its deeply religious motives, it is clear that there are social structural influences on the decision to perform the pilgrimage. In particular, in rural Makassar communities, the pilgrimage represents a risky but ambitious strategy for achieving prestige — a dominant cultural concern in this society, perhaps more so than in any other Indonesian society. Although religious interests may motivate people independently, it is a fact that the pilgrimage raises one's rank faster and more markedly than any other social activity.

This perspective on the pilgrimage's status implications is, in fact, widely shared among villagers. Most comment that the pilgrimage is deeply related to aspirations for wealth and status. Yusup, a religious teacher in a neighboring primary school, explained the matter in the following blunt terms: "Why do people make the pilgrimage? Because they want to show that they have money. And most important is that, as someone who has performed the pilgrimage, you are respected. Maybe you are stupid and don't know how to read or write, but everybody will honor you. People think that you are at the top of society, even if you are an illiterate descendant of slaves. That is why Makassar like the hajj." Yusup stated further that the last thing he would do was to perform the pilgrimage. If he had lots of money, he averred, he would instead buy as much land as he could because that, in his eyes, was something very useful, unlike the hajj, which he designated as an additional "pleasure." In contrast to what he said before, this sounds surprising. However, his attitude may be explained by the fact that Yusup is not only highly respected for his education at an Islamic college in Ujung Pandang and for his position as a school teacher of Islam, but also as the son of a high-ranking karaeng regarded as the most famous ruler in the eastern highlands since the end of the war.

Yusup's opinion is widely shared. However, as Hasan's case illustrated, this strategy of raising one's status by performing the pilgrimage is not always successful. Haji Hasan is still a person of low social rank, a man who "counts for nothing," just as he was before making the hajj.

## Case of Fatimah

Fatimah is a thirty-six-year-old woman of noble descent who also lives in Bontolowe. During the fasting month of 1984, she told me that she was too lazy to join the tarâwîh-prayers every night, though as a person who was trained as a school teacher of Islam, she was actually obliged to attend. Seven years later, she was the second person from the village to perform the hajj. Understanding her motivations for making the pilgrimage requires a brief look at her life history.

There are now only three members of the nobility living in the village. While Fatimah's mother is of commoner background, her father was a son of the noble Imam Daeng Bunding, who, after the Dutch had gained control of the region around the year 1910, had been the main agent for spreading Islam in the highlands. A crucial event in Fatimah's life history was her marriage to an outsider, whom she subsequently discovered to be already married — a fact that nobody had known before and that was the cause of Fatimah's rapid social decline, especially among her noble kin. Immediately after her marriage, she moved back to Bontolowe, where she lives with her mother. Notwithstanding this dramatic experience, in recent years she has proved to be a woman of extraordinary economic skill. Primarily by lending money to peasants at high rates of interest, Fatimah has become the wealthiest person in the village. Earlier, in 1989, her father's brother, a former district head and the highest-ranking noble in the region, had announced that in 1991 he would make the pilgrimage. The expense of such an excursion represented no problem for Fatimah, so she saw an opportunity to raise her status by joining her uncle.

Other villagers commented that Fatimah had always used Islam to mark herself off from her neighbors. Though she had long claimed noble descent, we learned shortly after meeting her that she was actually of commoner descent. Much later, in 1990, we learned that she had not in fact been trained as a school teacher of Islam, as she had earlier assured us. When we discussed this fact with some other people, they laughed, and one said: "That is typical for Fatimah. She performs the daily prayers (salat) regularly, and her mouth talks about Islam day and night. But inside her heart she is very different. Her heart thinks of money and status. She wants us to recognize that she is of higher standing."

There is a curious continuity to this association of Islamic piety with high status. In the kingdom of Gowa and its subordinate principalities, it should be recalled, the nobility had earlier been the primary agents for the diffusion of Islam. For centuries Islam was for the nobility a significant motivation for expanding political power. After Fatimah's grandfather had started his missionary activities at the beginning of this century, the local nobility of Kasepekang and adjacent regions adopted Islam. Islam spread through marriage alliances and other social strategies concerned with hierarchy and status mobility. However, the new faith was of only marginal significance for commoners, especially those in the highlands.

These considerations also relate to the pilgrimage today. Fatimah's uncle is the son of the "founder of Islam" in the region and a man of great political influence. He is in close contact with the high nobility in Ujung Pandang, many of whom are also haji. The pilgrimage, then, was one of the few things still missing from this man's high-status portfolio. Status concerns seem to have influenced Fatimah's decision to make the pilgrimage as well. In 1993, whenever he visited Bontolowe, Fatimah's uncle spent the night in her house. Before their hajj, he would not even set foot in it.

In their efforts to mark off their superior position from commoners, it seems likely that the local nobility will continue to draw on Islamic symbols. The status of haji is the most effective such instrument since, for financial reasons, it is out of reach of most peasants. Traditionally Makassar nobles were distinguished by their habit of bearing two names, their clothing styles, houses, language patterns, kinship terminology, ritual celebrations, and even eating habits. Many of these features, however, no longer unambiguously mark noble status. No longer in a position simply to prohibit commoner imitations of noble symbols, the nobility cling to a cultural trait that still clearly distinguishes them from most commoners: Islam.

Though the cases presented here seem to suggest that Islam now challenges hierarchical social arrangements, I would suggest that this is not, in fact, the case. Identity is still closely tied to hierarchical thinking; only the empirical content of the ranking structure has been modified. Although it may appear that Islam and supralocal identity are changing societal structures, they apparently are not; they are only filling them with new meanings.

A final example may serve to illustrate this argument. In 1984, on the occasion of the feast of immolation (îd al-qurbân), the feast requiring every pious Muslim to sacrifice an animal for the sake of God, six cows were donated for sacrifice. Since Islam demands that the meat be distributed among the poor and needy, the village chief and the imam had prepared a list of some fifty households to which meat portions should be given. However, not a single representative from these households appeared on the scene. For the leaders, the reason was evident. They knew that cultural values, in particular the concept of self-respect (Mk. siri'), made the distribution of the meat according to Islamic precept impossible. For a Makassar, accepting a donation of meat is to admit that one cannot afford its purchase, which is to lower one's position within the social hierarchy. Where continuous redefinitions of status constitute the most significant basis for social relations, notions deriving from an exogenous religious tradition may still seem inappropriate, despite the new religion's identification with modernity and progress. The meat was thus distributed among people whose status was not likely to be negatively affected: the wealthy, nobles, and resident anthropologists.

## Conclusion

It has long been asked whether the diffusion of Islam to Southeast Asia or other parts of the world was in one way or another related to local societal structures. The arguments presented here suggest that people in the Gowa highlands were more passive "victims" than active agents in the face of Islamization. I am convinced that this is how the majority of the local population assess their recent history. With victims, social theorists expect to see evidence of some kind of resistance. Yet I am not sure whether emptying the mosque or refusing to contribute alms to officials can be labeled resistance in the strict sense of the term. People are ambivalent but rarely engage in overt resistance – much like the Malays described by Michael Peletz in this volume.

Yet, there are individuals who clearly benefit from presenting themselves as "better Muslims." Political changes during the last thirty years contributed to the increasing importance of official styles in religion. In addition, growing numbers of individuals use Islam to challenge traditional hierarchies. Typically they do so, however, without repudiating the principles underlying hierarchy itself. Such individuals are still few, but the fact that their discourse is positively sanctioned by the government gives them influence beyond their numbers.

From an analytic perspective, the process I have described here is a familiar but important one in situations of socioreligious transformation. Religious change is being determined by individual choice among divergent clusters of norms and values. That there is individual choice does not mean, of course, that the decisions individuals make are unaffected by local notions of hierarchy and social order. On the contrary, individual choice has always been deeply affected by the status order and the avenues for mobility it allows. To some degree, people could always compensate for low descent ranking through demonstrations of personal bravery, education, and religious knowledge. Now, the process of Islamization has added new norms and options, which people take into account in evaluating every individual's position within hierarchically structured networks of social relations.

Certainly the assimilation of Islam into such small-scale communities affects and is affected by the complex relationships existing between the individual and his or her sociocultural environment. I argue that it takes place mainly through agents whose thoughts and actions are not only shaped by their cultural background, but who in the long run also shape and modify that wider cultural system, including local views of Islam. Such a concept of agency focuses not only on how individuals construct meanings out of specific social situations, but also on how the cultural system allocates capability for action. Here in the highlands, agency is evident when an individual sees Islamic devotion as a strategy for achieving prestige or redefining his or her social position. This fact does not exclude the ability of religious ideas to motivate actors independently of social constraints; my experience with this society, however, indicates that the structural principles underlying these strategies are far more profoundly influenced by the rules and preoccupations of everyday life than by religious ideals alone.

These arguments should neither be misunderstood in the sense of postulating a generalized repertoire of communitywide shared knowledge, nor should they be seen as equating culture with clusters of norms and values. Norms and values, representing a specific, action-related aspect of culture, are primarily selected as regulative guidelines for action. They therefore represent an important feature of social life, stimulating and shaping empirical events. Aside from notions regulating action, however, culture implies above all knowledge and meaning. There is an ongoing debate about where "meaning" is to be found in culture and what it does: "Meanings represent the world, create cultural entities, direct one to do certain things, and evoke certain feelings". In this chapter, however, I have been particularly concerned with the constructive and the directive functions of cultural meanings. If the members of a society accept and appeal to specific meanings as directive guidelines for social action and for constructing new elements of culture, these meanings appear to be more than something static or definite that could be "simply internalized". In the process of internalizing new cultural meanings, individual actors modify them by adding or removing something, while at the same time thinking and acting within the framework of their cultural knowledge. These considerations render labels such as "essentialist" or "universalist" Islam a fiction and instead direct attention to the strategies by which agents possessing varied interests and motivations both shape and are shaped by "received" and "local Islams".

Any discussion of world religion must go beyond local peculiarities, since it implies a range of concepts and meanings greater than those found in small-scale societies. I strongly agree with Dale Eickelman's proposal that the "middle ground" between the village context and that of the "Islam of all times and places" be taken as the basis for comprehending Islam as a world religious tradition. Yet it has also been stressed that the local form a world religion assumes may differ considerably from its wider normative structure. I have tried to show that such differences result from complex constructions and transformations of meaning systems. These transformations are themselves consequences of the coincidences of cultural history, only some of which are empirically observable. I have suggested, then, that we can best understand this complex process from the perspective of the "folk tradition" in local context, even if, as we know, these constructions of local meaning systems also shape the "great tradition" of Islam or any other world religion.

In Bontolowe these individual strategies for reshaping identity have become increasingly linked to the larger society as a result of several historical processes. Incorporation into the kingdom of Gowa, colonization, administrative reforms, resettlement, and Islamization — all of these comprised an "opening" of the local social system in the face of which individual strategies were devised.

Let me provide a final illustration of this interaction of local contexts with supralocal religion. In this chapter I have for the most part avoided any direct discussion of ethnic identity because of the profound differences between the coastal Makassar and the mountain population. I noted that in this mountain region there was in premodern times no more encompassing notion of identity than that associated with small territorial units; after the incorporation of the region into the kingdom of Gowa, however, "to be a Makassar" for the local people also became significant. On the occasion of the ritual that was performed before Hasan's departure for Mecca in 1984, a haji originating from a village across the river valley narrated his experiences during the pilgrimage. He addressed his words to me, but the audience included many more people: "When I was in Mecca, there were many fellow Indonesians with me. One day a man from Java came up to me and said: 'You just made a mistake. What you just did was not in accordance with the precept (aturan) of the hajj.'I answered: 'Do you want to teach me Islam?' And then I thrashed him soundly. He was bleeding all over. That is how we orang Makassar deal with such folk. How can a Javanese (orang Jawa) dare to say that a Makassar (orang Makassar) does not know Islam?" The audience lauded his behavior. This story became extremely popular and was retold on numerous occasions during the weeks and months that followed. It was the only oral comment I ever heard linking Islamic identity to Makassar ethnicity.

Is it then possible to apply the concept of identity to a situation as complex as that I have described here? Or should we rather label the case an example of an "identity in between," an aggregate of continuously changing meaning systems on the level of both the individual and the group? Personal strategies for constructing identities are shaped by cultural meaning systems, but the latter are also primarily the products of individual thought and action. From a local social perspective, identity defined in terms of adherence to a world religion is an artifact deeply informed by local structures and opportunities. Admittedly, beyond this empirical reality, the identity of the Muslim community of the faithful (umma) also provides directive and evocative meanings. Below the surface, however, religious identity appears to consist of a conglomerate of meaning systems of more varied origins, continuously interpreted and reconstructed by individual agents – with much the same evocative complexity as the concept of nation. It is this characteristic of cultural meaning, and in particular the complex ties linking individual action to the cultural whole, that makes identity one of the most dynamic aspects of human existence and makes processes of Islamization in contemporary Sulawesi so richly complex.

# 6

# Islamic Movements in Indonesia

## Introduction

There is no doubt that al-Raniri had an irreversible impact. Before long the renewal again gained a crucial stimulus in al-Sinkili, one of the most important early mujaddids in the archipelago. We have already established that al-Raniri in one way or another had connections with the core of networks in the Haramayn. al-Sinkili surpassed al-Raniri in this respect. He possessed direct and undisputed links with the major scholars of the networks. For the first time we find, in al-Sinkili, a clear picture of intellectual and spiritual genealogies, putting Islam in the Malay-Indonesian world on the map of the global transmission of Islamic reformism.

Al-Sinkili has been the subject of several important studies. However, these mainly concentrate on his teachings. Some of them do mention in passing his teachers in the Middle East, but no attempt has been made to trace further his intricate intellectual connections with the cosmopolitan scholarly networks centred in Mecca and Medina. There is no study either that seeks to examine how his involvement in the networks influenced his thought and intellectual disposition. Furthermore, no critical study has been done to assess his role in stimulating Islamic renewal in the Malay-Indonesian world. An attempt will be made in this chapter to deal with all these questions. In that way we shall be able to gain a better understanding not only of his position in the historical course of Islam in the archipelago but also of the interplay between Islam in the Malay-Indonesian world and Islam in the Middle East.

## Al-sinkili'sinkili Early Life

'Abd al-Ra'uf b. 'AH al-Jawi al-Fansuri al-Sinkili, as his name indicates, was a Malay of Fansur, Sinkil (modern Singkel), on the southwestern coastal region of Aceh. His birth date is unknown, but Rinkes, after calculating backwards from the date of his return from the Middle East to Aceh, suggests that he was born around 1024/1615. This date has been accepted by most scholars of al-Sinklll. We do not have very reliable accounts of his familial background. According to Hasjmi, ancestors of al-Sinklll came from Persia to the Sultanate of Samudra-Pasai at the end of the thirteenth century. They later settled in Fansur (Barus), an important old harbour on the coast of western Sumatra. He further argues that al-Sinkili'Sinkili father was the older brother of Hamzah al-Fansuri. We are not sure whether al-Sinklll was really a nephew of Hamzah, as there is no other source to corroborate it. It appears that he did have some familial relationship with him, for in some of his extant works al-Sinkili'Sinkili name is followed by the statement: 'who is of the tribe of Hamzah Fansuri' ('tyang berbangsa Hamzah Fansur -f).

Daly, on the other hand, maintains that al-Sinkili'Sinkili father, Shaykh 'AH [al-Fansuri], was an Arab preacher who, after marrying a local woman of Fansur, took up residence in Singkel, where their child, 'Abd al-Ra'uf, was born. There is of course the possibility that al-Sinkili'Sinkili father was nonMalay, as we know that Samudra-Pasai and Fansur had been frequented by Arab, Persian, Indian, Chinese and Jewish traders from at least the ninth century. But as far as the accounts of al-Sinkili'Sinkili father are concerned, there is no other source to substantiate them.

It appears that al-Sinklll acquired his early education in his native village, Singkel, mainly from his father, a supposed 'alim, who, Hasjmi believes, also founded a madrasah that attracted students from various places in the Acehnese Sultanate. It is also very likely that he continued his studies in Fansur, as it, as Drakard points out, was an important Islamic centre and a point of contact between Malays and Muslims from western and southern Asia. According to Hasjmi, al-Sinkili later travelled to Banda Aceh, the capital of the Acehnese Sultanate, to study with, among others, Hamzah al-Fansuri and Shams al-Din al-Samatram. It is clear that al-Sinklll could not have met Hamzah, as the latter died around 1016/1607, at which time al-Sinklll was not even born. However, we cannot rule out the possibility of al-Sinklli'Sinklli studying with Shams al-Din. If we assume that he studied with Shams al-Din (d. 1040/1630) in his final years, al-Sinklll must have been in his teens at that time. There is no indication whatsoever that al-Sinklll met and had personal contact with al-Raniri, who was in Aceh in the period 1047/1637 to 1054/1644-45. However, he must have been aware of the teaching of Hamzah al-Fansuri and Shams al-Din as well as of al-Raniri'Raniri persecution of their followers. Al-Sinklll, as we will see later, apparently attempted to disengage himself from the controversies.

## Al-sinkili'sinkili Arabian Networks

Although al-Sinklli'Sinklli early years were obscure, we are fortunate that he has left us a biographical codicil of his studies in Arabia. In the codicil attached to the colophon of one of his works, 'Umdat al-Muhtajin ila Suluk Maslak al-Mufridln, he provides us with information on the tariqahs he was affiliated with, the places where he studied, the teachers from whom he learned, and the scholars he met. Although the account is rather concise, it nonetheless gives us a good picture of how a Malay-Indonesian 'alim travelled in search of 'Urn (religious knowledge). It discloses not only the crisscrossing of our scholarly networks but also the process of transmission of Islamic learning among Muslim scholars.

Al-Sinklll most probably left Aceh for Arabia in 1052/1642. He lists 19 teachers from whom he learned various branches of Islamic discipline, and 27 other 'ulama' with whom he had personal contacts and relations. We are not going to give accounts of all his teachers; we will examine only the most prominent among them. Al-Sinklll studied in a number of places, scattered along the hajj routes, from Duha (Doha) in the Persian Gulf region, Yemen, Jeddah, finally to Mecca and Medina. Thus he began his studies in

Duha, Qatar, where he studied with 'Abd al-Qadir al-Mawrir, but it appears that he stayed there for only a short time.

Leaving Duha, al-Sinklll continued his studies in Yemen, chiefly in Bayt al-Faqlh [ibn ' Ujayl] and Zabld, although he also had several teachers in Mawza', Mukha, al-Luhayyah, Hudaydah and Ta'Ta. Bayt al-Faqlh and Zabld were certainly the most important centres of Islamic learning in this region. In Bayt al-Faqlh he studied mostly with scholars of the Ja'Ja family, such as Ibrahim b. Muhammad b. Ja'Ja, Ibrahim b. 'Abd Allah b. Ja'Ja and Qadi Ishaq b. Muhammad b. Ja'Ja. In addition, he established relations with Faqlh al-Tayyib b. Abi al-Qasim b. Ja'Ja, the Mufti of Bayt al-Faqlh, and another Faqlh, Muhammad b. Ja'Ja. The Ja'Ja, an eminent sufi-'ulama' family in Yemen or, as al-Muhibbi puts it, 'A prop of the people of Yemen', initially lived in Zabld before finally moving to Bayt al-Faqlh. Several of the Ja'Ja scholars, mentioned earlier, were students of Ahmad al-Qushashi and Ibrahim al-Kuram.

Among al-Sinkili'Sinkili teachers from the Ja'Ja family, the most important was Ibrahim b. 'Abd Allah Ibn Ja'Ja. Mostly known as a muhaddith and faqlh, he appears to have studied largely in the Yemen region before settling down in Bayt al-Faqlh. He was a prolific author of fatwas and, therefore, one of the most sought-after scholars in the area. He also had connections with leading 'ulama' in the networks. al-Sinklll relates that he spent most of his time with Ibrahim b. 'Abd Allah Ja'Ja studying what he calls "Urn al-zahif (exoteric sciences), such as fiqh, hadith and other related subjects. It was ' with his blessing that this faqir, poor [al-Sinklll] was able to continue his studies under the feet [tapak] of the enlightened wall (saint] who was the authority and Qutb of his time; that is, Shaykh Ahmad al-Qushashi in the City of the Prophet, peace be upon him'.

Ishaq b. Muhammad b. Ja'Ja (d. 1014-1096/1605-1685) was another major scholar of the Ja'Ja family with whom al-Sinklll studied. Born in Zabid, he got his early education, in Yemen, from his uncle, Ibn alTayyib b. Ja'Ja, among others. Later he travelled to the Haramayn, where he became a student or rather a friend of Ibrahim al-Kuram, 'Isa al-Maghribi and Ibn 'Abd al-Rasul al-Barzanji. Returning to Bayt al-Faqlh, he gained fame as a leading faqlh and muhaddith in the region. He died in Zabld.

Ja'Ja, who introduced him to al-Qushashi, it is not unlikely that Ishaq b. Ja'Ja also recommended him to study with al-Qushashi as well as with al-Kurani. The network of al-Sinkili'Sinkili clearly becomes more complex on the continuation of his studies in Zabid. Among his teachers in Zabid were 'Abd al-Rahim b. al-Siddiq al-Khass; Amm b. al-Siddiq al-Mizjaji, who was also a teacher of Muhammad al-Qushashi; and 'Abd Allah b. Muhammad al-'Adani, whom al-Sinkili calls the best reciter of the Qur'an in the region. He also came into contact with prominent Zabidi or Yemeni scholars such as 'Abd al-Fattah al-Khass, the Mufti of Zabid; Sayyid al-Tahir b. al-Husayn al-Ahdal; Muhammad 'Abd al-Baqi al-Mizjaji, a celebrated Naqshbandi shaykh (d. 1074/1664), who was also a teacher of al-Maqassari; Qadi Muhammad b. Abi Bakr b. Mutayr (d. 1086/1675); and Ahmad Abu al-'Abbas b. al-Mutayr (d. 1075/1664). Most of these scholars, especially of the Ahdal and Mizjaji families, as we have shown, played an important role in linking scholars in the networks.

Al-Sinkili does not inform us as to when he left Yemen. Following the pilgrimage route we now find him in Jeddah, where he studied with its Mufti, 'Abd al-Qadir al-Barkhali. He then continued his travels to Mecca, where he studied with Badr al-Din al-Lahuri and 'Abd Allah al-Lahuri. al-Sinkili'Sinkili most important teacher in Mecca was 'AH b. 'Abd al-Qadir alTabari. al-Sinkili was introduced to 'All al-Tabari by one of his teachers in Zabid, 'All b. Muhammad al-Dayba', a muhaddith who had close relationships with the Tabari family and other Haramayn leading scholars. 'AH al-Tabari, like his brother Zayn al-'Abidin was a leading Meccanfaqih. 'AH, or the Tabari family, had extensive networks with other Yemeni scholars, especially of the Ja'Ja family, who may also have recommended al-Sinkili to study with 'AH al-Tabari and other prominent Haramayn scholars.

In addition to studying with scholars whom he mentioned specifically as his teachers, al-Sinkili established contacts and relations with other prominent scholars in Mecca, both resident and visiting. He does not specify the nature of his relations with them, but there is little doubt that he gained great advantages from them. They can be assumed, at least, to have inspired him and brought him a much wider intellectual perspective. Most of these scholars are familiar names in the networks: they include 'Isa al-

Maghribi, 'Abd al-'Aziz al-Zamzami, Taj al-Din Ibn Ya'Ya, 'Ala' al-Din al-Babili, Zayn al-'Abidm al-Tabari, 'AH Jamal al-Makkl and 'Abd Allah b. Sa'ld Ba Qashir al-Makkl (1003-1076/1595-1665).

The last leg of al-Sinkili'Sinkili long journey in his search of knowledge was Medina. It was in the City of the Prophet that he felt satisfied that he had completed his studies. He studied in Medina with Ahmad al-Qushashi until the latter'latter death in 1071/1660, and with his khallfah, Ibrahim al-Kuram. With al-Qushashi, al-Sinkili learned what he calls the 'interior' sciences ('tUrn al-batin); that is, tasawwufwd other related sciences. As a sign of his completion of studying the mystical way, al-Qushashi appointed him his Shattariyyah and Qadiriyyah khallfah. al-Sinkili'Sinkili relationship with al-Qushashi was apparently very cordial. An account of the Shattariyyah silsilah in West Sumatra tells us that al-Sinklll studied with and served al-Qushashi for several years. One day the teacher ordered him to return to Jawah, for he considered that al-Sinklll possessed sufficient knowledge to enable him to carry out further Islamisation in his homeland. Having heard the order, al-Sinklll burst into tears, as he felt the need to learn more. As a result, al-Qushashi changed his mind and allowed him to stay with him as long as he wished.

Intellectually, al-Sinkili'Sinkili largest debt was to Ibrahim al-Kuram. This is obvious not only in his thought, reflected in his writings, but also in his personal demeanour, as we will elaborate shortly. In his accounts, al-Sinklll makes it clear that it was with al-Kuram that he completed his education after the death of al-Qushashi. He had no tariqah silsilah with al-Kuram; therefore, what he learned from him apparently were sciences, promoting an intellectual understanding of Islam rather than a spiritual or mystical one. In other words, for al-Sinklll, al-Qushashi was a spiritual and mystical master, while al-Kuram was an intellectual one.

There is no doubt that al-Sinklli'Sinklli personal relationship with al-Kuram was very close. We have mentioned earlier that Ibrahim wrote his masterpiece, the Ithaf al-Dhakl, on the request of his unnamed 'ashab al-Jawiyym'. Considering their close intellectual and personal ties, it is no surprise that Johns suggests that it was al-Sinklll who asked al-Kuram to write it. This suggestion becomes more plausible if one takes into account the fact that al-

Sinklll, after returning to Aceh, asked al-Kuram'Kuram opinion on the way al-Raniri launched his reform in Aceh. Furthermore, it was apparently not the only question sent across the Indian Ocean by al-Sinklll to al-Kuram. In the concluding notes to his Lubb al-Kashf wa al-Bayan li ma yarahu al-Muhtadar hi al- ' lyan, which deals with the best type of dhikr for the dying, he writes:

Let it be known, my disciples, that after I wrote this treatise, I sent a letter to the City of the Prophet, to our enlightened Shaykh in the science of Realities ('tUrn al-haqa'haqa) and in the science of secret details of things ('tUrn al-daqa'daqa), i.e., Shaykh Mawla Ibrahim [al-Kuranl], asking [his opinion] about all matters described in the beginning of this treatise whether it is correct in the opinion of the [leading] sufis, and whether this matter on the best dhikr is discussed in hadith books or in any [other] books. After a while, his treatise entitled Kashf al-Muntazar was sent by [our] Shaykh, in which he answers all the questions.

Al-Sinkili notes that he spent 19 years in Arabia. The fact that most of his teachers and acquaintances are recorded in Arabic biographical dictionaries indicates the incontestable prominence of al-Sinkili'Sinkili intellectual milieu. Coming from a fringe region of the Muslim world, he entered the core of the scholarly networks and won the favour of the major scholars in the Haramayn. His education was undeniably complete from shari'shari, fiqh, hadith and other related exetoric disciplines to kalam, and tasawwuf or esoteric sciences. His career and works after his return to the archipelago were the history of his conscious efforts to implant firmly the idea of harmony between sharl'sharl and tasawwuf.

Like many other scholars in the networks, al-Sinkili appears to have begun his teaching career in the Haramayn. This is no surprise, as by the time he came to Mecca and Medina he already possessed sufficient knowledge to be transmitted to his fellow Malay-Indonesian Muslims. It appears that al-Sinkili also initiated Jawl disciples into the Shattariyyah tariqah. But there were also Shattariyyah silsilahs in Java which went straight back to Ahmad al-Qushashi, instead of by way of al-Sinkili. Snouck Hurgronje maintains that al-Qushashi appointed his Malay-Indonesian khallfahs during the pilgrimage. If we accept this, then we can believe that al-Sinkili played a crucial role in introducing them to al-Qushashi.

## Al-sinkili'sinkili Teachings and Renewal

Al-Sinkili supplies no date for his return to his homeland. However, he indicates that he returned not long after the death of al-Qushashi, and after al-Kuram issued him an ijazah to transmit what he had received from him. Therefore, most scholars of al-Sinkili are in accord that he returned to Aceh about 1072/1661. It is useful to recall that Sultanah Safiyyat al-Din, who had patronised al-Raniri for about two and a half years before turning to Sayf al-Rijal, still occupied the throne of the Acehnese Sultanate. We do not know for sure whether Sayf al-Rijal, powerful exponent of the wujudiyyah type of SUFIsm, was still alive nor how far the doctrine could be revived by him.

In any case, the arrival of al-Sinkili from Arabia naturally created curiosity, particularly among court circles. Before longal-Sinkili was attended by a court official, Katib Seri Raja b. Hamzah al-Ashi, who put unspecified religious questions to him. Voorhoeve points out that al-Ashi'Ashi office was 'Reureukon Katiboy Mulo'; that is, the Secret Secretary of the Sultanah. Therefore, Voorhoeve believes that al-Ashi was assigned by the Sultanah to assess al-Sinklli'Sinklli religious views. It is clear that al-Sinklll passed the 'examination', as he soon won the favour of the court. He was appointed by the Sultanah to the office of the Qadl Malik al- 'Adil or Mufti who was responsible for administering religious affairs.

Before we proceed with al-Sinkili'Sinkili teachings and his renewal, it is appropriate to discuss briefly the political developments in the Acehnese Sultanate during his career. The most striking feature of the period was that the Sultanate was ruled by four successive Sultanahs, well until the close of the seventeenth century. We already know that the first sultanah was Safiyyat al-Din, who succeeded her husband, Iskandar Thani, in 51/1641. Under her long rule until 1086/1675, the Sultanate'Sultanate authority substantially dwindled; much territory under its control in the Malay Peninsula and Sumatra soon broke away. In addition to its political decline, the Sultanate under Safiyyat al-Din was marked by religious turmoil.

The next Sultanah, Nur al-'Alam Naqiyyat al-Din, after reigning for only three years (1086-88/1675-8), was succeeded by Zakiyyat al-Din (1088-98/1678-88). Despite the Acehnese political troubles, the Sultanate was still apparently a respected Muslim political entity in the region. Thus in 1096/1683 Sultanah Zakiyyat al-Din received a delegation from the Sharif of Mecca. The delegation was initially dispatched by the Sharif Barakat to meet the Moghul Sultan Aurangzeb, who reportedly refused to entertain them. As a result, the delegation came to Aceh instead, bringing letters and gifts for the Sultanah. Feeling very pleased, she asked them to stay for a while in the capital city, while preparing gifts for the Sharif of Mecca. It is reported that the Acehnese sent gifts and sadaqah (charitable gifts), consisting of, among other things, a statue made of gold taken from the ruins of the palace and the Bayt al-Rahman Mosque, which had both been destroyed by fire during the period of Sultanah Naqiyyat al-Din.

It is clear that al-Sinkili was involved in events surrounding the delegation. However, we have no information on his exact role in entertaining the envoys of the Sharif of Mecca. The delegation finally returned to Mecca, bringing numerous gifts to be presented not only to the Sharif of Mecca, and the Prophet Mosque in Medina, but also to the poor population in the Haramayn. There was dispute among the sons of the deceased Sharif Barakat concerning the distribution of the gifts. The events surrounding the delegation, the coming of the gifts from 'Bandar AshT (Banda Aceh) and the dispute among members of the Sharifian family are not ignored by Arab historians. Based on a chronicle written about 1700, Ahmad Dahlan, an eminent scholar and historian of Mecca, gave a detailed account of the events.

The coming of the delegation from Mecca was to a certain extent a boost to the prestige of the Sultanah. But it was also taken as a good opportunity for some Acehnese to ask for an opinion on the question of whether it was permissible according to Islamic law for a woman to be a ruler. The question had long been an unsolved problem among the Acehnese. Al-Sinklll himself appears to have failed to answer it explicitly. In his fiqh work Mir'Mir al-Tullab, he does not address the issue directly. Discussing the requirements for the hakim (judge by extension, the ruler), al-Sinklll seems deliberately to provide no Malay translation for the word dhakar (male). He could possibly be accused of compromising his intellectual integrity, not only by accepting the rule of a woman but also by not addressing the issue more properly. On the other hand, this case could be a further indication of his personal tolerance, a trait al-Sinklll certainly possessed.

Similarly, the Meccan delegation gave no answer to the matter but apparently brought the question to the attention of the Haramayn 'ulama'. The answer finally came from Mecca to the Acehnese court during the reign of Sultanah Kamalat al-Din (1098-1109/1688-99). The Chief Mufti of Mecca reportedly sent a fatwa, declaring that it ran contrary to shan'shan for an Islamic kingdom to be ruled by a woman. As a result, Kamalat al-Din was deposed from the throne, and ' Umar b. Qadi al-Malik al-'Adil Ibrahim was installed as Sultan Badr al-'Alam Sharif Hashim Ba al-'Alawi al-Husaym, establishing the 'Arab Jamal al-Layl dynasty in Aceh.

Thus, in his entire career in Aceh, al-Sinklll was patronised by the Sultanahs. He wrote about 22 works, dealing with fiqh, tafsir, kalam, and tasawwuf. He wrote in both Malay and Arabic. He appears to have preferred to write in Arabic rather in Malay, acknowledging that his Malay was not very good because of his long sojourn in Arabia. Therefore, he was helped by two teachers of the Malay language to write his works in Sumatran Malay or, as he puts it: 'in the lisan al-Jawiyyat alSamatra'Samatra.' Throughout his writings al-Sinklll, much like Ibrahim al-Kuram, demonstrates that his main concern is the reconciliation between the shan'shan and tasawwuf, or in his own terms, between the zahir and bdtin sciences.

The major work of al-Sinklll in fiqh is Mir'Mir al-Tullab fi Tashil Ma'Ma al-Al-Ahkam al-Shar'Shar li al-Malik al-Wahhab. Written on the request of Sultanah Safiyyat al-Din, it was completed in 1074/1663. Unlike the Sir at al-Mustaqlm of al-Raniri, which deals solely with 'ibadat (devotional services), the Mir 'At al-Tullab sets out the mu 'Amalat aspect of fiqh, including the political, social, economic and religious life of the Muslims. Covering so many topics, it is a substantial work in the field. Its main source was the Path al-Wahhab of Zakariyya al-Ansari, a major predecessor in the networks discussed earlier. But al-Sinklll also derives materials from such standard books as: Path al-Jawwad and Tuhfat al-Muhtaj, both of Ibn Hajar al-Haytami (d. 973/1565); Nihayat al-Muhtaj of Shams al-Din al-Ramli; Tafsir al-Baydawi of Ibn ' Umar al-Baydawi (d. 685/1286); and Shark Sahlh Muslim of al-Nawawi (d. 676/1277). With these sources al-Sinklll makes clear his intellectual connections with the networks.

Al-Sinklll was the first scholar in the Malay-Indonesian world who wrote on the fiqh mu'amalat. By way of the Mir'Mir al-Tullab he shows his fellow Muslims that Islamic legal doctrines are not confined to purely devotional services ('ibadat) but include all aspects of their daily life. The Mir'Mir al-Tullab is no longer used in the archipelago today, although in the past the work was widely circulated. Hooker has pointed out that the Luwaran, 'Selections', used by the Muslims of Maguindanao, the Philippines, since the middle of the nineteenth century, made the Mir 'At al-Tullab one of its main references. Another work of al-Sinklll in fiqh, Kitab alFara'Fara, presumably taken from the Mir'Mir al-Tullab, was apparently used by some Malay-Indonesian Muslims until more recent times.

The significance of Al-Sinklll to the development of Islam in the archipelago is irrefutable in the field of Qur'an commentary (tafsir). He was the first 'alim ever in this part of the Muslim world to take on the enormous task of preparing tafsir of the whole Qur'an in Malay. A number of studies have discovered that before him there was only a fragment of commentary on surah 18 (al-Kahf). That work, supposedly written during the period of Hamzah al-Fansuri or Shams al-Din al-Samatram, follows the tradition of al-Khazin'Khazin commentary. But the style of translation and interpretation was different from that of Hamzah or Shams al-Din who, as a rule, interpreted passages of Qur'an verses cited in their works in a mystical sense.

Although al-Sinklll gives no date for the completion of his acclaimed tafsir work, entitled Tarjuman al-Mustafid, there is no doubt that he wrote it during his long career in Aceh. Hasjmi maintains that it was written in India, when he allegedly travelled there. This is a wild supposition, as there is no indication whatsoever that al-Sinklll ever set foot in India. Furthermore, it would have been impossible for him to undertake such a huge work while travelling. The patronage he enjoyed from the Acehnese rulers makes it more plausible that he wrote the work in Aceh.

Being the earliest tafsir, it is not surprising that his work was widely circulated in the Malay-Indonesian world. Editions are found to be among the Malay community as far away as South Africa. Of various MSS available in many collections, Riddell has established that the earliest extant copy of the Tarjuman al-Mustafid dates back to the late seventeenth and early eighteenth centuries. More importantly, the Tarjuman al-Mustafid lithograph and printed editions were published not only in Singapore, Penang, Jakarta and Bombay but also in the Middle East. It was published in Istanbul by the Matba'Matba al-'Uthmaniyyah as early as 1302/ 1884 (and in 1324/1906); and later also in Cairo (by Sulayman al-Maraghi) and Mecca (by al-Amiriyyah). The fact that the Tarjuman al-Mustafid was published in the Middle East at various times reflects the importance of the work as well as the intellectual stature of al-Sinklll. Its latest edition was published in Jakarta as recently as 1981. This indicates that the work is still in use among Malay-Indonesian Muslims today.

The tafsir has long been regarded as simply a translation into Malay of the Anwar al-Tanzll of Baydawl. Snouck Hurgonje, apparently without having studied the work in greater detail, concludes in his typically cynical way that it was merely a bad rendering of al-Baydawi'Baydawi commentary. With this conclusion Snouck was responsible for leading astray two other Dutch scholars, Rinkes and Voorhoeve. Rinkes, a student of Snouck, creates additional errors by stating that al-Sinkili'Sinkili works, in addition to the Tarjuman al-Mustafid, include a translation of the Baydawl Tafsir and a translation of a section of the Jalalayn Tafsir. Voorhoeve, after following Snouck and Rinkes, finally changed his conclusion by stating that the sources of the Tarjuman al-Mustafld were various Arabic exegetical works.

Riddell and Harun, in their studies, have shown convincingly that the work is a rendering of the Jalalayn Tafsir. Only in rare instances did al-Sinklll make use of the commentaries of al-Baydawi and al-Khazin (d. 41/1340). This identification is important, not only for disclosing the line of transmission from the centres, but for showing the approach al-Sinklll used in transmitting what he received from his teachers in the networks to his Malay-Indonesian audience.

The Jalalayn Tafsir, it is worth noting, was written by the two Jalals; that is, Jalal al-Din al-Mahalli (d. 864/1459) and Jalal al-Din al-Suyup (d. 911/1505), a major figure to whom most of our leading scholars in the networks traced their intellectual and spiritual genealogies. al-Sinkili'Sinkili selection of this tafsir as the major source of his own commentary, therefore, must be because he possessed isnads connecting him to Jalal al-Din al-Suyup through both al-Qushashi and al-Kuram. Having had ijazahs to transmit from al-Kuram all the sciences he received through successive chains of transmission, which included al-Suyup, al-Sinklll could be expected to prefer the Jalalayn Tafsir to other commentaries of the Qur'an. This argument becomes more plausible when we take into account the fact that al-Sinklll also took the Path al-Wahhab of Zakariyya al-Ansari as the main source for his Mir'Mir al-Tullab. His tendency to rely heavily on the works by scholars in the networks is also clear in his works on kalam and tasawwuf.

Furthermore, as Johns argues, although the Jalalayn Tafsir was often considered as contributing little to the development of the tradition of Qur'an commentary, it is a masterly, lucid and succinct exegesis of the Qur'an. Furthermore, it provides asbab al-nuzul (the backgrounds to revelation) of the verses, which are very helpful for a fuller comprehension of the commentary. With these characteristics, the Jalalayn is a good introductory text for novices in the science of tafsir among the Malay-Indonesian Muslims. In rendering the Jalalayn into Malay, al-Sinkili makes it simple or comprehensible to his fellow Malays in general. As a rule, he translates the Jalalayn word for word, and restrains himself from giving his own additions. Furthermore, he leaves out the Arabic grammatical explanations and long commentaries that might distract the attention of his audience. Thus, it is clear that his intention is that the Tarjuman alMustafid should be easily understood by his readers and, as a consequence, become a practical guide for life.

One can hardly overestimate the role of the Tarjuman al-Mustafld in the history of Islam in the archipelago. Johns maintains that 'it is in more than one way a landmark in the history of Islamic learning in Malay'. It has contributed significantly to the study of Qur'an commentary in the archipelago. It lays the foundation for a bridge between tarjamah (translation) and tafsir, and thus stimulates further study on the tafsir works in Arabic. For almost three centuries it was the only full rendering of the Qur'an in Malay; only in the past 30 years have new commentaries in MalayIndonesian made their appearance, but without necessarily detracting from the Tarjuman al-Mustafld. Therefore, this work continues to play an important role in promoting a better understanding of the teachings of Islam.

We need no long argument to prove that al-Sinkili inherits the tendency from the scholarly networks of emphasising the importance of the hadith. He wrote two works in this field. The first was a commentary on the Arba'un HadITh of al-Nawawi, written at the request of Sultanah Zakiyyat al-Din. The second was al-Mawa'Mawa al-Badl'Badl, a collection of hadith qudsl that is, God'God revelation communicated to the believers by the Prophet'Prophet own words. Again, al-Sinkili'Sinkili selection of these works reflects his genuine concern for his fellow Muslims at the grassroots level; all he wants is to lead them to a better understanding of the teachings of Islam. It is worth noting that the Forty HadITh of al-Nawawi, a small collection of hadiths concerning the basic and practical duties of Muslims, is clearly intended for a general audience rather than specialists pursuing religious studies.

Al-Sinkili'Sinkili collection of the hadith qudsl possesses a similar nature. It delineates 50 teachings (pengajaran) concerning God and His relation to creation, hell and paradise, and the proper ways for the individual to achieve God'God favour. al-Sinkili particularly emphasises the need for each Muslim to find harmony between knowledge ('tUrn) and good deeds ('tamal); knowledge alone will not make a better Muslim: he must do good deeds as well. He thus appeals to Muslim activism. The Mawa'Mawa al-Badi'Badi was published in Mecca in 1310/1892 (fourth or fifth edition). It was also reissued in Penang in 1369/1949, and it is still used by Muslims in the archipelago. With these works, al-Sinkili set an example for later Malay scholars to undertake works on small collections of the hadith, as since the nineteenth century such works have been very popular in the archipelago.

Al-Sinkili writes not only for common Muslims (al-'awwam) on the zdhir sciences but also for the elite (al-khawwas) on topics related to the batin sciences, such as kalam and tasawwuf. He wrote several works dealing with these topics. But the works are still not sufficiently studied, and, as Johns lamented more than three decades ago, there is a lack of interest among scholars in exploring them. The works of Hamzah al-Fansuri and Shams al-Din al-Samatram, however, whom Johns calls ' the foremost exponents of heterodox pantheistic mysticism', have been published. al-Sinkili'Sinkili orthodoxy, he laments further, appeals less to the imagination of scholars than heresy.

To begin our discussion of his mystical teachings, al-Sinkili, in his Kifayat al-Muhtajln ila Mashrab al-Muwahhidln al-Qa'Qa bi Wahdat al-WujUD, insists on the transcendence of God over His creation. He refuses to adhere to the notion of the wujudiyyah, which emphasises the immanence of God in His creation. This teaching reminds us of the doctrines developed by the leading scholars discussed earlier. al-Sinkili argues that before God created the universe (al- 'Alam) He always thought of Himself, which resulted in the creation of the Nur Muhammad (the Light that is Muhammad). It is from the Nur Muhammad that God created permanent archetypes (al-a'yan althabitah), namely, the potential universe, which became the source of the exterior archetypes (al-a'yan al-kharijiyyah), the creation in its concrete form. al-Sinkili concludes that although the a'yan al-kharijiyyah are the emanation of the Absolute Being, they are distinct from God Himself: it is like a hand and its shadow. Although the hand can hardly be separated from its shadow, the latter is not identical to the former. With this explanation, alSinkili establishes the transcendence of God over His creation.

The same argument is presented in his short treatise entitled Daqa'Daqa al-Huriif. The work is a commentary on the so-called ' two pantheistic verses' of Ibn 'Arab!. There is no need to dwell on al-Sinkili'Sinkili discussion of the verses, as Johns has shown us that al-Sinkili knowledgeably interprets them in an orthodox sense, proving that God and the universe are not identical. Although al-Sinkili also makes use of the quasi neo-Platonic emanation system, also closely associated with the pantheism of Shams al-Din, he carefully distances himself from an unorthodox interpretation. Johns concludes:

> *He [al-Sinkili] affirms at once the intuition of the mystics and the rights of orthodoxy, recognising the incapacity of human words to express adequately the dependence of the world upon God and its existence through Him, and the unspeakable reality of the Divine transcendence.*

Al-Sinkili'Sinkili interpretation is clearly reminiscent of Ibrahim al-Kuram, who emphasises the importance of intuition (kashf) in the mystical way, while recognising the limit of reason in understanding the Realities of God. al-Sinkili expresses his intellectual links with al-Kuram in a more than implicit way. In discussing the Unity of God in the Daqa'Daqa al-Huruf, he relies heavily on al-Kuram'Kuram concepts of Tawhld al-Uluhiyyah (Divine Unity), Tawhld al-Af'al (Unity of God'God Act), Tawhld al-Sifat (Unity of Attributes), Tawhld al-WujUD (Unity of Being), Tawhld al-Dhat (Unity of Essence) and Tawhld al-Haqlql (Unity of Absolute Reality).

Like Ibrahim al-Kuram, al-Sinkili proposes that the most effective way to feel and grasp the Unity God is by performing 'ibadat, particularly dhikr ('tremembrance' of God), both silently (sirr) and vocally (jahr). According to al-Sinkili, the aim of the dhikr more specifically is to achieve al-mawt al-ikhtiyarl ('tvoluntary' death), or what is called by al-Kuram almawt al-ma'nawl ('ideational' death), as opposed to al-mawt al-tabi'l (natural death). In his detailed method of dhikr, however, al-Sinkili, largely follows that of Ahmad al-Qushashi, as described in his work alSimt al-Majld. He also follows al-Qushashi'Qushashi teachings on the obligation of disciples towards their master, as he shows in his two treatises called respectively Risalah Adab Murid akan Syaikh and Risalah Mukhtasarah fi Bayan Shuriit al-Shaykh wa al-Murld.

Having discussed al-Sinkili'Sinkili teachings, it is clear that he transmitted the doctrines and tendencies in the scholarly networks in order to renew the Islamic tradition in the Malay-Indonesian archipelago. The most salient feature of his teachings indicates that what he transmitted is neo-SUFIsm: his works make it clear that tasawwuf should go hand in hand with the shari'shari. Only with total obedience to the shari'shari can aspirants of mystical ways gain the true experience of the haqlqah (realities).

It is important to keep in mind, however, that al-Sinkili'Sinkili approach to renewal was different from that of al-Raniri: he was a mujaddid of an evolutionary type, not a radical. Therefore, like Ibrahim al-Kuram, he preferred to reconcile opposing views rather than to take sides. Even though he was against the doctrines of wujudiyyah, only implicitly does he make clear his views. Similarly, he shows his dislike for the radical approach of al-Raniri'Raniri renewal quite simply and not explicitly. Again, without mentioning al-Raniri'Raniri name, he wisely reminds Muslims in the Daqa'Daqa al-Hurufof the danger of accusing others of unbelieving by citing a hadith of the Prophet, stating ' let no man accuse another of leading a sinful life or of infidelity, for the accusation will turn back if it is false'. Considering al-Sinkili'Sinkili gentleness and tolerance, Johns rightly concludes that he was a mirror image of his teacher, Ibrahim al-Kuram.

## Al-sinkili'sinkili Malay-indonesian Networks

The Acehnese have long been proud of their country; they have always called their country, with pride, 'Serambi Mekkah', or the front yard or gate to the Holy Land, not only because of its crucial role in Islamic learning but also for its position as the most important transit point for the MalayIndonesian pilgrims in their journey to and from the Haramayn. Aceh'Aceh special position was among the main reasons why works of scholars like Hamzah al-Fansuri, Shams al-Din al-Samatram, al-Raniri and al-Sinkili became widely circulated in the archipelago. The fact that all these scholars lived in Aceh, together with extensive relations and contacts between the Acehnese and foreign Muslim scholars, contributed substantially to the establishment of the identity of the Acehnese as one of the most ardent Muslim ethnic groups in the archipelago.

Al-Sinklll appears to have begun teaching while he was in the Haramayn, but we have no information on his disciples there. It is only after he returned to Aceh that we are able to trace his Malay-Indonesian network of disciples. These disciples, in turn, were responsible for spreading al-Sinkili'Sinkili teachings and tariqahs, particularly the Shattariyyah order, in many parts of the archipelago.

There is no doubt that the type of the Shattariyyah order, so often associated with the Indian type of SUFIsm, that was implanted by al-Sinklll in the archipelago was the one that had been reformed by such leading scholars in our networks as Ahmad al-Shinnawi and Ahmad al-Qushashi. Archer, in his classical study, calls the Shattariyyah introduced by al-Sinklll the ' orthodox way'. Although in his silsilah al-Sinklll refers to the tariqah as the Shattariyyah, he also calls it the ' Qushashiyyah' tariqah. The Shattariyyah tariqah was also known as the 'Ishqiyyah in Iran and as the Bistamiyyah in Ottoman Turkey, but is not generally known as the Qushashiyyah. The Qushashiyyah tariqah was another name for the reformed Shattariyyah and became a unique Malay-Indonesian phenomenon.

This can be taken as an indication of al-Sinkili'Sinkili attempts to disengage his tariqah from the early Shattariyyah. The Qushashiyyah tariqah was and can still be found in certain parts of the archipelago.

The most celebrated of al-Sinkili'Sinkili disciples in Sumatra was Burhan al-Din, better known as the Tuanku of Ulakan, a village on the coast of the Minangkabau region (now West Sumatra). Local accounts of the development of Islam in Minangkabau relate that Burhan al-Din (1056-1104/ 1646-92) studied with al-Sinklll for several years before returning to his home region. Burhan al-Din was, of course, not the first scholar to introduce Islam to the Minangkabau area, but he undoubtedly played a crucial role in the intensification of Islamisation among its population.

Soon after his return, Burhan al-Din established his Shattariyyah surau, a ribat-type educational institution, in Ulakan. Before long it gained fame as the sole religious authority in Minangkabau. The Ulakan surau attracted numerous students from throughout the region; they specialised in various branches of Islamic discipline, and in turn established their own suraus when they returned to their home villages. By the fourth quarter of the eighteenth century several leading students of Burhan al-Din began in earnest to launch their reforms, which reached a climax at the turn of the century.

Another eminent student of al-Sinklll was 'Abd al-Muhyi of West Java. It is through the latter'latter efforts that the Shattariyyah gained a large following in Java. Although our sources provide no date of birth, they are in accord in reporting that 'Abd al-Muhyi studied with al-Sinklll in Aceh before embarking on a pilgrimage to Mecca. He was reported also to have travelled to Baghdad in order to visit the tomb of 'Abd al-Qadir al-Jaylam.

Returning from the hajj pilgrimage, on the request of the local leader he settled in Karang, Pamijahan, West Java, where he played a substantial role in converting people from animistic beliefs to Islam. 'Abd al-Muhyl was also very active in preaching the Shattariyyah tariqah, for many silsilahs of the order in Java and the Malay Peninsula went through him which he received directly from al-Sinklll.

Al-Sinklll also had a prominent student in the Malay Peninsula: he was 'Abd al-Malik b. 'Abd Allah (1089-1149/1678-1736), better known as Tok Pulau Manis, of Trengganu. Abdullah points out that 'Abd al-Malik studied with al-Sinklll in Aceh, and later continued his studies in the Haramayn. According to local tradition, he studied there also with Ibrahim al-Kuram. But this is hardly plausible, because at the time of the latter'latter death (1101/1690) 'Abd al-Malik had not even been born. At best, he may have met with al-Kuram'Kuram students. Apart from this problematic account, 'Abd al-Malik was obviously a scholar of some distinction. His works deal mainly with the sharl'sharl orfiqh; he was also very active in teaching.

The closest disciple of al-Sinklll, without doubt, was Dawud al-Jawi al-Fansuri b. Isma'Isma b. Agha Mustafa b. Agha 'All al-Ruml. The importance of citing his long full name is to indicate that he was most likely of Turkish origin. His father was probably one of the Turkish mercenaries who came in large numbers to assist the Acehnese Sultanate in their contest with the Portuguese in the early sixteenth century. The attribution al-Jawi indicates that his mother was probably a Malay, or that he was born in the archipelago.

Despite the obscurity surrounding his origin, Dawud al-Jawi al-Ruml was the most favoured student of al-Sinklll. There is a strong indication in the colophon of al-Sinkili'Sinkili Tarjuman al-Mustafid that he was ordered by the teacher to make some addition to the tafsir. And there is also a suggestion that he did so under the supervision of al-Sinklll himself before the latter'latter death. Hasjmi maintains that Dawud al-Jawi al-Ruml was the main khallfah of al-Sinklll. Together with his master, he founded a dayah, a traditional Acehnese Islamic educational institution, in Banda Aceh. He was also reported to have written several works.

Al-Sinklll died around 1105/1693 and was buried near the kuala, or the mouth, of the Aceh River. The site also became the graveyard for his wives, Dawud al-Ruml and other disciples. It is after the site of his tomb that al-Sinklll later came to be known as the Shaykh of Kuala. Al-Sinklli'Sinklli tomb has become the most important place of religious visitation (ziyarah) in Aceh until the present time.

It is important to note that al-Sinkili was also associated with al-Maqassari. They were in fact friends, studying together with, among others, al-Qushashi and al-Kuram. It is to al-Maqassari that we now turn.

# 7

# Islamic Renewal in the Eighteenth Century

## Introduction

The differences among modern scholars over the definition and boundaries of the terms ' reform' and ' renewal', it is clear that not all of the Malay-Indonesian scholars proposed radical doctrinal changes of Islam that can be categorised as reform. Their endeavours are more appropriately called renewal *(tajdld)* than reform. Their central theme is a return to an orthodoxy that finds its most salient feature in the harmony between *sharl'sharl* and *tasawwuf.* With this, these *mujaddids* contributed substantially to the strengthening of the Islamic identity of their societies. The immediate result of this process was the intensification of Islamisation in the archipelago.

I have argued that Islamic renewal began in the Malay-Indonesian world as early as the seventeenth century, rather than at the beginning of the nineteenth century or the early twentieth century, as maintained by some scholars. Hamka and Federspiel, for instance, believe that Islamic reform or renewal began in the archipelago only with the rise of the Padri Movement in West Sumatra at the beginning of the nineteenth century. Although Geertz recognises that what he calls 'A more precisian Islam' (or 'scripturalist Islam') was introduced to the archipelago before the nineteenth century, he is of the opinion that it gained momentum only after the early nineteenth century with the rise, for instance in West Sumatra, of what he termed 'A band of religious zealots, outraged by the heterodoxy of local customs'. In this reference to the Padri Movement, Geertz clearly views Islamic reforms very simplistically.

The Padri Movement, as we will discuss briefly later, in fact originated from the scholarly networks. The birth and growth of this movement reflect a complicated process of the transmission of reformist ideas, including a 'tug of war' between the forces of reformism and local factors such as *adat* (custom). The Padri Movement is an excellent example of how reformism generated by the networks found one of its extreme manifestations in the archipelago.

Deliar Noer, on the other hand, maintains that Islamic reformism started only in the early twentieth century. Noer overemphasises Islamic reformism in the period he discusses, concluding without hesitation that Indonesian Islam before the twentieth century was dominated by *tasawwuf* and was thus no more than a hybrid of Islamic mysticism and remnants of local Hindu-Buddhist beliefs. He does mention the influences that had come from Mecca since the eighteenth century, but by using Snouck Hurgronje'Hurgronje framework Noer views this influence mostly in political terms, or more precisely as pan-Islamism.

As we will see shortly, this view can no longer be maintained, because there is no evidence in the eighteenth century, among scholars in the centres of the Haramayn or among our Malay-Indonesian scholars, that points to any attempt to forge a feeling of pan-Islamism in the archipelago. What they transmitted to this part of the Muslim world was for the most part, indeed, reformist or renewalist religious ideas rather than political ones.

Our three *mujaddids* did not explicitly declare that they were launching reform, nor did they employ the organisation of the *tanqah&* in order to pursue their ends, but the central theme of their teaching leaves no doubt about their commitment to renewalism. It is important to note that reformism or renewal is not an overnight process. Therefore, although by the second half of the seventeenth century reformist ideas had been introduced to the archipelago, they took root only slowly and sporadically. There is no doubt, however, that the momentum of renewalism sparked by al-Ranin, al-Sinkili and al-Maqassan was irreversible. Thus, as Federspiel rightly points out, over the past four centuries Islam in Indonesia has slowly altered its form: ' the heterodox religious trends of the early period have slowed in momentum, and more orthodox Islamic practices and patterns have slowly gained in importance'.

Federspiel recognises that contacts between the Malay-Indonesian world, by way of *Jowl* students and pilgrims, and the Middle East greatly contributed to the rise of Islamic renewalism in the region. Again, however, like Hamka, he simply points to the famous example of the Padri Movement, which gained crucial stimulus from the return of three *hdjjis* from Mecca in the early nineteenth century. But as we have already noted, and will discuss further later, the origins of the Padri Movement can be traced back to al-Sinkili and to reformist movements in the centres of the networks in Mecca and Medina.

In the final analysis, the roots of Islamic renewal in the MalayIndonesian world are tő be found in the teachings of al-Raniri, al-Sinkili and al-Maqassari. Like reformism in the Haramayn, the renewal is genuine and born as an internal response to prevailing religious conditions among Muslims themselves. But from the eighteenth century outside factors, especially increasing colonial encroachment, also contributed to the acceleration of Islamic renewal and reform in the archipelago.

## *'ulama'* In The Eighteenth Century Networks

If al-Ramri, al-Sinkili and al-Maqassari have commanded much attention from scholars, the *'ulama'* in the eighteenth century have been less studied. Furthermore, the few sources available, mainly in Malay and Indonesian, simply narrate biographies, without critical examination of their positions vis-a-vis Islamic developments in the Malay-Indonesian world or their relationship to the teachings introduced by al-Raniri, al-Sinkili and al-Maqassari. No attempt has been made to trace their connections with the scholarly networks of the larger Muslim world, which should give us a better picture of the continuing religious and intellectual relations between the archipelago and the Middle East.

The *'ulama'* involved in the eighteenth century scholarly networks indeed had traceable connections with earlier networks. While they did not have direct teacher-student connections with al-Raniri, al-Sinkili and al-Maqassari, their teachers in Mecca and Medina were among the prominent figures of the networks in their period and had direct connections with earlier scholars to whom the three predecessors had also been linked. Malay-Indonesian scholars in the eighteenth century, moreover, were well aware of the teachings of their three precursors, and they established intellectual connections with them by making reference to their works.

We have seen how, through al-Maqassari and his disciples, the regions of South Sulawesi and West Java, following Aceh, came into the picture of Islamic learning in the archipelago in the seventeenth century. In the eighteenth century, South Sumatra, South Kalimantan (Borneo) and the Patani region in the northern part of the Malay Peninsula came to prominence. Therefore, I would argue that the birthplaces and ethnic origins of Malay-Indonesian scholars in a way reflect the historical course of Islam in the archipelago through centuries. This points to the fact that appreciation of the importance of Islamic learning as well as the need for renewal and reform began to gain ground among various ethnic groups in the archipelago. These scholars, having acquired substantive credentials in Islamic learning, in turn stimulated further intensification of Islamisation, particularly among their respective ethnic groups. In the eighteenth century such developments continued, so as to become one of the most distinctive features in the transmission of Islam in the archipelago.

There were several major Indonesian-Malay 'ulama' who came from various regions and ethnic groups in the archipelago in the eighteenth to the early nineteenth centuries. A prominent group came from the Palembang region of South Sumatra. The most important among them were Shihab al-Din b. 'Abd Allah Muhammad, Kemas Fakhr al-Din, 'Abd al-Samad al-Palimbam, Kemas Muhammad b. Ahmad and Muhammad Muhyl al-Din b. Shihab al-Din. Then came Muhammad Arshad al-Banjarl and Muhammad Nafls al-Banjari from South Kalimantan; 'Abd al-Wahhab alBugisI from Sulawesi; 'Abd al-Rahman al-Batawi al-Masrl from Batavia and Dawud b. 'Abd Allah al-Fatam from the

Patani region (South Thailand). Although information on several of these scholars is sketchy, their careers and teachings make it clear that they were involved both socially and intellectually in the networks. Taken together, they constituted the most important scholars of the archipelago in the eighteenth century.

## Al-palimbani and Other Palembang Scholars

The fact that there were several scholars of the Palembang region who rose to prominence in the period under discussion is an interesting example of the relations between Middle Eastern Muslims and the growth of Islamic learning in the archipelago.

Arab migrants, particularly from the Hadramawt, began to come to Palembang in increasing numbers from the seventeenth century. Al-Palimbam'Palimbam father, although he stayed in Palembang for only a relatively short time, was among the Arab sayyids who came to this region in the early seventeenth century. By the middle of the eighteenth century, some Arab scholars had gained prominent positions in the court of the Palembang Sultanate. In 1168/1754-5 a certain Sayyid al-'Aydarus was reported to have married Sultan Mahmud'Mahmud sister, and several unnamed sayyids came to control the religious hierarchy in the Sultanate: they became 'senior priests', and one of the sayyids was called 'Tuan Besar' (great lord).

These Arabs clearly played an important role in the growth of the tradition of Islamic learning in the region. They stimulated and encouraged the Sultans of Palembang to pay special attention to religious matters, but apparently did not go much further. They did not take any initiative, for instance, to establish religious educational institutions at the popular level, for there is no evidence that such institutions as madrasah or pesantren existed during this period. Instead, they concentrated on the court, and apparently contributed to the rise of the court as the centre of learning. As a result, the court of Palembang become the centre for an extensive collection of religious works by local scholars. This further indicates the importance of the court in the scholarly discourse in the Malay-Indonesian archipelago.

Most of the Palembang scholars, such as Shihab al-Din, Kemas Fakhr al-Din, Muhammad Muhyl al-Din and Kemas Muhammad, are known mostly from their works, preserved initially in the court of the Palemban Sultanate before being taken by the Dutch and the British. Drewes has correctly concluded that they lived throughout the second half of the seventeenth and the early eighteenth centuries. There is insufficient information on their lives, although it is known that Kemas Fakhr al-Din (1133-777 1719-63) travelled to India and spent a good deal of his life in Arabia, most probably in Mecca or Medina, where he wrote his works. Most of the works of these scholars deal with mysticism and theology and are based largely on the teachings of al-Junayd, al-Qushayri and al-Ghazali. They clearly embraced teachings belonging to neo-SUFIsm.

Without doubt, the most prominent among these Palembang scholars was 'Abd al-Samad al-Palimbam. He was also the most influential, especially through his works, which were widely circulated in the archipelago. We have a rather complete account of his life and career, unlike his fellow Palembang scholars, so that we are able to reconstruct his biography. So far, accounts of al-Palimbam'Palimbam life are based on the scattered information he supplied in his works, which have been supplemented by Malay accounts and Dutch sources. However, there is ample information on him in Arabic biographical dictionaries, which throw some light on this major Malay-Indonesian scholar. This is an important finding, for never before had accounts of a Malay-Indonesian scholar been given in Arabic biographical dictionaries. This also indicates that al-Palimbani enjoyed a respected career in the Middle East.

According to Malay sources the full name of al-Palimbam was 'Abd al-Samad b. 'Abd Allah al-Jawi al-Palimbam, but Arabic sources call him Sayyid 'Abd al-Samad b. 'Abd al-Rahman al-Jawi. We have every reason to believe that 'Abd al-Samad b. 'Abd al-Rahman al-Jawi was indeed 'Abd al-Samad al-Palimbam. As we will show in this chapter, the picture of the career of 'Abd al-Samad b. 'Abd al-Rahman al-Jawi in Arabic sources almost entirely describes that of 'Abd al-Samad al-Palimbam given by other sources.

Of all the available sources, only the Tarlkh Salasilah Negeri Kedah supplies the date of al-Palimbam'Palimbam birth and death. According to this work, al-Palimbam was born about 1116/1704 in Palembang to a sayyid father and a Palembang woman. This, therefore, corroborates the Arabic sources, which mention that al-

Palimbani was a sayyid. Al-Palimbani'Palimbani father is said to have come from Sana'Sana, Yemen, and travelled widely in India and Java before taking up residence in Kedah, where he was appointed Qadl. About 1112/1700 he went to Palembang, where he married a local woman and returned to Kedah with his new born son, al-Palimbani. It is believed that al-Palimbam acquired his early education in Kedah and Patani, probably in apondok (local traditional Islam educational institution), about which more follows. Later, his father dispatched him to study in Arabia. We have no information on when he left the archipelago.

Although we cannot resolve the conflicting dates surrounding his life, all sources are in accord that al-Palimbam'Palimbam life span was from the first decade well into the late eighteenth century. Al-Baytar points out al-Palimbam died after 1200/1785. But most probably he died in 1203/1789, the date of completion of his final and most acclaimed work, the Sayr al-Salikln. When he completed this work he would have been 85 years old. In the Tarlkh Salasilah Negeri Kedah, it is reported that he was killed in the war against the Thais in 1244/1828. It is difficult to accept this account, as there is no evidence in other sources to indicate that al-Palimbam ever returned to the archipelago. Furthermore, he would then have been about 124 years old too old to go to the battlefield. Although al-Baytar does not mention the place where al-Palimbam died, there is a strong suggestion that he died in Arabia.

Al-Palimbam almost certainly established his career in the Haramayn and never returned to the archipelago. He nevertheless maintained a deep concern for Islam and Muslims in the Malay-Indonesian world. In the Haramayn, al-Palimbani was involved in the Jowl community and was a fellow student of Muhammad Arshad al-Banjan, 'Abd al-Wahhab Bugis, 'Abd al-Rahman al-Batawi and Dawud al-Fatani. His involvement in the Jowl community kept him fully aware of the religious and political developments in the archipelago.

Al-Palimbani and his group all had the same teachers. The most famous among them were Muhammad b. 'Abd al-Karlm al-Sammani, Muhammad b. Sulayman al-Kurdl and 'Abd al-Mun'Mun al-Damanhuri. Al-Baytar, in addition to mentioning Muhammad [b. Sulayman] al-Kurdl, lists other teachers of al-Palimbam: they were Ibrahim al-Ra'Ra, Muhammad Murad,

Muhammad al-Jawhari and 'Ata' Allah al-Masri. Some of these scholars were also teachers of the four friends of alPalimbani.

It is important to examine briefly the biographies of these last four teachers, as they further show us the connections al-Palimbam and his fellow Malay-Indonesians had with the extensive scholarly networks.

[Abu al-Fawz] Ibrahim [b. Muhammad] al-Ra'Ra [al-Zamzami al-Makki] (1110-94/1698-1780) was evidently another important scholar from the Zamzami family. As al-Jabarti points out, Ibrahim al-Zamzami al-Ra'Ra was well versed in various religious sciences; one of his special subjects was 'Urn al-falak (astronomy). Among his teachers were 'Abd Allah alBasri, Ibn al-Tayyib, Ahmad al-Jawhari, 'Ata' Allah al-Masri and Hasan al-Jabarti, the father of the historian al-Jabarti; he took the Khalwatiyyah order from Mustafa al-Bakri and the Naqshbandiyyah from 'Abd alRahman al-'Aydarus. No less importantly, he was a student of Murtada al-Zabidi and Salih al-Fullani, both major figures of the scholarly networks in the eighteenth century. Ibrahim al-Ra'Ra was also closely connected with Mustafa al-'Aydarus and with scholars of the Ahdal and Mizjaji families, including the father of Sulayman al-Ahdal, one of alPalimbam'Palimbam students.

As for Muhammad Murad, there is strong evidence that he was Muhammad Khalil b. 'All b. Muhammad b. Murad al-Husaym (1173-1206/ 1759-91). My research on Muhammad Murad in several biographical dictionaries of the period points to Muhammad Khalil al-Muradi. Better known as al-Muradi, primarily for his four-volume biographical dictionary Silk al-Durar, he was a contemporary of al-Palimbam. Al-Jabarti, his good friend, points out that al-Muradi mainly lived in Damascus but travelled extensively, including to the Haramayn, in order to collect information on the scholars he would write about in his biographical dictionary. In the course of his travels, al-Muradi not only advanced his knowledge but taught students as well. Therefore, it is highly probable that al-Palimbam took the opportunity of al-Muradi'Muradi visits to the Haramayn to study with him.

Although al-Muradi was renowned mostly as a historian, al-Jabarti reports that he was a ' prop of the shan'shan and a ' house of knowledge' in Syria during his time, who had mastered both exterior and interior sciences to the fullest extent. As al-Baghdadi also tells us, he was the Mufti of the Hanafl school of law in Damascus, and a Naqshbandi shaykh. He had wide connections with such major scholars in the networks as Murtada al-Zabidi, not only because he had met them in the course of collecting biographical data but more importantly because of hadith scholarship; his was considered a 'superior' isnad in hadith studies.

The next teacher of al-Palimbam, Muhammad [b. Ahmad] al-Jawhari [al-Misri], was the son of a leading Egyptian muhaddith, Ahmad b. al-Hasan b. 'Abd al-Karim b. Yusuf al-Karimi al-Khalidi al-Jawhari al-Azharl (1096-1181/1685-1767). Muhammad al-Jawhari (1132-86/ 1720-72), like his father, Ahmad al-Jawhari, was known mainly as a traditionist. Although he lived mostly in Egypt, Muhammad al-Jawhari often travelled to the Haramayn, where besides performing pilgrimages he taught students. In addition to receiving hadith from his father, he possessed isnads through his father which connected him with such scholars as 'Abd Allah al-Basri and Ahmad al-Nakhli. Therefore, he was among the most soughtafter isnads in the networks during this period. He had also extensive networks through hadith studies down to more recent times.

The last scholar in the list of al-Palimbam'Palimbam teachers was 'Ata' Allah [b. Ahmad] al-Azhari al-Masri al-Makkl, mentioned earlier as a teacher of Ibrahim al-Ra'Ra. 'Ata' Allah was a renowned muhaddith and a colleague of Muhammad al-Sammam, Muhammad al-Jawhari and Murtada al-Zabidi. Al-Zabidi even lists 'Ata' Allah as one of his numerous teachers. It appears that after completing his education at the Azhar, later in his life 'Ata' Allah migrated to Mecca or, in al-Kattam'Kattam terms, he was 'nazil alHaramayrC, where he was very active in teaching. Among his students were Abu al-Hasan al-Sindi al-Saghir and Salih al-Fullam, and a number of Yemeni scholars. Like Muhammad al-Jawhari, 'Ata' Allah is considered a superior isnad in hadith studies.

Thus, as al-Sinklll earlier, al-Palimbam reaped great profit from visiting scholars in the Haramayn, especially during the pilgrimage season. One visiting scholar from whom al-Palimbam gained great benefit was Ahmad al-Damanhurl. The latter, whose biography has been provided by Zabldl, lived mostly in Cairo, though he often travelled to the Haramayn. Based on notes he took when he attended lectures given by al-Damanhuri in Mecca, al-Palimbam was able to write one of his earliest works, entitled Zuhrat al-Murldfl bayan Kalimat al-Tawhld. The work, in Malay, deals with logic (mantiq) and theology (usul al-din), and it was written at the request of one of his friends, obviously a Malay, in order to better understand al-Damanhun'Damanhun lectures.

Considering the status of the scholars he studied with, it is certain that al-Palimbam'Palimbam education was a thorough one; he studied hadith, fiqh, shan'shan, tafsir, kalam and tasawwuf. Al-Palimbam had a strong disposition towards mysticism, and it is evident that he studied tasawwuf mostly with al-Sammanl, from whom he also took both tariqahs of Khalwatiyyah and Sammaniyyah. Abdullah believes that al-Palimbanl studied with alSammam for five years in Medina. During the course of his studies with al-Sammanl, he was entrusted to teach some of al-Sammani'Sammani students of Arab origin. So far as his adherence to tariqah is concerned, al-Palimbam was deeply influenced by al-Sammam. Conversely, it is through alPalimbanl that the Sammaniyyah tariqah found fertile ground not only in the Palembang region but in other parts of the archipelago; al-Sammanl and the Sammaniyyah tariqah became principal subjects in the writings of later Palembang scholars.

Al-Palimbanl never returned to the archipelago. He devoted his time in the Haramayn to writing and teaching. Al-Baytar reports that in 1201/1787 he travelled to Zabld, where he taught students, particularly of the Ahdal and al-Mizjaji families. This report is in accord with Abdullah'Abdullah accounts of al-Palimbani'Palimbani travels to Zabld and his meetings with local scholars and students. One of his students in Zabld was Wajlh al-Din 'Abd al-Rahman b. Sulayman b. Yahya b. ' Umar al-Ahdal (1179-1255/1765-1839), a muhaddith who later occupied the post of Mufti of Zabld. Wajlh al-Din al-Ahdal evidently considered al-Palimbanl one of his most important teachers, as he included his biography in his dictionary, al-Nafs al-Yamanl wa al-Ruh al-Rayham.

According to al-Kattanl, Wajlh al-Din al-Ahdal in his biographical dictionary put al-Palimbanl into his third category (al-tabaqat al-thalithah); that is, major scholars who visited Zabld and spent their time there primarily as teachers. It is interesting to note that, in addition to studying with al-Palimbam, Wajlh al-Din learned from such scholars as Ahmad b. Hasan al-Muqn al-Zabldl,

Amr Allah b. 'Abd al-Khaliq b. Muhammad alBaql al-Mizjaji, Sulayman al-Kurdl, 'Abd al-Rahman Mustafa al-'Aydarus and Murtada al-Zabldl. Thus, through Wajlh al-Din al-Ahdal, al-Palimbam was connected to a much wider networks of scholars.

Because of his scholarly connections, al-Palimbam was, without doubt, the most prominent Malay-Indonesian scholar in the eighteenth century networks. However, his importance in light of Islamic development in the archipelago lies not only in his involvement in the scholarly networks but more importantly in his writings, which were widely read in the MalayIndonesian world, particularly in the 'ulama' circles, in the pesantren, pondok and other Islamic educational institutions. In his works al-Palimbam disseminated the teachings of neo-sufis, but he also appealed to his fellow Muslims to launch a jihad against Europeans, particularly the Dutch, who had intensified their attempts to subdue Muslim political entities in the archipelago.

## Al-banjari

With Muhammad Arshad al-Banjari we now come to South Kalimantan (Borneo), a region where the development of Islam is still insufficiently studied. As elsewhere in the archipelago, studies of Islam in South Kalimantan have so far mainly concentrated on the questions of when, how and whence Islam came to this region; there is almost no discussion of the growth of Islamic institutions and the tradition of learning among its Muslim population. With regard to this, the importance of Muhammad Arshad lies not simply in his involvement in the scholary networks but also in the fact that he was the first scholar to establish new Islamic institutions as well as to introduce new religious ideas to South Kalimantan.

Islam came to South Kalimantan at a much later period than, for instance, North Sumatra or Aceh. It is assumed that there had been some Muslims in the coastal region since the early sixteenth century, but Islam gained momentum only after the Demak Sultanate'Sultanate troops in Java came to Banjarmasin to assist Pangeran Samudra in his struggles with the court elite of the Dana Kingdom. On his victory, Pangeran Samudra converted to Islam around 936/1526 and was installed as the first Sultan of the Banjar Sultanate. He was given the name of Sultan Surian Shah or Surian Allah by an Arab teacher.

With the establishment of the Sultanate of Banjar, Islam appears to have been officially regarded as the religion of the state, although Muslims constituted a minority of the population. Adherents to Islam, by and large, were confined to the Malay population; Islam only very slowly made inroads among the tribal population, commonly called the Dayaks. Even among Malay Muslims, the adherence to Islam was evidently nominal and did not go beyond the utterance of the confession of faith. Under successive Sultans down to the period of al-Banjari, it is evident that there was no substantial attempt made by the rulers to advance Islamic life. However, they did adopt the Arabic script for the Sultanate'Sultanate correspondence with other Malay-Indonesian rulers, the Dutch and the British. There are also accounts of attempts by wandering scholars to further Islamisation in the region, but apparently they made little progress.

A substantial drive for further Islamisation was launched by Muhammad Arshad b. 'Abd Allah al-Banjan (1122-1227/1710-1812), one of the best-known scholars of Kalimantan. Born in Martapura, South Kalimantan, Muhammad Arshad acquired a rudimentary religious education in his own village, apparently from his father and local teachers, for there is no evidence that surau or pesantren existed during this period in the region. When he was seven years old he is reported to have been able to read the Qur'an perfectly. He became famous for this, which led Sultan Tahlil Allah (1112-58/1700-45) to take him and his family to live in the court of the Sultanate. Later the Sultan married him to a woman, but almost immediately he sent Muhammad Arshad to the Haramayn in order to pursue further studies at the Sultanate'Sultanate expense. The Sultan seems to have financed him generously; Muhammad Arshad was even able to buy a house in the Shamiyyah quarter of Mecca, which is still maintained by the Banjar immigrants even today.

As we noted earlier, Muhammad Arshad studied with al-Palimbam and several other Malay-Indonesian students. However, while al-Palimbam had a good number of teachers, Muhammad Arshad'Arshad known teachers included only al-Sammam, al-Damanhuri, Sulayman al-Kurdi and 'Ata' Allah al-Masri. It is possible that he studied with other teachers, especially with Ibrahim al-Ra'ls al-Zamzami, from whom Muhammad Arshad most likely studied 'Urn al-falak (astronomy), a field in which he was a leading authority among Malay-Indonesian scholars.

With regard to his works and activities after his return to the archipelago, one might assume that Muhammad Arshad was simply an expert mfiqh or shan'shan, especially due to the fact that his best-known text, entitled Sabll al-Muhtadln, is afiqh book. But this does not necessarily mean that he was not learned in SUFIsm; it is known that he also wrote a work entitled Kanz al-Ma'Ma, dealing with tasawwuf. Thus Muhammad Arshad was well versed in the exterior (al-zahif) and interior (al-batiri) sciences or, as Steenbrink writes, he was an expert mfiqh as well as in tasawwuf. Muhammad Arshad received the Sammaniyyah tariqah from al-Sammam, and he is considered the scholar most responsible for the spread of the Sammaniyyah tariqah in Kalimantan.

Muhammad Arshad studied for about 30 years in Mecca and five years in Medina before returning to the archipelago. Several years before his return it is said that he began to teach students in the Haram Mosque of Mecca. However, Muhammad Arshad felt that he did not yet have sufficient knowledge. Together with al-Palimbam, 'Abd al-Rahman al-Batawi and 'Abd al-Wahhab al-Bugisi, he asked permission of their teacher, 'Ata' Allah al-Masri, to advance their education in Cairo. While appreciating their good intention, 'Ata' Allah suggested that it would be much better for them to return to the the archipelago, as he believed they already possessed more than sufficient knowledge to be effective as teachers in their homeland. They decided to travel to Cairo anyway, but simply for a visit, not to study. It was probably a sign of their connection with 'Ata' Allah and their visit to Cairo that one of Muhammad Arshad'Arshad friends, 'Abd alRahman al-Batawi, added the laqab (surname) of 'Al-Masn' to his name.

Like other Malay-Indonesian scholars, Muhammad Arshad maintained constant contact and communication with his homeland while he was in the Haramayn, so that he was well informed about the developments of Islam there. In this connection he is reported to have asked the opinion of his teacher, Sulayman al-Kurdl, about the religious policies of the Sultan of Banjar. The Sultan, he had heard, imposed heavy fines on his Muslim subjects for failing to perform the Jum'ah (Friday) prayer. Muhammad Arshad also asked Sulayman al-Kurdl to explain the differences between zakah (obligatory 'Alms') and tax, for the Banjar Sultan had required the population to pay tax instead of zakah. It is unfortunate that we have no information on Sulayman al-Kurdi'Kurdi responses to these questions, but this account reflects the genuine concern on the part of Muhammad Arshad about the correct application of the sharl'sharl.

Muhammad Arshad, together with 'Abd al-Rahman al-Batawi al-Masn and 'Abd al-Wahhab al-Bugisi, returned to the archipelago in 1186/1773. Before he proceeded to Banjarmasin, at the request of al-Batawi, Muhammad Arshad stayed in Batavia for two months. Although in Batavia for a relatively short time, he was able to launch an important reform for the Batavian Muslims. He corrected the qiblah (the direction Muslims face when performing prayers towards the Ka'bah in Mecca) of several mosques in Batavia. According to his calculation, the qiblah of mosques in Jembatan Lima and Pekojan, Batavia, were not directed correctly at the Ka'bah, and therefore had to be changed. This created controversy among Muslim leaders in Batavia, and as a result the Dutch Governor summoned Muhammad Arshad to explain the matter. The Governor, impressed by Muhammad Arshad'Arshad mathematical calculations, happily presented him with several gifts. Later, the correction of the direction of the qiblah was proposed by 'Abd al-Rahman al-Batawi in Palembang when he travelled there around 1800; this incited heated discussion as well.

The reformist impulse in Muhammad Arshad'Arshad personality to introduce new religious ideas and institutions is obvious after his return to Martapura, South Kalimantan. One of the first things he did after his arrival was to establish an Islamic educational institution, which was crucial to the education of Muslims in advancing their understanding of Islamic teachings and practices. To that end Muhammad Arshad asked Sultan Tahmld Allah II (r. 1187-1223/1773-1808) to grant him a large plot of wasteland outside the capital of the Sultanate. He and 'Abd al-Wahhab al-Bugisi, who was now married to Muhammad Arshad'Arshad daughter, built a centre for Islamic education, which was similar in characteristics to the surau in West Sumatra or pesantren in Java. Like many suraus and pesantrens, Muhammad Arshad'Arshad centre of learning consisted of lecture halls, students' hostels, teachers houses and libraries. This centre was economically self-sufficient, as Muhammad Arshad together with other teachers and students transformed nearby lands into productive rice fields and vegetable gardens. Before long, the centre had established itself as the most important locus for the training of students, who later became leading scholars in Kalimantan society.

Muhammad Arshad took another important step in intensifying Islamisation in his region by reforming the administration of justice in the Sultanate of Banjar. In addition to making Islamic legal doctrines the most important reference in criminal courts, Muhammad Arshad, with the support of the Sultan, established separate Islamic courts to deal with more purely civil legal matters. He also initiated the establishment of the office of Mufti, who was responsible for issuing fatwas on religious and social matters. With these initiatives, Muhammad Arshad managed to put Islamic law into effect in the realm of the Sultanate of Banjar.

Another important Kalimantan scholar is Muhammad Nafls b. Idris b. Husayn al-Banjari. Although we do not have much information on his life, there is no doubt that he was second only to Muhammad Arshad in terms of the influence he exerted on the Kalimantan Muslims, especially in the field of tasawwuf. If Muhammad Arshad was known primarily as an expert in shan'shan, Muhammad Nafls was famous as a sufi scholar by virtue of his well-known work, al-Durr al-Nafis fl Bayan Wahdat al-Af'al al-Asma' wa al-Sifat wa al-Dhat al-Taqdls, which circulated widely in the archipelago. This work was printed several times in Cairo by Dar al-Taba'Taba (as recently as 1347/1928) and by Mustafa al-Halabi (1362/ 1943), in Mecca by Matba'Matba al-Karim al-Islamiyyah (1323/1905), and in various places in the archipelago.

Muhammad Nafls was born in 1148/1735 in Martapura into the Banjar royal family. Thus, he lived in the same period as Muhammad Arshad. There is no evidence of the date of his death, although it is known that he died and was buried in Kelua, a village about 125 kilometres from Banjarmasin. His early education is not known, but he was most probably taught the basic principles of Islam in his own region. Later, we find him studying in Mecca, as he writes in his introductory notes to his al-Durr al-Nafis: '...he who writes this epistle...that is Muhammad Nafls b. Idris b. alHusayn, who was born in Banjar and lives in Mecca'. There is no hard evidence that he studied together with al-Palimbam, Muhammad Arshad or their colleagues, but it is highly probable that his period of study in the Haramayn coincided with that of al-Palimbam and others. I would suggest that they studied together at one time or another, particularly if we consider the following list of Muhammad Nafls' teachers.

Abdullah mentions that Muhammad Nafls studied with a number of scholars in the Haramayn, the most famous of whom were al-Sammam, Muhammad al-Jawhari, 'Abd Allah b. Hijazi al-Sharqawi, Muhammad Siddiq b. ' Umar Khan and 'Abd al-Rahman b. 'Abd al-Aziz al-Maghribi. Muhammad Siddiq b. ' Umar Khan was a student of al-Sammam and 'Abd al-Aziz al-Maghribl, and was apparently a close friend of al-Palimbanl. The latter even includes the titles of several works of Muhammad Siddlq in the list of works that he recommends to be read by aspirants of the sufi path.

We have already mentioned both al-Sammam and Muhammad al-Jawharl, who were among the teachers of al-Palimbanl and his fellows. The fact that Muhammad Nafls studied with al-Sammanl, al-Jawhari and Muhammad Siddlq indicates that he was indeed a fellow student of al-Palimbam, Muhammad Arshad and their other Malay-Indonesian counterparts.

As for 'Abd Allah b. HijazI [b. Ibrahim] al-Sharqawi al-Azharl (1150-1227/1737-1812), he was Shaykh al-Islam and Shaykh of the Azhar from 1207/1794. Al-Sharqawi was two years younger than Muhammad Nafls. As al-Sharqawi mostly lived in Cairo, it is very likely that Muhammad Nafls studied with him during his frequent visits to the Haramayn. We are not so certain whether al-Palimbam, Muhammad Arshad, 'Abd al-Rahman al-Batawi and 'Abd al-Wahhab al-Bugisi also studied with al-Sharqawi. But, as we will see shortly, al-Sharqawi had another important Malay-Indonesian student, namely Dawud al-Fatanl.

Al-Sharqawi, it is worth mentioning briefly, was himself a student of important scholars in the networks, including Ahmad al-Damanhurl, Mahmud al-Kurdl and Ahmad al-Jawharl. Mahmud al-Kurdl appointed him as the khallfah of the Khalwatiyyah tariqah in Cairo. Al-Sharqawi then established himself among reformists of the order. He was well versed in various branches of Islamic discipline, although he was mainly known as a leading expert in the sharl'sharl and hadith. Like most scholars in the networks, he emphasised the importance of hadith, in terms of its position not only as the second source of Islamic legal doctrines but also as the indispensable source of proper moral conduct. Therefore, in addition to being a reformist, and a sufi with numerous khallfahs, al-Sharqawi was among the most respected isnads in the networks. It is important to note in passing that Muhammad Mahfuz al-Tarmisi (from Termas, East Java 1285-1338/1842-1920), an important Malay-Indonesian hadith scholar who lived and died in Mecca, traced his isnads to al-Sharqawi, among others. Having studied with al-Sharqawi as well as with al-Sammanl and Muhammad al-Jawharl, Muhammad Nafls clearly had strong links with the networks in the period under discussion.

Muhammad Nafls al-Banjarl, like all Malay-Indonesian scholars, followed the Shafi'Shafi school of law and Ash'ari theological doctrines. He was affiliated with several tariqahs: Qadiriyyah, Shattariyyah, Sammaniyyah, Naqshbandiyyah and Khalwatiyyah. Muhammad Nafls was an expert in kalam and tasawwuf. His Durr al-Nafis, while stressing the absolute transcendence and Unity of God, refused the notion of the Jabariyyah, who maintained fatalistic determinism as opposed to free will (Qadariyyah). In Muhammad Nafls' opinion, Muslims must strive to achieve a better life by doing good deeds and avoiding evil. Thus, Muhammad Nafls was clearly a proponent of activism, one of the basic characteristics of neo-SUFIsm discussed earlier. With its strong emphasis on Muslim activism, it is no surprise that his book was banned by the Dutch, who feared that it would incite people to launch & jihad.

There is no information on when Muhammad Nafls al-Banjari returned to the archipelago. It appears that he proceeded straight to South Kalimantan. Like Muhammad Arshad, who was the pioneer of the Islamic educational institution, Muhammad Nafls devoted himself to the pioneering work of propagating Islam in the interior of the South Kalimantan region. He was indeed a typical wandering sufi teacher and played a crucial role in expanding Islam in Kalimantan.

## Rise of Patani Scholarship

To conclude this chapter, we will examine the Patani scholars who by the end of the eighteenth century increasingly came into the picture of Islamic learning in the archipelago. With the rise of Patani scholars, we can observe not only the proliferation of the tradition of Islamic learning but also the further dissemination of renewal and reformism in the Malay-Indonesian world.

The conversion of the Patani region in South Thailand to Islam took place from roughly the twelfth to the fifteenth century. The Patani Sultanate was a populous and prosperous Muslim kingdom in the Malay Peninsula until it fell under Thai control in 1202/1786. Its harbour was also an important centre of trade for Asian and European traders.

There have been numerous studies on Patani Muslim separatism after World War II but little attention has been paid to the growth of Islamic tradition and institutions among the Patani Muslims in the earlier period.

Despite Patani'Patani political weakness as a border state, wandering teachers, mainly sufis, continually frequented the Patani region. The Hikayat Patani reports the coming of scholars such as Shaykh Gombak and his student 'Abd al-Mu'Mu from Minangkabau, and Shaykh FaqIH Safl al-Din from Pasai in the second half of the sixteenth century. They played a crucial role in the religious life of the Sultanate. Safl al-Din, for instance, urged the construction of a royal mosque and later became adviser to Sultan Muzaffar Shah on religious matters. Again, in the middle of the seventeenth century, a number of scholars came to Patani: Sayyid 'Abd Allah from Jerusalem via Trengganu, Haji 'Abd al-Rahman from Java, FaqIH 'Abd al-Manan, a Minangkabau from Kedah, and Shaykh 'Abd al-Qadir from Pasai. They are reported to have carried out concerted efforts to spread the hukum Allah (shan'shan) into Patani.

An important point conveyed by these accounts is that the Patani Muslims were not isolated among their fellow Muslims in the archipelago. With the coming of scholars to their region, Patani Muslims were made aware of developments in religious ideas and institutions in other parts of the Malay-Indonesian world. It is highly plausible that it was such scholars who stimulated the establishment of the traditional Islamic educational instititution known in Patani as pondok. Furthermore, it is suggested that the pondok system, which also developed in other parts of the Malay Peninsula, originated from Patani. al-Palimbani, as mentioned earlier, is said to have had his early education in Patani, probably in the pondoks there, but little is known about them in the period before the nineteenth century. Matheson and Hooker point out that the pondok?, in Patani were very prestigious and that their more advanced students were welcomed as teachers elsewhere. I would argue, however, that this was true only in the nineteenth century, when native Patani scholars increasingly came onto the scene and contributed significantly to the growth of the pondok?.

Shaghir Abdullah, a grandson of Ahmad Zayn al-'Abidm al-Fatam, a leading Patani scholar, lists Muhammad Tahir b. 'All al-Fatam (914-78/ 1508-78), the author of the famous Tadhkirat al-Mawdu'Mawdu? as among the earliest and most famous scholars of Patani. This is incorrect, as Muhammad Tahir also had a laqab (nickname) of al-Hindi (from India), to be exact, from Patan in the Gujarat region. If this claim were true, Muhammad Tahir al-Fatam would have been the earliest Malay scholar involved in the scholarly networks of the Haramayn; that is, a century ahead of al-Raniri, al-Sinkili and al-Maqassan.

The best-known Patani scholar was Dawud b. 'Abd Allah b. Idris alFatam; but he was neither the earliest nor the only scholar from this region involved in the networks. At least from Dawud al-Fatam'Fatam silsilah of the Sammaniyyah tariqah we know that he received the order not directly from Muhammad al-Sammani but by way of two other Patani scholars, namely 'All b. Ishaq al-Fatam and Muhammad Salih b. 'Abd al-Rahman alFatam. They probably came to the Haramayn earlier than Dawud al-Fatam, but Abdullah suggests that the three were contemporaries, with Dawud al-Fatani the youngest among them.

Thanks to research done by Abdullah, published in his Syeikh Daud bin Abdullah al-Fatani, we know more about Dawud al-Fatam'Fatam life and career. According to Abdullah, records kept by families related to Dawud al-Fatam give the date of birth of this great scholar differently; that is, 1724,' 1153/1740 and 1183/1769. He died in Ta'Ta f, and one of the records gives his date of death as 1265/1847. There is no way we can be certain which of the dates is the correct one. But because of his studying with the teachers listed below, I think al-Fatam was most probably born in 1153/1740; he is reported to have studied with al-Barrawi (d. 1182/1768), as will be seen shortly. Furthermore, his earliest dated work was completed in Mecca in 1224/1809, when he was 69 years old and had established himself as a learned scholar. The date of his last work is 1259/1843. This means that he lived a relatively long life. The height of his career was certainly in the early decades of the nineteenth century beyond the period of our discussion. However, as he had direct connections with the eighteenth century scholarly networks, he must be included in this discussion.

According to Abdullah, Dawud al-Fatam was born in Kresik (also spelled Gresik), an old harbour in Patani, where Mawlana Malik Ibrahim, one of the famous Wali Sanga, reportedly preached Islam before he proceeded to East Java. There he built a centre of Islamic propagation also named Gresik. It said that Dawud al-Fatam had ancestral relations with Malik Ibrahim. Abdullah believes that Dawud al-Fatam'Fatam grandfather was a certain Faqlh 'All or Datuk Andi Maharajalela, a prince of the Bone Sultanate, South Sulawesi, who came to Patani in 1047/1637 from the court of Bone as a result of political unrest. Later he married a Patani woman and rose to influence in the Patani Sultanate. Although it is difficult to substantiate these accounts, they at least indicate that, in addition to intellectual connections in the various Muslim ethnic groups in the archipelago, there existed some kind of blood relations among them.

Dawud al-Fatam acquired his early education in his own region, apparently from his father. But Abdullah suggests that Dawud al-Fatam also studied in the pondoks in Patani. He later travelled to Aceh, where he studied for two years with Muhammad Zayn b. Faqlh Jalal al-Din al-Ashl. Muhammad Zayn al-Ashl, as Hasjmi tells us, was a leading scholar of the Acehnese Sultanate during the period of Sultan 'AlA' al-Din Mahmud Shah (r. 1174-95/1760-81). Al-Ashl appears to have inherited his father'father expertise in fiqh, for he wrote several works in this field. There is strong evidence that al-Ashl also studied in the Haramayn. Two of al-Ashi'Ashi known works, the Bidayat al-Hiddyah and Kashf al-Kiram, were prepared in Mecca in 1170/1757 and 1171/1758 respectively, and were apparently completed in Aceh.

In all probability, Dawud al-Fatam travelled from Aceh directly to the Haramayn, but we have no information on when he reached the Holy Land. In the Haramayn, he immediately joined the circle of Jowl students already there. Among them were Muhammad Salih b. 'Abd al-Rahman al-Fatam, 'All b. Ishaq al-Fatam, al-PALIMBANI, Muhammad Arshad, 'Abd al-Wahhab al-Bugisi, 'Abd al-Rahman al-Batawi and Muhammad Nafis. Abdullah tells us that Dawud al-Fatam was the youngest of these scholars. All the older students were also teachers of Dawud al-Fatam, or at least assisted him in his studies with non-Malay teachers.

Abdullah argues that Dawud al-Fatam, like al-PALIMBANI, Muhammad Arshad, 'Abd al-Rahman al-Batawi and 'Abd al-Wahhab al-Bugisi, studied directly with al-Sammani. He is also reported to have learned from 'Isa b. Ahmad al-Barrawi, who died in 1182/1768, seven years earlier than al-Sammani (d. 1189/1775). In other words, when Dawud al-Fatam studied with al-Barrawi, presumably in the last years of his life, al-Sammani was at the height of his career. Because of his studying with al-Barrawi and al-Sammani, Dawud al-Fatanl must have reached the Haramayn in the second half of the 1760s, or when he was in his late 20s.

'I sa b. Ahmad [b. 'Isa b. Muhammad al-Zubayn al-Shafi'I al-Qahiri al-Azhari], better known as al-Barrawi, was a muhaddith wdfaqih who had a special expertise in legal hadiths and in the comparative study of schools of Islamic law. He lived mainly in Cairo, where he died in 1182/1768. He was also a frequent visitor to the Haramayn, performing pilgrimage and involving himself in scholarly activities. He received hadith through isnads which included 'Abd Allah al-Basri. Al-Barrawi was also a teacher of Murtada al-Zabidi and Muhammad b. 'All al-Shanwam. Al-Shanwam, as we will see shortly, was also a teacher of Dawud al-Fatanl. Al-Fatanl mostly studied usul al-Dln (lit. 'roots of religion') with al-Barrawi. He possessed an isnad in this science, which ran from al-Barrawi to include such major network scholars as 'Abd Allah al-Basri, 'AlA' al-Dln al-Babili, Shams al-Dln al-Ramli and Zakariyya al-Ansari. Considering the fact that al-Fatanl wrote a number of works onfiqh, it is highly probable that he also learned this science mostly from al-Barrawi.

More than any other Malay scholar who preceded him, al-Fatanl had many teachers either of Egyptian origin or with a strong Egyptian connection. As there is no evidence that al-Fatanl ever travelled to Cairo, he must have studied with them during their visits to the Haramayn. In addition to studying with al-Barrawi, al-Fatanl continued his studies with alSharqawi, the Shaykh of Azhar and celebrated Khalwatiyyah reformist mentioned earlier as a teacher of Muhammad Nafls. As al-Sharqawi was an expert in hadith, shari'ah, kalam and tasawwuf, it is probable that al-Fatanl also learned these sciences from him.

The next teacher Dawud al-Fatanl studied with was the successor of al-Sharqawi as the Shaykh of al-Azhar. He was Muhammad b. 'All Al-Shanwam (d. 1233/1818), better known simply as Al-Shanwam, who was elected President of the Azhar University on al-Sharqawi's death. During his youth, Al-Shanwam studied with most of the leading scholars of Egypt, including Ahmad al-Damanhun, al-Barrawi, al-Sharqawi and Murtada al-Zabidi. He was an outstanding scholar of hadith, fiqh, tafsir and kalam. Although he taught mostly in Cairo, he had a number of students in Mecca, who studied with him during his visits there. With Al-Shanwam, al-Fatanl advanced his studies mfiqh and kalam.

In addition to studying with the scholars mentioned above, al-Fatanl learned from Muhammad As'As, Ahmad al-Marzuqi and Ibrahim al-Ra'Ra s al-Zamzami al-Makki. The latter, as we have seen, was also a teacher of al-Palimbani. Dawud al-Fatanl studied various branches of Islamic discipline with Ibrahim al-Ra'Ra s as well as receiving the Shadhaliyyah tariqah from him. It is interesting that Ibrahim al-Ra'Ra s in turn took this tariqah from Salih Al-Fullam, who got it from his teacher, Ibn Sinnah.

'Muhammad As'As' was most probably Muhammad As'As al-Hanafi al-Makki, a muhaddith who is said to have been very proud of having a hadith isnad that went back to 'Abd Allah al-Basri. Interestingly enough, al-Fatam did not take the isnad but instead took the Shattariyyah tariqah from Muhammad As'As al-Makki, who took it from Muhammad Sa'Sa b. Tahir, who took it from his father, Abu Tahir, who in turn took it from his father, Ibrahim al-Kurani, who took it from Ahmad al-Qushashi, who took it from Ahmad al-Shinnawi, who took it from Sibghat Allah. This silsilah is different from that of al-Sinkili, who received the tariqah not from al-Kurani but from al-Qushashi.

We do not have much information on 'Ahmad al-Marzuqi' the last in the list of al-Fatam'Fatam teachers. This scholar very likely was Ahmad al-Marzuqi [al-Makki al-Maliki], a student of Al-Shanwam. Ahmad alMarzuqi was known as a muhaddith who taught mostly in Mecca. Both Muhammad As'As al-Hanafi and Ahmad al-Marzuqi al-Maliki were alFatani'Fatani teachers of non-Shafi'I madhhabs. This indicates that the differences among scholars in their adherence to schools of Islamic law, as in the previous century, were not barriers in the networks of 'Ulama' in the eighteenth century.

Considering all the teachers he studied with and the sciences he got from them, it is clear that Dawud al-Fatani'Fatani education was complete and comprehensive. He possessed more than sufficent knowledge to earn him fame as a major Malay-Indonesian scholar in the period of transition between the eighteenth and nineteenth centuries. Al-Fatam seems never to have returned to Patani or elsewhere in the Malay-Indonesian archipelago. Instead he devoted himself to teaching and writing in the Haramayn until he died in Ta'Ta f. His numerous Malay-Indonesian students came from all over the archipelago. He has been claimed as a pivotal figure in the history of Islam in Patani.

There can be no question that al-Fatam was one of the most prolific among Malay-Indonesian scholars. He wrote at least 57 works, dealing with almost all branches of the Islamic disciplines. The works themselves, however, some printed in various places in the Middle East and the Malay-Indonesian world, have not been sufficiently studied.

The careers of Malay-Indonesian scholars in the eighteenth century, from al-Palimbani to al-Fatam, have shown us that the networks among Middle Eastern and Malay-Indonesian scholars continued to gain momentum. More importantly, these indicate the incessant transmission of reformism from the centres of learning in the Middle East to various parts of the archipelago. The wide circulation of the writings of these MalayIndonesian scholars pushed Islamic reformism in this part of the Muslim world even further.

# 8

# Reshaping in Muslim Society

## Introductrion

Replacing the clash of economies is a clash of civilizations: the secularized West versus overreligious Islam. This dichotomy rests on a particular construction of what it is to be modern, a construction that arose from the European Enlightenment and that celebrates the ideal of a secular public sphere of deliberative discourse. A modern society, in this view, must draw a sharp boundary between the religious values of the individual and the political values of the public.

From this perspective, social movements that urge people to become more steadfastly religious in order to become more modern are internally contradictory, if not outright threatening to modernity itself. Secularizing states throughout the world have taken this view seriously, arrogating to themselves the right to define the modes and manners of public behavior, and to view religious-based public norms (of dress, legal standing, or education) as anathema. Here, post-Enlightenment political theory converges conveniently with the interests of those in power.

Ironically, these state actions have made all religious movements "modern" by dictating the terms by which they must operate. In shaping their activities, religious movements must take account of modern state structures, ideologies, and forces, as well as international economic exchanges and transnational communication flows. Culturally, as well, religious movements have redefined their own ideas in engagement with European modernity and in particular with ideas of agency, individual responsibility, and subjectivity. As Charles Taylor has argued, European modernity has historically entailed a radical detachment of subjectivity from the outer world, including the social world, and a consequent refocusing inward. This process of fashioning a cultural model of individualized subjectivity has been religious as well as political in the Euro-American world.

Taylor's analysis leads us to ask what kinds of cultural subjectivities modernity-making may have engendered elsewhere in the world. Such an inquiry builds on the long-standing concern of cultural anthropologists with local ideas of self and subjectivity but asks what challenges to these ideas are posed in the name of a "modernity" that is also religious.

I examine here one such confrontation between older and newer religious practices where notions of subjectivity became central. The broader context for the case is the set of movements for religious reform that animated many Muslims throughout the Dutch and British East Indies (and elsewhere), beginning early in the twentieth century. I consider what has been at stake in Gayo society in the highlands of Sumatra, where, beginning in the 1930s, heated disputes arose over whether a worshiper should recite a statement of intent before worship. The debates implicated ideas about subjectivity, persons, and actions, and contained a strong critique of local thinking about religion. The dispute was carried out along many channels; I examine here the religious poetry created to disseminate the reformers' views. Finally, I consider what other courses the reform movement might have taken, drawing on materials from neighboring societies to do so. I use this case to suggest strategies for proceeding beyond the single ethnographic study to a comparative study of Muslim modernist projects.

Through this case study I wish to underline the importance of strategy, beliefs, and rhetorics to religious phenomena, religious in the narrowest sense of matters of worship and liturgy. These strategies, beliefs, and rhetorics are highly responsive to social and cultural features and processes. Religious actors select from a variety of ideas and emphasize those that offer the best chances of success in a particular social environment, or so I argue. Such a claim is commonplace in studies of the social and political aspects of Islamic movements. But debates about worship or liturgy have generally been left to the text-based Islamicist, whose training leads him or her to focus on the origins of particular ideas in normative texts. This unfortunate division of labor has at times led scholars of religion to respond to field studies of religious ideas with some hostility. My own assumption, one shared by most anthropologists, is that we do wish to understand how people have interpreted and debated particular religious issues, and why they have emphasized some matters over others. This kind of knowledge allows us to understand why transnational movements (such as Islamic reformist movements) catch on at some times and places and not at others; local studies give us a window onto the rhetorics and forms that mediate between "local" and "translocal" phenomena. Indeed, the more we (quite rightly) turn our anthropological attentions to "transnational" phenomena – whether religion, migration, or music – the harder – we must work to retain the particularities and diversities in our analytic frame, lest all blur into generalized World Culture.

In what follows I seek to explain the particular set of religion-oriented acts taken by specific individuals and groups by identifying the social frameworks in which they acted, their own intentions and interests, and their sense of the relative cultural force of various alternative ways of discussing religious matters. An account of a set of actions thus derived may in turn be made more plausible by contrasting them with other sets, chosen to be as controlled as possible, that is, as close to the original set in terms of period and cultural features – the old anthropological strategy of "controlled comparison."

## Disputes over Intent

When I first heard about the religious controversies that had animated many Gayo earlier in this century, I found it difficult to understand why these disputes had been so prominent and why, in the 1980s, they continued to occasion discussion and debate. Beginning in the mid-1930s, a group of Gayo religious teachers who had recently returned to their Sumatran homeland from schooling elsewhere in the Dutch East Indies began to urge their fellow men and women to purify their religious activities of nonIslamic elements. These teachers emphasized the unique authority of the Qur'an and hadit, and associated themselves with the general movement for religious reform called the "young group" (kaum muda). The kaum muda drew extensively from the Salafi movement in the Middle East, inspired by the Egyptian scholar Muhammad Abduh. Other Gayo teachers resisted the "young group" position, affirming long-standing religious practices and the authority of prominent religious scholars of the past. These scholars increasingly identified with the general Indies-wide "old group" (kaum tua) position. These two labels were of general archipelagic currency and are usually glossed as "modernist" and "traditionalist."

In the main Gayo town of Takengen, these teachers engaged in public and private debates over such liturgical matters as how many times to bend down in worship, whether or not to offer a distinct prayer at morning worship, or whether to remind a just-buried corpse of the main tenets of Islam. But no debate occasioned as much hurt and discord as that concerning the statement of intent to worship. Many Gayo (and other Muslims), just before beginning to worship (proclaiming Allahu akbar), state to themselves their intent to worship, usually reciting a one-sentence formula (in Gayo, Indonesian, or, for the more learned, Arabic), such as: "I worship at daybreak with two cycles on account of God, may He be exhalted." Those who do pronounce the formula consider it to be an aid to worship; most modernists see it as an illegitimate addition to the actions dictated by scripture. The opening pronouncement "I worship" in Arabic is "ushalli," and the dispute has been called the "ushalli controversy."

One traditionalist scholar in Takèngën recalled the disputes over the usballi that began in the 1930s. "They [modernists] kept telling us we were wrong, and the disputes led to some divorces. Some people moved from Takèngën to Bireuën [on the northern coast] because they were ashamed at all the disputes." These early debates over the ushalli made it emblematic of the traditionalist position, as in the following couplet linking the ushalli to the holding of ritual meals (also critized by modernists):

*semiyang berushalli*
*Molut berkenduri*

*At worship, say the ushalli;*
*On the Prophet's Birthday, hold a ritual meal.*

Of all the issues that increasingly embroiled traditionalists and modernists in Takèngën, "it was the ushalli that caused the most turmoil," he said. Such was the degree of local antagonism that the principal imam of the mosque in Kota Raja (today Banda Aceh) intervened in the mid-1930s, instructing scholars on both sides to quell their enthusiasm. But the disputes continued, and the ushalli question was central in a public debate held in 1941 between the chief spokesmen for the two camps.

Why was the controvery over the ushalli the hardest felt of these disputes? What was it about a preliminary pronouncement of intent that was so objectionable to modernists and so important to others? It alone of the disputed aspects of worship raised the issue of subjectivity in worship, and part of the answer to this question will lie in the notions of subjectivity and action that underlie ideas of religious modernism. But not all Indonesian societies were as touched by this particular controversy; another part of the answer thus must lie in the specific history of Gayo modernists' efforts at persuasion.

Now, having the right intent when engaged in ritual activity is generally important to Muslims. Specifically, most Muslims, whether Gayo, Egyptian, or British, would agree that one must form the correct intent before beginning ritual worship. It thus seems strange that modernists, who urged Muslims to purify their religious practice by returning to the Qur'an and hadith, would argue that one should not express the intent to worship. But they did so argue, on the grounds that there was insufficient textual evidence that the prophet Muhammad himself ever stated a formula of intent to worship and that, following the general principle of strictly following Muhammad in matters of worship, we should therefore refrain from uttering such a statement.

This particular issue might have been a minor one were it not that early on it became a token of the larger controversy. Modernism began to take root in the Indies in the first few years of this century, when several scholars returned from study in Mecca to their homes in West Sumatra. In 1906 one such scholar, ' Abd al-Karim, began to criticize established ritual practices, including the practices of holding an additional worship session after the Friday congregational worship and adding a separate section (the qunut) to morning worship, along with a long list of other matters having to do with delivering recitations to the deceased or to God on his or her behalf. ' Abd al-Karim directed his criticisms at the organized religious orders (tariqa) of West Sumatra, whose members engaged in precisely these practices. These orders were important political bodies as well as associations for religious learning and worship, and these criticisms launched an extensive and hardfought series of public debates over knowledge and authority. About this time ' Abd al-Karim asked Ahmad Khatib, his teacher in Mecca (and of Sumatran origin himself), for an opinion (fatwa) on the ushalli question. Ahmad Khatib complied, coming out in favor of the practice, but ' Abd alKarim rejected the fatwa, issuing his own counter-fatwa. His rejection of the venerated Meccan stirred up a storm of protest in West Sumatra and generated a great deal of hostility toward him.

Thereafter, the practice of saying the ushalli came to index one's acceptance of a larger package of positions; it thus became quite salient among the disputed practices. But in most Sumatran societies it did not become the main issue. The rhetorics adopted by modernists varied. In much of lowland Aceh, for example, reform-oriented groups underscored the importance of the individual's rationality as a weapon against the passions. In West Sumatra itself, ideas of socially liberating modernity permeate much influential writing by Muslim reformers. But in the Gayo highlands it was the ushalli that provided the encompassing framework for critiques and replies on a wide variety of topics. Why this issue in this place? It is not enough to identify the general Muslim sources or the general archipelagowide currency of the ushalli; the long-lasting importance of the ushalli and of the issue of intent in Gayo religious rhetoric requires a local explanation.

## The Social Frameworks for the Disputes

One place to begin is with the social history of religious life in the highlands. Although Gayo probably converted to Islam during the expansion of the Acehnese kingdom in the sixteenth and seventeenth centuries, little is known about religious ideas and institutions in the highlands before 1900. Dutch forces invaded the area during the period from 1901 to 1904 as part of their effort to occupy Aceh. By the 1920s they had turned their attention from pacifying the countryside to encouraging export agriculture, and the town of Takèngën in northern Gayoland soon became a center for trade, government, and education. The town took on a marked multicultural character, as traders and teachers from elsewhere in the Dutch East Indies came there to settle. Many of them came from West Sumatra, where they had studied in the new style of religious school. In Takèngën they were joined by a new class of Gayo merchants and civil servants, who had to learn what was beginning to be called Indonesian in order to speak with them.

By the mid- 1930s, Gayo and other Sumatran teachers of both modernist and traditionalist persuasions had established their own religious associations and schools in or near Takèngën. Their emerging doctrinal differences attracted widespread public attention, and their spokesmen engaged in public debates, particularly over the correct ways to worship and whether to speak with the dead. Friday preachers took sides on these issues, and disagreements among preachers led to the building of new mosques. People carried the arguments away from the mosques into town coffee shops and village prayer houses.

Out of these developments emerged a new public sphere of Islamic discourse in Takèngën. This sphere was defined by religion (agama; Ar. dîn) and religious practice (ibëdët; Ar. 'ibâdât) as warranted by explicit prescriptions in the Qur'an and hadith. The participants in this sphere included Gayo, Acehnese, and other Sumatrans who shared a set of religious ideas and practices detached from any particular place. Indeed, to retain their legitimacy as properly religious, these practices needed to be explicitly distinguished from purely local forms of ritual. The immigrant character of the town contributed to its flavor: the people who arrived there brought forms of social, religious, and economic life that could exist apart from a village base. Moreover, the two largest groups of Muslim immigrants, the West Sumatran Minangkabau and the Acehnese, both came from cultures where circular migration was part of the life course. Men in both regions typically spent years away from their homelands. These migratory traditions probably accentuated the sense of detachment from place that characterized the new socioreligious ideas.

But if many Gayo modernists participated in town life, they also maintained ties to the surrounding villages. Many continued to live in the villages and work in the town; others visited their natal villages frequently for feasts and celebrations. No migratory culture emerged here. This particular combination of networks and allegiances has given a distinctive stamp to highlands modernist culture. Gayo modernists participate in a supraethnic, pronationalist, Arabic-language-based religious culture, but they also aim at reforming established rural social practices from within. Their specific social orientation has led Gayo modernists to carve out a distinct religious sphere of activity, in which people of diverse backgrounds could participate (in town life) but that would also allow for the continuation of older cultural activities and social ties (largely in the villages).

Gayo modernists thus have underscored the contrast between matters of religion, where one must follow scriptural norms, and all other matters, where, in the words of Muhammad, "you know best your affairs." This position has allowed them to urge practicable reforms in village religious life without calling for the abandonment of other social practices, something neither they nor their audience would have welcomed. Their stance has led them to accent certain features of the general modernist position over other features. They have emphasized the scriptural constraints on interpretation rather than the process of independent reasoning (ijtihad), usually claiming that there is one correct interpretation of scripture and vehemently denouncing all innovation (bid'a) in ritual affairs. By stressing the boundary between religious ritual (ibadat) and the rest of life, they have played down claims that a particular set of religious orientations should guide all activities (such as reason aqal ], so prominent in the modernist discourses of Aceh, Malaysia, and North Africa).

Within the religious domain, Gayo have emphasized the direct, unavoidable link between the subjectivity of the individual worshiper and the reception of the ritual act by God. The intent associated with an act defines it: an act of sacrifice, worship, or pilgrimage to Mecca counts as such only if one undertakes it for the sake of God (rather than in hope of gaining wealth or prestige). The degree of concentration during the act also gives it more or less value: the individual thus must strive in a mental battle against distraction and the Devil. The merit that results from religious practice accrues only to the actor, and so all claims that actions can create merit for others are illegitimate.

As I often heard modernist friends declare: "Everything depends on intent." Now, the term "intent" (Gayo niët; Ind. niat; Ar. niyyâ) has a broad range of meaning in Gayo life, much broader than what is meant by the modernists. It refers to a general sphere of communication: for example, a vow that one will sacrifice an animal or offer a meal to a spirit in return for the spirit's help in healing a child or securing a bountiful harvest. Or it can refer in negative fashion to the "hidden intentions" behind an ostensibly good act.

In modernist usage, however, "intent" is intended to define the subjective component of a more narrow view of religion and ritual. Against older notions of ritual as a wide field of powerful communication, modernists assert a conception of ritual as the tightly defined range of ways in which an individual can fulfill God's commands, and thus as obedience. This shift can be seen in Weberian typological terms as a shift away from instrumental rationality toward value rationality. It reaches widely into domains of agricultural ritual, liturgical form, and treatment of the dead. Emphasizing the importance of intent in itself does not constitute a critical intervention into preexisting religious discourse. What is specific to the Gayo case is how the emphasis on intent can be used as a foundation for a sweeping modernist critique of ritual practices.

If ritual is primarily about communicating with God, then anything that serves to clear the way and the mind must be in God's service and thus properly part of worship. If, however, ritual is primarily about obeying God's commands, then two objections to the ushalli follow. First, because scripture does not explicitly order worshipers to pronounce the ushalli, we should not pronounce it. In religious matters we must strictly follow scripture, using our powers to reason but not adding or subtracting one iota of information. (Modernists emphasize the religious importance of translating scripture into vernaculars not so that people can judge and interpret freely on their own — for that you need specialists — but so that they will know what they say in worship and thus have the correct intent.) Altering what scripture says is improper "innovation" (bid'a).

Secondly (and here is what is especially stressed in Gayo society), adding the ushalli to the prescribed ritual pattern implies that intent is not already part of every ritual act, that it is something extraneous to religious action (as in certain social science circles "ideas" are seen as detached from "behavior"). Because you must perform all your religious acts with the correct intent (in order to serve God), intent should suffuse all acts. As several Gayo modernist scholars put it, we express the intent to worship by preparing for worship: by walking to the mosque, by performing ablutions, and so forth, even before we begin to worship. If one's subjective formation of intent defines and constitutes an act as a religious act of a particular nature, then the notion that one can have action apart from intent is false and misleading. Including the ushalli in worship may dangerously weaken the principle that actions have built-in intentions precisely because it implies that such a statement is needed.

The ushalli controversy thus provided the Takèngën modernists a chance to stress that intent is a quality that accompanies all actions and renders them valid or invalid. But why did traditionalists feel compelled to defend the ushalli? At first glance it seems odd that the couplet quoted earlier included the ushalli as one of two practices that defined the traditionalist position. Part of the answer is undoubtedly historical. Because modernists criticized traditionalists for the ushalli relatively early in the history of highlands debates, the practice became a traditionalist emblem. Traditionalists also see that a broader issue is at stake here. The ushalli represents clearly the central idea that worship is communication with God and that a separate act of stating intention is necessary to effect that communication. Traditionalist scholars criticize a broad array of modernist ideas about ritual on this general point. For example, modernists speak too quickly, so that their half-intoned words run together and they end up saying ridiculous things to God. Communication needs to have a channel opened for it, and the ushalli does just that, directing worship to God. In their view, modernists seek to deny them a way of creating this personal pathway.

## Rhetorics of Persuasion

I have said that my task is to try and account for the particular shape of modernist interventions and the responses to those interventions. But this accounting should include, at least to the anthropological way of thinking, not just what issues arose, but how modernists set out to persuade people to change what they did. The history of persuasion is not simply the reflection or translation of high-level scholarly disputes; it also involves the strategic creation of rhetorical forms by those seeking to persuade.

In order to change the ways the less educated among the Gayo understood religious ritual, modernists created an entirely new genre of poetry, which in its formal features as well as its content underscored the separateness of religious matters from secular ones. The poetry, called saèr, embodies the particular highlands mixture of socioreligious emphases. Most poems feature one or more lines of Arabic scripture, followed by an elaboration of the scriptural message in Gayo verse. This juxtaposing of languages and styles may be unique in the Islamic world. It underlines the scriptural dependence of religious understanding and addresses a Gayo-speaking audience. The poetry was generally sung by local poets, some of whom were also popular singers in other genres. It soon became a highly popular performance genre.

In these poems modernists stress the importance of forming and holding the correct intent, a task that requires remaining attentive, having faith, and correctly formulating, to oneself, the act's religious purpose. They argue that intent is necessary to create any religious merit and that, therefore, one cannot create merit for others. Based on this proposition, they eliminate from the sphere of religious activity (ibadat) practices that were (and still are) important to many Gayo, including reciting verses for the benefit of the deceased.

Once they have narrowed the field of permissible ritual action to exclude certain older practices, modernists then ask: What are the conditions for worship to be effective? Here modernists refocus the question of efficacy on the worshiper's subjectivity rather than on the social conditions surrounding the event. The poems attack three specific elements of an older subjective stance toward worship: ignorance, blindly following others people's teachings, and following Gayo norms rather than religious ones. Following others people's teachings without thinking through the matter yourself is usually referred to as taqlid, a term that can otherwise be used to convey the more neutral idea that one follows established teachings, usually of a particular religious legal tradition. Sometimes the practice is attacked as taqlid buta, "blind obedience." Following established Gayo cultural norms or ëdët (Malay adat) is also incorrect in religious matters; one should instead think things out for oneself after consulting those with religious knowledge. Thinking for oneself is sometimes referred to as ijtihad, "independent legal reasoning." The poets link ignorance, blind obedience, and following ëdët as all signaling that the actor does not have the proper intent. Herein lies the link between religious reform and modernity: backwardness, ignorance, and traditions are all viewed as hindering the progress toward proper religious action.

Much of the religious poetry written in the 1930s and 1940s argues that knowledge is required for acceptable worship, since only with knowledge can one formulate the correct intent for each act of worship. The first poem in a handwritten manuscript dating from about 1950, written by the foremost poet, Tengku Mudë Kala, directly addresses this multiplex problem. The poem links the problem of "blind obedience" (and the critique of ëdët) to the absence of intent and reminds the listener that God will not accept such worship. As with all the poems, it begins with a quotation from scripture; in this case, verse 36 of Qur'an 17, which reads: "Follow not that of which you have no knowledge. The hearing and the sight and the heart: each of these will be questioned."

The first two stanzas of the poem provide a vernacular gloss of the Arabic verse, adding the explanation that what the Qur'an condemns as mere "imitation" is carrying out worship according to past practice or the dictates of so-called teachers. The poem then returns to the original gloss to effect a persuasive closure midway through the poem.

*telah berkata Allah ta'ala*
*menegah jema buët uru-uru*
*enti itunung ko sara buët*
*ikë gërë dëpët ningko ilmu*
*So spoke God the highest,*
*forbidding people to imitate.*
*Do not follow a practice*
*if you do not have the knowledge.*
*kerna penengé orum penèngon*

*ikunëi tuhën barang ngë tentu*
*demikian ku atas até*
*oyapé besé periksë mutuju*
*amal ibëdët enti menurut ëdët*
*mungikut buët si ngë telah lalu*
*tanih-temanih turun-temurun*
*kunë perbuëtën ni muyang datu*
*Because about your hearing and sight*
*God will surely enquire,*
*and similarly for your heart,*
*He will inspect it closely.*
*Religious practice, don't [carry out]*
*according to ëdët*
*following practices of by-gone days:*
*handed down, passed along,*
*however it was done by our*
*ancestors.*
*berbuët ibëdët gelah karna Allah*
*enti ërëp tung ijazah*
*ari tengku guru*
*berbuët ibëdët kë malé ibuëtën*
*dalil keterangan ikunëi*
*ku tengku*
*Practice religion solely for God,*
*not just for a diploma*
*from the honored teacher.*
*Practice religion; when ready,*
*ask for justifications*
*from a teacher.*
*enti lagu jema ikut-ikutën*
*sana ibuëtën ërëp itetiru*
*olok pedi sesat taqlid bota*
*iharapé pahla nisé delé demu*
*Don't be like those who just follow;*
*whatever is done, they just imitate it.*
*They are far astray, the blind imitators;*
*they hope to get lots of merit.*
*padahal tuhën ngë munegah*

*gërë iosah buët uru-uru*
*Yet God has forbidden;*
*has not allowed us to merely imitate.*

After further elaborations of this message, the poet then introduces a second voice, that of an uninformed Gayo person who worships in an unthinking, uncaring fashion:

*naku ngë beta iëjër awan*
*pasal ipinahan sëbër mi tengku*
*sebëb awanku pé mubaca kitëb*
*mungaji sirët munapal nahu*
*For me, grandpa taught me just so.*
*Straying [from scripture]? Don't*
*worry so much about it, teacher.*
*For grandpa also read the book,*
*recited the Prophet's life,*
*memorized Arabic.*
*tentang aku gërë asal menuntut*
*melèngkan mengikut manatni*
*awanku*
*As for me, no need to learn;*
*just follow grandpa's legacy.*
*dowa ni sembahyangku pé jadi*
*konot-konot*
*jadi singkët-singkët enti mi naru*
*The worship prayers I just keep short;*
*keep brief, never long.*
*kuatas kutuyuh kubaca Fatihah*
*ngë meta kutamah tikik ni Qul hu*
*kë iterimëë keta terimëë*
*ikë gërë pé sana kené aku*
*Up and Down, I recite the Fatihah;*
*finished, I add a bit of "Qul hu"*
*If it's accepted, then it's accepted;*
*if not, what can I say about it?*

These passages use the notion of blind obedience (taqlid buta) to link following tradition to not forming the correct intent during ritual: absence of intent signals the twinned negative characteristics of merely following others (taqlid; Gayo uru-uru) and being blind or without knowledge. The willingness to renounce past practices and detach oneself from past authority becomes the necessary condition for authentic religious practice.

The requirements of intent in worship also include attentiveness, the subject of a number of poems. Poem number 45 in Mudë Kala's 1950 collection is one of several making the further claim that those who worship without proper intent will find that their worship does not count. The poem begins with a hadith: "Be informed that God does not respond to a prayer from an inadvertent and oblivious heart." Mudë Kala then depicts the unthinking way in which many people just run through their worship, with their minds floating off elsewhere, for example, to the state of their ricefields. I give the complete poem here:

*berkata nabi Muhammad*
*munerangan ku umët*
*do'a gërë makbul*
*Said the Prophet Muhammad,*
*explaining to his people [about]*
*prayers that are not received.*
*ara-kë ibetèhko bèwèné jema*
*tentang ni do'a si gërë makul*
*Do you all know*
*about prayers that are ineffective?*
*gërë iterimë tuhën do'a ni jema*
*kedikën ara do'a iapal*
*God does not accept people's prayers*
*if prayers are learned;*
*awah berdo'al atéwé lalé*
*lagu si lengé peningëté muraul*
*gërë sunguh até muniro do'a*
*ërëp ngë ara gërë dalih betul*
*the mouth prays; the heart is lazy*
*as if it is weak; thoughts wander.*
*Besseching is not done earnestly,*
*just so that there is [a prayer],*
*it does not have to be straight.*
*kedikën até ngë mujejawans*
*biër sembahyang ngë wët kunul*

*awah mubaca até berkekirë*
*If the heart is roaming,*
*even though worship has begun.*
*The mouth is reciting, the heart*
*is figuring*
*bèwèh si rikë ngë telam-timul*
*all sorts of matters, up and down.*
*tengah ibëdët pikirné terbang*
*In the middle of worship,*
*thoughts are flying*
*lagu lelayang si gërë berkampul*
*isoné até ngë mutetayang*
*isi kin pematang ngë teridah*
*buntul*
*like a kite no longer held down.*
*So the heart is long gone:*
*"there are the hills, the knoll*
*is in view,*
*isi kin sagi méh jëjëp lengkék*
*there is the field's edge, with every*
*little row;*
*isi kin relèt ngë teridah arul*
*there is the corner, the stream's*
*come into view."*
*enta isihën tekebir isihën wajah*
*Who knows where is the takbîr*
*or the wajah;*
*enta isihën Fatiha orum atahyatul*
*who knows where is al-Fâtiha*
*or the atahyatul.*
*gërë ibetèh arti ni baca*
*He does not know the meaning*
*of what is read;*
*sana dië makna iprinné kul*
*whatever its meaning, he says*
*it's deep.*
*enta isihën ujung enta isihën raliq*
*Who knows where is the end*

*or the beginning,*
*ngë mubabalik ngë dabuh kancul*
*turning all around, becoming all*
*confused.*
*cubë itimang orum pikirën*
*mera-kë memangan ikë parang*
*tumpul*
*Try and weight it yourself;*
*does a dull knife ever bite?*

The poet then draws a sharp contrast to the intense way in which these same people would utter doa intended as spells. He draws the picture in such a way as to clarify the result people intend spells to have, without claiming either that they do have that result or that it is appropriate to say such spells:

*dup do'a kebël mera mejadi*
*Whereas an invulnerability spell*
*would work*
*karna sunguh até iopul-opul*
*because earnestly the head shakes*
*back and forth,*
*karna perasané ara berpa'èdah*
*waktu bertengkah mera wë semul*
*because it's felt to be worthwhile,*
*that when fighting, knives*
*won't cut.*
*do'a pengokop orum pegempar*
*do'a tegër orum penimul*
*tapé tekebir sawah ku salam*
*Spells to unnerve or create confusion,*
*to make tough and strong;*
*but from the takbîr all the way*
*to the salam,*
*até wé belayar ngë mugerupul*
*His heart flies and shakes.*
*ngë mari sembahyang dabuh berdo'a*
*ikecèpën mata lagu jema sugul*
*After worshiping, he sets in to pray,*
*closing the eyes like someone*

*meditating.*
*ngë mungë gernang ibubuh geritik*
*The drum has sounded, now*
*he shakes;*
*ngë lepas depik itama cangkul*
*the fish are gone, now he sets*
*the net.*
*apabilë sembahyang si mengoh n'oya*
*nabi berkata mana bisa makul*
*If worship is done in that way,*
*the Prophet said: How can it*
*be effective?*
*kitë muniro numë ku jema kucak*
*kitë bercerak orum jema kul*
*We make requests not to a little guy;*
*we speak with a big guy.*

While in the midst of worship, "from the takbîr all the way to the salam," his heart is still in his fields, but the minute worship ends and he has a chance to ask for a favor from God through petitionary prayer, he instantly becomes intensely focused on what he is doing. Not that this is proper – Mudë Kala ridicules the shaking and eye shutting to underscore the person's intensity while not making it seem as if the prayers will be effective. God is not receiving these prayers: "the fish are gone, now he sets the net."

This sort of criticism offended many Gayo, some of whom indeed knew little more Qur'an than the short verses mentioned here. But such was the intent of the poems: to shake people up, so that they would realize their errors and "come to taubid" (God's essential oneness), as one poet put it. Even the manner and vocal timbre of some modernist teachers was grating – famously so in the case of Tengku Jali, the modernist teacher who initiated public debates on ritual matters in the late 1930s and founded the leading modernist school in the Takèngën area, called Islamic Education. Even modernist-leaning Gayo men and women remember his loud manner, his shrill voice, and his punishment, generously meted out to lazy students. I knew one of his successors, Tengku Mukhlis, and found him a man of generous heart and deep religious devotion, but irritating in his unwillingness to let a matter drop and his quickness to anger when someone failed to follow what he considered to be correct religious procedure. "That is not religion!" was his frequent cry. Such direct challenges to others were (and are) quite contrary to the general Gayo tendency to avoid public confrontations or accusations and, I am convinced, were made with that sense of purposive transgression very much in mind.

The sarcasm, shrillness, and confrontational style were all, I believe, aimed at shaking up ideas taken for granted about the world, at interrupting the normal social fabric and etiquette, so that it could be replaced by something else. Gayo modernists did not seek to construct a city on a hill, but to reform the behavior of villagers and townspeople without removing them from their social context. They did so by insistently drawing them back to scripture, underlining both the Arabic source and the vernacular gloss, and on the basis of these truths assaying villagers' behavior in the religious sphere.

In its tone and specific textual links, Gayo modernist rhetoric links following scripture to throwing off the past. In this it echoes the broad thrust of Indonesianist modernist writing during the first half of the twentieth century, from the shrill blasts aimed at other religious scholars by Ahmad Hassan of the Persis movement to the novels of the religious scholar Hamka and other, principally West Sumatran, authors who celebrate the release that Islam provides from the constraints of tradition.

But traditionalist scholars have been able to reinterpret the implications of intent for ritual criticism. Indeed, they have used the modernist emphasis on intent as the basis for a counterreformation within traditionalist practice and commentary. Granted, they say, that intent determines what a practice is and thus whether or not it is acceptable. But we cannot know the intent of another, so we should not be quick to criticize the practice of another person. Here the scholars draw on a general Gayo tendency to acknowledge the possibility that intent is other than what one sees in behavior. As Tengku Ali Salwany, a noted traditionalist scholar in Takèngën, explained to me, when people hold ritual meals with special foods and incense, they may conceive of these objects as objects of devotion or they may understand them as ways of bringing people together to worship God. The only difference between the two possibilities is the (unobservable) intent of the actors. The former intent is incorrect from a religious point of view, but the latter is perfectly acceptable to God. Incense, for example, is fine if it is intended as a way of making things fragrant (Muhammad himself used it for this purpose), but not as a way of calling a person's soul or making requests to angels.

Not only has this line of reasoning enabled traditionalist scholars to defend older practices, both in private and in public meetings of the district Council of Ulama, it also enables some modernist-leaning individuals to attend controversial ritual events and interpret their own participation as consistent with their general religious principles. This possibility of multiple interpretations is facilitated by the general tendency to minimize public exegesis of rituals or to offer only the most general account of what the ritual is all about.

In the village of Isak, for example, nearly all residents attend the recitations for the dead described earlier. Sometimes no public speech is given about the ritual (other than formulaic speeches of welcome). When such speeches are given, they usually simply say that the chanting "helps the spirit of the deceased." The explanation allows each individual to figure out just how this help reaches its destination. Some think that the food eaten and the words recited travel straight to the spirit of the deceased, who enjoys their benefit. Others reject emphatically such an idea but believe that the words reach God, who then relieves the burdens on the deceased because he is pleased by the recitations. Still others participate in the recitations on the assumption that they are simply recitations for the glory of God and that it is entirely up to God, whose will is unfathomable, what he does about the deceased. Such, for example, is roughly the position held by one modernist teacher who does attend these sessions. Other modernists, however, find no possible interpretation acceptable and avoid these events. These ambiguities of exegesis allow people to resist, or at least to deflect, demands that they turn away from older ritual practices. The very focus on intent in Gayo modernist discourse may have contributed to the maintaining of liturgical pluralism within villages and neighborhoods.

## Explanations and Comparisons

My argument so far has stayed within the confines of Gayo history. I have indicated how the concept of intent has been invoked in Gayo religious debates and with what effects. I have also argued that Gayo modernists focused on narrow religious reform rather than broader societal issues at least in part because they retained a strong identification with their villages even as they became actors in a new religious sphere. The town of Takèngën became a multiethnic center for modernist thinking and thus encouraged both the development of a transethnic formulation of religious concerns and early alliances with nationalism. Yet because Gayo reformers continued to be deeply involved in village affairs, they focused on transforming village religious life. This set of social commitments led them to carve out a distinct religious sphere for reform, and this sphere defined the limits of public debate.

This line of argument emphasizes the role of social ties in channeling religious reform strategies in one direction rather than another. An alternative, ultimately complementary line of reasoning would have begun from cultural features rather than social relations. I might have argued as follows: Gayo generally emphasize the power of internal, unobservable events, and so a reformist emphasis on the problem of intent enjoyed a good cultural fit. Gayo practices of healing and sorcery, for example, rest on the possibility of effecting bodily transformations entirely through powerful depictive imagination, with no public activity. This intensely private sort of healing contrasts with very public practices found elsewhere in the region; the theories behind it ensure that one cannot reach any conclusions about someone's activities from his or her observable characteristics or actions.

These social or cultural arguments ought to lead me (and all other analysts of such things) to make comparisons with other cases. In saying that Gayo did such and such because of certain social or cultural features, I am also, at least implicitly, stating that in the absence of those features things would have gone otherwise. Cultural arguments, for example, require us to consider the ways that other cultural frameworks might have shaped religious discourse. For example, the Gayo cultural view contrasts with that described for Morocco by Lawrence Rosen, in which one can read from social characteristics of persons to the attendant mental states. The Moroccan view asserts that persons have essential differences in their mental characteristics, depending on such critical social differences as gender and place of origin. Where Gayo culture emphasizes practices and allows for a great deal of circumstantial variability and contingency in intent, Moroccan culture emphasizes the social construction of persons and a lesser degree of variability. Consistent with this difference is the importance of gender-based contrasts of (male) reason versus (female) passion in Moroccan religious discourse vis-à-vis the virtual absence of such contrasts in Gayo discourse.

This sort of comparison – in which different cultural patterns explain, by contextualizing, different religious histories – is that usually followed in cultural accounts. For the study of Islam the best known of such patterncomparisons is Clifford Geertz' Islam Observed, which, however right or wrong it might be, set out a cultural contrast in style and focus between North African and Javanese ways of being Muslims.

My starting point has, however, been less the styles and patterns characteristic of a society or region than the particular intentions, strategies, and rhetoric of actors, the issues they chose to emphasize, and the ways they formulated and expressed their ideas so as to influence various audiences. Comparisons might, then, emphasize differences in projects and strategies. Such comparisons could be broad in scope, as when William Roff depicts the contrasting ways that movements adapted "Wahhabi" ideas to particular circumstances in the nineteenth century. But one can also look at controlled comparisons, where microvariation in social conditions, conversion strategies, and cultural forms emerge within a more specific region. I can only suggest the lines of such a comparative analysis here, working outward from the Gayo case to that of lowland Aceh (and suggesting a potential contrast with the earlier reformist struggles in West Sumatra). When more fully fleshed out, such comparisons may illuminate both the highly differentiated projects of modernist persuasion and the relations among social structures, religious change, and cultural forms.

The contrast with Aceh is particularly telling for the frequent cultural contacts between the two peoples, especially in religious affairs, and the development in both societies of a modernist Islamic consciousness in the 1920s and 1930s. The social context for religious modernism in lowland, northern Aceh differed from that in the highlands in two major ways. First, the context was all-Acehnese. The most important organization was not the pan-Indonesian

Muhammadiyah but the Aceh-specific association of religious teachers called PUSA (Persatuan Ulama Seluruh Aceh), AllAceh Association of Religious Scholars, led by a future governor of Aceh, Daud Beureueh. Modernist imaginings thus primarily concerned a new Aceh rather than Aceh's place in a new Indonesia.

Second, modernists developed their social critique in terms of the opposition of village life and the world beyond, the rantau. "They appealed to men to act not as villagers but as Muslims; to the ulama, this meant forgetting traditional social identities". This opposition was also strongly linked to oppositions of gender and religious values. Most Acehnese men spent years away from their village at study or work, in allmale settings. Women, by contrast, were at the center of village life, remaining in their natal villages after marriage, receiving houses from their fathers, and managing ricefields. Men felt they were treated as children by their wives when at home; the high divorce rates of the area followed from these tensions. Male religious spokesmen identified women with emotions and desires, hawa nafsu, which the properly religious (male) individual must transcend through the strengthening of reason, aqal. Men could best develop reason and control passions away from the village, on the rantau.

The Acehnese social fabric in which modernism developed was thus one of a male/female opposition within an ethnically specific framework. Acehnese modernists sought to transcend village life rather than, as in the Gayo highlands, reforming it. They did so in the idiom of struggle: for selfmastery through worship and for economic success through individual labor, both in some sense a continuation of the earlier struggle against the Dutch through war. These struggles involved individuals, joined in "mechanical solidarity." A powerful image of the properly religious society was found in congregational worship, where all Acehnese worshiped side by side and in precisely the same way. The social and political importance of this image led provincial leaders to feel particularly threatened by particularistic, inward-looking, local forms of worship.

The earlier struggles as conceptualized by ulama were embodied in the poetry of holy war. The epic of the Acehnese war, the Hikayat Prang Sabi (Story of the Holy War), relates the journey from this world to the next. Arabic scripture also appears here, and, as in Gayo poetry, it is foregrounded against the background metrical scheme. Here, too, scripture has an "unvarying message" to convey. But scripture serves not as a source of correction for wayward villagers, as in highlands verse, but as a source of promise, of the reward that awaits the fighter in paradise.

From the 1930s on, Acehnese religious forms looked at the possibility for creating a new society on earth rather than in paradise. These new forms of religious persuasion include sermons and newspaper articles. They emphasize not the reform of village life in a strictly demarcated religious sphere, but the building of a new society on socioreligious principles. If Gayo modernists stress the boundary of religion and the rest of society, their Acehnese counterparts emphasize "the idea of society as a manifestation of ibadah (religious duty)". Acehnese modernist writings point to the tone that worship gives to all of life, not the reform of specific acts (as in the Gayo poetry). They portray Aceh as a once and future glorious nation, in which struggle strengthens reason and reason orders men in their actions.

The tone of the earlier poetry and the later sermons and articles is redemptive, future-looking. These forms take men out of their current social surrounds and turn them toward a future promised society. The dominant metaphor is an awakening from sleep, not the interruption of current social practices. And it is a message that is directed at men, not women. Thus Gayo modernists urge their fellow men and women to transcend ethnic identity in favor of a scripture-based life in their village surrounds; Acehnese modernists urge their fellow men to transcend village identity in favor of an ideal Acehnese unity of supralocal male individuals.

A third, geographically close contrast is in Minangkabau society, where men have lived on the margins of the village, rather than fully in it, as in Gayo, or apart from it, as in Aceh. Christine Dobbin has shown how, in the early nineteenth century, the combination of a growth in coffee cropping and a new, highly reformist Muslim ideology led to sharp attacks on village practices by these marginal men and to attempts to establish new, purified communities. In the early twentieth century, modernist teachers created distinct school communities in greater tension with the villages than was the case in Aceh. One might argue that these marginal schools continued the social heritage of the earlier reformist movement, in contrast to Acehnese ideals of total separation and Gayo direct involvement in village reform.

These brief remarks point toward an ethnological, comparative study of religious modernisms that would underscore the local particulars of putatively universalistic projects. It also might lay the groundwork for a general framework of comparison. For one can discern other emphases in Gayo modernism that, given different social conditions, could emerge as dominant and that indeed in other parts of the world have become the dominant form of modernist intervention. Let me suggest three specific associations between social situations and religious emphases:

First, certain struggles revolve around efforts by a reforming group to distinguish itself from others, either from other religious streams within Islam or from other groups in a broader, non-Islamic cultural framework. In such cases Muslims may emphasize public self-definition, especially through congregational worship but also, potentially, through fasting, the keeping of rules regarding purity, and so forth. An early phase of Gayo modernism was, indeed, characterized by reformers' concern with establishing separate mosques as signs of their distinction from the older tradition. Muslims in similar situations in West Africa and China have played up worship or ritual purity as markers of social (including ethnic) distinction.

Second, other reformers place at the forefront the struggle against preexisting socioreligious hierarchies and thus underscore the egalitarian (and possibly also the latitudinarian) messages of "scripturalism." In such cases, such as the South Asian movements studied by Barbara Metcalf, one would expect to find an emphasis on tafsir (interpretation) and ijtihad (independent reflection) and the antielite values they can be seen as promoting. And, in those Gayo places where traditional rulers sought to suppress modernist teachers, it was indeed the right to appeal directly to scripture that was stressed; this emphasis was absent in those places where such teachers obtained rulers' backing or achieved power themselves. The specific effects of colonial rule must be factored into these accounts: for example, British and Dutch colonial suppression of social reform discourse may have pushed reformists to emphasize the reform of individual religious practice.

Finally, with the Gayo/Aceh and Gayo/ Morocco contrasts in mind, one might expect that broad differences in the cultural construction of personhood would shape religious reform movements and that, in particular, a strong male-female ideological contrast might support movements for the wholesale reworking of society (in order to change individuals) rather than the reform of specific liturgical practices.

## Why Emphasize Diversity?

I have argued that comparing religious histories allows us to study specific ideas, practices, and strategies in a way that avoids two common reductionisms: the normative essentialism that reduces religious phenomena to the elements that fit the Great Tradition and the ethnographic particularism that reduces them to the elements that fit the local cultural logic. Both kinds of reductionism continue to plague the study of Islam and other "world religions"; both are understandable outgrowths of disciplinary training. Textually trained historians of religion find it natural to look for text-based similarities across societies, while field-trained anthropologists find it equally natural to highlight the differential patterning of religious cultures.

Neither approach, taken by itself, can make much sense of movements — religious or otherwise — that appeal to members of diverse societies precisely because of their rhetorics of transcending cultural differences. Rather, because such movements themselves strategically incorporate both local and translocal ideas, so should their analyses. Comparisons involve, or should involve, paying attention to the multiple social levels at which religious phenomena exist: from norms and practices found in nearly all Muslim societies (worshiping, even if the forms vary, or avoiding pork, even if not all comply), through the texts and histories that characterize regions, to the ways specific individuals and groups select from the broader-scale phenomena those that fit their own ideas, intentions, and interests.Keeping these levels distinct and tracing the myriad choices and reasons of distinct groups of Muslims will, I trust, make difficult the labeling and lumping of movements that appears to characterize current popular studies of religious movements and especially studies of so-called fundamentalisms. The problem is not just the social-scientific one, that this labeling obscures much more than it discloses about Muslim and other reform movements. The problem is also political and moral, because, as I think most of us would admit, the more we can consider others to partake of an undifferentiated Other (whether communism, terrorism, or Islâm), the less we feel obliged to treat them as morally equivalent to ourselves. We, of course, are composed of complex, intersecting motives; they do everything out of their singular Otherness.It thus becomes especially incumbent upon those of us who write about current Others to stress their particularity of ideas, their complexity of motives, and their general humanity. And herein lies a possible contribution of comparative studies, even studies of small and far-off places, to social life. It only makes sense if there is some relationship between social science writing and political acting, if the more particularity that bleeds through portraits of current political Others, the greater the humanity that will surface in foreign (or domestic) policy. This hope may be naive, but it has the advantage of being hope.

# 9

# Islam in Southeast Asia

## Introduction

We look for "Islam" in the late twentieth century, one arena of central importance turns out to be the institutions of the nation-state. The meaning of being "Muslim" in that sense, as the marker of a citizen or of a politicized ethnic group, is profoundly new. And just as many of the specifics of the debates described in this volume are much the same as those conducted by Muslims elsewhere, the kinds of issues engaged in these debates are ones shared by modern societies everywhere.

This argument stands in marked contrast to what is perhaps the characteristic Western interpretation of Islam in public life. That interpretation insists above all on quintessential difference and continuity, failing to recognize what is new in the meaning and deployment of Islamic symbols and failing to recognize what is shared. In that regard, Dale Eickelman's argument recognizing the modernity of the very concept of "the Islamic state" is particularly important. Europeans and Americans on the whole have a blind spot in relation to Islam and tend to posit it as a retrograde, oppressive, and anarchic threat. The essays in this volume belie that interpretation and, far from suggesting that Southeast Asia is unique ("not really Muslim"), should encourage us to rethink our approach to Islamic societies overall.

In the American case, a distorted view of Islam continues to be a serious handicap to a rational Middle Eastern policy. Nor is this interpretation only Western: there are Indians who justify the virulent anti-Muslim behavior in their country in terms of the great danger of worldwide Islamic "fundamentalism" from Israel to India itself. The essays in this volume provide lines of analysis that challenge the interpretation of a frightening, monolithic Islam, ones that are relevant to Muslim societies generally, not only to Southeast Asia. They encourage us to ask two sets of questions: How and in what settings is an Islamic language deployed? And is "Islam" in fact different from other historic religious traditions?

At first blush, the chapters seem to fit into the narrative of Islamic power and difference, many structured around themes of Islamic "resurgence," "reactualization," "renewal," and so forth. In each of the countries studied, the Philippines, Malaysia, and Indonesia — whether the Muslim population is 5 percent, 52 percent, or 90 percent of the whole — the story in the last two decades seems broadly the same. In each case, states or provinces have increasingly supported Islamic programs in such arenas as law and economics; individuals increasingly demonstrate public behavior marked as Islamic in behavior and dress; and Islamic organizations directed to politics, social welfare, and preaching seem to proliferate. One might well conclude that these changes demonstrate an Islamic identity and power long waiting to emerge. But by examining these changes in detail we learn, on the one hand, of the historical shallowness of politicized Islamic communities and, on the other, of the complexity and, indeed, often the familiarity of the social and ideological projects — not reducible to state terrorism or "jihad" — in which Islamic symbols find expression.

## Narrating Histories

Nothing makes clearer the power of the historical myths that shape political loyalties than the fact that they are taken as natural and prima facie factual. Histories are at the core of nation-state identities and form a major strand in constructing, sustaining, and contesting those identities. Benedict Anderson has pointed to the essential irony in these stories: they are new in modern times but they must be told as if they were very old. In these stories a religion may even be equated with citizenship itself.

To cite a comparative case, India is particularly striking in the extent to which a historical myth, its fundamental lines evolved during the colonial period, has come to the fore in public life. In that story, part of virtually everyone's "common sense," "Muslims" and "Hindus" are taken as the significant markers of identity throughout the long period of the past thousand or so years. "Muslims" are "foreigners," who "penetrate" and "invade," and their monuments are deemed an extrusion symbolizing the shame of invasion. Forgotten are the pluralism and fuzziness of earlier societies, the shifting boundaries of cultural regions that render problematic notions like "foreign," the presence of Muslims in the subcontinent from roughly the same period as other migrants/invaders from what is now outside India, the shifting alliances defined not by religion but by interest, and the intermarriage and conversion that make it impossible to equate genes and culture. The British first told the story of two communities and foreign invasion as they constructed a history of "India" and justified their place in it; nationalists in turn utilized the story to explain cultural decline and to claim nationhood.

History has since become a basis for political argumentation on moral grounds by making "original" occupation (already problematic, as noted above) a justification for entitlements and rights. Against this basis, other arguments that ignore this "history" — current legal claims, the social good, justice, archeological conservation — have little play. The story ceased to be abstract on December 6, 1992, when Hindu nationalists destroyed the sixteenth-century mosque at Ayodhya and justified their action, and even the anti-Muslim violence that followed, as necessary to restore the pristine cultural shape of the nation as a whole.

In Southeast Asia, particularly in Malaya and the Philippines, colonizers and colonized have told similar stories in which "Muslims" as a historically continuous community have played a part. The chapters on the Philippines richly illustrate the modernity, "inventedness," and utility to ethnic and national projects of this kind of linear narrative. Thomas McKenna convincingly argues that the notion of a coherent Muslim identity, forged in religious wars with Spain, contravenes substantial evidence of long periods of peace, of the lack of an ulama class ranged against the Spanish, and of intersultanate rivalry that meant frequent alliances on the part of the sultanates with Spain. Instead, the colonial power, in this case the United States, saw a coherent "Moro" identity — assumed on Orientalist grounds to be of necessity embryonic and only needing encouragement — as a fundamental fact of Filipino history and sought to use it as the foundation for democratic participation.

It is modern education and the opportunities of modern politics, not atavistic religious antagonism, that forge a Muslim identity, at least among certain elites, in the colonial and postcolonial state. Despite an officially secular school policy, we hear of Carpenter wanting to educate Muslims "in the positive aspects" of their religion and Kuder again pushing education and links to cultural artifacts like the Arabian Nights so that students in colleges come to see themselves as "Mohammedan Filipinos." Boundaries are drawn to create an area with "Moro" courts and a Moro municipality. With independence, Muslim leaders focus on "rationalized emblems of a single Muslim ethnic identity," as McKenna puts it, as a way to project Muslim power; and, whether as politicians or as rebels, they deploy the heretofore pejorative Spanish label "Moro," a label Patricia Horvatich (n.d.) shows to be largely irrelevant to ordinary Muslims in everyday life.

Thus Muslim politicians and civil servants and, after 1972, rival elites give legitimacy to their claims for political clout or autonomy by reading back into history a solidarity only now, haltingly, having any meaning at all. Even today, according to Horvatich (n.d.), a Maranao, a fellow Muslim Filipino, is as foreign and frightening to a Sama as is a Christian Filipino. Sama depend on the Filipino state to protect their interests against the longdominant Muslim Tausug. Yet Muslim politicians claim a primordial, essential Muslim nation, even as they contend with the claims of Filipino nationalists who counter with an equally primordial, pre-Christian and pre-Muslim, identity that they call on "backward" Muslims to embrace.

Although only alluded to in the essays in this volume, Malay history bears much the same burden of reified communities and the moral claims of presumed prior residence of Malays, in contrast to putative immigrants, who bear the further taint of colonial association. "Malays" are homogenized and elevated to privilege by their status as "sons of the soil." A Sumatran who arrived yesterday achieves that distinction. A Chinese whose ancestors came five hundred years back is a mere migrant.

These narratives set the framework for defining the nations in which Islamic symbols, institutions, and communities have become so significant. Even in Indonesia, whose national myths typically allowed for more pluralism, an Islamic discourse and Islamic programs have in the past two decades increasingly come to the fore.

## National Politics

In each of these settings, underpinned to varying degrees by historical stories of primordial community, there has been a move from "vertical" identifications as subjects of patrons and notables to "horizontal" ethnoreligious community. Roy Ellen, speaking of Malaya, called precolonial Islam an "idiomatic convenience" deployed, for example, in festivals used to reaffirm loyalty to chiefs. In the Indian case, the Mughal Empire, far from being an "Islamic state," operated like other early modern polities on the fundamentally secular basis of loyalty. Only if a non-Muslim went into opposition would he be signaled as a kafir; and Muslim as well as non-Muslim opponents in warfare would be subject to jihad.

The settings conducive to moving from this kind of sociopolitical organization to a pattern of religiously defined community identity are those of modernity: the colonial state, the nationalist movements, the ethnic competition characteristic of interest competition in nation-states with limited resources, and the cultural bonds forged in transnational flows of education, travel, personnel, and resources. Although some chapters in this volume treat the deeply important colonial context as laying the foundation for the new religious communities, most focus on the frameworks offered by the contemporary states that provide a context and even support for the new ethnicities.

That these Islamic movements and identities flourish in modern social contexts is suggested by the importance of educational centers, including international centers, for fostering a self-conscious Islamic religious style. It is in colleges in the Philippines that young men come to think of themselves as Muslim Filipinos. Nur Misuari got his start through a university scholarship, and the public school supervisor, Haji Hussein, spread the teaching of the

Ahmadiyya movement to receptive teachers in Tawi-Tawi. It is at al-Āzhar, in the 1960s and after, that a new Filipino clerical class is forged with a vision of Islamic reform. In Malaysia, higher education not only provides the context in which modern Muslim identity is forged, but, as Shamsul A. B. shows, the academic discipline pursued actually influences individuals' response (moderate or radical) to the dakwah movement. The dominant figures in Islamic intellectual circles in Indonesia all seem to have U.S. advanced degrees. Beyond travel for education, we hear of travel for work to Sabah and the Middle East, and travel for pilgrimage and business. While the setting for Islamic reform and ethnicization is the nation-state, what happens in the nation-state is profoundly influenced by what happens outside its borders.

As significant as the newness of these communities is the fact that the bonds may be as much ethnic as Islamic. Here too the Philippines serves as a useful example, since the "Moro" rebellion was initially driven by a nationalist/regional program, not an Islamic program, at the elite level and by bonds of kin and community at an individual level. Outsiders may often impute a religious program — the genesis of Pakistan is a good example - when in fact goals are primarily the political interests of those who happen to be Muslim.

All three states, Malaysia, the Philippines, and Indonesia, have seen their interests bound up in patronizing and controlling expressions of Islam. Malaysia, as Clive Kessler has argued, may be "secular" at the federal level, but it contains a system where provinces may well be engaged in religious activities, and, at the central level as well, there have been recent initiatives in support of an Islamic university, Islamic economics, Islamic courts, and a civil law that "implicates" shari'ah at the expense of a shared "life world" for all Malaysians. In the Philippines a 1976 settlement brought federal support for Muslim personal law, Islamic banking, and even a mosque built by patronage from Marcos himself. In Indonesia, after what appeared to be suppression of Islamic symbols in the first decade of the New Order, there have now been a range of initiatives supporting Islamic practices, restricting Christian missionaries, building mosques and madrasahs, and identifying state officials with voluntary Islamic organizations.

There has been in each state a kind of homogenizing of what is defined as Islamic, rather like what Romila Thapar has spoken of as "syndicated Hinduism" in the Indian case. In both cases, the "flattening" of local and sectarian differences is intimately linked to the project of forging a national culture. In this respect, the quotation from Wilkinson that Michael Peletz cites – "The native...is becoming less of a Malay and more of a Mussulman...his racial laws are being set aside.... His allegiance is being gradually transferred from national to Pan-Islamic ideals" – is, in fact, quite wrong, for the process has turned out to be the invention of the Malay "Mussulman" race as metonym precisely for the nation.

An Islamic discourse has come to dominate public space so that resistance, as Peletz argues for Malaysia, becomes the morally ambiguous resistance to Islam itself. In this Malaysia would appear to resemble Pakistan in the period inaugurated by Zia ul Haq in 1977, when all participants in public life had to embrace an Islamic vocabulary lest they be charged with opposing Islam. In the cases described by Peletz, it would appear that people come to associate Islam with state control, tainted by U.S. government support, intruding into intimate dimensions of individual lives, including family law, surveys of economic transactions, limits on women's dress, imposition of corporal punishment, and restrictions on local customs. Martin Rössler's village-level study in Indonesia seems much the same: villagers empty the mosque when an official enjoins Ramadan attendance, and everyone resists turning over the îd al-fitr offerings to officials. Islamic movements, like Nahdlatul Ulama in Indonesia, that disassociate themselves from formal participation in government thus remove themselves from association with distasteful state control.

A corollary to state use and "syndication" of Islam would appear to be the traditionalizing and encapsulating of local cultural forms. Wayang produced in hotels and theaters, described as the embodiment of "tradition," or, in Whalley's example, Minang clothes regarded as "ethnic dress" worn on special occasions, are no longer culturally central except as a necessary foil to "modernity," here in the form of "Islamic modernity."

In the case of Indonesia, it would appear that the withdrawal of organizations from active politics or the creation of new organizations with "constructive" rather than political programs has made it possible for Islamic activities and ideologies to flourish without the taint though the tension is always there — of undue association with the state, its at least potential oppression, and its apparently inevitable corruption. Andrée Feillard argues that by this disassociation with politics since 1984, Nahdlatul Ulama has gained considerable legitimacy, proliferating organizations for women and youth, serving as a moral force to shape government policy, and stimulating Islamic change at the local level ("more mosques, fewer dogs"). Robert Hefner similarly charts the influence of ICMI, the new Association of Indonesian Muslim Intellectuals, which declares itself apart from politics even while involving government figures in the quest to capture the moral imagination of the urban middle class living in a context of rapid economic change and polarization and the spread of consumer culture. It is in the context of this activity that the Indonesian state, whatever its Pancasila rhetoric, has successfully identified itself with a range of Islamic symbols and institutions.

If these Muslim communities are new, so too are the other identities, national and local, with which they interact. Patricia Horvatich has underlined how being Sama must not be understood to be the old, primal identity but is itself the result of active fostering — drawing boundaries, writing books, staging performance, creating university study programs — in the context of economic and political rivalries within the nation-state. The contested statement "I was a Malay before I was a Muslim," described by Kessler, recalls another widely quoted statement by a Pakistani politician, "I am a six thousand years old Pushtoon a thousand year old Musalman, and a twenty-seven year old Pakistani." The truth is that, as markers of politicized communities, all these terms are equally new.

## Moral Communities

Both the activist movements and the nation-states they operate in are engaged in defining the principles of behavior, law, and morality that guide everyday life. Overall there has been an increasing utilization of Islamic idioms within the institutional structure of the nation-states coupled with a transition within the society to more self-conscious scrutiny of what are taken to be normative Islamic practices.

In part this transition is linked to greater mobility and sociopolitical integration within a society as a whole. Put simply, there are a range of practices engaged in uncritically that serve to structure rural society: patterns of feasting and reciprocity that define social relations among the living and the dead. These practices are "Muslim" in that Muslims engage in them and may, in an unsystematic, even unself-conscious way, see them as conducive to sustaining the moral community. In contrast are a range of practices that are anything but unself-conscious: they are measured against rationalized principles of what is taken to be "Islam" properly understood. Those who identify with these "reformist" principles may often be people engaged in larger social arenas. In John Bowen's Gayo setting, those who espoused these principles as early as the 1930s typically were engaged in commerce, lived in multiethnic settings, and were fluent in the language that was coming to be called "Indonesian." Both systems can be seen as underpinned by values, even Muslim values. Both offer status and prestige in one setting but not the other.

The new values were defended, in a characteristically Islamic style but not by a defense of "Islam" as such – that comes later. Rather, arguments were conducted at a more fine-grained level. Thus, to take John Bowen's issue of ushalli, the objection might be that "it is against the shari'ah to make requisite that which is optional." The objection to feasting or wayang might be "it is against the shari'ah to waste money," "to go into debt unnecessarily," "to create a venue where men and women mix inappropriately," "to absorb people in activities that distract them from required worship," and so forth. This goal of such critical weighing, in which the issue of acting always out of good intent (ikhlas) and obedience, and not out of self-interest in any sense, including the pursuit of a good reputation based on following old customs, is to foster a religion of individual responsibility and "portability" delinked from local bonds of time, place, and ritual specialists. This process and the modes of argumentation are ones that cut across Muslim societies.

Muslim religious styles may seem to vary infinitely, but there are shared languages, institutions, and approaches that some members of societies may share across wide geographical boundaries at any given time. This style of shari'ah-based reasoning is certainly one, and may not be as specific to Gayo, for example, as it seems. Thus, the Fatiha for the dead, with accompanying food, in the Indic context is subject to much the range of interpretation as death ceremonies in Gayo. Critics will insist that it is an attempt to reach the dead, to bring them their favorite foods, or, in the case of powerful figures, an effort to win their goodwill and intervention in worldly needs, all this in ways that risk the worship owed to God alone. Those committed to the practice might insist on normatively acceptable arguments: that the Fatiha merely seeks intercession with God who is alone powerful or that it is the recitation of sacred texts whose merit accrues only to the reciter, and so forth. In the course of contention, the meaning and moral underpinnings of customary practices also change.

The issue of the salience of social context for different religious values is nicely illustrated in Martin Rössler's vignette of the funeral of the sister of Banci, the former traditional priest who by 1991 had become involved in the "new Islam," which the local imam insisted was inappropriate in the village and belonged in the towns. Banci, it turned out, had been influenced by his own town-based brother, and, while he managed to conduct the funeral as he wished, other relatives, for whom such behavior threatened their values and networks, performed the traditional rituals secretly. Adherence to normative practices can also be a route to social mobility when those practices are associated with the pious and the well-born. Correct practice distinguishes one from peasants. We may well use Bowen's Weberian language of "elective affinity" of certain social realities for certain religious styles.

"Reformist modernism," again to use Bowen's term, may also distinguish one from the cosmopolitan, or secular, or Westernized elites, a fault line illustrated in Whalley's discussion of Minangkabau. In Indonesia, as described by Hefner, a goal of the Islamically oriented has been to "convert" the secular Javanese elites. Educated professional women can distinguish themselves from such suspect values in part by their dress. This has also been true in Pakistan, where a particular target of the Islamists has been the Westernized women who are seen as a threat to all society.

The focus of much moral argument, in both Southeast Asia and the Subcontinent, has, in fact, been issues of gender. Control of women's behavior and restrictions on women's dress have become centrally important public symbols of an Islamic society. Whalley has described the choices of dress styles available to urban, educated women, especially unmarried women, as they seek to manage a public image of themselves as both modern and moral. On the whole deeply concerned with sustaining the status of their natal lineage, they now do so not in the old way of marrying appropriately, but in a new way by behaving and dressing in a morally acceptable style while earning an independent livelihood. Whalley, citing Errington, underlines that elaboration of female difference through dress is a recent development in Southeast Asia in contrast to an emphasis on distinction by class.

Bowen's study of reform in Gayo, like my own of Deoband in India, finds – surprisingly, given our stereotypes about Islam and women – that women and men are conceptualized as essentially identical, open to the same kind of teaching, responsible for the same kind of behavior. The elaboration of female difference, both bodily (undergirded with Western pseudoscience on subjects like menstruation) and moral, attributing to women the heretofore unknown quality of innate spirituality, comes with the more political movements of the twentieth century, like that in the Subcontinent led by Maududi. In Gayo, women were apparently not only invited to participate in the reformist religious style, but were themselves among the poets who spread the teachings. In Minangkabau, as early as the 1920s women were being trained to be good Muslims and civil servants and professionals: it is the Indonesian state that now wants to narrow the scope of women's activities primarily to the home. Even so, in Indonesia today women are active and well known among public preachers and preach not only to other women but to mixed audiences. The contemporary attention to distinctive women's roles is not "traditional" but embedded in the construction of national states.

## Nature of Islamic Difference

This brief review of some of the themes in this wide-ranging collection of essays may suggest some points to counter the kinds of assumptions that are so widespread in our society. First, the fact of "horizontal" Muslim solidarities, of "ethnic" or "nationalist" Islam, is as modern as the nationstates in which Muslims are embedded. Muslim communities, above all communities motivated by ideological programs, are not age-old. If many Muslims today talk of the distinctiveness of Islam as a "complete way of life," we must recognize that as one contemporary trope and then take account of the multiplicity of Islamic positions that range from those who envisage utopian communities to those who insist that to sacralize the state is shirk. Christianity is no more uniformly committed to a separation of religion and politics than Islam is to a single religious order. What is more totalistic than the Puritan fathers, the Spanish inquisition, or the pre-Emancipation British exclusions?

Second, the public use of Islamic symbols and the forging of Islamic solidarities are often part of profoundly modern projects shared across nations. We have seen in the Philippine case the extent to which Muslim solidarities are used as a basis for participation in the modern state, much as other ethnic solidarities are elsewhere. The Moro Islamic Liberation Front uses the language of democratic egalitarianism in opposing the datus: "good people with good minds have had little chance for success" — this resonates more with America as a land of opportunity than with the Qur'an. The datu answer similarly reflects a liberal democratic view, in this case directed to the separation of religion and politics: "if the ulama form the political leadership, there will be no one to preach. We do not want to create ayatollahs." Islam provides a language for political participation and competition.

It also provides a language for debating values in public life and for defining the respective authority of individuals, civil society, and the state. Even without invoking Harvey Cox, the ICMI vision of individual personal ethical cultivation and the espousal of issues like "human rights" bespeak cosmopolitan moral values and would be at home with other movements challenging states and societies dominated by corruption and consumerism everywhere. An ICMI leader like Nurcholish Madjid is part of a transnational conversation, engaged in in the United States by intellectuals like Robert Bellah, who seek to foster the institutions of civil society as the locus of transcendent values and commitments that in turn influence the state. Robert Hefner suggests that Indonesia provides "an alternative ideology of what the nation should become" for those who expect secularism inevitably to triumph. But Islamic movements like this one in Indonesia are also an "alternative" to those who identify Muslim movements only with reaction and terror. It matters that these societies are Muslim above all because of the awareness and links they have with each other. But it is, in the end, the participation in patterns common with other cultural, religious, and nationalist groups, not their specificity, that comes out most clearly in this collection. Bowen, with his interest in whether there are universal forms of the modern person; Hefner, exploring the nature of Indonesian civil society; and the authors of all these essays invite us to make the kinds of investigations of contemporary Islamic movements and styles that can profitably be compared with other, non-Muslim societies. The very process of doing that, in contrast to the stereotyping and demonizing of Islam that is so widespread, will illuminate our study of Southeast Asian societies as well as of other societies, including our own, engaged with common problems of social change and pluralism.

# 10

# Islamic Movement in Philippines

## Introduction

The primary participants in the debate were the Moro National Liberation Front (MNLF)--a militant separatist movement officially recognized as representative of Philippine Muslims by the Islamic Foreign Ministers' Conference--and the Marcos government, which denied the MNLF's representativeness and opposed its assumptions and goals. This study attempts to describe the positions taken by the participants during two periods: (1) the years from 1972 through 1976 when the MNLF successfully challenged existing government structures and policies and negotiated a tentative agreement outlining the institutions for its own agenda and (2) the years from 1977 to approximately 1984 when the government "implemented" the tentative agreement in ways that institutionalized its dominance.

Because the debate included divergent interpretations of history and of the current status of Philippine Muslims, it is difficult to describe its context without using information that is itself controversial. Hence, in this study, where assumptions are presented, they describe the perspectives on history and current status held by Muslims and the Marcos government, respectively.

These assumptions, in turn, shaped the goals and tactics of the protagonists and must be evaluated in assessing their successes and failures.

Some basic information can, however, be stated at the outset. Islam came to the islands that now constitute the Republic of the Philippines in the fourteenth century; by the time the Spaniards arrived in the sixteenth century, Islam had affected socioeconomic and political structures in the southern islands and was spreading northward. Because the Muslim sultanates in the south were better organized than the more localized structures in the north, the Muslims were successful in staving off Spanish conquest and, hence, Christianization. The Spaniards, however, persisted in their effort to subjugate the sultanates, with help from Filipino converts.

Weakened by centuries of warfare, the Muslims finally succumbed to the Americans' superior military strength. The Americans then attempted to consolidate control over the Muslim region in the south and integrate it into the governmental system of the Philippines. After independence in 1946, integration continued (at least superficially). Muslim politicians participated in government processes; Muslim students attended government-provided schools in both the south and the north; Christians, with government encouragement, migrated south to Muslim areas.

Meanwhile, most Muslims remained divided among themselves and alienated from Christian Filipinos. The most obvious division among Muslims was linguistic, but language differences were reinforced by differences in territorial identifications, economic activities, social and political structures, art forms, and hierarchies of values. On these bases, thirteen different Muslim groups were identified, though four predominated: in Mindanao, the Maguindanaon of the Cotabato region and the Maranao-Ilanun of the Lanao region; in Sulu, the Tausug and the Samal. Internally, these groups were further divided by clans and by status within clans.

Although the Islamic resurgence increased Muslim consciousness in ways that to some extent transcended the traditional identifications among Muslims, it and other factors--primarily the political and economic consequences of migration--exacerbated relations between Muslims and Christians. These developments, moreover, coincided with a general deterioration in the capabilities of Philippine political structures to meet the demands of the entire population. Thus the stage was set for the emergence of a protest movement among Muslims; particular circumstances determined the timing of its emergence and the nature of its leadership.

## Moro National Liberation Front

The MNLF dates its beginning from a massacre that occurred on Corregidor island in 1968. Here is the account given by MNLF Chairman Nur Misuari on the fifteenth anniversary of the massacre:

> *That event occurred on the black night of 18th of March 1968. Over twohundred of our innocent youths, mostly unlettered ones, were lured into a clandestine politico-military organization known as "Operation Merdeka" and its military arm "the Jabidah" with the sinister intention of infiltrating the brotherly state of Sabah so as to create internal commotion preparatory to the launching of full-scale military invasion by the armed forces of the Philippines for the seizure of the territory from Malaysian rule. Two naval boats with some helicopters were readied at Corregidor island to be used to transport the supposed saboteurs to Sabah.*

This evil scheme, however, boomeranged against Marcos and his regime owing to the cold-blooded execution of our brothers who, upon knowing the ulterior motives behind their highly secretive recruitment and training, refused to embark on their mission. They demanded their enlistment papers into the armed forces of the Philippines as promised and their monthly pay or salary as well. The Chief of the Operation Major Eduardo Martelino, reportedly tried to sort out those demands, particularly the matter of payment of salary, but to give in to the demand for official enlistment was contrary to the credo of the Operation, for obvious reasons.

So tense and explosive the outlook had became so much so that Marcos, the blood-thirsty evil-incarnate, summarily ordered that all evidences of the sinister plan be suppressed and destroyed, with the obvious implication that all those who had potential to expose the treacherous scheme be done away with.

But Allah in His infinite wisdom did not allow the criminals to pursue their conspiracy successfully. And so one wounded survivor, after going through the ordeal of floating in a driftwood for several hours in the shark-infested channel of Corregidor, following his miraculous escape from the scene of the execution, was rescued from the sea by some fishermen and the lid of secrecy imposed on the invasion plan was exposed most glaringly to the peoples of world.

And in the ensuing crisis and the series of demonstrations by the youths from various parts of our homeland, the MNLF and the Bangsamoro Revolution came to life, rising as it were from the womb of our colonial society. With the birth of the MNLF and the Bangsamoro Revolution, the decision to form the Bangsamoro Republik, as an independent and sovereign political entity, distinct and separate from the nations of the world including the Philippines, was unanimously reached.

Some of Misauri 's information is presented with a certitude not characteristic of other accounts, but he has not overstated either the intensity of Muslims' emotional reactions or the pivotal role the massacre played in Muslim political mobilization. Whoever authorized the Jabidah force, or whatever its real purpose, it was clear that the force had been secretly organized, that the recruits had been told they were being trained for a mission in Sabah, that at least twenty-eight of them were killed, and that the Marcos administration did everything it could to cover up the incident, including some things that made it look foolish. Muslim historian Cesar Majul recounts how "platoons of young army recruits from Luzon were organized to march through the hall of Congress, avowing they were the trainees who had been at Corregidor, and, lo, here they were, very much alive." The ploy failed when Muslim university students queried the recruits in Muslim dialects, which, of course, they could not speak, so the government tried again, herding truckloads of Muslims from regular army units into a Manila mosque for prayers. The purpose, according to Majul, was to "prove to the faithful that Muslims in the armed forces were not only alive but also encouraged to keep their faith strong and to attend congregational prayers." The soldiers were embarrassed, however, and admitted that the army was using them to deflect attention from the massacre.

The government did succeed ultimately in controlling both congressional investigations and military trials and in securing acquittal of all the accused. The cost of this success was high because the verdict increased the outcry among Philippine Muslims and encouraged them toward further political organization. The cover-up also confirmed the conviction of Malaysian officials that Marcos had, indeed, intended to take Sabah by force. The result was a recognized congruence of interests between young Muslims in Manila--who had heretofore directed their political energies toward radical student organizations and/or subsumed them in the entourages of traditional Muslim leaders--and Muslims in Malaysia, particularly in Sabah--who felt Marcos had betrayed them after they had made significant compromises to restore good relations with the Philippines. Malayan confidence in the goodwill of Philippine officialdom had been shaken badly by President Macapagal's announcement of a Philippine claim to Sabah in 1962 and by his subsequent efforts to mediate between Malaya and Indonesia during their confrontation over the formation of Malaysia. Marcos's actions--in the perception of the Malaysian leadership--were simply further examples of Philippine perfidy.

Among the Muslim students, the cooperation that had begun during the Corregidor protests in Manila was given informal structure later in 1968 in Zamboanga City. There was further consolidation in 1969 when groups of young Muslims began going to Malaysia for military training. A central committee of seven members was constituted. They named Nur Misuari--an instructor from Sulu at the University of the Philippines-as chairman and agreed to call their organization the Moro National Liberation Front.

The trainees' return from Malaysia coincided with other developments. Also reacting to the Corregidor massacre, an old Muslim political leader in Cotobato, Datu Udtog Matalam, had formed the Muslim Independence Movement (MIM) with the goal of gaining independence for Mindanao and Sulu, the areas in the southern Philippines that Muslims had traditionally dominated. Mindanao, however, and specifically Cotabato, had had a large Christian migration in recent decades that had caused endless disputes between Christians and Muslims over land ownership and that threatened Muslim political control. Matalam 's MIM appealed to Muslims but frightened Christians; both reactions resulted in the creation of armed bands, outbreaks of violence, and a buildup of government armed forces.

The situation deteriorated further as politicians began to mobilize for the 1971 elections.

Because of escalated fighting by the end of 1970--Ilagas and Christian armed groups against Blackshirts, Barracudas, and other minor Muslim armed groups--there were other signs of discord everywhere. Schools in many towns had closed; farms were left abandoned; commerce had stagnated; the number of refugees was increasing. One report has given a very conservative estimate that at least 30,000 Muslims, Christians, and Tirurays [a tribal group] had left their homes for safer areas.

June 1971 brought another massacre. Armed "Christians" entered Manili, a barrio in North Cotabato, when most of the men were out working their fields; they summoned the remaining residents--old men, women, and children--into a mosque for a "peace conference" and killed at least seventy of them with grenades, guns, and knives.

Again, the massacre had both internal and international ramifications. It convinced Muslim leaders that "there was collusion among Christian politicians, settlers, and some commanding officers of the Philippine constabulary in Cotabato and Lanao" and that the plight of Muslims was likely to worsen because many of these Christians had strong connections with the Nacionalistas (Marcos's party). Hence, Muslim leaders--"a senator, a former senator, congressman, high government officials, heads of Muslim associations, religious and academic scholars and intellectuals, professionals and businessmen, and student leaders"--met in Manila and drew up a manifesto in which "they pledged before God that if justice could not be brought by legal or peaceful means, they would do their best to preserve their community and lands, regardless of their personal ambitions or political differences." The manifesto reassured Muslims, irritated the government.

Of equal importance was the effect of Manili on Libyan leader Colonel Muammar Qaddafi, who heard of the massacre, expressed his concern to the Philippine government, and began a program of aid for Muslim refugees and religious activities that subsequently expanded to military and diplomatic support for the Muslim cause.

The conclusions of the 1971 elections did not resolve the escalating unrest in the south or elsewhere. Most of the critical Muslim-Christian contests resulted in Christian victories; the violence continued, though apparently at a lower level. In other areas of the Philippines, election results were interpreted as a major loss for Marcos. Debates in the Constitutional Convention--called in an effort to secure order and justice through institutional changes--were bitter and had pro- or anti -Marcos implications. Bombings and shootouts occurred in the Manila area. Marcos attributed them to Communists; his opponents charged his own men with having started them. Floods deluged areas of Luzon and threatened a nationwide rice crisis.

Finally, under seige on every front, unable to maintain control through traditional mechanisms, and unwilling to trust democratic processes to produce new ones, Marcos declared martial law in September 1972. The declaration cited the revolutionary goals and activities of lawless elements motivated by "Marxist-Leninist-Maoist techniques and beliefs" supported by a foreign government, and the "equally serious disorder in Mindanao and Sulu." Martial law, he said, would allow him both to remove anarchy and maintain peace and order and to reform the country's institutions.

In the south, however, martial law had effects contrary to Marcos's intentions. Violence escalated from sporadic local conflict with specific economic and political causes to intense and widespread fighting that was, from the Muslim perspective, explicitly antigovernment in its objectives. Muslims saw martial law as excluding them from decision making by centralizing power in Christian hands and as leaving them only two options: accepting the regime and its promises or resorting to armed rebellion. In this context, the regime's immediate moves to collect guns from civilians were incendiary. Having already identified collusion between local Christian adversaries and government forces and officials, Muslims had no intention of giving up the weapons they regarded as essential for self-protection, and they fought to keep them. The government sent in additional troops, thereby increasing both the Muslims' feeling of vulnerability and their determination to defend themselves. In 1973, fighting spread through Cotabato, Zamboanga, Basilan, Sulu, and Tawi Tawi, and armed Muslim bands and Philippine armed forces maintained an uneasy equilibrium in Lanao.

At this stage the MNLF emerged. Its dominance over both spontaneously formed partisan groups and the private armies of Muslim politicians was secured by the fact that its ideology and organization provided the basis for cooperation among Muslims divided by language, culture, and clan. Equally important, it established connections with Libya and Malaysia that provided it with funds for guns and ammunition and a refuge. In 1974, the MNLF leadership made a further move, an effort to gain recognition and support for its cause from the Islamic foreign Ministers' Conference.

## Assumptions and Goals

The cause, as articulated in the position papers prepared for the Foreign Ministers' meeting in Kuala Lumpur, is essentially a nationalist struggle against colonial domination. According to the account given, the Moros (the term is Spanish, transferred from a familiar Muslim enemy--the Moors of Spain and North Africa--to the new enemy in the Philippines in the sixteenth century) constitute a distinct people, a nation, with a traditional homeland--Mindanao, Sulu, Basilan, and Palawan. They had "among the first independently organized communities in the Malay world," even before the coming of Islam at the end of the thirteenth century. Thereafter, the migration of a series of "Muslin princes" introduced "a new awareness in their spiritual life," "a new direction in their ethical outlook," and "innovations in social and political relationships." Islam and its concomitant social and political structures had spread as far as Manila when the Spaniards arrived in the sixteenth century, conquered the isolated settlements in the north and central islands, and co-opted the inhabitants into what they intended to be a final, triumphant struggle against the infidel Moros to the south.

For three hundred years, the Moros resisted Spanish domination, determined (the account continues) "to defend not only the integrity of their national homeland, but also the dignity of their Bangsa and the preservation of the Islamic Faith." Throughout this period the Spaniards portrayed the Moros "as pirates, savages and barbaric only because they were steadfast, brave, fierce and courageous in battle."

At the end of the nineteenth century a new force appeared on the scene, the United States. The MNLF claims that "the Bangsa Moro people, lacking in sophistication to understand American expansionism, cordially accepted the presence of the Americans as friends and equals because of the latter's insidious display of goodwill and cordiality." Indicative of their peaceful attitude was the Muslims' refusal to cooperate with General Aguinaldo against the Americans. But the Americans "treacherously" changed policies after their victory in the north and began to interfere in the internal affairs of the Muslim areas. Although some of the Muslim leadership capitulated, others resisted. For ten years, the United States was "locked in armed conflict with the Bangsa Moro people." Then U.S. policy changed again. The MNLF's explanation is that "the mailed first approach was rendered futile in the face of Moro invincibility in battle. And so the much publicized policy of attraction was launched by the colonial government."

The Muslims then entered a new era, which the MNLF describes:

> *. . . the American colonial soldiers gained an attitude of cooperation from some Moro leaders. Sultans and Datus accepted monetary annuities and land grants. The irony of it was that the lands parcelled out by the Americans to them were originally Moro lands. Their sons and daughters accepted scholarships to Washington, contributing further to American brainwashing efforts and propaganda balderdash. They forgot the superior ethical basis of Islamic education which had moulded the Moro spirit and character for centuries. The great masses of the Bangsa Moro people were left in the dark but still fiercely yearning to preserve the national homeland. Under this situation, history took its course shifting the character of Moro resistance to a more complex form. Some who were co-opted by the American colonial dispensation, took the path of parliamentary struggle, but others, especially those from among the humble masses, continued the armed defiance against American rule.*

The parliamentary efforts were as unsuccessful as the armed defiance. Two parliamentary efforts were made, in 1926 and again in 1935. The first was an attempt by Datu Piang of Cotabato to gain support for the Bacon bill, which sought to separate Mindanao and Sulu from the rest of the Philippines. It failed, the MNLF says, because Congressman Bacon was motivated by "colonial vested interests" who wanted only to exploit Mindanao's resources and because "Quezon, Osmena, Roxas and the other colonial stooges, a vexatious lot, were always in Washington wailing on the walls of the United States Congress and the White House, to beg for Philippine Independence that would incorporate Mindanao and Sulu, no matter how bogus and arbitrary."

The second attempt was significant primarily because of its powerful articulation of Muslim perceptions:

> *... we want to tell you that the Philippines as it is known to the American people is populated by two different peoples with different religions, practices and traditions. The christian [sic] Filipinos occupy the island of Luzon and the Visayas. The Moros predominate in the islands of Mindanao and Sulu. . . . Should the American people grant the Philippines an independence, the islands of Mindanao and Sulu should not be included in such independence. . . . Our public land should not be given to people other than the Moros. Our practices, laws and the decisions of our Moro leaders should be respected. Our religion should not be curtailed in any way. All our practices which are incidents to our religion of Islam should be respected because these things are what a Muslim desires to live for. Once our religion is no more, our lives are no more.*

This attempt also failed, and the Philippine Commonwealth government was inaugurated. The incorporation of Mindanao and Sulu in it, in the view of the MNLF, was "the most monstrous crime not only against the Bangsa Moro people but also against the Filipino people of Visayas and Luzon." The Bangsa Moro people were thus delivered "to a more vicious form of oppression, i.e., to the Christian Filipino oppressive rule, thus setting the Bangsa Moro people and the Filipinos on a collision course."

The Japanese invasion provided an interregnum; Moro resistance reemerged with the establishment of the Philippine Republic after the war. The resistance, as earlier, took two forms, parliamentary efforts to gain independence and isolated instances of armed defiance. Neither was sustained until the Corregidor massacre and the subsequent escalation of fighting in the south, which the MNLF attributed to the actions of the Marcos administration and described as "colossal and heinous crimes." Genocide now joined earlier and continuing manifestations of "Christian Filipino injustice and discrimination" as well as "economic and political aggression," thus no alternative was left to the current revolutionary struggle.

On the basis of these historical assertions and assumptions, the MNLF issued its manifesto and called for the support of the Islamic Foreign Ministers' Conference. Speaking for "the five-million oppressed Bangsa Moro people, wishing to free ourselves from the terror, oppression, and tyranny of Filipino colonialism which has caused us untold sufferings and miseries by criminally usurping our land, threatening Islam through wholesale destruction and desecration of its places of worship and its Holy Book, and murdering our innocent brothers, sisters and old folks in a genocidal campaign of terrifying magnitude," the MNLF declared the establishment of the free and independent Bangsa Moro Republik in Mindanao, Basilan, Sulu, and Palawan. The republic would have a democratic system of government that tolerated neither exploitation nor oppression, an ideology and legal system based on Islam, an economic system encouraging foreign investment, and a foreign policy committed to world peace and the principle of national self-determination. Filipinos wishing to stay in the "Bangsa Moro national homeland" after independence would be welcome and given equal rights and protection, including property rights and the free exercise of their political, cultural and religious rights--if they renounced their Filipino citizenship and "wholeheartedly" accepted Bangsa Moro citizenship.

The MNLF asked for political, economic, and military aid from the Islamic foreign ministers. Specifically, it wanted formal recognition of the republic, support for the MNLF in the United Nations and in Third World activities, military assistance for the Bangsa Moro army, the channeling of all refugee aid through the MNLF, and the breaking of all diplomatic, economic, and cultural ties with the Philippines. It identified an oil boycott as being of primary significance: The boycott accompanying the Middle East war in 1973 had greatly reduced the Philippines' military operations against Muslims, and the pro-Arab diplomatic initiatives that had resulted in the lifting of that boycott were motivated solely by opportunism.

The Islamic foreign ministers gave the MNLF considerably less than its leaders asked. They did not give formal recognition to, or support for, an independent Muslim state; they did not call for military support for the Bangsa Moro army; and they did not agree to break diplomatic, economic, and cultural ties with the Philippines. However, they condemned as inadequate the socioeconomic measures proposed by the Philippine government as a solution to the Muslims' problems, called on the Philippines to negotiate a political and peaceful solution "to the plight of Filipino Muslims within the framework of the national sovereignty and territorial integrity of the Philippines," and identified the MNLF as an appropriate participant in negotiations. They also appealed to "peace loving states and religions and international authorities" to use their good offices to insure the safety and liberty of Philippine Muslims.

Thus the Kuala Lumpur meetings gave both the MNLF and the Philippine government clear notice of the intent and extent of Islamic Conference involvement. In subsequent months, while the MNLF consolidated its military organization and extended the scope of its military operations against the rapidly augmented Philippine armed forces, the Islamic Conference continued to take initiatives designed to facilitate a solution to the conflict. The conference's secretary-general made several trips to Manila and succeeded in arranging a meeting between the MNLF leadership and a Philippine delegation in Jedda, Saudi Arabia, in midJanuary 1975. After that meeting deadlocked, a four-member committee (from Saudi Arabia, Libya, Somalia, and Senegal), representing the Islamic foreign ministers, prepared a draft agenda for further negotiations. That draft, in turn, was rejected by Muslims whom Marcos had assembled in Zamboanga City. Instead, they endorsed a Marcos plan that the foreign ministers then considered. Not surprisingly, the foreign ministers preferred their committee's agenda and instructed the committee and the secretary-general to arrange negotiations as soon as possible.

That negotiations did not occur immediately was also not surprising because consensus seemed limited to an agreement that "autonomy" was the solution. The MNLF had agreed to give up independence as a goal, substituting in its stead a demand for an internally sovereign, politically "autonomous" Bangsa Moro State that would include all of Mindanao, the Sulu Archipelago, Basilan, and Palawan. This state would have its own security force and exclusive responsibility for maintaining internal order, and it would be loosely associated with the Philippines. The foreign ministers' agenda (which the MNLF supported) provided for Islamic self-government in the territory owned by Muslims before 1944, including that taken from Muslims since then; Christians and non-Christian minorities historically present in Islamic territories would have the status of minorities in a Muslim land. The Marcos plan, in contrast, involved the creation of four "autonomous" regions in the southern Philippines that would be headed by commissioners appointed by the president and directly responsible to him; the appointment (by him) of Muslims to economic and social welfare offices; and the absorption of "sincere" higher ranking Muslim defectors into the armed forces. There was, in short, agreement on the use of the word autonomy, not on its substance.

Negotiations were, however, finally resumed in Tripoli, Libya, in December 1976, after talks between Imelda Marcos and Qaddafi. The preliminary agreement signed on December 23 appeared to indicate that the MNLF, with the help of its Islamic Conference supporters, had achieved most of its objectives. The terms provided for an "autonomy for the Muslims" in thirteen provinces. The "autonomy" was to have Muslim courts as well as a legislative assembly, executive council, and administrative system. In addition there would be special regional security forces; representation in the central government; control over education, finance, and the economic system; and a right to a "reasonable percentage" from the revenues of mines and minerals. The central government was to maintain responsibility for foreign policy and national defense. The role of the MNLF forces in the Philippine armed forces and relationships between structures and policies of the "autonomy" and those of the central government were to be discussed during further talks. In the meantime, there was to be a cease-fire, supervised by a committee representing the Philippine government, the MNLF, and the Islamic Conference's committee of four.

The MNLF's success was short-lived. Negotiations to implement the cease-fire quickly foundered, and Marcos proceeded to hold a plebiscite on critical provisions of the agreement itself. The plebiscite produced the mandate he wanted. Henceforth, the Philippine government "implemented" the agreement as it chose, until in 1980 a spokesperson declared it no longer "in force." The Islamic Conference complained about Philippine bad faith, called on the government to resume negotiations, and occasionally tried to negotiate through its secretary-general. Fighting resumed after the cease-fire collapsed in late 1977, but it eventually subsided. The MNLF's supply of arms decreased markedly after the change in the government of Sabah in 1975 and after a reduction of Libyan aid apparently beginning in 1976. A combination of exhaustion and government policies of attraction encouraged MNLF's troops to defect, and its leadership was factionalized.

## Assessment

But what accounts for the MNLF's decline after so rapid an ascent? Why did the combination of ideology, organization, and access to outside resources--elements that originally gained it leadership of the Muslim protest movement and subsequently allowed it to achieve both military and diplomatic success--prove so ineffectual over time? Answers are difficult because the issues are complex and because it is important not to underestimate the MNLF's achievements and its remaining potential. Nevertheless, it seems possible to suggest that there were flaws in the MNLF's ideology and in its organization and that its reliance on outside assistance was a source of weakness as well as strength.

The appeal of the MNLF's ideology was that it articulated an alternative to a social order that Muslims found intolerable. Muslims saw Islam as the essence of their identity and of their way of life, were proud of their history, and felt keenly the loss of their homeland. Many (probably almost all) shared the MNLF's perception of Filipinos as alien and threatening and as contemptuous of their religion and covetous of their land. They opted for separatism as a natural solution.

The problem was that it was an excessively simplistic solution. MNLF writings reflect part of the dilemma. The use of the word Moro rather than the word Muslim suggests two needs: (1) to place religious identity in space (the homeland) and time (history) and, hence, to give it the legitimacy of nationalism and (2) to include those non-Muslims history had placed in the homeland. Abdurasad Asani, a member of the MNLF's Central Committee, writes in a pamphlet entitled, Moros--Not Filipinos:

> *. . . the fact remains that the Bangsamoro people, honed by their historical and cultural experiences, are nonetheless fortunate to be heirs to distinct social and moral values which characterise them as a nation, proud of its own heritage. . . .*

Originally, the use of the term Moro by the colonialists was meant to perpetuate an image of the Muslim people of Mindanao, Basilan, Sulu and Palawan as savage and treacherous, while they are simply daring and tenacious in the defense of their homeland

and faith. But despite its colonial origins the Moro National Liberation Front (MNLF) has cleansed the term of its unpleasant connotation by propagating the more correct view that the tenacity with which the natives conducted their war of resistance against foreign intrusion was a classic exercise in heroism.

The term is not only common to all the indigenous tribes of the region but includes Muslims, Christians and those still adhering to traditional religious values--in a word all those who share common aspiration and political destiny. Hence, the MNLF had adopted Bangsa (nation) Moro as a national identity and implants it in the consciousness of the masses. Today, it is rooted in the heart of every man and woman and the defense of its integrity has become a national duty.

Asani's own description seems to have an internal contradiction; certainly contradictions appear when one considers other aspects of the MNLF ideology and population statistics. Christians are apparently included among the Bangsa Moro if they feel they have "common aspiration and political destiny" with Muslims and are willing to accept minority status in an area of "Islamic self-government." Yet, even if one concedes that government figures have consistently understated Muslim numbers, Muslims are clearly a minotiry not simply in the Muslim "homeland" originally claimed by the MNLF--Mindanao, Basilan, Sulu, Palawan (a total of twenty-one provinces)--but also in most of the thirteen provinces specified at Tripoli. Professor Majul, whose pro-Muslim sympathies are strong, says:

> *The population of only a few of these provinces--Lanao del Sur, Sulu, and Tawi-Tawi--was almost wholly Muslim, that is, over 90 percent. The population of Basilan and North Cotabato was about 70 percent Muslim. That of Lanao del Norte, Maguindanao, and Sultan Kudarat, however, was less than 50 percent Muslim, and that of Zamboanga del Norte, Zamboanga del Sur, South Cotabato, Davao del Sur, and Palawan less than 20 percent. Of the total population of the thirteen provinces--at least six million--an estimated three million were Muslims, or about 50 percent.*

Thus, the MNLF's demand for Muslim domination of the "homeland," as originally defined in its manifesto in Kuala Lumpur or subsequently in the Tripoli negotiations, was unrealistic. Presumably, it could have broadened its ideological base to include non-Muslims also alienated by the Marcos government or reduced its territorial goals; by doing neither, it undermined its achievements.

The MNLF's radicalism was also an issue, partly because it was unclear. Front spokespersons have accused both Christians and Muslims of corruption, abuse of power, and exploitation (particularly land grabbing), and they have rejected the leadership of Muslim sultans as well as of the "Christians" in Manila. There is talk of Islamic socialism, but what it means is not defined. According to Ulangutan, an MNLF commander in Tawi Tawi, who was interviewed in 1974, "Islamic socialism means that everything must conform to the norms, customs and traditions of the Muslims. Socialism comes in specifically in the Islamic practices--not exactly in the economic side. Among Muslims, Islam is a way of life."

Front spokespersons have consistently distinguished themselves from the "Maoists" of the New People's Army (NPA). An early manifesto insisted that the activists were not Communist but "God-fearing people" and demanded freedom to practice Islamic laws and customs without restrictions. Misuari allegedly left the Kabataang Makabayan--a radical student group identified with the NPA--because the Maoists in it were unsympathetic toward Muslims. It was reported in 1975 that a group of Communist insurgents from the north visited Mindanao to arrange a meeting with the MNLF central committee, which they hoped would lead to a military alliance between the two, but the Muslims refused because they felt that the movements were ideologically incompatible and that a link with Communists would weaken relationships with the Islamic world. An MNLF spokesperson interviewed in 1975 was quoted as saying that, although the Front represented an internal social revolution within Moro society, it was not Communist and would have nothing to do with Communists. The Front's leadership has maintained this position, though there is some evidence of at least local cooperation between non-Muslim (specifically NPA) and Muslim resistance groups.

The dilemma of the Front's leadership has been that for ideological and practical reasons they have wanted to emphasize both their Muslim identity and their radicalism. Each of these emphases has attracted particular followers and excluded others. Combining the two has tended more to subtract than to add potential recruits, a tendency Front spokespersons may have tried to counter with vague and inconsistent statements.

Joel de los Santos, in an undated article (apparently written in 1976 or 1977), takes the critique a step farther. In his analysis, the MNLF's problem was less the substance of its ideology than its failure to communicate an ideology. "Only a few MNLF leaders had a high level of ideological commitment and political consciousness," because, he claims, there was an "early emphasis on military training at the expense of political training." He attributes this emphasis to the fact that the MNLF's mass base was provided by the "depredations and dislocations" resulting from the confrontations between Christian armed bands and Muslims and by the heightening of Muslim insecurities caused by the presidential decree ordering the surrender of firearms. With the growing buildup of government forces and the consequent expansion of conflict, there was a natural emphasis on military activities--specifically for preparation for guerrilla warfare. Institutions--such as village and town committees on finance, propaganda, intelligence, and supplies--remained rudimentary, with heavy reliance placed on the personal charisma of local leaders. Loyalty, not ideology, provided the Front's internal cohesion. Because loyalty was prompted by various motives, the links of the local leaders to the MNLF's structure and of the leaders' followers to them had varying degrees of reliability.

Obviously, de los Santos's analysis identifies organizational as well as ideological problems. Formally the MNLF had (and has) parallel political and military structures, topped by a Central Committee of about twenty. The Central Committee regarded itself as setting broad policy outlines and leaving to local units the maintenance of discipline and specific tactical decisions. For reasons de los Santos indicated, it could not do otherwise. The MNLF never managed to bring into its structure all the Muslim groups fighting the government, and it could not control the behavior of many groups nominally fighting along side it. Moreover, some of its early accomplishments--for example, an ethnically balanced central committee and connections between its overseas leadership and its forces in the field--proved difficult to maintain.

Finally, events seem to have demonstrated that the MNLF was excessively reliant on external support. Originally military assistance from Malaysia (particularly Sabah) and later from Libya was significant in subsidizing a level of warfare that would not otherwise have been possible and that put considerable pressure on the Philippine government. The diplomatic support of the Islamic Conference (when coupled with the potential for an oil boycott) was also significant and, undoubtedly, was responsible for securing agreement at Tripoli on terms much more favorable to the MNLF than it could have achieved alone. Yet Islamic support may also have inflated the expectations of the MNLF's leadership and diverted it from developing an institutional base among Muslims and linkages with non-Muslims in the Philippines. Clearly, post-Tripoli, it was Philippine realities, not pan-Islamic ones, that proved dominant. Malaysia had earlier curtailed its military support for the MNLF as its perceived interests changed; Libya later limited its aid. Other Muslim states gave no priority to the achievement of the MNLF's political objectives, even ones they had helped to negotiate.

## Philippine Government, 1977-84

If the Marcos government after 1977 dominated the debate over appropriate political structures and policies for Muslims, it was not simply because of MNLF weaknesses. During the early years of the martial law regime, when the MNLF was successfully challenging both the regime's legitimacy and its control in the south, the government began to develop a series of strategies that provided a basis for its actions in the period following the Tripoli Agreement. In part, the regime's counterattack was ideological, an alternative to the MNLF's efforts at defining its cause as nationalist. Primarily, however, the regime concentrated on devising structures and policies that would attract and/or appease those Muslims at home and abroad sympathetic to the MNLF's critique while consolidating its own control and maintaining the loyalty of both Muslims and Christians who had benefited from the old order.

### Assumptions

The MNLF's manifesto was an assertion that the Moros were a distinct nationality, set off by religion, history, and identification with their homeland. They had resisted both Spanish and American colonial efforts but had finally succumbed and had wrongfully been included in the Republic of the Philippines. The Filipino Christian government, in their perspective, was simply a successor to the earlier colonial regimes. It aimed at discrediting Muslims' faith and practices, depriving them of their patrimony, and finally, under Marcos, endangering their very existence. Hence, there was no alternative to a form of separatism, preferably independence--but at least autonomy. Muslims must have control over their own destinies--and specifically over political and military institutions that would protect their religion, land, and lives.

The government, in response, identified the MNLF's view of history as inaccurate, its goals as inappropriate, and its leadership as lacking in integrity. Its version of history was that "the problems in the Southwestern Philippines are the result of several centuries old inequities and misunderstandings caused primarily by the Western colonization of the country." Before the coming of the Spaniards the Malay population of the islands was organized in communities that were separate ("autonomous," in one version) but essentially similar, equal, and peaceful. The coming of the Spaniards began "four centuries of protracted struggle by the Filipinos against colonization [that] bifurcated their historical orientation as a people and left a legacy of social instability in the country." The "Southern Filipinos" started the fight against the Spanish conquistadores and continued it for three hundred years. It was the "Northern revolutionaries," however, "who later succeeded in liberating the entire Philippine Archipelago that resulted in [sic] the declaration of independence on June 12, 1898."

With the coming of the Americans, according to the government's account, roles reversed. Whereas the northern Filipinos continued to fight the Americans to preserve Philippine independence, the southerners signed the Bates Treaty in 1899, thus exchanging sovereignty over Sulu and portions of Mindanao for pensions given to ruling members of the Sulu sultanate. Later, southern Filipinos opposed the Americans, but ineffectually. The Americans then created, in succession, "two regional autonomous governments" in the south, both aimed at providing governance for Muslims and integrating them into the political system. Since then, the government claimed, "despite recurring inter-ethnic conflicts, Filipino Muslims have lived peacefully as part and parcel of the Filipino body politic," with exactly the same constitutional rights as non-Muslims, including guarantees of religious freedom.

The government conceded that tension did break out in "small pockets of rebellion" in some parts of Mindanao during late 1972 and early 1973. The government's analysis was that these were caused by the fact that political warlords and subversive elements had successfully exploited ancient grievances," which had been aggravated by land conflicts and economic opportunism.

Because conditions elsewhere in the country were similar to those in the south, Marcos declared martial law. In the south, however, according to the government, rumors spread that martial law had been declared to convert Muslims forcibly to Christianity; this resulted in Muslim resistance to efforts by the armed forces to collect all guns in civilian hands. These rumors and other "baseless suspicions" were fomented by a variety of groups who hoped to gain from disorder:

> *Their aims were varied. Some were ambitious politicians who sought the secession from the Republic of the islands of Mindanao, Basilan, Sulu, Tawi-Tawi and Palawan to coalesce with Sabah in order to form an indeterminate political state. Others were the Communists who sought to divert military pressure from the Luzon guerrilla bases. Others were simply bandits and brigands who took advantage of the general confusion to rob and to plunder. Others were adventurist youths. And still others were political radicals who manipulated the religious fervor of many Muslim communities as one more lever for overthrowing the national government.*

The government placed the MNLF among these latter groups. Stripped of rhetoric and some of its inconsistencies, the government's account was that the MNLF's membership was recruited from discontented Muslim students educated at home or abroad, influenced by Maoist ideology, and trained and armed by foreign powers. Its leadership chose to downplay its Maoist influences and to seize the banner of Islam for two reasons. First, an Islamic identification enabled it to emphasize the deeply felt grievances of Muslims in the Philippines and thus to mobilize them for its secessionist ends. Second, identifying religion as the cause of its conflict with the government misled Muslims outside the Philippines into providing support.

In response, the government claimed to have developed a "two pronged approach of conciliation and development for the Southwestern Philippines" and a policy of "open diplomacy." Conciliation involved dialogues with groups engaged in the rebellion to arrive at solutions to perceived problems and development committed the government "to the provision of economic, social, cultural, and educational facilities and to the expansion of citizen participation in nation-building." Open diplomacy was based on the following premises: that the condition of Filipino Muslims was more advanced than that of Muslim minorities elsewhere, therefore the government had nothing to hide; that the majority of Filipino Muslims were loyal to the government, not to the MNLF; that the MNLF was composed of a handful of young radical rebels, living comfortably in self-exile abroad, who were actually working for the dismemberment of the republic; that the MNLF was in active alliance with the NPA; and, finally, that the Islamic Conference wished to use its good offices to help resolve an internal problem for the benefit of Filipino Muslims.

In short, the government asserted that Muslims--Southern Filipinos, in its argot--shared with other Filipinos a common history and land. They also shared an "intrinsic piousness," which manifested itself in a variety of religions, as well as strong loyalties to ethnolinguistic groupings (eighty-seven in all). The state was defined as secular with the Constitution guaranteeing freedom of religious belief and worship to all citizens. Muslims had suffered in the past, partly because of the malfeasance of their own traditional leaders and politicians, partly because of inadequacies in the political system throughout the country. Martial law was proclaimed to correct such problems, and the Marcos regime was committed to redress any wrongs. According to the government the MNLF's secessionist goals were a threat to national sovereignty and territorial integrity as well as to the welfare and lives of Muslims.

## Structures and Policies

The government's outline of its efforts to respond to the needs of Muslims is helpful if one remembers that conciliation and development were accompanied not simply by open diplomacy, but also by a massive expansion of the Philippine armed forces and by the deployment of about seventy percent of them in the south. Their operations there ranged from aerial bombardments and full-scale ground assaults to skirmishes and drunken shootouts. On balance, they probably contributed as much to disorder as to order because their indiscriminate firing and other undisciplined behavior encouraged Muslims to flee their lands (and hence the source of their livelihoods) and/or to join the rebels in the hills. Certainly through most of the 1970s, they constituted the most obvious government presence in the south.

It is, however, true that by 1973 the government was also placing considerable emphasis on conciliation and development programs for the south. The agency primarily responsible for early initiatives was the Presidential Task Force for the Reconstruction and Development of Mindanao, which was chaired by Alejandro Melchor, then Marcos's executive secretary and the regime's top technocrat. The task force had on its staff a number of well-trained young Muslims who shared Melchor 's objective of developing an "all out, well-planned program designed to expand all facets of Philippine Muslim participation in the national society." The result was not simply the coordination of the regime's investments of borrowed funds in various activities aimed at economic development in the south, as Marcos's original charge to the task force indicated, but a series of decrees, research projects, and agencies. Among the decrees was a proclamation of Islamic holidays in Muslim areas, provisions for asserting ownership of "ancestral lands," and permission for the resumption of barter trade between Sulu and Sabah. Staff members were involved in a project to develop a Muslim law code. Cotabato, Zamboanga, and Sulu provinces were partitioned, ostensibly to allow greater representation of Muslims. The Philippine Amanah Bank was created. Operating on the Islamic concept of banking following the "no-interest and partnership principles," it was to improve socioeconomic conditions in the economically depressed provinces of Mindanao.

Meanwhile other efforts were underway, some compatible with the task force's activities, others either not coordinated or apparently contradictory. Among other moves, the Department (Ministry) of Education allowed the use of Arabic in schools, and the government took steps to develop a new area for Muslim housing in Manila. But the government also began to consult with, and appoint to office, older, traditional Muslim leaders, some of whom were responsible for the warlordism Melchor regarded as one of the infirmities of the old society.

By 1975, however, the Islamic Foreign Ministers' meeting in Kuala Lumpur and the negotiations with MNLF in Jedda had provided a new focus for government initiatives. Melchor's opening statement at the Jedda meetings stressed that the "New Society" had not been given a chance to institute reforms and development plans because of a lack of peace and order--a lack for which Misuari was blamed--and argued that the logical move was to stop the "senseless enmity" and proceed to implement reconstruction and development. Melchor rejected any form of autonomy, except local administrative autonomy, as incompatible with the Philippine Constitution. Sometime thereafter, Melchor's staff apparently began drafting possible schemes for local and/or regional "autonomous" structures. One of these, a truncated proposal for the creation of four regions in the southern Philippines and for additional appointments of Muslims, was first announced at the "peace talks" held in Zamboanga City in June 1975 and subsequently communicated to the Islamic foreign ministers in Jedda in July. By the time negotiations resumed in Tripoli in December 1976, Marcos had already created two regional offices in areas of heavy Muslim population and appointed commissioners to head them. Western Mindanao (Region 9) included the five provinces of Sulu, Tawi-Tawi, Basilan, Zamboanga del Norte, and Zamboanga del Sur, with headquarters in Zamboanga City. Southern Mindanao (Region 12) included North Cotabato, Maguindanao, Sultan Kudarat, Lanao del Norte, and Lanao del Sur, with headquarters in Cotabato City.

During the meetings in Tripoli, the Philippine position was that these two regions and the ten provinces they included should constitute the "autonomous" area under discussion. The MNLF (and apparently the Islamic Foreign Ministers' team) had proposed twenty-one provinces and a single "autonomy for the Muslims." The agreement on thirteen--with Palawan, Davao del Sur, and South Cotabato added to the Philippines' already constituted regions--and on vocabulary referring to "the autonomy for the Muslims in the Southern Philippines" appeared to be a compromise. Yet, the Philippine government had also insisted on the inclusion of a clause in the preliminary agreement that it would take "all necessary constitutional processes for the implementation of the entire Agreement." According to Philippine documents, it was understood by all parties that "constitutional processes" included a referendum ("to determine various questions including the administrative nature of the government") and elections for public officials. Marcos announced immediately after the preliminary agreement was signed that a plebiscite was "under study," then announced on February 11, 1977, that a referendum would be held on February 21 to get the consent of the people in the thirteen provinces to the territorial scope of the "autonomy"; on February 16 the referendum was postponed until March 17; on March 16 it was postponed until April 17.

Meanwhile, the Tripoli talks had reconvened and deadlocked. The Muslim version of the deadlock was that after the MNLF and the Philippine government had presented their positions, the conference chairman suggested an adjournment for each side to work out a compromise; the MNLF was prepared to do so, the Philippine panel was not. The Philippine government charged that the MNLF was reverting to earlier demands for a separate state and insisted on a referendum, which the MNLF considered unnecessary. Finally Imelda Marcos flew to Tripoli again to work out another compromise. Her efforts produced an exchange of cables between Qaddafi and Marcos on March 18 and 19. Once more, however, the apparent agreement dissolved in claims and counterclaims. Finally, despite objections from Qaddafi, the Islamic Conference's secretary general, and Misauri, the Philippine government held the referendum it wanted, with the questions of its choice. An overwhelming majority of those voting rejected the merger of the thirteen provinces into one region (which had been agreed to at Tripoli) as well as other proposals based on an MNLF draft prepared for negotiations (which someone on the Philippine team had allegedly leaked). Instead, the majority approved a proposal that the administration of the "autonomy" be under the general supervision and control of the Philippine government, with ten provinces clustered in two regions. Representatives from the Islamic Conference, the MNLF, and the Philippine government then met in Manila in an attempt at saving the negotiations; talks ended at the end of April with mutual recriminations.

Thereafter, the Philippine government proceeded to implement the Tripoli Agreement as it chose. By its description, the referendum was followed by: the establishment of the provisional Regional Government in Southern Philippines and an invitation to Misuari to chair it; the promulgation of the Muslim Code as the nucleus of an Islamic judicial system; the strengthening of the Amanah Bank and the Southern Philippine Development Authority as the core of the regional financial and economic system; the establishment of a new university, to strengthen the autonomous educational system; the creation of regional security commands; the addition of the Philippine Pilgrimage Authority to existing Muslim-oriented agencies, to preserve Islam as an integral part of Filipino culture; the reinforcement of the regional commissions as agencies for administration; and the election of members to the regional assemblies and the impending appointment (by Marcos) of members of the regional executive councils.

The government's list was misleading because it suggested a smoothness of implementation and an efficacy of institutions that did not exist. Melchor's task force team on Muslim law had, for example, originally produced a "Proposed Draft of the Administration of Muslim Law Code" on April 4, 1974. The draft raised strong objections from the Philippine judicial heirarchy:

> *Instead of introducing progressive new practices, it would serve to institutionalize existing practices. It would answer Muslim demands that their religion and customs be preserved, but it would not serve to "inculcate new habits and attitudes among Muslims." Inclusion of adat considerations lessened the possibility that "old customs" would be eliminated. On top of that it created a multiple level judicial hierarchy, the operations of which would be effectively out of the control of the regular judicial bureaucracy.*

Consequently, Marcos established a review commission chaired by Professor Cesar Majul, a Muslim, but dominated by non-Muslims. The commission produced a much more conservative code (e.g., it was rooted in Middle Eastern Islam rather than Philippine Muslim customs and it established a compartment within the existing Philippine judicial system rather than a semiautonomous judicial structure). However, this code was ignored from its submission in August 1975 until the Tripoli Agreement apparently encouraged its promulgation in February 1977. Marcos decreed that administrative preparations were to begin immediately and that its provisions were to take effect in forty-five days. As of 1984, administrative preparations continued in the form of training institutes in sharima law, but the code was not yet in force.

As for the Amanah Bank, it was "strengthened" because mismanagement and nonpayment of loans had threatened its solvency. Moreover, according to an article in a publication of the Ministry of Muslim Affairs in 1982, it was not scheduled to start its Islamic (i.e., interest-free) operations until 1983, nine years after the bank's creation. The Southern Philippines Development Authority, the other agency cited as constituting the region's financial and economic core, was headed by Imelda Marcos.

There were also difficulties with the regional governments. In Western Mindanao (Region 9) the major opposition grouping refused to field candidates in the polls to elect candidates to the regional assembly. In Southern Mindanao (Region 12) the KBL (the government party), the opposition party, and self-identified MNLF candidates (the MNLF boycotted the election) decided to merge into one party and allow Marcos to choose the candidates for its regional assembly. Nevertheless, the government claimed that the election was significant because it implemented the Tripoli Agreement.

There was, however, a more fundamental problem if the issue was whether or not the government would be said to have implemented the Tripoli Agreement as it claimed. If one compared the texts of the Tripoli Agreement with the MNLF's proposed draft of a presidential decree with Presidential Decree No. 1618 (signed by Marcos on July 25, 1979), it appeared that the MNLF's draft attempted to institutionalize Muslim dominance (specifically MNLF dominance) to a degree neither required by the Tripoli Agreement nor realistic, given population statistics. Nevertheless, it was considerably more in accord with both the letter and spirit of the Tripoli Agreement than the Government's subsequent version.

The first clauses of the English (for the Philippines) and French (for the Islamic Conference) versions of the agreement differed markedly: The English stated agreement on "The establishment of Autonomy in the Southern Philippines within the realm of the sovereignty and territorial integrity of the Republic of the Philippines"; the French version of the same sentence declared agreement on "internal autonomy for the benefit of Muslims in the Southern Philippines" ("autonomie interne au profit des muselmans du Sud des Philippines"). Nevertheless, the English version subsequently resembled the French in its reference to "autonomy for the Muslims," its specific provisions that Muslims shall have the right to set up their own courts and administrative system in the autonomy, and its implication that the "authorities of the autonomy" who are to have the right to establish schools, their own economic and financial system, and so on are also understood to be Muslims.

There is no doubt that the questions submitted for a referendum were intended to modify the terms of the Tripoli Agreement as well as to counter MNLF interpretations of appropriate implementation. Yet Presidential Decree No. 1618 went beyond referendum results to depart in a fundamental way from the essence of the Tripoli Agreement: Neither the Muslims nor Islam were mentioned in the entire document, nor was there the substance of autonomy (if normal usage of the word is adhered to). Rather, there were provisions for the kind of regional government one might expect in a secular, centralized state. The regional assemblies consisted of a mixture of members elected from provinces (seventeen) and sectors (four--youth, agricultural workers, nonagricultural workers, and professionals), and those appointed by Marcos (up to five). These assemblies have limited powers, including oversight of the activities of certain national ministries, and the right to initiate certain kinds of programs of their own so long as the programs do not conflict with national plans. Fiscal constraints provided even more stringent limits.

But if the regional institutions seemed to provide neither for the special representation of Muslim interests nor for autonomy, Marcos did supplement those institutions with a Manila-centered Commission on Islamic Affairs, described in a government publication as "the President's arm for the direct assistance to Muslims in Southern Philippines." In 1981, the commission was given ministry status as the Ministry Affairs and the minister was made a member of the Batasang Pambansa (the National Assembly) and of the presidential cabinet. The functions of the Agency for the Development and Welfare of Muslims were transferred to the ministry, so that is became responsible for handling assistance from the Organization of Islamic Conference. Because the minister (Admiral Romulo Espaldon) and deputy minister ( attorney

Michael Mastura) also headed the Philippine Amanah Bank, the ministry's influence extended there. Finally, the ministry's mandate was sufficiently broad (or its leadership sufficiently energetic) to allow its involvement in a variety of programs initiated but not yet implemented, for example, the Ancestral Land Decree of 1974, presidential decrees regarding sharia law (1974 and 1977), and a presidential letter of instruction (1982) that provided for the development of Muslim community schools and the strengthening of programs in Islamic studies and Arabic.

The government, then, provided structures and policies that deal with many of the issues outlined in Tripoli. In that sense, and in that sense alone, it could be said to have implemented the agreement. Indeed, what it most seemed to have implemented were the proposals it made in Tripoli that were rejected in favor of compromises reflecting Muslim initiatives and interests as Muslims defined them--a point made, at least indirectly, in successive meetings of the Islamic foreign ministers.

The Marcos government was, however, justified in claiming that its moves were supported not simply at home, but also abroad. Its assertion in one of its publications that "Philippine bilateral relations with the 42member states of the Islamic Conference are good and in most cases, excellent" had some basis in fact. That at least the appearance of good relations existed was the result of a recognized congruence of interest as well as the Philippines' open diplomacy. Certainly, some Islamic states had had reservations over the MNLF's goals and/or ideology and over setting precedents to support interference in the internal affairs of states. Clearly, Indonesia and Malaysia felt they benefited from cooperation with the Philippines on particular objectives and were unwilling to jeopardize ASEAN. Although Middle Eastern states could find other markets for their oil or other sources for their imports of foreign labor, they had established trade and labor exchanges with the Philippines that served their interests. Hence, so long as the Philippines made gestures toward meeting Muslim needs and so long as it refrained from escalating warfare to a point resembling genocide, Islamic states (separately or together) were unlikely to use the forms of leverage they possessed to bring about optimal objectives, such as those they affirmed in yearly meetings.

## Assessment

If the Marcos government succeeded in countering the MNLF's assumptions and goals by substituting its own nationalist ideology for that articulated by the MNLF and by institutionalizing its dominance through new structures and policies, it--like the MNLF-had problems of both ideology and organization. Ideological problems were exemplified by a quotation from former President Marcos on the back of a government publication that described "infra-structure development in Muslim Mindanao":

> *The challenge before us today is the same challenge that faced all generations before us: that of permanently integrating the nation. We need to build a nation in which no one will see himself as a Tagalog, Ilocano or Pampango, Tausug, Maranaw or Maguindanao, much more than he sees himself as a Filipino; in which no citizen of the land will identify himself by his religious faith or his ideological persuasion rather than by the common patrimony of nationality which he shares with all Filipinos.*

Data from a recent survey of Muslim college students suggested the extent of the challenge, as Marcos posed it; other data called into question its wisdom. The survey, which provided the data for master's thesis for a research intern at the Gowing Memorial Research Center in Marawi City, queried five hundred students about their "self-images and intergroup attitudes." Specifically, it asked them to indicate their citizenship, their nationality, and their preference for "identifying names." The results were startling, both in students' manifestations of alienation from the Philippine/ Filipino identifications and in their revelation of differences among Muslim ethnic groups.

Most Maranao, Maguindanaon, and Samal students, for example, listed their "primary citizenship" as "Muslim," but a high percentage of Samal and most Tausug claimed "Bangsa Moro" as their citizenship-undoubtedly both cause and result of the strength of the MNLF in the Sulu Archipelago. The Maranao--the most "integrated" geographically into the Philippines--had the highest percentage identifying as Muslim Filipino (9% of Maranao informants) and Filipino (12%). The totals were 54.6% Muslim, 28.6% Bangsa Moro, 12% ethnic name, 4.2% Muslim Filipino, 3.8% Filipino, and 2.6% not stated.

When asked to indicate whether Filipino (in one question) or Moro (in another) was an appropriate designation for Muslims, a strong majority (89.4%) disagreed that Filipino was accurate. Regarding Bangsa Moro, 43.2% agreed it was accurate, with marked differences among Maguindanaoan (13.6%), Maranao (2.4%), Samal (75.27%), and Tausug (81.6%). On questions asking for identifying names, a majority of students preferred Muslim (58.6%); 31.2% preferred Bangsa Moro; 6.4% preferred an ethnic name; and 3.8% preferred Filipino. Again, however, the totals masked differences among groups, roughly paralleling the findings regarding citizenship identification. Maranao and Maguindanaoan most strongly preferred Muslim (83.2% and 69.6%, respectively), whereas Samal (44.8%) and Tausug (62.4%) had strong preference for Bangsa Moro. Only the Maranao had a significant percentage (12%) identifying as Filipino.

The thesis contained intriguing explanations of the figures, based both on survey data and on interviews, but only the strong identification as Muslim, the comparatively weak identification with ethnic group, and the almost nonexistent (except among Maranao) identification as Filipino deserve emphasis here. Although there was no way of knowing the extent to which the data were reflective of opinion among all Muslims, it seemed reasonable to assume that they were reflective--certainly one would assume that older Muslims would be more traditional (i.e., more religious) in their identifications. In any event, the opinions of an emerging professional class were important. They clearly suggested that the government's goals of subordinating ethnic identifications and eradicating religious identifications are likely to founder. Both the survey findings and the writings of Philippine Muslims would seem to dictate other goals: specifically a definition of Filipino nationality that included both ethnic identification and religion. Certainly, any definition of nationality that forced Muslims in the Philippines to make choices or even to set priorities was destined to lose to Islam.

There was another aspect to the Marcos regime's ideological problems. If divide and rule was not a deliberate tactic, the regime took full advantage of Muslim divisions--ethnic, clan, personalistic, ideological. Clearly, it emphasized and encouraged factionalism among the MNLF's adherents and supporters. In place of the

MNLF's ideology it substituted what appeared primarily as a spoils system, with loyalty bought by benefits and cohesion achieved through mutual dependency. But neither the loyalty nor the cohesion so gained was a basis for development, if that could be taken seriously as a goal.

Again as with the MNLF, ideological problems became organizational ones. Without a common sense of purpose, without some loyalty to a greater cause, participants in the regime's projects found more limited goals--personal enrichment through commissions or cuts, political position through publicity. Projects once initiated were not finished; programs were poorly planned and, hence, nonproductive; corruption was rampant. Marawi City had water pipes but no reliable water supply, telephone lines but no functioning phone system. The power from Maria Cristina Falls provided power for plants and for houses around Lake Lanao, but the resultant pollution and the drop in the lake's water level upset the area's ecology and economy. Therefore, Muslims had no money to pay for electricity.

Under the circumstances the Marcos regime's success was dependent on a constant flow of pesos to MNLF defectors, to refugees, and to politicians and their clients. Yet, the regime's delivery capacity was severely curtailed by fluctuating prices for exports, drought, and mismanagement.

Ironically, the regime's chief assets -- in the short run -- may have come from programs to which it gave little significance. In recent years, the Ministry of Muslim Affairs contributed to the strengthening of a number of institutions that mattered to Muslims and to the development of a cadre of professionally competent and committed Muslims whose potential usefulness would transcend their current assignments. Michael Mastura, while deputy minister of the ministry, talked of communal autonomy in ways reminiscent of post World War II statesmen promoting the Common Market as a step toward European integration. Yet his focus was really a variant of the Islamic resurgence -- his goal was to strengthen Muslim institutions and self-help mechanisms and thereby to build a more cohesive and effective Muslim community rather than to expend energies on the apparently futile effort to secure political autonomy for Muslims. Others in or out of the Ministry of Muslim Affairs made similar efforts. Despite the exacerbation of Muslim-

Christian relations caused by the fighting and by government programs resented by Christians, there was an impressive amount of Muslim-Christian cooperation in the southern Philippines. Catholics and Protestants, for example, participated in programs designed to educate Christians about Islam, and Christians and Muslims met frequently for dialogues. Research centers and community development programs had Muslim and Christian staff members.

But if these efforts suggested both problems and the possibility of short term stability, other problems were more acute, and were ultimately responsible for the collapse of the Marcos government. Hence, when Corazon Aquino emerged triumphant in February 1986, she inherited not simply an unresolved debate with the MNLF over appropriate political structures and policies for Muslims. The new government faced a national debate over appropriate political structures and policies for the country, while at the same time it attempted to cope with divisions within its own leadership, a devastated economy, and organized opposition from both the left and Marcos loyalists. The MNLF had splintered, its own internal flaws exacerbated by Marcos's tactics.

Under the circumstances, it was understandable that six months after assuming power the government had not begun the negotiations with Muslims to which it had committed itself. Two Muslims had been appointed to the new Constitutional Commission; others had been appointed to replace officials identified with the Marcos era; but Muslims were quite obviously not being given priority on the national agenda. Mrs. Aquino explained that she was waiting for leaders of different groups in the MNLF to decide who would represent them and whether the Tripoli Agreement was to provide the basis for talks. Other officials commented that the government was taking advantage of the factionalism Marcos had encouraged to deal with other issues it regarded as more pressing.

Meanwhile, Muslims grew increasingly restive. Many were sympathetic initially not only because they opposed Marcos but also because Senator Benigno Aquino, and later his brother Agapito ("Butz"), had sought out Muslim leaders for conversation and had been openly supportive of Muslim demands for increased autonomy. Even the sympathetic, however, were concerned about the role of the Catholic Church and of the military (specifically Defense Minister Enrile and General Ramos) in Mrs. Aquino's victory and subsequently in her government's actions. Delay in the announcement of a specific agenda for dealing with Muslim issues encouraged their skepticism; among the more alienated, it encouraged violence.

For Muslims and the government, then, the Marcos government had left a legacy. If it made Muslims more conscious of their Muslim identities and more assertive of what they believed to be their rights than they had been before, it also left them more divided and perhaps less capable of concerted, effective action. For the government, the costs of conflict and of co-operation were clear. The issue of appropriate political structures and policies for Muslims seemed likely to remain a central feature of Philippine political life.

# 11

# Islamic Society in Malaysia

## Introduction

The very pluralism of the system has led to a society in which ethnicity and religion have become intimately entwined and in which social policies, politics, and economics are all heavily influenced by communal considerations. This chapter initially describes the character of this diversity and then discusses the role of Islam within the Malay community; the place of that religion in education, government and political activities; and recent efforts to expand the place of Islam in the nation.

## Pluralism and Ethnicity

Malaysia is administratively and geographically divided between Peninsula Malaya and the Borneo states of Sabah and Sarawak. The population of the nation as a whole includes approximately forty-five percent Malays, thirty-five percent Chinese, ten percent Indians, and ten percent others, with the peninsula being approximately fifty percent Malay, thirty-five percent Chinese, ten percent Indian, and five percent others. Several important factors tend to be correlated with this ethnic balance and each tends to reinforce both actual differences and perceptions. Geographically, the Chinese primarily live on the west coast of the peninsula and on Borneo, where they are concentrated in urban areas. The more rural Malays are to be found in greater numbers outside the cities on the peninsula, although they are beginning to move into urban settings. The non-Malay indigenous population lives principally on Boreno, whereas the Indians are usually to be found in cities and on plantations on the peninsula.

Historically, the Chinese and, to a lesser extent, the Indians have tended to control local commercial and professional activities, and the Malays have tended to control small-scale agriculture and higher administrative posts. Plantation workers have generally been Indians. This relationship of occupation to race has led to disparities in income between the Chinese and Malays and to efforts by the government to raise the economic conditions of the poorer Malays. Finally, almost all Muslims are Malays. Only a relatively small number of the other groups accept Islam; instead, they maintain the traditions they brought with them from China and India or they follow indigenous beliefs. Thus, with many individual exceptions, ethnicity has historically correlated with geography, occupation, economic status, and religion.

The manner in which Islam came to Malaya and past colonial policies may help to explain some of these relationships. Although Arab tombstones have been found on neighboring Java from as early as the eleventh century, Islam first arrived in Malaya through the peaceful penetration by Indian and Arab traders, with the first recorded conversion occurring in the early fourteenth century. Then, in 1414, the ruler of Malacca, Muhammad Iskander Shah, was reportedly converted, leading to the spread of Islam through the peninsula. The power of Malacca made the acceptance of the religion politically and economically desirable and conversion of the general population followed through state sponsorship and individual missionary activity. Islam was thus established in a relatively isolated environment insofar as the influence of centers of theological learning in the Middle East is concerned. It was fostered initially by individuals lacking religious sophistication, a condition that lasted into the twentieth century.

The period of British colonialism (from the end of the eighteenth century to the middle of the twentieth) promoted a new environment. While attempting to "protect" the Malay and his religion, the British, as had the Dutch before them, allowed the local sultans to retain responsibility over religion and did not encourage the Malays to enter the modern commercial world. Meanwhile, increased mining and plantation activities demanded heavy manpower commitments and through the years of a gradual influx of Chinese and Indians expanded to a precipitous flow. The non-Malay population of over 500,000 at the turn of the century reached almost 3.5 million at the time of independence in 1957. The religious complexion of the society was thus changed by the immigration of Taoist, Confucian, and Buddhist Chinese as well as mostly Hindu Indians. In addition, a small minority of Arabs, Indians, and Pakistanis became influential commercial and religious members of the Muslim population. The result was that by the first census after independence, the Malays, who to all intents and purposes were also Muslims, were but half the total number of people in the new nation.

When Sabah and Sarawak were brought into the Federation in 1963 to form Malaysia, the percentage of Muslims was further diluted. Coastal Malays form only a small percentage of the peoples of the two states, which have a heterogeneous indigenous population that includes sizable Chinese elements. In 1960, Sarawak was only 23.4 percent Muslim and Sabah 37.9 percent. For a period after its incorporation, there were efforts to convert the people of Sabah to Islam under the political leadership of Tun Mustapha and a number of well-publicized conversions took place. However, although the Muslims have dominated the political and cultural life of the nation as a whole and have continued to be the largest religious group, they only now compose slightly over 50 percent of Malaysia's population.

This plural character of Malaysian society permeates politics, economics, and religion in the nation, complicating and intensifying communal relationships. On the one hand, it presents the Islamic activist with a heterogeneous environment, unlike that in the Middle East, which leads to pressure for some form of accommodation. On the other hand, the history of a seemingly ever-increasing non-Muslim population in a modern environment and the resultant challenge to Malay traditions and values have made the Malay-Muslim even more conscious of his ethnoreligious identity and dampened divisions within the community. The perception of Islam as the religion of an endangered indigenous population that has been primarily rural, poor, and noncommercial in its character has also fostered a sense of defensiveness that has been the foundation for Malay sponsored politics, public policy, and attitudes. This welding of Malay and Islamic identity has been further strengthened by the religious and cultural cohesion of its adherents.

If the plural nature of Malaysia is one major force in explaining the role of Islam, the other force is the interactive relationship between religion and ethnicity to most Malays. According to the Constitution, "Malay means a person who professes the Muslim religion, habitually speaks the Malay language, conforms to Malay customs." As we shall see, this legal definition has important political and economic connotations. At this point, it is important to note the general and sturdy acceptance among Malays of the concept of the identity of Islam with being Malay. Observers over the decades have regularly commented on this relationship. Recently, writing of literary responses, T. S. Chee states, "Religion or the belief in Islam is not the end result of rational analysis, but a symbol of Malayness." S. Siddique wrote that to become a Malay and to become a Muslim are inseparable, and M. Nash said of the rural Malay, "Religion in the context of Kelantan is an interesting cognitive term. For Malays, it is not separable from ethnic identity or cultural heritage. In Kelantan, Malay equals Muslim."

## Malay Religious Beliefs

This perception of the unity of ethnicity and religion has a number of important ramifications. Muslims from the Arab world have emphasized the universal elements of Islam, underscoring the concept of the ummah. The Malay Muslim, although he takes considerable pride in being part of the world of Islam, also reflects, particularly in the rural setting, a certain parochialism and ethnoreligious nationalism. This parochialism, when combined with the challenges brought about by the non-Muslim communities, has led to an emphasis on particular rather than universal issues and provided obstacles to those seeking to employ religion as a unifying force in Malaysian Muslim society. According to one observer, "Traditional Malay identity was and is defined not so much in terms of universalistic membership in a world religion as it was and is in terms of more specific sorts of contexts and associations--family, kampong [village], state, people (bangsa Malayu) and perhaps in the past chief and ruler." Thus, the Malay seeking ready models for local solutions is not as likely to find them in the context of issues and actions elsewhere in the Muslim world.

Second, this identification of Islam and Malayness has provided an obstacle to Islamic unity within Malaysia. Although Arabs, Indonesians, Indians, and Pakistanis have been legally and, to a limited degree, socially incorporated into the indigenous (bumiputra) community, the more culturally distinct Chinese have had a more difficult time being received into the Malay society. Chinese converts may be publicized in the media, change their names, and live as Muslims; but their ethnic identity continues to provide an obstacle to full acceptance for many Malays.

Third, the interrelationship of Islam and being Malay has led to perceptions among the Malays of an integrated whole that includes lifestyle, values, language, and religion. Attacks on one part are viewed as endangering the whole. Thus, secular education, Western materialism, urbanization, and other aspects of modernization are perceived by many Malays to be challenges to both the religious and ethnic foundations of their society. This correlation of Malay and Muslim provides a powerful tool to Malay politicians who seek to unite the community. Defectors from the party can be charged with weakening a Malay Islamic community that is endangered by nonbelievers. Economic policies to aid the Malays can be described as means of defending and strengthening Islam. The development of Malay as the national language is also perceived as reinforcing the Malay role.

## Malay Beliefs and Practices

Prior to analyzing Islam as it relates to political issues, religious law, and education, it is necessary to describe briefly Islam as it has affected the average Malay. Today, as increased urbanization and mobility make it more difficult to define Malay society as a whole, the Malaysian Muslim is no longer almost entirely the product of the traditional rural village. What we wish to present is a modal description of the more central Malay Muslim religious patterns as they are still to be found in a rural population within which even the urban Malay has generally lived his formative years. In doing so, we shall concentrate on only two aspects of a complex environment: basic Islamic tenets and practices and non-Muslim elements.

Malay Muslims are Sunnis, with a complex set of influences derived from Sufi, Hindu, and animistic sources. At the village level, non-Muslim ways interact more with "purer" Islamic beliefs and practices, whereas those educated in the urban areas or with better religious training are more likely to display belief patterns more akin to orthodox Islamic teachings. In general terms, the rural Malay may be described as conservative and ritualistic in religious belief. He is influenced and circumscribed by individual expectations regarding the strong impact of fate and luck on his personal success or failure and community norms within which he is expected to act. These practices and beliefs are important guidelines in defining his place in the world. As one observer noted, "They see Islam or at least certain aspects of Islam as enveloping them in a set of ritual relationships, and as being a major dimension of community life and organization. Along with this there is a set of constraints which reflect an emphasis on social obligation, particularly of a ritual or ceremonial nature."

If we accept the common description of the Malay as oriented toward ritual, we can turn to four of the ritualistic Pillars of Islam: prayer, fasting, pilgrimage, and tithing. (We bypass the first, which relates to belief in the unity of God.) Although this description is brief and provides only a glimpse into Islamic elements of religious belief, it is meant to illustrate basic patterns. Islam calls for prayer five times a day and special services at midday on Friday; in rural Malaysia, these precepts are generally followed, not so much because of the sanctions established by law as to personal belief and peer-group pressure. Although urban Malays are less regular (some would say lax) in their practices, there are signs that more attention is being paid to this pillar among politicians, students, and religious organizations, in part owing to an increasingly religious environment.

Fasting during Ramadan (Puasa as the Malays term it), is the most important happening in the Malay religious calendar. The restrictions during the fast are widely followed; legal sanctions and notices in urban hotels and restaurants are generally not the controlling factors as much as individual attitudes and peer-group influences. At the end of the fast, Hari Raya, the most important

Malay celebration of the year takes place. It is a time for special foods, gatherings, and visiting cemeteries and relatives; in urban areas, there are special sales, exchanges of greeting cards, and a crush at airports, train stations, and bus depots as celebrants travel back to their towns and villages.

The hajj, the pilgrimage to Mecca, has become considerably more possible to the Malay Muslim since independence, as the government has aided in developing savings for the hajj, organizing the trip (now also made available to neighboring Muslim minorities), and seeing to the comfort and safety of pilgrims. The Malay, even more than the Indonesian, has looked on the hajj as an important religious act to fulfill during his lifetime; a higher percentage of Malays now make the hajj than any other major Muslim country in the region. Given the distance from the traditional centers of Islamic activity, this gives the Malay an opportunity to be part of the wider world of Islam. It also may give social and religious prestige to the returning pilgrim, although the fact that hajjis tend to be older and more affluent reinforces a status already present to a degree.

Zakat is a religious tax on agriculture and property, whereas fitrah is a personal levy. Traditionally it was an accepted practice in the village and was considered an important part of one's religious obligations. Collected by the local imam (leader of the mosque), it is normally used for maintaining and constructing mosques, religious education, and charities. Such levies are no longer unanimously accepted in rural areas; in urban centers, the more atomized community makes collection more difficult. Generally, then, the Malay Muslim has carried out the basic rituals of Islam in a conscientious and orthodox manner.

Although the rural Malay considers himself a Muslim and part of the world brotherhood of Islam, he is also deeply influenced by a set of primarily non-Islamic beliefs, a folk Islam that often combines Islamic elements with animist and Hindu factors. Rites of passage--birth, circumcision, marriage, death--each have their syncretic ceremonies. Magic with its acceptance of special powers, sorcery, amulets, and formulas are mixed with forces derived from a more orthodox religious framework. The rural Malay has also incorporated into his belief system a wide-ranging spirit life that necessitates propitiation through various ceremonies. For example, there are evil spirits of animate and inanimate objects as well as spirits that can inhabit a man's body and influence his actions. Illness can be the result of spells, spirits, and magic, and treatment can be provided through reliance on special magical cures. In rice-growing areas, the rice soul has necessitated particular ways of harvesting and storage. The syncretic nature of many of these acts brings together animist, Hindu, and Islamic elements and can involve local Muslim religious leaders, verses from the Quran, thoughts of God to ward off spirits, and so on.

There has been some decline in these more traditional beliefs and practices as religious leaders have urged the populace to give less emphasis to spirits and magic; the influence of Islamic modernism has challenged these "impure" views and ways; and the process of education, modernization, and urbanization has weakened traditional ties. However, there is no doubt that a substantial portion of the rural population as well as less educated urban migrants retain and accept these beliefs.

## Postindependence Issues

We now turn to a description and analysis of Islam as it has related to politics, religious law, and education in Malaysia. Although there have been other arenas in which Islam has been important, these have been the central national issues that have received attention over the years since independence.

## Politics

To understand the role of Islam in Malaysian politics, it is necessary to recognize two levels of interaction, that among the country's political parties and that within the Islamic community itself. Malaysian national and state politics cannot be understood outside the communal basis of the society. Since independence the governing elite has recognized the need to maintain a delicate balance between retaining the political dominance of the Malay Muslim in the political arena and placating other communities. Thus the ruling coalition in Kuala Lumpur has always had at its helm the Malay-Muslim United Malay National Organization (UMNO), the party from which all prime ministers, deputy prime ministers, and home ministers have come. Other members of the coalition (originally the Alliance, now called the National Front) have been drawn from largely Chinese- and Indian-based parties. The opposition historically has been composed of dissatisfied socialist-oriented Chinese and Indian elements that have expounded greater rights for non-Malays and for conservative Malays unhappy with the government's multiracial policies. The latter were concentrated in what was first the Pan-Malayan Islamic Party (PMIP), now called PAS.

The issue of religion has thus necessitated a balance that has the leadership of the coalition, on the one hand, espousing a pluralistic society guaranteeing the rights and privileges of all Malaysians and, on the other hand, attempting to assuage its Malay-Muslim constituency. Too heavy handed Malay-Muslim chauvinist rhetoric and policy endangers the maintenance of the coalition and possibly national stability. At the same time, it is necessary to hold the loyalty of a Malay-Muslim constituency that remains deeply conscious of its ethnoreligious roots and fears the encroachment of other races and cultures. From the early days of independence, parliamentary backbenchers of UMNO, youth organizations, and local traditional leadership have called on their national leaders to increase the role of Islam in Malaysian society and to use the power of the state to advance Islamic goals. Frequently UMNO politicians on the rise have found it desirable to pander to these views in order to attain power. UMNO must also consider its Malay-Muslim opposition, which has long espoused more religiously chauvinistic policies and is able to drain away voters if the government does not appear to be giving sufficient attention to Malay interests. During the first dozen years, national policy and rhetoric were weighted toward a more pluralistic approach. In its first dozen years after independence, the Alliance leadership fostered pragmatism, even spoke of the need to develop the Protestant work ethic and placated its more religiously oriented constituents with rhetoric more than action. The year 1969 was a watershed for rhetoric and policy as the racial riots of that year led to a shifting of the balance toward a government emphasis on Malay-Muslim goals while not rejecting pluralism. On the economic front, greater attention was given to bringing the Malay into the modern sector. Through subsidies, quotas, and other "affirmative-action" programs, the Malay was encouraged to compete in the marketplace, education, and the factory. Politically, this increased emphasis on religion, and ethnicity became even more central to Malaysian party politics than was previously the case. UMNO backbenchers and often UMNO youth attempted to push the National Front more actively into the defense of Malay-Islamic interests. As the government sought to meet these pressures, its Islamic opposition found it difficult to compete at the ballot box. This continued inability to increase its political role helped to lead PAS toward an even more narrowly Islamic Malay chauvinist position and finally into a basic change in leadership in which older, more traditional party leaders gave way to younger activists. Events in contemporary Malaysia have exacerbated differences within the Muslim community itself. On politicoreligious grounds, it is possible to divide Malaysian Muslims into four categories:

1. Radicals
2. Traditionalists
3. Fundamentalists
4. Accommodationists

**Radicals.** At one end of the spectrum may be found small fringe elements who have demanded basic changes in the relationship between Islam and Malaysian society. They have received considerable publicity because of both the dramatic violence of their acts and the opportunities they gave the government to illustrate the dangers of extremism. Two of the most well-known examples of such actions were the depredation of Hindu temples by a small group of primarily south Indian Muslims and the 1980 attack on a local police station by fifteen white-robed individuals crying, "Allahu Akbar"--("Allah is Great"). In the latter case, some twenty-six police and civilians were wounded and eight of the attackers killed. The leader of the assault, one Mohammed Nasir, said that the era of Mohammed was over and that he would lead the crusade to rid the country of all evil. Radicals of this sort have received little public support and are condemned by all other major Muslim groups.

**Traditionalists.** This category includes the bulk of the Malay rural community and provides much of the membership of both UMNO and its Islamic party opposition. These people identify themselves with the synthesis of Islam and Malay ethnicity, and they seek to maintain traditional patterns of life. Although their religious consciousness is infused with animistic beliefs, this does not weaken their vigorous support for a strong role for Islam in

Malaysian government and society. Religiously, they also tend to be suspicious of new and foreign influences on Islam. Politically, they tend to be divided between UMNO and PAS. At the local level, contests between these two parties can be based on economic differences within the local Malay community personalities, charges against opponents for being "un-Islamic," and communal issues as each candidate seeks to out-Malay the other.

**Fundamentalists.** By fundamentalist or revivalist we mean those who actively seek to expand the role of Islam in Malaysian economic, religious, and political life. Employing education, public forums, the printed media, and other nonviolent means, the fundamentalists seek to make Malaysian Muslims more conscious of their faith and to foster an understanding of Islam that goes beyond mere adherence to ritual and practice. In a religious sense, they tend to situate themselves alongside many of the historic basic goals of Islamic modernism.

The most articulate exponent of this position has been Anwar Ibrahim, former head of the Islamic Youth Organization, Angkatan Belia Islam Malaysia (ABIM), and minister of culture, youth, and sports in Dr. Mahathir's cabinet in 1983, later minister of agriculture and now minister of education. His economic and political goals have emphasized equity, pluralism, and social welfare. He has sought a greater role for Islam in the state and a strengthening of the religious consciousness of believers, but not at the expense of non-Muslims. Not all fundamentalists, even within ABIM, accept Ibrahim 's pluralist approach, but there are those who want to see non-Muslims educated in, and finally converted to, Islam. Their end goal is the establishment of a totally Islamic society.

The core of the fundamentalist movement in Malaysia comes from educated youth who have come into contact with Western values and material culture during their schooling in Malaysian and foreign universities and have increasingly become part of the country's urban population. Unlike the older and more traditional local leadership of the rural Malays, these young people are more sophisticated in their use of the media, development of modern organization, and ability to employ the technological tools of the West.

**Accommodationists.** Malay politicians, on reaching national leadership, have publicly espoused what can be called the accommodationist approach. They have emphasized the necessity of a multiracial, mutireligious society in which all elements can freely practice their own religions without government interference. Prior to the 1969 riots, these leaders articulated an almost secularist position in which religious considerations were downplayed in favor of pluralism and pragmatism. Men like the first prime ministers, Tunku Abdul Rahman and Tun Razak, appeared more comfortable in a less sectarian environment (although Tunku became involved in domestic and international Muslim activities after leaving office). While the next two prime ministers, Hussein Onn and Dr. Mahathir still proclaim a multireligious Malaysia, secular rhetoric has given way to a greater emphasis on Islamic values. The accommodationists do not include a large segment of the Islamic community, but they hold key political and bureaucratic offices and are reinforced by the paucity of other alternatives if Malaysia is to remain a peaceful nation. Some fundamentalists, such as Anwar Ibrahim, fall into this group.

It should be noted that secularists, in terms of those declaring that religion should not play a public role in society, are not included as a major force within the Malay community. Although there are nonreligious Malays and secularism has developed, an influential, publicly secular Malay sector simply does not play any important role in political life.

## Religious Laws

Historically, Islamic law in Malaysia has been a local rather than a national matter. During the British period, the Malay sultans were accepted as protectors of Malay religion and culture and within their jurisdiction an Islamic court system was established largely limited to civil cases dealing with marriage, divorce, and inheritance. These courts also enforced various regulations regarding prayer, fasting, and so on, although punishment was limited in all cases to a fine of M$10. Those states with a hereditary ruler also had a head khati (qadi) (religious magistrate)--as did each district--who was responsible for administering Islamic justice. The British on their part attempted to prohibit proselytizing among Muslims while guaranteeing freedom of belief to other faiths.

With independence came many other changes. However, it is important to recognize that Malaysia has been both a constitutional and federal system. In the first instance, this means that there has been a rule of law and generally religious rules have been codified and operate through a system of courts. Fundamental issues are written into the Constitution. Second, the country is federal, with primary responsibility for religion resting at the state level. Each of the sultans has retained his role as protector of Islam, whereas the states of Malacca and Penang come under the king (Yang di-Pertuan Agong). The Borneo states of Sabah and Sarawak have no official head of religion.The Constitution of 1957 firmly puts Islam within the state structure while guaranteeing religious freedom to other religions. Its key provisions provide for

1. The establishment of Islam as the religion of the country. "Islam is the religion of the Federation."
2. The sultan as head of the Islamic religion. In every State that has a ruler, he is recognized as the "Head of the Muslim religion in his State."
3. The protection of Muslims from proselytizing. "State law may control or restrict the propagation of any religious doctrine or belief among persons professing the Muslim religion."
4. Freedom of worship for other religions. "Other religions may be practiced in peace and harmony in any part of the Federation. Every religious group has the right (a) to manage its own religious affairs; (b) to establish and maintain institutions for religious and charitable purposes; and (c) to acquire and own property and hold and administer it in accordance with the law."

Each of these constitutional provisions has become the focus of further debate, refinement, and in many cases new laws and interpretations. Regarding the role of Islam in the state: There has been considerable debate as to whether Malaysia should become or already is an Islamic state. Elements within both UMNO and PAS have called for some form of an Islamic state for many years, although there has been a certain vagueness about the meaning of the concept beyond having the government following the precepts of the Quran and shariah. Both the new leadership of PAS and spokesmen for ABIM have been somewhat more specific in terms of the structure and goals of such a state, but again this has not been completely spelled out.

The government, under cross pressures from both within and without the United Front, has sought to continue to guarantee religious freedom while at least rhetorically meeting Islamic demands. This has led the prime minister and his deputy to argue that Malaysia already is an Islamic state and Dr. Mahathir has given tacit approval to the vague concept of Islamic rule for the country. However, at this point the strategy appears to be to forestall any move toward a well-defined constitutional amendment creating an Islamic state while political rhetoric and limited actions would increase the perceived role of Islam within the nation.

**Role of the Sultans.** After independence the role of the states and sultans in protecting Islam was reinforced. Departments of religion were retained or formed in all the states with hereditary rulers and the Islamic courts were able to expand both their jurisdiction and the punishments they could mete out. At the federal level, the Council of Rulers attempted to cooperate on national religious matters.

Two problems arose out of this increased role: A conflict between the sultans and federal authorities over jurisdiction and a lack of uniformity in religious statutes. In the first instance, the federal government has steadily moved into religious issues, engaging itself in areas of conversion, Islamic religious education, international Islamic cooperation, Islamic banking and economics, the hajj, and so on. There have also been efforts to become involved in local affairs through the education of Muslim religious leaders and schoolchildren and through support for religious schools and other Islamic institutions. Also, the close association between UMNO and lower level Islamic leaders has long been a fact of political life, leading often to bitter local party conflicts during local and national elections. The sultans have become quite concerned with what they perceive as government efforts to weaken their powers, and there has been increasing tension on several levels. For example, in 1983, the sultans of Perak and Johore proclaimed different periods for the Ramadan than those presented by the federal authorities, leading to both confusion and tension.

Another issue that has disturbed national authorities has been obvious inconsistencies in religious laws and sanctions across states. Although there have been efforts to develop some uniformity over the years, federal officials have privately complained that the unity of Islam and the state has been weakened by the hodgepodge of regulations now in existence. Certainly nowhere in South or Southeast Asia does one find the breadth of rules formulated to assure that Muslims properly follow the precepts of their religion regarding prayer, fasting, morality, and purity of the faith. Historically, Malay Muslims have emphasized the importance of ritual, and these laws reflect this concept of religious obedience. Even the more conservative Indonesian Muslims when discussing the Malaysian situation find these legal strictures on the faithful too demanding; some Malaysian fundamentalists have complained that they detract from a necessary emphasis on more central issues. The provision for Muslim law in the state lists reads:

Muslim Law and personal and family law of persons professing the Muslim religion, including the Muslim Law relating to succession, testate and intestate, betrothal, marriage, divorce, dower, maintenance, legitimacy, guardianship, gifts, partitions and non-charitable trusts; Muslim Wakfs and the definition and regulation of charitable and religious trusts, the appointment of trustees and the incorporation of persons in respect of Muslim religious and charitable institutions operating wholly within the state; Malay custom; Zakat, Fitrah and Bait-ul-Mal or similar Muslim revenue; mosques or any Muslim public place of worship, creation and punishment of offences by persons professing the Muslim religion against precepts of that religion, except in regard to matters included in the Federalist; the constitution, organization and procedure, of Muslim courts, which shall have jurisdiction only over persons professing the Muslim religion and in respect only of any of the matters included in this paragraph, but shall not have jurisdiction in respect of offences except in so far as conferred by federal law: the control of propagating doctrines and beliefs among persons professing the Muslim religion; the determination of matters of Muslim Law and doctrine and Malay custom.

One author collected a representative list of specific state statutes, although these may vary in detail and punishment and may or may not be implemented:

- failure to attend Friday prayers at the mosque;
- consumption of intoxicating liquor;
- sale to a Muslim or consumption by a Muslim of any food or drink during daylight during the month of Ramadan;

- any Muslim male found in suspicious proximity with any woman who is not his close relative [this is the khalwat law that, if strictly enforced, outlaws unchaperoned dating practices];
- any female Muslim abetting the offence of khalwat;
- sexual intercourse between husband and wife in a manner forbidden by Islam;
- willful disobedience by a woman of an order lawfully given by her husband;
- teaching any doctrine of the Muslim religion without written permission of the Malay ruler;
- propagating religious doctrines other than Islam among persons professing the Muslim religion;
- teaching false doctrine;
- printing or distributing books or documents repugnant to any lawful Fetwa or contrary to orthodox belief;
- contempt of religious authorities or officials;
- contempt of the law of Islam or its tenets.

More recently there have also been pronouncements by religious leaders that argue there should be laws against Muslims calling one another infidels over political differences and to have women sit in the back of buses to avoid khalwat (close proximity between the sexes) as well as government warnings that "deviant" Muslims could lose their special privileges as bumiputra and prohibitions against Muslims working in the gambling casinos at Genting Highlands, outside Kuala Lumpur.

**Proselytizing and Freedom of Worship.** Every state took advantage of the Constitution by prohibiting efforts to convert Muslims; this in itself has not led to problems. What has been at issue has been the perception of leaders of religions other than Islam that their efforts to propagate their beliefs among non-Muslims have been restricted and that the government has become a vehicle for conversion to Islam of their fellow believers. Certainly, the media has largely been closed to other faiths in terms of religious programs, advertisements, news stories, and so on, and a close watch is held over material that might be detrimental to Muslims. The identity between religion and ethnicity among Malays and the special privileges that come with remaining Muslim would certainly limit conversion and, although legally possible, such rare cases of apostasy have not been recognized by religious authorities.

Also disturbing to other religions are efforts to propagate Islam, arguably the faith of only a bare majority of Malaysians, by way of the media, public forums, official pronouncements, subsidies to Islamic institutions, attempts to make Muslim holy days national celebrations, support of dakwah (missionary) organizations in their work to convert non-Muslims, news programs rejoicing at such conversions, and so on. Programs to raise the religious consciousness of Muslims is one thing, but perceptions that there is increasing pressure for the Islamization of the population as a whole have obviously created uneasiness among non-Muslims. These fears were heightened when Islamic courts called for the punishment of non-believers caught in khalwat with Muslims, when state governments demanded a ban on non halal meat in all hotels and restaurants (later rescinded), or when a deputy within the prime minister's office discussed a morals law with leaders of other faiths, even though he said it would be based on all religions and the government later backed down.

Difficulties in these areas often arise because national political leaders find it necessary to talk to two constituencies: their Muslim base and their multiracial partners. Thus, Musa Hitam, former deputy prime minister, or Anwar Ibrahim, former head of the Islamic Youth Organization, might both support some form of Islamic state before one constituency. Yet, at another time and to another constituency, the former deputy prime minister could also say, "Malaysian leaders are aware that this is a multiracial and multi-religious society. Islamization as in other countries. cannot be done." And Ibrahim could also argue that Islamization "is not aimed at mass conversion of Malaysians to Islam. It's a process to inject more spiritual values into our lives." Neither man probably sees any incompatibility in these statements, although their audiences may hear or want to hear differently.

## Islamic Education

Prior to independence, education in Malaya was characterized by its considerable variety in mode of instruction and means of support. English, Malay, and vernacular Indian and Chinese languages were all used as the means of instruction, and state and charitable contributions were the bases of school budgets. As one author noted, education for the Malay and Indian was primarily to attain literacy, for the Chinese to maintain ties to China, and for those studying in English to pass the Cambridge Overseas School Certificate examinations. All of this changed after 1957 when the government placed its highest budgetary priority on education as it sought to Malaysianize the educational system through regulation of the curricula and teacher training as well as fostering Malay as the national language.

Until a quarter of a century ago, Malay Muslim education was, with the exception of that available to the aristocracy, not given high priority by the state or national governments and was left to local efforts. The British colonial administration, although prepared to counter illiteracy, did not want to interfere with what it saw as a stable Malay lifestyle. On their part, Malay parents were unsure as to the benefits of furthering the education of their children. The boys were needed on the land and education for females was considered largely unnecessary. The Malay schools that did exist for the average student were generally of a very low quality, and the English-medium schools were usually taught by non-Muslims who appeared to be, at best, unsympathetic to Malay Muslim values. Religious education did not have many of these drawbacks.

Traditionally, the young Malay boy received his initial religious training at the age of seven or eight from a local teacher from whom he learned to chant and memorize the Quran. Further Islamic education, if available and desired, came from local religious schools or individual teachers, with ultimately a very few going abroad for advanced work in the Middle East. Much of the early instruction was by rote with comparatively little understanding of the content or the Arabic language in which it was presented.

With the expansion of education in recent decades, more boys found a greater variety of education available and turned to secular schools or religious institutions, such as the Arab Schools. Here they learned to read and write Arabic and gained a limited elementary education. Or they turned to the Majlis institutions that combined religious and secular training. Most Malays in either a secular or an Islamic system received some instruction in Islam. After independence, if there are fifteen or more Muslims in a school, by law a Muslim religious teacher, supported by the state and federal governments, must be employed. This teaching takes place within school hours and is in Malay.

Islamic education has expanded at the tertiary level as well, with Islamic studies programs at both the University of Malaya and Universiti Kebangsaan. At both of these institutions, a wide range of courses in Arabic as well as Muslim theology, history, law, and so on, is offered to a largely Malay Muslim student body. In 1983, a government-sponsored international Islamic university was opened in Kuala Lumpur that seeks to present a curricula in which Islam permeates all subjects. The language of instruction is English, and it is open to students from all countries and religions.

Thus, what we are seeing in education for the Malay is a complex interaction between expanding secular training and increased government effort to advance Islam in the schools. (Some opponents argue that this is, in part, in order to take education out of the hands of local religiopolitical PAS teachers.) Elementary education is no longer limited Quranic instruction for boys, but a primarily secular education for both sexes that reaches over ninety percent of the school age population. In the first six standards, the children take geography, history, mathematics, science, civics, physical education, and art from teachers much better trained than their predecessors. At the tertiary level, Malay Muslims, aided by government quotas and subsidies, are encouraged to enter the sciences, business, and engineering, formerly the preserve of the Chinese and Indians. At the same time, "Islamic religious knowledge" is required in the lower standards and religious studies at advanced levels have become broader and comparatively more sophisticated. This educational policy has not solved the problem of the often rudimentary rote-learned knowledge of Islam of the rural student, yet it has engendered disquiet among many parents that the secular nature of the rest of their children's education could dilute religious and traditional values.

## Contemporary Patterns and Policies

The past decade has seen important real and symbolic changes in the traditional role that Islam played in Malaysian society. It has become far more obvious in public rhetoric, government policies, and even dress. Our discussion will address some of these changes, but first it is useful to assess some of the reasons for this development. Three factors would appear to be paramount: modernization, international influences, and domestic politics.

## Modernization

The process of modernization, reinforced by government efforts to raise the economic level of Malays, has brought an increasing number of Malays into settings where their traditional beliefs and practices have been challenged. The largely rural Malay coming to the city or experiencing modernization in his own traditional environment has often displayed disgust or antagonism against what he has perceived to be questionable elements inherent in Western values and activities. It can be argued that this confrontation with modernization has reinforced the sense of religious and ethnic identity among the Malays. From time to time there have been dramatic outbursts against aspects of this new milieu, such as the individual who threw his television out the window because of the offensive material broadcast on it. However, television ownership is rapidly increasing among Malays.

At the elite level, we have also seen an increased sense of religious identity for somewhat similar reasons. Young Malays entering universities in Malaysia and abroad have been confronted with new ideas and values.

Overseas they have been influenced by other Muslims, often with radical or fundamentalist views. It is from many of these well-educated youth that the intellectual and organizational base for the fundamentalist movement in Malaysia has been formed. The perceived dangers of these "deviate" ideas has obviously made the government nervous; thus efforts have been made to prepare these students to deal with differing Islamic ways of thinking.

## International Influences

The past decade has seen a worldwide resurgence of Islam, which has not been ignored in Malaysia. The apparent increased power of Islamic countries since the oil crisis has reinforced pride in their religion among the Malay Muslims. Events in Iran and the Middle East have kindled interest in the new ideas and movements that have swept those areas; and the government has become worried about the possible consequences of the spread of the ideas of the Iranian revolution, Libya's Colonel Qaddafi, and unauthorized international Islamic organizations. With the increased mobility of young Malays, the old, often relatively static, quality of Islam in Malaysia is being infused with concepts from the outside as never before.

## Domestic Political Forces

As we have noted, Malaysian politics have always had a communal base and UMNO and PAS have each responded to their Malay and their Muslim constituencies. In a fashion, the contemporary interplay of Islam with the aforementioned domestic and international factors has been circular. As the government has attempted to react to increased demands to defend and develop Islam, it has helped to establish a religious environment in which such religious pressures have had a greater legitimacy and Malay-Muslim expectations of government support have been higher.

There has been a tendency among outside observers and domestic political opponents to describe government actions and rhetoric in this sphere as instrumentalist and manipulative. Although political motives cannot be denied and would be surprising if nonexistent, it would also appear that the general character of the Weltanschauung of the Malay elite and community has changed since 1969. The Malay political and bureaucratic leadership no longer lives in the almost totally Chinese and Indian enclave that defined much of urban Malaysia in the past. Malay migration to the cities, their large-scale enrollment in the universities, their domination of the media, and their place in the international world of Islam have all helped to create an atmosphere reinforcing a sense of identity and self-confidence. This, in turn, has been translated into the kind of Malay-Islamic actions and rhetoric that pervades Malay politics today.

There have been numerous examples in recent years of increased government response to these pressures. A regular visitor to Malaysia is struck by the increased time given Islamic subjects on nationally controlled television, the number of women wearing conservative Muslim dress (at one time encouraged in government offices), the greater emphasis on Islamic holidays, constant references to Islamic subjects in the printed media and by politicians, and the proliferation of organizations dealing with Islamic issues and projects. Here we can note three examples of these changes: Malaysia's involvement in the Islamic world, interest in Islamic economics, and the growth of dakwah movements.

Malaysia has not simply been the passive recipient of internationally defined ideas and movements. The government has taken advantage of its membership in the wider Islamic community to seek aid for domestic activities, such as the new international Islamic university. It has also attempted to reinforce the perception of its position as defender of the faith and as an important actor in the world of Islam. Malaysia has been a regular participant in a wide variety of international Islamic activities and has hosted numerous such gatherings, Quranic reading contests, and other interactions with the world Islamic community. These are often done with considerable style, such as the international Quranic reading contest that is televised nationally, attended by top UMNO politicians, and held in a large stadium. The government has also involved itself in international Muslim appeals, resolutions, and demands, such as those related to the Soviet Union's occupation of Afghanistan and Israel's activities on the West Bank. There has been some caution in handling such issues so as not to allow non government Islamic groups to take advantage of them to develop their own organizations and goals.

## Domestic Economic Issues

Islam and contemporary economic issues interact on two levels: efforts to improve the economic role of the bumiputra and recent rhetoric and actions to formulate Islamic economic policies. In the first instance, we return to an earlier discussion of the interplay of religion and ethnicity. Following the 1969 riots, the government of Malaysia set out to develop programs to increase the role of the Malay in the modern economy and to raise his social and economic position in the society. The centerpiece for this effort was the New Economic Policy, which called for the reduction and eventual eradication of poverty and acceleration in restructuring Malaysian society to reduce and eventually eliminate the identification of race with economic function.

To achieve these goals, a multifaceted program was initiated that included efforts to have national racial patterns more accurately reflected in employment and ownership in the modern sector. Thus employers were encouraged to have their work force at all levels reach approximately forty percent bumiputra, and strenuous efforts were made to bring ownership in the modern sector by the bumiputra from less than two percent in 1970 to thirty percent in 1990. This is not the place to go into detail with regard to the complex set of programs used to implement these goals. Suffice it to state that among them were special subsidies to Malay businesses, training programs for indigenous entrepreneurs, priorities in obtaining contracts, education programs to increase Malay participation in business and modern technological pursuits, the formation of government and quasi-government institutions to aid the expansion of Malay capital, and so on.

The relationship between the betterment of the Malay under the NEP and Islam has not always been clearly articulated by the government, but it has not been lost on many Malay-Muslim politicians. Thus, UMNO tracts have urged the need to develop a more modern, competitive Muslim if Islam is to thrive in the modern world. If Islam is to be defended and develop, the Muslim must be able to compete with the Chinese and the Indians. Politicians have warned that attitudes and habits need to change to reflect more discipline, hard work, and innovation. These policies have been challenged by both the fundamentalists and traditionalists who both argue that this stress on materialism is injurious to Islamic principles or that it is creating class differences among the Malays, thus weakening the unity of the Malay-Islamic community. For some socialist-oriented fundamentalists, the NEP is also viewed as encouraging capitalist tenets and adherents within the Malay society. Certainly the success attained by the NEP at this point has brought more and more Malays into urban settings that challenged their traditional values. Urban attractions, the entrance of Malay women into the factory, and a weakening of ties with the more integrated rural community have all been of concern to those desiring to maintain the integrity of Malay-Islamic life.

A second and quite recent aspect of the interplay of religion and economics has been the attempt to move the state closer to what is perceived to be the tenets of Islam in the economic sphere. For a number of years there has been considerable discussion within UMNO, PAS, ABIM, and Muslim intellectuals of such issues as zakat, usury, insurance, lotteries, and banking. For example, when the question arose as to the use of revenues from lotteries to build mosques, a group of theologians were called in to decide the issue. It was agreed that such funds should go into general revenue and then be disbursed for such construction. Until recently, these were issues that usually generated more rhetoric than action. In the past two years, a series of new, and some would argue largely symbolic, moves have been made. In 1982, an Islamic insurance company and Islamic pawnshops were approved. In 1983, the first no-interest Islamic bank was opened in Kuala Lumpur with great fanfare; major Malay politicians publicly deposited money in the new institution. Although there were earlier statements to the effect that a large number of banks would follow, it appears that the government intends moving cautiously. As the prime minister stated,

> *There should not be any fear that suddenly there is the intrusion of a very radical system. It is not going to hurt anybody. But it will certainly satisfy a group of Moslems who feel that it is wrong for them to accept interest.*

One of the more interesting and, to many establishment politicians, most worrisome new actors has been the dakwah movement. Certainly missionary activities in Islam are not new; their organizations have been about for centuries in Southeast Asia. However, in Malaysia today they are taking an active role beyond traditional conversion. At this time, there are two major types: those seeking to convert nonbelievers to Islam and the fundamentalists who seek to combine demands for social and economic change with missionary work among the Muslims themselves. In the first group, the most noteworthy organization has been Perkim, which has received funding from the government and overseas Muslims. Perkim not only has involved itself in proselytizing, but has also sought support for new converts in terms of economic aid as well as helping Muslims among the Indochinese refugees coming to Malaysia.

It is the second type of dakwah movement that has led to some negative government reactions. Within this category there are a wide variety of organizations, including radical groups employing violent means to achieve their goals. Dural Arqam is interested in establishing a cooperative, communally oriented system among Muslims in economic, social, educational, and health areas; and the Jaamatul Tabligh is targeted in on Indian Muslims, for example. ABIM has received the most attention, however. Growing from less than 200 members when it was inaugurated in 1971, it now claims 35,000 or more. Under its former charismatic leader Anwar Ibrahim, the organization sought to move the Malay Muslim from his emphasis on ritual to a better understanding of the relationship of Islam to basic economic and social issues facing the nation. Ostensibly apolitical, nonetheless, its leadership has supported an Islamic state and economic and social reform within an Islamic mode, including attaining greater equity for all Malaysians. It has argued that the formation of an Islamic state would strengthen rather than weaken democratic society in Malaysia. These reformist goals, when combined with the strong attraction to the organization and its leadership among young educated Malays, is seen as a political danger by many within UMNO, particularly if ABIM and Anwar Ibrahim join with the opposition PAS. This problem has been partially ameliorated by co-opting Ibrahim into the government, where he has quickly risen to prominence. This has also led to some negative reactions among fundamentalists who feel that the pluralist designs of present UMNO leadership are unacceptable and PAS has made inroads into ABIM's strength on the campuses.

## Conclusion

Malaysia remains a pluralist state in which the majority non-Muslim population can practice its own religion freely. But it is a state with a national flag showing the star and crescent, a Constitution that describes Islam as the official religion, a prime minister who gives highest priority to uniting Muslims, a government whose top ministers are all Muslims, and a national ideology, the Rukunegara, that is clarified by a government that claims it is the "sacred duty of a citizen to defend and uphold" a constitution that guarantees a special position to the Malays, the role of the sultans, and the maintenance of Islam as the official religion. Not only is Malaysia a society in which ethnicity and religion have become intimately intertwined, but also one in which communal identification has been historically associated with geography, occupation, and economic position as well as rural-urban lifestyles. Finally, there is both an increasing sense of Malay-Islamic identity and of rapid modernization. Within this changing and complex environment, several (perhaps inconsistent) patterns have developed. Each one puts added strain on a people attempting to form a nation out of a highly heterogeneous population.

There has been a slow weakening of the traditional syncretist practices and beliefs that have characterized village life in the past. Better education, mobility, communications, influence of "purer" Islamic views, and other broadening forces are making inroads into what was once a much more homogeneous belief system. Yet, this very mobility and modernization is helping to increase ethnic and religious identity among many Malays who are being confronted with new lifestyles and values as well as finding themselves in direct competition with the Chinese and Indians who have been the majority population of urban Malaysia. As more Malays leave the village or have modernization thrust upon them, there is likely to be a continued adverse reaction to those attributes of the new environment that are found undesirable.

The present prime minister, deputy prime minister, and minister of education all want to see the development of an Islam that looks beyond ritual. When he was deputy prime minister, Dr. Mahathir said,

> *Unfortunately, there are still many of us who place more importance on form rather than on substance. Practices required by religion, such as brotherhood, pursuit of knowledge and equipping oneself for defense are unheeded. Priority is given to things like beard, turban, and robe.*

About the same time, then Prime Minister Hussein Onn criticized the narrow views of fundamentalist students educated abroad.

Yet, the dilemma the government may find itself in is related to the extent to which the giving up of traditional and politically stable ritual for a more socially involved faith may open Pandora's box: that is, a more fragmented politicized Islam. After all, it was ABIM's "non-political" demands for reform based on Islam that frightened the government when Anwar Ibrahim was its head.

The political reality of UMNO/PAS politics necessitates continued support for at least symbolic rhetoric and actions in defense of Islam and the Malays. With PAS always ready to challenge moderate pluralistic policies as un-Islamic or un-Malay, the National Front leadership must maintain its public stance as the protector of Muslim and Malay interests. It is difficult to channel rising fundamentalism and Malay-Islamic identity while assuaging the fears of non-Muslims. However, to this point, the government appears ready to move cautiously toward a deeper commitment to domestic and international Islamic policies. Yet, some of these very policies, such as expanding Malay as the national language and bringing in more Malay-Muslims into the universities may lead to increasing interaction among communal groups. Thus, Malay, Indian, and Chinese youths can now be seen conversing and exchanging views with little apparent tension. In 1980, moderate student organizations won elections at the Universiti Kebangsaan and the University of Malaya, in part, because (as one successful candidate said), "We are not for one group or race, but all Malaysians."

Much depends on whether young Islamic fundamentalists are willing to follow a more pluralistic approach or narrower Islamic goals, the government can channel religious demands, and non-Muslims can see their future in a Malay-dominated Malaysia with a commitment to protect the beliefs and goals of all its peoples.

# 12

# International Relations of Asian Islam and Its Impact

## Introduction

On the contrary, the first is generally thought of as putting one out of touch rather than in conflict with the modern world. What is meant, of course, is that Islam is advancing values that are at odds with many of those of Western Christian civilization at the same time as these values are able to work against Western interests. Islam, it is thought, is able to pose these challenges because of the power that comes partly from possessing vast amounts of oil wealth but mostly from the newfound religious and political self-consciousness of many millions of Muslims throughout the world. It is assumed that these Muslims are fostering instability and perhaps revolution in countries ruled by secular, modernizing regimes and, hence, are working against Western interests. Because the Asian Muslim as well as Middle Eastern Muslim countries are strategically located, any weakening of these secular regimes will invite either Soviet or local Communist intrigue.

This perception of tears in the regional fabric fits in with the larger assumption, often held in the West, that Muslims are moving toward greater unity among themselves. The emergence of an Islamic bloc is seen as contrary to Western interests because it would lessen the ability of the West to influence or to pressure Muslim countries. It is assumed that the disposition of mind that leads one to veil women or to apply traditional legal penalties also leads to a commitment to unite all Muslims and even to supersede the current nation-state system. There may or may not be a relationship between the two patterns of thought. But one cannot deny that national borders are proving to be permeable to the chiliastic language of Khomeini or to the antiestablishment violence of such radical groups as the Islamic Jihad Organization. In fact, Muslims in every part of the Muslim world are hearing the message that Islam must accept "neither East nor West" and must reject the blandishments of both superpowers and their respective ideologies.

The question of what Muslims want is a large one and extremely important, but the American and the Westerner also need to look at what is actually happening, to look at the trends and patterns of activity, and then to judge whether we are, indeed, in a threatening or revolutionary era. The obvious first thing to realize is that Islam is not a monolith, neither wishing one wish nor acting in one way. In this chapter, I shall concentrate on the Asian Muslim states. Then, on the basis of these examples, I will look at the extent to which Islam may be said to be a significant international factor today and a stimulus to Muslim economic and political integration.

What constitutes a Muslim state is the obvious first problem. I recognize that there is a large literature and much controversy on what constitutes a proper Islamic state and, hence, my use of the adjective Muslim, rather than Islamic, is designed to avoid any normative implication and to be simply descriptive. Muslim states are those states where Muslims are in the majority. Yet, even when this definition is accepted, it must be noted that there is considerable variation in their Islamic self-consciousness. The spectrum ranges from Pakistan and Iran, the only two to have proclaimed themselves Islamic states, at one end, to secular Afghanistan and Indonesia at the other end; in between are Bangladesh, Malaysia, and Brunei, where Islam is the "first principle" or "the religion" of the state. Other Asian countries neither have Muslim majorities as do Iran or Bangladesh, nor have extremely small Muslim minorities as do Japan or Vietnam, yet they play an important part in the political consciousness of modern Muslim elites. These states have significant Muslim minorities and include India, the Soviet Union, China, the Philippines, Thailand, and Burma, among others.

In this discussion, I shall look at the general subject in terms of three categories of relationship: (1) the relationship among the Asian Muslim states themselves, and that between them and the states with significant Muslim minorities; (2) the relationship between the Asian Muslim (including the minority states) and the non-Asian Muslim states, particularly the Arab states; and (3) the relationship between the Asian Muslim states and the Western states.

## Economic Cooperation of Asian Muslim States

If ties of sentiment among Asian Muslim and Muslim minority states exist, they do not translate into concrete economic ties. It is perhaps only to be expected that the major trading partners of at least the Asian members of the Organization of the Islamic Conference (OIC) are the industrialized giants. This pattern is particularly true of imports, with the Asian states notably importing from the United States and West Germany. Among Asian regional states, Japan is clearly important: In 1981 it was one of the top three exporting countries to each of the states listed in Table 12.1, and it was one of the top three importing countries from all of these Asian Muslim states, with the exception of Bangladesh. The only other regional states to have prominence are Singapore, not surprisingly important as an import and export partner of Malaysia, and China, a longtime friend of Pakistan and a top customer for Pakistan's goods. The Soviet Union falls in the top three export customers only in the case of Bangladesh, which it has traditionally supported to offset Chinese support of Pakistan, and falls not at all in the listing of important partners. Although I have not looked at the trading pattern of the states with significant Muslim minorities, I doubt that it would reveal a fundamentally different conclusion -- that is, there is not significant economic integration.

## Institutional Development

Institutional cooperation among Asian Muslim states is somewhat more developed than economic cooperation. Coordination of activities has occurred among Asian youth groups, such as happens elsewhere in the Muslim world under the aegis of the World Assembly of Muslim Youth. This organization, for

Table 12.1 Main Sources of Imports of Asian OIC Countries

| Importing | Top Three Exporting Countries (in order of precedence) | | | | Share of Total imports (percentage) | | | |
|---|---|---|---|---|---|---|---|---|
| Countries | 1975 | 1978 | 1980 | 1981 | 1975 | 1978 | 1980 | 1981 |
| Bangladesh | U.S., Canada, W. Germany | Japan, U.S., Canada | Japan, U.S., UK | Saudi Arabia, Japan, UAE | 38.0 | 27.6 | 36.6 | 29.6 |
| Indonesia | Japan, U.S., W. Germany | Japan, U.S., W. Germany | Japan, U.S., Saudi Arabia | Japan, U.S., W. Germany | 52.6 | 51.4 | 51.1 | 53.3 |
| Iran | U.S., W. Germany, Japan | U.S., W. Germany, Japan | Japan, W. Germany, UK | W. Germany, Japan, Italy | 53.5 | 55.2 | 36.5 | 33.4 |
| Malaysia | Japan, U.S., UK | Japan, U.S., Singapore | Japan, U.S., Singapore | Japan, U.S., Singapore | 40.8 | 45.6 | 49.6 | 52.1 |
| Maldives | New Zealand, Japan, UK | Japan, Pakistan, India | Japan, India, W. Germany/UK | Singapore, Japan, India | 64.3 | 66.4 | 58.7 | 68.1 |
| Pakistan | Japan, U.S., Saudi Arabia | U.S., Japan, Saudi Arabia | U.S., Japan, Saudi Arabia | Saudi Arabia, Japan, U.S. | 33.9 | 33.8 | 34.0 | 35.8 |

example, sponsors "International Islamic Youth Training Camps for the Muslim Youth of Asian Countries," whose purpose is to bring together Asian Muslims "from different ethnic groups" to learn about each other's "interests or perhaps problems" and, in doing so, to "help promote and develop genuine understanding among themselves." A periodical publication, Islamic Vision, which, although closely tied to the Malaysian youth group, Angkatan Belia Islam Malaysia, reports on the activities of other groups in the Asia-Pacific region. From this one would learn, for example, of the activities of the Assembly of Muslim Youth of Singapore; and, more important, of how Muslim youth in one Asian country interact with those in other Asian countries.

This interaction occurs in such programs as the training program in dakwah that the Pakistani government runs for Muslim students in Pakistan coming from ASEAN countries.

More noteworthy is a second type of institutional development. In November 1980, delegates from sixteen Asian states met in Kuala Lumpur to launch a new regional coordinating body, the Regional Islamic Da'wah Council of Southeast Asian and the Pacific (RISEAP). The Malaysian and Saudi governments are the main financial supporters, and, as one might expect of an organization with such patronage, it is specifically not intended "to interfere with the political" situation of the regional states. Rather, its purpose, according to its secretary-general, Tunku Abdul Rahman, is "to help Muslims to help themselves." In practical terms, this means the establishment of an Islamic training center, the publication of a regular magazine called Al-Nahdah (The Renaissance) that reports on various regional activities and events, and the production of books on Islam in the thirteen languages used in the area. Over sixty groups are now members of RISEAP, and Tunku Abdul Rahman seems to have found in this population a platform for urging better treatment of Muslim minorities in Asia. He has made not only relatively ordinary trips in this regard, such as to Australia in 1981, but also more noteworthy ones, such as to China in 1982, where he offered assistance to the China Islamic Association. In December 1984 the General Assembly of RISEAP endorsed the resolutions of the OIC Conference on Muslim Minorities, which was held in Perth in September 1984, and specifically endorsed the idea that zakat revenues should be used

**Table 12.2 Main Export Customers of Asian OIC Countries**

| Exporting | Top Three Importing Countries (in order of precedence) | | | | Share of Total Exports (percentage) | | | |
|---|---|---|---|---|---|---|---|---|
| Countries | 1975 | 1978 | 1980 | 1981 | 1975 | 1978 | 1980 | 1981 |
| Bangladesh | U.S., USSR, Mozambique | U.S., Pakistan, USSR | UK, U.S., USSR | U.S., Singapore, Mozambique | 29.0 | 32.6 | 32.1 | 24.8 |
| Indonesia | Japan, U.S., Singapore | Japan, U.S., Singapore | Japan, U.S., Singapore | Japan, U.S., Australia | 79.3 | 75.3 | 81.3 | 83.1 |
| Iran | Japan, U.S., Netherlands | U.S., Japan, W. Germany | Japan, W. Germany, Brazil | Japan, Bahamas, Spain | 44.6 | 45.1 | 46.9 | 42.9 |
| Malaysia | Singapore, U.S., Japan | Japan, U.S., Singapore | Japan, Singapore, U.S. | Singapore, Japan, U.S. | 50.7 | 56.4 | 58.2 | 56.2 |
| Maldives | Japan, Sri Lanka, Pakistan | Japan, Mauritius, Denmark | Mauritius, Japan, Switzerland | Japan, Sri Lanka, Malaysia | 97.2 | 81.8 | 72.9 | 65.4 |
| Pakistan | Hong Kong, Japan, Saudi Arabia | Japan, Hong Kong, UK | China ( PRC), Japan, Iran | China ( PRC), Japan, U.S. | 24.3 | 25.2 | 23.9 | 39.0 |

to improve the status of minorities. It also called upon the governments of Australia and New Zealand to show as much generosity to Afghan refugees as they have to refugees from Southeast Asia.

I would not want to argue that RISEAP has the potential to make great changes in the status of Muslims in the area. It is too diffuse and too self consciously apolitical for that. But it is the first attempt at the linkage of dakwah groups anywhere in the Muslim world, and the bringing together on a regular basis of Muslims in the same general region is bound to enhance their knowledge of each other and to create a greater sense of community. It is a way of making the abstract notion of Islamic fraternity, the umma, take on more concrete significance. Yet, even as Muslims gain a greater sense of community, they may also more clearly see what concerted action can do -- and this, despite the avowed apoliticism, is a political perception. Very definite political ideas could well creep in, especially given that member groups, such as the Muhammadiyya of Indonesia, which are supposedly nonpolitical, have very definite political ideas and the desire to spread them; and given that states less conservative than Malaysia and Saudi Arabia might occasionally provide funds and thus influence the organization. Both the Burmese and Thai governments have recently recognized the potential political importance -- and menace -- of RISEAP. In 1982, the Burmese government denied an entry visa to Tunku Abdul Rahman, who wanted to attend an Islamic conference, presumably out of the fear that his visit would encourage Burma's dissident Muslims. In 1983, the Thai government banned a RISEAP meeting in Bangkok because, it charged, Libya was behind the meeting as it was behind the separatist movement of southern Thailand.

Whether or not the Libyan regime, in fact, sees value in trying to use RISEAP, in at least one instance it is clear that some Muslim governments rate secular regional organizations higher than specifically Islamic ones. This is the case in the reaction of the Malaysian and Indonesian governments to the Muslim minority problem of the southern Philippines and, to a lesser extent, of southern Thailand. Both these governments have consistently tried to keep the minority question from the top of the agenda of the OIC for fear of antagonizing the Philippines and Thailand, fellow members of ASEAN. Indonesia and Malaysia plainly want to preserve good working relations with their ASEAN partners, even at the cost of failing to seem assertively Islamic, as they might have if they had encouraged the OIC to take definite action in support of the Filipino and Thai Muslims. They have even been acting against an Islamic consensus.

The Islamic community's concern over the Filipino Muslims in particular has been growing since the early 1970s when armed clashes between the army and the Moro National Liberation Front (MNLF) occurred with some regularity and when martial law was declared. Libya was especially strong in its support of the Muslims and condemnation of the Marcos regime. For example, at the fourth Islamic Foreign Ministers' Conference, which was held in Banghazi in 1973, there was a considerable effort by Libya to put the Filipino matter at the top of the agenda. Indonesia tried to prevent it being considered at all, however, arguing that it was an internal concern of a sovereign state and therefore beyond the legitimate interest of the OIC. Malaysia countered a Libyan draft resolution, which was very critical of the Filipino government and called for the suspension of diplomatic relations, with its own draft centered on the idea that the problem was fundamentally a Filipino one, not an international or even Islamic one, and that the OIC's proper role was to encourage communication between the protagonists. After rather intense debate, the ministers adopted a compromise resolution that could not have been displeasing to Malaysia and Indonesia. In addition to setting up a committee of four states to discuss the problem with the Filipino government, it called on Malaysia and Indonesia to use their good offices through their common membership in ASEAN. The resolution conceded that the "problem is full of complications, the more so as it concerns the internal affairs of an independent sovereign state."

At the fifth Islamic Foreign Ministers' Conference in Kuala Lumpur in 1974, Indonesia continued to exert a moderating influence, arguing that any call for a "just solution" be "within the framework of the national sovereignty and territorial integrity of the Philippines." However, the trend toward greater support of the Muslim rebels and impatience with Manila was quickly establishing itself. At this 1974 meeting, the ministers specifically mentioned the MNLF for the first time; in 1977, in an "exceptional measure," they admitted it as an observer and called on member states to support it "by all ways and means"; in 1978, they invited members to extend their "moral and material support" to it; in 1980, they called on Muslim states to "exert the appropriate economic, social, and political pressure" on the Filipino government to induce it to abide by the Tripoli Agreement of 1976, which had set out the basis for regional autonomy. In recent meetings, the ministers have reaffirmed their support for the Tripoli Agreement but have refused to be drawn into the internal fighting within the MNLF that has been acute since 1977. More important, they have refused to back the change of strategy of Nur Misauri, leader of the MNLF, who now advocates full-scale independence for the Muslims rather than the autonomy most Muslim states advocate. An indication that OIC members do not wish to go further is the fact that although a special committee was set up to look at the question during the sixteenth Foreign Minister's Conference in Fez in January 1986, no report was issued or resolution passed.

The point here is that Malaysia and Indonesia have been instrumental in keeping the OIC from a complete break with the Philippine government, which would have helped to isolate it internationally. There is no doubt, though, that the consensus of the OIC has shifted toward greater criticism of the Philippines. The OIC became more openly critical of the Marcos regime than it was in the early and mid-1970s, and it is no longer inclined to accept that the problem is purely an internal affair. But as the refusal to support Misauri 's call for independence shows, the OIC is still firmly behind the idea of preserving the territorial integrity of the Philippines. This position must be considered a victory for Malaysia and Indonesia, both of which have an obvious self-interest in defeating the idea that minorities have a right to secede from multiethnic and multi religious states.

However, the preeminent concern of both countries has been to preserve good working relations with an ASEAN partner, and thus to preserve ASEAN itself, from which they feel they derive the substantial benefit of subregional stability in an unstable region. According to former Deputy Prime Minister Datak Musa Hitam, Malaysia's commitment to ASEAN is paramount, and its commitment to the OIC is secondary (with the Non-Aligned Movement and the Commonwealth coming third and fourth). It is not surprising that this is so when one bears in mind the not very distant past of hostility between Malaysia and the Philippines over rival claims to the island of Sabah. It is also not surprising that the Malaysian government will not help the Muslim rebels in southern Thailand when one bears in mind that it needs the cooperation of the Thai government to control the Communist insurgents in the north of Malaysia. The Indonesian government shares a similar perception of the need to ensure ASEAN harmony above all. The era of Indonesia's confrontation with Malaysia is never far from the consciousness of the elites, and the general fear of Communist penetration of the region guarantees that Jakarta will not wish to do anything that might weaken its anti-Communist neighbors. This concern, along with the fear of being considered an "Islamic State" with all the unacceptable ramifications that such a designation would have in domestic politics for the secular elite, accounts for Indonesia's decision not to apply for full membership in the OIC but rather to accept associate membership.

## Foreign Policy

As the discussion so far indicates, to nongovernmental groups, institutional Islam seems sometimes to have a life of its own, yet, to governments, it seems to be of secondary interest. As a foreign policy matter, Islam is often a concern to Asian governments. But it is a subsidiary, and perhaps complicating, but rarely by itself a determining, factor in the clash of national interests. There is no question, of course, that genuine outrage at the plight of the Afghan mujahidin accounts for the condemnation of the Soviet Union by the governments of the Muslim states, but this outrage has not led them to break diplomatic relations. Nor has this outrage prevented them from working toward an accommodation with Soviet interests similar to the one sought by the Pakistani government.

That Islam does not very often determine foreign policy is best shown in such a highly ideological state as revolutionary Iran. Until recently, despite what one might have expected from an assertively Islamic regime, the relationship with the Soviet Union was lukewarm. Although the Ayatoullah from the beginning had called for a foreign policy of equal antagonism toward both superpowers and in spite of the strong reaction against the Soviet invasion of Afghanistan, Iran's trade with the Soviet bloc increased as relations with the Western states deteriorated during the American hostage crisis. Moreover, the Soviet-backed Tudeh party was free to operate until early 1983. In recognition of the rather unexpected toleration they received, the Soviets moderated their initial attacks on the Shi'ite ulama; at the time of the 26th Party Congress in February 1981, Brezhnev deemed it prudent to make a relatively generous concession: "The main thing is what aims are pursued by the forces proclaiming various slogans. The banner of Islam may lead into the struggle for liberation. This is borne out by history, including very recent history." The reversal of fortunes since 1983 has had nothing to do with Islam, but has been due to the Iranian government's belief that it is stable enough to act against the Tudeh and that the Soviets have moved from a kind of neutrality in the Gulf war to active support of Iraq, with which they have a Treaty of Friendship and Cooperation.

Yet, it must be said that Iranian Islamic ideology probably determines Iranian foreign policy in the case of exporting the revolution. The media are full of reports of "Islamic terrorism," and although the term is certainly objectionable, as "Catholic terrorism" would be when talking of the activities of the Irish Republican Army, there is no doubt that the Islamic revolution of Iran has been for export. The Iranian regime distanced itself from a number of terrorist acts in 1985, such as the attack on the Kuwaiti amir in May and the hijacking of the TWA airplane in June, but major figures have consistently argued the need to spread the message of Ayatoullah Khomeini and to have others follow the example of a successful revolt against Westernized regimes.

Very little hard information is available, but it is widely believed that the Islamic Jihad Organization, which has taken responsibility for terrorist acts in Lebanon, Kuwait, and other places in the Middle East, is not one single group but rather a convenient label for a number of groups whose main inspiration, if not also source of funding, is Iran. The Jihad name surfaced in Jakarta in March 1984 in connection with threats made to the British, American, French, and Italian embassies that promised: "From now on, neither you nor your wives and children will find peace on Muslim soil." Malaysia has also been worried about the activities of the Iranian embassy in Kuala Lumpur, which had distributed revolutionary leaflets and could, the government fears, be encouraging dissent among the growing number of activist Muslims there.

The Philippine government has also been worried about the Iranian factor in its domestic politics. It was reported in August 1983 that Tehran had sent a hit team to eliminate opponents of the Ayatoullah among the five hundred to nine hundred Iranian students in the Philippines and in December 1983 that a bomb wrapped in Iranian newspapers was defused outside the American embassy in Manila. A pro-Khomeini group also claimed to have distributed more than 5 million pamphlets calling for revolution: "We have succeeded in effectively provoking the Filipino masses -- Moslems and Christians alike -- to take overt action against the corrupt regime of prostitutes and dictators." Even more worrisome for the government is the belief of many that Iran has displaced Libya as the main financial backer of the MNLF.

Iranian activism, however, is probably the exception that proves the rule and, in general, rather than determining policy by itself, Islam tends to play three other roles: confirming the national interest, contradicting the national interest, and facilitating the implementation of policy. In saying this, though, I may seem to imply that Islam is a monolith and that it is an independent variable, able to take action on its own, to play roles. But this is not always the case, or even often the case. More exactly, the role of Islam varies according to those who use its name, and, although there are values that are generally perceived and shared, specific interpretations of these values might sometimes differ among Muslims.

First, Islam may add to or confirm considerations of realpolitik. This tendency is clearly seen in Pakistan's dispute with India over Kashmir. There is no doubt that Pakistanis genuinely feel an affinity with the Muslims of the Kashmir valley and are aggrieved by what they view as the historical injustice of a Hindu ruler calling upon the Indians to preserve his throne against the wishes of his Muslim subjects. The majority of the Indian state of Jammu and Kashmir, who are Muslim, ought to have their say, the Pakistanis insist. Their concern about the plight of Muslims in the Indian federation can only have intensified since the bloody Assam riots in 1983. But other, more practical, considerations also explain the Pakistanis' insistence. They look upon Kashmir as of vital strategic importance because it is located in an area of relatively greater Indian vulnerability than elsewhere along their common border. Indeed, in the Indo-Pakistani wars of 1965 and 1971, which were fought in part over this issue, the only major successes for Pakistan occurred along the Kashmiri frontier. Moreover, since the Soviet invasion of Afghanistan, as indeed before, it cannot have been lost on the government in Islamabad that only a thin strip of Afghanistan separates Pakistan from the Soviet Union. Although control of the whole of Kashmir would obviously not eliminate this strip, it would enhance Pakistan's security in a very unsettled region and, more concretely, deprive India, which has close relations with the Soviet Union, of about 3.5 million people and of a forward staging post for its troops. It would also extend the border with China, with which Pakistan has close relations. The skeptic will say that these geostrategic considerations are the only ones that count in Islamabad, but I think it would be wrong to deny that Islam is also a consideration, though admittedly not necessarily an equal consideration.

Second, Islam may provide a reason for not doing what the national leaders were intending to do, and, although this may not cause them to alter their conduct, it may embarrass them. This tendency is seen, for instance, in the dilemma that the Malaysian and Indonesian governments face in their policy toward the Filipino and Thai Muslims. The sense of community that all Muslims share and the engrained sense of obligation to come to the aid of maltreated coreligionists stand in powerful contrast with the official hands-off approach. As Peter Gowing wrote, "The fact is, there is a common feeling of solidarity among the Muslims of the Malay world where, after all, Islam is the predominant religion." This contrast between popular opinion and government policy is particularly strong in Malaysia, and it could account, in part, for the fact that the government there cannot afford to be seen as insensitive to demands for greater Islamization at home.

Third, Islam could be important in the implementation of policy rather than in its formulation, as in the first and second points, because it can be used to legitimate. One can point to the rather remarkable proposal by the government of Brunei to settle by reference to Islamic law (fiqh) the long-standing dispute with Malaysia over the Limbang district in Sarawak. Brunei sees the issue as vital because the loss of Limbang has meant the effective partition of the country into two unconnected zones. There is a historical argument that Limbang had been an integral part of Brunei until 1890, when British imperialism caused the division. But the government seems to feel that invoking fiqh is a more attractive defense. Thus, in its view, Malaysia as a Muslim state is bound to give up the territory because it is stolen property. The reference to Islamic law here is not designed to influence the opinion of Muslims within Brunei -- they do not need to be convinced of the merits of the sultanate's case -- but rather to influence the opinion of Muslim activists within Malaysia, who just might then lobby for Islamic justice to be done.

A better example of how governments use Islam as a legitimating -and, indeed, delegitimating -- force in international relations is found in the rivalry between the Soviet Union and China. Both countries aim propaganda blasts at each other's significant Muslim minorities in order to convince them of how badly they are treated at home. It is in each state's interest to engage in this kind of activity because Muslim dissension would turn the attention of its rival inward and probably also induce the diversion of scarce resources to efforts at pacification of the Muslims. The stakes seem all the higher when one realizes where the Muslims are located in each country: The Soviet Muslims inhabit the soft underbelly of the Central Asian republics, what neighboring Khomeini refers to as his cordon sanitaire; the Chinese Muslims are located in areas bordering the Soviet Union, particularly the uranium-rich Xinjiang (Sinkiang) province, which also borders on Mongolia, Afghanistan, Pakistan, and India.

The Soviets have accused the Chinese government of moving non Muslim, Han people en masse into these border areas in order to make them more dependable and to militarize them, and, in the process, the Soviets charge, perpetuating Mao's "great-Han, chauvinistic policy" that is harmful to the indigenous, often largely Muslim, people. The Chinese government is, indeed, worried about the stability of its border regions and vividly remembers that in 1962 some sixty thousand Kazakhs from Xinjiang crossed into Soviet Kazakhstan. It is reported that China currently keeps three hundred thousand troops in Xinjiang. It certainly sees the hand of Soviet intrigue there, denouncing "Soviet revisionists" for trying to initiate rebellion and warning of the "danger that Xinjiang faces from Soviet revisionist social-imperialism." Taking the offensive, Beijing accuses the Soviet regime of trying to suppress the identity of its own Muslims. Moreover, Beijing is clearly trying to enhance its own legitimacy in the eyes of the Muslims in Asia and elsewhere by its repeated denunciation of the Soviet invasion of Afghanistan as "criminal," and by suggesting that this invasion is but the thin edge of the wedge for the Muslim world: "The Soviet Union has not halted since its military occupation of Afghanistan, and during the past twelve months and more, the Islamic countries have suffered a great deal from intensified Soviet infiltration and expansion, particularly in the Gulf and Red Sea areas, and through the continuously enhanced Soviet military forces in the Indian Ocean and the Pacific." I shall say more about this competition for legitimacy later on.

## Asian Muslim States and Other Muslim States

This second category covers the relations between the Asian Muslim states and the rest of the Muslim world. In practical terms, the relationship of the Asian Muslims with the Arab states is what matters. Islamic theory suggests that a community of interests as well as of spirit exists between them, and certainly the public rhetoric of leaders and the media and the talk of ordinary Muslims are full of references to Islamic brotherhood. There is some reality to this fraternal sentiment, but there are also real differences between Asian and non-Asian Muslims. These differences are revealed in several ways.

First, despite the increasingly pronounced activity among Muslim states, particularly within the OIC system (i.e., the OIC itself and its many affiliated organizations, such as the Islamic Chamber of Commerce and the Islamic Broadcasting Organization), little economic integration has occurred among member states. Specifically, there has been little economic integration between the Asian member states and the non-Asian member states of the OIC. Whereas not all statistics on these countries can be viewed as entirely reliable, what figures we do have clearly show that trade between the Asian Muslim countries and the non-Asian Muslim countries is insubstantial. Table 12.3 shows, for instance, that, of the countries listed, Pakistan has the highest level of economic integration with other Muslim states, with perhaps thirty (or more) percent of its 1981 exports going to OIC member states and about thirty-five percent of its imports coming from member states. Bangladesh and Afghanistan (the latter with regard to exports only) are next, with Iran and Indonesia coming at the bottom of the list. Indonesia, for example, is reported to have only one percent of its exports going to OIC states and under two percent of its imports coming from these states. However, it must be noted that the Islamic statistical office based in Ankara reports a figure of nine percent for the 1982 imports. It is also to be noted that, although the trend is generally upward over the years reported, the movement is certainly not dramatic. Take the case of Malaysia. Whereas its export figure for 1970 was about two percent, it was only about four percent for 1981, and its import figure for 1970 was eight percent, which was roughly the same as in 1981. These trends are only to be expected, though, because these countries (as the developing countries generally) are dependent on the industrialized countries for the bulk of their trade.

Political integration has also been minimal between the Asian Muslim and other Muslim states. The one significant exception is the fact that the Palestinian issue has clearly become an Islamic issue. Over time, almost all Muslims everywhere have come to accept that the question of self determination for the Palestinian people cannot be separated from the liberation of Jerusalem, the third holiest city of Islam. Strong feelings along these lines can be found in Indonesian society, but the government's pro-American conservatism has kept it from active support of the Palestinian Liberation Organization (PLO). By way of contrast, the Mahathir government in Malaysia, which has been developing broad and warm contacts with the Arab Gulf states, has moved to a position of more open support of the PLO. The PLO was allowed to open an office in Kuala Lumpur in 1981, and in July 1984 Yassir Arafat paid an official visit during which he was received by the king and spoke to a rally of fifteen thousand people. The prime minister has said that the government's only motivation is to help see justice done, but these moves must also be seen as useful signals to the Arab states that Malaysia is diplomatically cooperative and to its own people that it is moving in tandem with their increasing Islamic self-assertiveness.

Table 12.3 Flow of Trade of Asian OIC Countries with Member Countries

| | Exports to Member Countries (percentage) | | | | | | Imports from Member Countries (percentage) | | | | | |
|---|---|---|---|---|---|---|---|---|---|---|---|---|
| Country | 1970 | 1973 | 1978 | 1979 | 1980 | 1981 | 1970 | 1973 | 1978 | 1979 | 1980 | 1981 |
| Afghanistan | 9.0 | 16.9 | 21.5 | 16.4 | 14.3 | 24.6 | 3.4 | 5.0 | 6.6 | 7.2 | 5.9 | 6.4 |
| Bangladesh | -- | 6.0 | 21.2 | 17.8 | 18.4 | 21.3 | -- | 4.3 | 11.8 | 12.0 | 13.6 | 25.9 |
| | | | (20.0)a | | (20.0) | (25.0) | | | (15.0) | | (18.0) | (26.0) |
| Indonesia | 3.3 | 1.1 | 1.3 | 1.2 | 0.9 | 1.0 | 2.1 | 3.6 | 4.5 | 6.0 | 7.8 | 1.8 |
| | | | (1.0) | | (1.0) | (1.0) | | | (5.0) | | (8.0) | (9.0) |
| Iran | ngb | ng | ng | ng | ng | ng | ng | ng | ng | ng | ng | ng |
| | | | (3.0) | | (3.0) | (6.0) | | | (2.0) | | (7.0) | (7.0) |
| Malaysia | 2.3 | 2.0 | 2.9 | 3.3 | 3.4 | 4.3 | 8.0 | 5.3 | 6.9 | 8.4 | 9.2 | 8.2 |
| | | | (3.0) | | (4.0) | (4.0) | | | (8.0) | | (9.0) | (9.0) |
| Maldives | -- | -- | 7.7 | 9.1 | 3.6 | 19.7 | -- | -- | 17.7 | 7.6 | 1.6 | 0.0 |
| | | | (--) | | (4.0) | (20.0) | | | (--) | | (2.0) | (1.0) |
| Pakistan | 11.1 | 19.9 | 29.1 | 27.4 | 25.8 | 29.9 | 5.9 | 10.9 | 18.9 | 22.9 | 35.0 | 35.1 |
| | | | (36.0) | | (32.0) | (36.0) | | | (18.0) | | (34.0) | (34.0) |

a The Islamic Development Bank says that its figures are derived from the International Monetary Fund's Direction of Trade Statistics Yearbook, 1982, but its percentages do not always seem to be derived from what is actually reported in the Yearbook. For example, my calculation of Afghanistan's exports to the OIC countries listed in the Yearbook for 1978 as a percentage of its total exports is 14.2 percent, not 21.5 percent.

b ng equals not given.

The Palestinian exception apart, national leaders pursue their own national interests regardless of opinion elsewhere in the Muslim world. This fact means that the OIC has not become a powerful, independent political actor. But to say this is not to make a damning indictment because international organizations, such as the OIC, the Arab League, or the Organization of African Unity, can do no more than the member states will let them do. The reality of any international organization is that it survives as long as it is useful to its members. Utility most of the time derives from the organization's ability to contribute to the long-term goal of regional stability, but often the organization is useful to a member because it advances its own foreign policy.

Pakistan, for example, has found the OIC useful in its more or less constant diplomatic competition with India. It was able to prevent India's admission to the organization in the first place and, since then, has been able to find a sympathetic hearing at OIC meetings. The Indian nuclear explosion of May 1974 prompted the Pakistanis to try to secure a resolution that, if it did not forthrightly condemn India, did specifically name it, and thereby implied that it was posing a threat to regional and world peace. Senegal tried to avoid the singling out of India, but Pakistan, although unable to secure a clause calling on India to accept nuclear inspection by the United Nations, was successful in having only India named and thus put again in the dock of the court of world opinion. That Pakistan was successful is partly due to that amorphous yet palpable thing, Islamic solidarity, and partly to the enormous sympathy that Pakistan won, particularly in the Arab world, as a result of India's role in the dissolution of a sovereign state in the 1971 Indo-Pakistani war. It is no wonder, then, that Pakistan regards the OIC as its most important commitment -- all the more so, it must be added, because its commitment to CENTO (Central Treaty Organization) and SEATO (Southeast Asia Treaty Organization) has evaporated. As a result, owing to the Arab majority in the OIC, Pakistan now primarily looks to the Arab world for diplomatic support.

Outside of the OIC, relations between the Asian Muslim states (and those with significant Muslim minorities) and other Muslim states are often complicated when the Islamic element is especially evident. For example, the Indian government, under domestic pressure, has been critical of Arab governments for pouring money into the country for the purpose of inducing the conversion of harijans, Mahatma Gandhi's word for the untouchables. After voicing concern about mass conversions in 1981, India said it would not ban foreign money from coming into the country's Islamic organizations but would amend the Foreign Contribution (Regulations) Act so that it could regulate the inflow. However, the Assam riots in 1983 prompted the government to prevent such organizations as the All India Muslim Majlis-Mushawarat, Jamaat-e-Islami, and Jamaate-Ahl-Hadis from receiving foreign money. When Mrs. Gandhi charged in the Indian Parliament that the violence was due to such foreign money, no one could have missed the implication that it was Arab money. For their part, many Arab Muslim states have been severely critical of the Indian government for failing to prevent the riots and generally for failing to protect the Muslim minority.

Another example of how contention over an Islamic issue sours relations between an Asian Muslim state and a non-Asian one involves the Iranian-Saudi dispute over the nature of the hajj (pilgrimage) to Mecca. This dispute must be seen as part of the general tension in the region created by the Iranian Revolution, but the issue of the pilgrimage has taken on particular significance. The Iranians believe that the pilgrimage is an opportune occasion to advance their views of Islam and thus their political views, whereas the Saudis, who are apprehensive about the events across the Gulf, insist that the pilgrimage must not be turned into a political rally with the unfortunate demonstration effect that it could create within Saudi Arabia. It is no mean problem from the Saudi perspective, given the approximately one hundred thousand Iranians who make the pilgrimage and the fact that the Iranian regime consistently condemns the Saudi dynasty as corrupt and un-Islamic. The Saudis, however, cannot even appear to try to exclude Iranian pilgrims lest that undermine their primary claim to legitimacy--being the protectors and guarantors of safe and open holy cities. But they have expelled some pilgrims who attempted to carry weapons into the sanctuary area or to distribute pamphlets, and they have tried to enlist the support of other Muslim states in condemning what Khomeini 's followers have done during the pilgrimage. As the Kuwaiti newspaper al-Anba' said, "Allah ordered the hajj to be a framework for cohesion among Muslims, not an arena for conflict and differences, and what Khomeini seeks is unacceptable to Allah and His Prophet." There would be bad relations between the Gulf countries and Iran in any event, but the pilgrimage issue is important because it affects something all Muslims everywhere feel strongly about and because it represents a challenge to the legitimacy formula of the regime that prides itself on administering the hajj for the rest of the Muslim world.

The Afghanistan invasion is the most notable instance of the souring of relations. It is seen as an Islamic issue because of the nature of the regime that the Soviets are trying to prop up and because the guerrillas have self-consciously called themselves mujahidin, fighters in a jihad against the godless Soviets. The OIC, in an extraordinary session of the Foreign Ministers' Conference in Islamabad in January 1980, condemned the Soviet invasion and suspended Afghanistan's membership. But few concrete actions, including the suspension of diplomatic relations with the Soviet government, have taken place since then. Humanitarian aid has been given to the refugees in Pakistan, certainly, and some money and arms have been channeled to the mujahidin, but notably absent is the willingness to be seen as militantly anti-Soviet. At the Islamabad meeting, for instance, the ministers passed a balancing resolution that condemned American "pressure" and "threats of punitive action" against Iran. Indeed, some Afghans are embittered by the lack of concrete help:

> *The Russian invasion at a time when all Muslim countries enjoyed advanced military facilities for defence and for waging Jehad, made it incumbent on all Muslim countries of the world to have mobilized Jehad against the Red heathen army. They should have taken [their] share in the Jehad against the great common enemy of Islam by helping their Afghan Muslim brethren in accordance with the valuable tenets of the Holy Quran. But unfortunately, not even a sound has been heard from most of these leaders. Contrarily some of them even continued their economic and social co-operation totally for the benefit of the Russians.*

Despite what these Afghans expect, it is obvious that there are political limits to Islamic outrage in the Muslim, particularly the wealthy Muslim, states. But the Soviets have felt defensive, and they, like the Chinese, with one eye on their domestic Muslim situation, have tried to convince Muslims throughout the world, especially in the Arab world, that, after all, they are not so objectionable. The most effective way to convince them of this, they believe, is to allow contacts between foreign Muslims and some of their own, albeit carefully vetted, Muslims. The Muslim Religious Board for Central Asia and Kazakhstan publishes a journal, Muslims of the Soviet East (in Persian, Arabic, Uzbek, English, and French) that is designed to show that the Soviet Union's enlightened policy toward its own Muslims is of a piece with its enlightened policy in international relations. Unsubtle language is used to condemn Israel and its American patron, but such bombast also makes the more subtle point that if we Russians seem to be bad because of Afghanistan, the other side is even worse: "[The] mufti, as well as all those who were present at the mosque, prayed before Almighty Allah that He may reprimand Israeli Zionists and their protectors in [the] USA who are conducting criminal actions against all the Muslims and those of Palestine in particular."

China, without the burden of Afghanistan, is more effective in the use of Islam in its relations with the Arab states. The China Islamic Association has been important in this respect not only because it arranges for foreign Muslims to visit China in order to see for themselves that Islam is not proscribed, but also because it sends its own delegations to the Arab world, which often meet political leaders there. Its chairman, Burhan Shahidi (Pao Erhan), for instance, met King Sa'ud of Saudi Arabia and King Husayn of Jordan in 1956, and, shortly after he met the Yemeni crown prince and his brother in Cairo, diplomatic relations were established between Yemen and the People's Republic of China (PRC). The association had also been instrumental in securing the recognition of Egypt and Syria. More recently, a delegation from the association visited Libya and Saudi Arabia, prompting one Soviet commentator to conclude that it might lead to the establishment of diplomatic relations between Saudi Arabia and the PRC. This event has not occurred, but such visits do provide an informal channel of communication. What is important is that the regime in Beijing believes that the use of Islam can help to legitimate it in the eyes of the Arab regimes, and the record shows that it has had some success at it.

Although the economic and political integration of the Asian and nonAsian Muslim states is not high, contacts are growing between them. The point about Soviet and Chinese delegations visiting the Arab countries is evidence of this, but so are two other points. First, the Gulf states give considerable amounts of aid to some of the Asian Muslim and Muslim minority states. Pakistan is a major recipient of aid, particularly from Saudi Arabia. Twenty-five percent of Saudi aid in 1976, for example, went to Pakistan and, roughly speaking about $100 million a year in Saudi aid went there until the decline in oil revenues in 1981-82. Saudi aid continues at a reduced level. Kuwait gave about $50 million and Qatar about $15 million in 1980 and 1981, and the United Arab Emirates (UAE) has given about $30 million a year. Part of these funds are outright grants and part loans.

**Table 12.4 Loans of Kuwait To Asian Countries Fund for Arab Economic Development**

| | April 1975-June 1980 (in thousand Kuwait dinars) |
|---|---|
| Afghanistan | 8,845 |
| Bangladesh | 15,450 |
| India | 24,400 |
| Indonesia | 13,800 |
| Malaysia | 15,400 |
| Maldives | 3,000 |
| Nepal | 7,000 |
| Pakistan | 25,300 |
| Philippines | 3,500 |
| Sri Lanka | 8,070 |
| Thailand | 13,000 |
| Vietnam | 2,900 |
| Total | 140,665 |
| Total Loans for Non-Arab Countries | 230,045 |
| Total Loans Worldwide | 500,399 |
| Loans to Asian Countries as Percentage of Total Non- Arab Loans | 61.1% |
| Loans to Asian Countries as Percentage of Total Loans Worldwide | 28.1% |

The Kuwait Fund for Arab Development, which had been originally set up to help only Arab states, has since 1975 been generous to several Asian states. Twenty-eight percent of its total loans have gone to Asian states, and this figure represents over sixty percent of its non-Arab loans. Eleven Arab/OPEC institutions also make concession disbursements. Looking at their total for 1981, one can see that Bangladesh received 7.9 percent, India 1.4 percent, and Pakistan 1.2 percent. This is not small, as it might seem, because only one country, the Sudan, received more than Bangladesh, and because the aggregate disbursements for the three countries came to more than US$70 million.

Second, the Arab states are host to large numbers of Asian migrant workers. Although the number of foreign workers generally will decline as oil revenues decline and as more of the indigenous population enters the work force, there will remain a need for unskilled and semiskilled foreign laborers for the foreseeable future. A great many of these will come from Asia. Recently, Asians have constituted the vast majority of migrant workers in Bahrain, Oman, Qatar, and the UAE. Malaysians, for example, have found lucrative jobs in the Gulf, particularly working on infrastructural development in Saudi Arabia. Because a shortage of manpower has existed in the oil-based economies generally, migrant workers have been important to their maintenance; this, in turn, has meant that the Asians in some Arab countries have been nearly indispensable. The benefits to the Asian countries have been obvious. They have disposed of large numbers of people who would be unemployed-drains on the social and economic system and potential recruits to political oppositional movements--and they have received considerable money in remittances--in the early 1980s $2.2 billion a year in the case of Pakistan, eighty-five percent of which came from the workers in the Arab countries. It has been estimated that in 1980 there were some 120,000 Filipino workers in Saudi Arabia who earned between $250 and $2000 a month and helped to provide the $700 million the Philippines had in invisible receipts from Saudi Arabia.

It is not clear at all, however, whether either of these developments suggests an emerging economic and political integration of the Asian and non-Asian Muslim states, despite the lack of substantial trade and political coordination that I have described. The aid and the migrant workers' patterns suggest Asian dependence on the Arabs. But when it comes to aid, there is really mutual dependence: The making of a loan ties the banker to the fortunes of the borrower and creates a kind of need for each other once the loan is made. But is there any political influence to be derived from the lending, or the granting, in the first place? It is hard to say, as it is hard to say when talking about Western aid to any Third World country. Many believe that President Marcos made concessions to Muslim demands out of fear that Saudi Arabia would cut off aid if he did not do this. In November 1980, the Saudis did terminate a contract to supply ten thousand barrels of oil per day specifically because of the Philippine government's policy toward its southern Muslims. In addition, there is no doubt that the Pakistanis, recipients of a great deal of aid, follow Saudi policy lines closely. But it is impossible to say in both cases if the aid, or the denial thereof, is the cause, and, in any event, the example of stubbornly independent India suggests that there are times when aid and political influence seem almost not correlated at all.

**Table 12.5 Asian Migrant Workers in Major Labor-Importing OIC Countries (in thousands)**

| Host | Indian Workers | | Pakistani Workers | | Other Asian Workers | | Asian Workers as Percentage of Total Migrant Workers | |
|---|---|---|---|---|---|---|---|---|
| Country | 1975 | 1980 | 1975 | 1980 | 1975 | 1980 | 1975 | 1980 |
| Bahrain | 8.9 | 11.0 | 6.7 | 10.0 | 3.0 | 10.0 | 63.5 | 68.9 |
| Iraq | 5.0 | 25.0 | 5.0 | 30.0 | 40.0 | 30.0 | 75.9 | 21.3 |
| Jordan | -- | 0.5 | -- | 5.0 | -- | 8.0 | -- | 22.5 |
| Kuwait | 21.5 | 25.0 | 11.1 | 16.0 | 30.1 | 45.0 | 30.1 | 30.7 |
| Libya | 0.5 | 6.0 | 4.5 | 50.0 | 0.5 | 10.0 | 1.7 | 16.5 |
| Oman | 26.0 | 30.0 | 32.5 | 40.0 | 0.6 | 4.0 | 83.6 | 82.2 |
| Qatar | 16.0 | 25.0 | 16.0 | 25.0 | 6.0 | 25.0 | 71.7 | 78.9 |
| Saudi Arabia | 15.0 | 80.0 | 15.0 | 110.0 | 18.0 | 180.0 | 6.2 | 26.4 |
| UAE | 61.5 | 80.0 | 100.0 | 120.0 | 23.0 | 43.5 | 73.4 | 73.8 |

There has been a dramatic increase in the amount of Arab-sponsored dakwah activities in Asia. Saudi Arabia has been particularly active as a patron, establishing mosques, training centers for Islamic officials, and institutes for the study of the Arabic language and the Quran. It funds these activities through direct government grants and also through the intermediaries of the Muslim World League and the Supreme World Council for Mosques, both based in Mecca and virtually appendages of the Saudi government. For example, in 1981 the league organized a training program for a thousand imams (mosque prayer leaders) in Indonesia and the Saudi government set up an Arabic language institute in Jakarta in conjunction with the Indonesian Ministry of Religious Affairs. In 1982, the Supreme World Council of Mosques devoted half of its budget of $29 million to the maintenance of mosques in Southeast Asia. In 1983, the Saudi government promised to provide $2.4 million for the transmission of a radio program, "Voice of Islam," to Southeast Asia in cooperation with the Malaysian government.

The Libyan Islamic Call Society is more active in Africa, but it, too, is involved in Asia. For example, it encourages and arranges visits of academics to Libya from such countries as Malaysia, sends teachers of Islam abroad, and offers scholarships to worthy students to study in Tripoli, as was the case in early 1984 with students from Sri Lanka. In addition, the Islamic Solidarity Fund of the OIC regularly contributes to the development of Islamic studies and provides for "humanitarian" aid to such groups as the MNLF, which was given a grant of $100,000 in 1983.

The result is that Muslims in the poorer areas of the Muslim world are increasingly beneficiaries of the sense of fraternal obligation that the richer Muslim states tend to feel. It is true that these wealthy states probably look upon dakwah aid as a way of maximizing their international influence, but they also see it as part of their Islamic duty. Moreover, there is no doubt that the beneficiaries feel increasingly part of the larger Islamic community, the umma. Yet, at the same time, this sentiment may have a negative effect on their loyalty to their own states. As the Mindanao Cross editorialized after an Arab delegation's visit to the southern Philippines in 1972: "The visit proved that the religious ties of the Muslims in Mindanao with other Muslim countries are as strong if not stronger than their allegiance to their government."

A linkage of ideas between the Arab and Asian Muslim worlds has also developed. The works of the Pakistani writer, Abul A'la Mawdudi, and the Indian writer, Abul Hasan Ali Nadvi, are now widely known in the Arab countries and elsewhere among the Asian countries. Sayyid Qutb Ma'alim fi'l-tariq (Signposts on the Road) has been translated into Thai and is also available to Soviet Muslims. Moreover, the library of the religious board in Tashkent is fairly well stocked with newspapers and periodicals from other parts of the Muslim world, and Arabic newspapers often carry lengthy pieces on the status of Muslim minorities in the Asian countries. This familiarization with writers from, and events in, faraway places is partly due to modern telecommunications and publishing and the resultant ease of dissemination. It is also due to the fact that the rich Arab countries, as we have seen, are funding the establishment of educational and language institutes throughout Asia that help to introduce young Muslims to major works of Arab writers and often also give them the ability to read them in the original Arabic.

But perhaps another reason why ideas are so shared now is that the greater ease of making the hajj brings together a vast number of people from all parts of the Muslim world in one place at one time in a highly charged, emotional atmosphere. In 1982, almost thirty-five percent and in 1984 over forty percent of the total number of pilgrims came from Asian countries (see Table 12.6). It is to be noted, however, that although the Saudi government has done a great deal to improve the conditions of the pilgrimage and has corrected many of the injustices perpetrated by the local guides and hoteliers, economic conditions still govern the ability of Asian Muslims to make the journey. For example, a study of the Thai hajjis shows that the fluctuating cost of fuel and hence airfares, the rate of inflation, and the price of rubber, the major local commodity, are all relevant factors affecting the Thai's decision to travel to Mecca, and this explains why there was a major decline in their numbers between 1975 and 1978.

**Table 12.6 Pilgrims from Asian Countries**

| Country | 1979 | 1980 | 1981 | 1982 | 1983 | 1984 |
|---|---|---|---|---|---|---|
| Afghanistan | 990 | 4,386 | 2,356 | 4,206 | 9,033 | 5,388 |
| Bangladesh | 7,435 | 10,522 | 11,296 | 12,258 | 24,508 | 22,188 |
| Brunei | 398 | 3 | 421 | 1,947 | 1,911 | 1,895 |
| Burma | 10 | 74 | 156 | 167 | 148 | 201 |
| Cambodia | -- | 3 | 55 | -- | -- | -- |
| China (PRC) | -- | -- | -- | -- | -- | 60 |
| Hong Kong | -- | 1 | 6 | 5 | 3 | 2 |
| India | 24,863 | 21,881 | 26,280 | 26,229 | 30,896 | 32,563 |
| Indonesia | 43,723 | 74,741 | 69,002 | 57,478 | 54,904 | 40,928 |
| Iran | 74,963 | 10,539 | 75,391 | 89,503 | 103,044 | 154,958 |

(Contd.)

| Country | 1979 | 1980 | 1981 | 1982 | 1983 | 1984 |
|---|---|---|---|---|---|---|
| Japan | 7 | 10 | -- | -- | -- | -- |
| Malaysia | 9,511 | 14,846 | 22,704 | 25,277 | 25,013 | 24,749 |
| Maldives | 46 | 144 | 13 | 278 | 354 | 476 |
| Nepal | 29 | -- | 25 | 28 | 6 | 59 |
| Pakistan | 74,296 | 78,624 | 69,343 | 72,844 | 85,019 | 91,872 |
| Philippines | 1,699 | 1,836 | 1,851 | 1,955 | 2,630 | 2,526 |
| Singapore | 1,838 | 2,490 | 3,103 | 2,328 | 2,998 | 2,947 |
| South Korea | 42 | 2 | 3 | 10 | 2 | -- |
| Sri Lanka | 594 | 520 | 728 | 836 | 715 | 999 |
| Taiwan | 86 | 123 | 73 | 114 | 252 | 832 |
| Thailand | 1,906 | 2,978 | 2,753 | 1,888 | 2,273 | 2,610 |
| USSR | 28 | 26 | 26 | 20 | 19 | 14 |
| Vietnam | 1 | -- | -- | -- | -- | -- |
| TOTAL | 242,415 | 223,749 | 285,579 | 297,371 | 343,728 | 385,267 |
| Total No. of Pilgrims Worldwide | 862,520 | 812,892 | 879,368 | 853,555 | 1,005,060 | 919,671 |
| Asian Pilgrims as Percentage of Worldwide Total | 28.1% | 27.5% | 32.5% | 34.8% | 34.2% | 41.2% |

The language barrier is another problem, but the level of education has generally so risen that growing numbers of hajjis, especially the younger ones, are able to communicate with Muslims from all over the world in French, and perhaps Arabic, or, more likely, English. Many Muslim leaders might prefer communication to be more difficult because these young Muslims could be introduced not only to Muslim Brotherhood ideas but also to those of the Islamic revolution in Iran. And, indeed, it must be pointed out that even though the numbers of hajjis are increasing, making the pilgrimage is increasingly organized by national bureaucracies, such as LUTH (Lembaga Urusan dan Tabong Haji) in Malaysia. This means that individuals often go to Mecca in "packaged tours," staying with their fellow citizens during the ceremonies and returning with them as a group. The contact with foreign Muslims, therefore, may not be as great as we tend to think in terms of this rite of ingathering.

## Relations Between Asian Muslim States and Western States

Islam is indirectly relevant to the international relations between Asian Muslim and Western states. It mainly affects people's attitudes, and, in this way, it can sometimes impinge on policy.

## Muslim Attitudes

Take, first, the attitudes of Muslims who have come into contact with the West. For some Muslims, this contact provides a positive experience because it offers an opportunity to organize themselves into Islamic organizations. They may be denied this opportunity at home, but, even if they have it there, the Western experience, usually at university, has an important advantage. It allows them to interact with Muslims from many parts of the world and to read Islamic literature of all kinds that might be unavailable at home. The Federation of the Students' Islamic Societies (FOSIS) in Britain is particularly active and has had a notable impact on Malaysian students. In the view of one writer, it has instilled "a sense of Islamic consciousness" in them: "FOSIS' Annual Conferences and Winter Gatherings [draws] hundreds of students to such places as Stanswick and Manchester where they [are] able to 'enhance [their] spiritual understanding of Islam' through readings and discussions." Parallel experiences in other Western countries can be found.

But the contact with Western societies can also prove to be a negative experience for Muslims. For example, students subjected to racist attack are not likely to forget or forgive it. It could be that just such a consideration would weigh heavily on their minds one day if they were to become important decision makers. The experience is more likely, though, to be less dramatic. For many, the moral and social climate of Western countries will simply confirm their inclination to regard the West as decadent and to try to revise Western models of politics and development for application to their own countries.

There is another way in which Muslim attitudes can be affected negatively by exposure to the West and Western organizations. This occurs when there is a feeling that Christian missionary work is a front for Western imperialism or, at least, that it is expanding to the detriment of Islam. This sentiment is often heard in Malaysia and especially in Indonesia, where at least one unpleasant incident occurred in which Muslims burned a new church in Aceh, a strongly conservative Muslim area of Indonesia. Public uproar was heard in 1978 when a Kuwaiti newspaper charged that Mrs. Suharto had become a convert and that her conversion was only the beginning of a Christianization drive. Others charged that Adam Malik, the former vice president, and many high military officials were perpetuating a Christian conspiracy to make secularism the official ideology of the state precisely in order to rob Islam of the central political role that its size would command in Indonesia. In response to attitudes such as these, the government issued a decree in August 1978 requiring foreign funding to be channeled through the Ministry of Religious Affairs and declaring that "the employment of foreigners in developing and propagating religion is limited." The government issued a further decree in January 1979 that put severe restrictions on the mobility and freedom of action of groups seeking to proselytize among those already professing a religion.

To give some idea of the sensitivity of the issue, let me note that Islamic groups have assumed that these restrictions are directed against them and their dakwah activities. Thus the decrees have had little impact on assuaging anti-Christian sentiment, and this fact only redounds to the disadvantage of the Indonesian government, which, with its official secularism, is seen by many as tolerant of Christianity or, worse, encouraging Christianization and, at any rate, as firmly pro-Western.

## Western Attitudes

With regard to the other side of the relationship, Western attitudes toward Muslims, there are also positive and negative experiences. Among the positive ones, one can say that the small Muslim community in Australia helps to make Australians generally, and thus the government, more aware of the plight of their coreligionists in the Asian countries to the north. The effect on policy, however, is not demonstrable.

If we consider Japan broadly part of the West, a kind of anti-Orientalism has also emerged among Japanese intellectuals that is analogous to that which has come to dominate the discussions among Western intellectuals in the past few years. The writings of

Anwar Abdel Malek and Edward Said on Orientalism have produced disquiet and even guilt in Western scholarly circles, but they and others have helped to advance the new orthodoxy of Islamic studies. The argument runs that Islam has been misunderstood, having been filtered through cultural prisms that made it seem inflexible and militant, and thus greater efforts must be expended to show Islam for what it is--adaptable and tolerant.

The Japanese, never far behind Western trends, are making the same types of arguments as those heard in the West: (1) Westerners think of Islam as inferior: "The average Japanese supposes Islam to be the religion of devout nomads, and an irrational obstacle to modernization"; (2) this way of thinking is due to cultural bias: "The Japanese perception of Islam is strongly colored by prejudice. It is seen as representing an anti-modernist, obscurantist way of thought and as totally alien to Japanese culture"; (3) Western scholars have not helped much to improve the understanding of Islam: "Shumei Okawa, a rightwing thinker who played an important role in Japanese Islamic studies during the 1930s and 40s, started his study not from contact with the realities of life and thought among Asian peoples, but by trying to apply to Asia the ideal types he had formed in his own mind." Moreover, "Islamic studies in Japan are handicapped in a number of ways"--that is, no university has a department of Islamic studies, only one university has a department of Arabic, and the Japan Association for Islamic Studies has no money--"and these handicaps must be quickly overcome."

A Japanese twist to these arguments emerges, however. It is that the Japanese view of Islam was derived from the Western one; therefore, what might be required is to go back to basics. Indeed, it is said, Japanese have an advantage in spite of themselves in the legacy of their historical lack of proximity to the Muslim world:

> *Europe has been in direct contact with the Islamic world; it has competed with Islam and attempted to build its own history by dominating it. Consciously or unconsciously, Europeans have been unable to throw off their colonialist mentality in their understanding of Islam. It will be difficult for them to break out of their habit of dealing, from an ethnocentric viewpoint, only with that part of Islam that has been absorbed by Europe. But we Japanese have the comparative advantage of greater distance and are in a position to examine and evaluate from*

*the perspective of world history. We can do this fairly and without prejudice, without forcing our own position on anyone.*

Much of this argument must be seen as self-serving when Japan's pre World-War II and wartime Islamic strategy is taken into account. Rather than a distant and benignly uninterested Japan, there emerges from the historical record a Japan actively concerned to use and to impose on Islam for Japan's own imperial interests. By the early 1930s, the government was convinced of the value of supporting its own association with Islam in order to win and to influence Muslim friends in the region and beyond in the Middle East. To this end, the Society for Islamic Culture gained official sanction and financial support, published abroad, and widely distributed copies of the Quran; mosques were built in Kobe and Tokyo; Asian students were granted scholarships to study in Japan; and legations were established in Kabul and Tehran as well as in Ankara, Cairo, Baghdad, Beirut, and Jerusalem. More covertly, the Japanese tried to make inroads among both the Soviet and the Chinese Muslim populations in order to destabilize both countries. The famous Muslim trials of 1929, 1935, and 1939 established the Japanese role in instigating several ultimately unsuccessful revolts in the Soviet Union, and the Japanese supported first Abdul Kerim and then P'u-Kuang, both unworthy of this confidence, as leaders of the Muslim revolt of Xinjiang (Sinkiang). During the war, the Japanese argued that they were the liberators of Islam and thus hoped thereby not only to pacify their new Muslim subjects in the Dutch Indies, Malaya, Burma, and the Philippines, but also to encourage the anti-British nationalist movement in India. The Japanese foreign minister declared in the Diet in 1943, "Japan is ready to consecrate all efforts in order to free these victims of Anglo-American tyranny and to support with energy the Muslim's political and cultural aspirations."

We have already seen how states with Muslim minorities of some magnitude, such as the Soviet Union and China, are able to use Islam as an instrument of diplomacy, but the Japanese case is remarkable for the same ability to use Islam without the benefit of a significant number of Muslims at home. According to one wartime American report, this was mostly due to the singular commitment of key figures in the elite to the advancement of Japan's sphere of influence, even if it meant converting to Islam themselves and holding out the hope of an Islamic Japan to Muslims abroad. Shintoism, the report maintained, would have presented no obstacle to such flirtations with Islam, even conversion. In any event, it was clear from the so-called Muslim Pact of the early years of this century that the promoters of Islam were above all patriots who saw Islam as a means to the realization of a greater Asian Japan. One of the adherents of the Muslim Pact, Tsuyoshi Inukai, became prime minister, and later the general policy came to have the support of such individuals as General Senjuro Hayashi, prewar minister of war and prime minister (and head of the Japanese Islamic Association, Dai Nippon Kaikyo Kyokai); General Sadao Araki, minister of education during the war and a confidant of Prime Minister Tojo; and General Iwane Matsui, once commander-in-chief of Japan's Central China army. The report concluded: "Small wonder, therefore, that with this kind of backing at the top Japan could count for the execution of this policy on a faithful and self-denying band of lieutenants, happy to devote their lives to the cause with the ecstatic abandon of a dervish."

Whether or not such a happy band of devoted men actually existed, Japan was somewhat successful in attracting support from Muslim groups abroad. More important, it was largely successful in governing Muslim societies under occupation. This success was partly due to the relief of the locals at having their European governors removed. It was also due to the cleverness of the Japanese in what is now Indonesia, for example, in recognizing the utility of the ulama and in cultivating both these religious scholars and the more modern-educated intelligentsia in preference to the priyayi (Javanese administrative class) whom the Dutch had favored and everyone else despised. But the Japanese were not able entirely to restrain the heavy hand. They tried, for instance, to Nipponize Indonesia, insisting that people bow in the direction of the divine emperor's palace, to forbid the reading of the Quran and the teaching of Arabic, and to control the curricula and personnel of private Islamic schools.

Perhaps because of the partial recognition of this background rather than, as the earlier quotation suggests, no recognition of it, contemporary Japanese intellectuals are intent on contributing to the critical self-examination--what can only be called the mea culpaism--among Orientalists today. In this manner, they are contributing to the significant change in the non-Muslims' perception of Islam that one can now begin to detect, and this intellectual lead must be seen as a positive experience.

Other contact between Westerners and Muslims, however, is often negative. For example, Western public opinion often turns against the presence of a minority in economically difficult times. This turn of public opinion is what has occurred in Europe with the rise of racism and resentment toward the guest-workers. It does not follow that such negative public attitudes translate into antagonistic state relations. They most often do not, but as Algerian President Chadli 's visit to Paris in November 1983 suggests, the matter of how one's nationals are treated is never far below the surface of diplomacy and can affect the quality of communication between governments. Moreover, a government might take advantage of negative public attitudes to adopt a restrictive immigration or educational policy that, in turn, would harm a state-to-state relationship. There is no question that the British government's policy of raising tuition for foreign students, for example, produced outrage in Malaysia, from where many thousands of students go to Britain for higher studies, and prompted the Mahathir government to formulate a "buy British last" policy.

There might also be a negative effect from the failure of Western statesmen to take the Muslim countries on their own terms. It is not surprising that whatever interest these statesmen show in Asian Islam, it comes mainly from concern over the stability of such pro-Western regimes as Indonesia, Thailand, and the Philippines, which, in varying degrees, face Muslim political agitation. Western leaders would not want these regimes undermined because they are strategically situated in an area where the Chinese, the Vietnamese, and the Soviets are all active (though in different ways and degrees) and supportive of local Communist groups. In the case of Indonesia, added concern stems from the possible loss of the presently secure supply line of oil--yet location, not oil as in the Middle East, primarily accounts for Western interest.

It is incumbent on statesmen and diplomats to think in terms of the worst; thus their thinking of Islam as a destabilizing factor is only to be expected. To assume that the worst will happen, however, might very well mean missing the fact that reality is somewhat different. Certainly a major block in Western perception in the past occurred when Westerners assumed that Islam was monolithic and monolithically anti-Western. But some evidence exists that the monolith might now have been replaced by a division of the world into good Islam and bad Islam. Good Islam is on "our" side, or at least tame; bad Islam is on "their" side, or at best destabilizing. Islam in Afghanistan is good, as it is in Pakistan; it is bad in Iran, as it seems to be in Indonesia and Thailand. Afghan Muslim fighters are said to be "freedom fighters" and to constitute a brave "resistance movement," but Thai or Filipino Muslims are "separatists" or "extremists." This kind of thinking could well lead Western decision makers to conclude that any attack or criticism of a pro-Western regime by an Islamic opposition means that the opposition is intent on working against Western interests.

Muslims themselves would find such logic amusing because many, if not most, of them envision their demands in terms of the promotion of social justice through Islamization rather than the rejection of the West itself or assistance lent to the West's political enemies. Some Muslims do speak of Westoxification (gharbzadegi), but such rhetoric is a direct response to both the overwhelming and often egregiously indiscreet physical and cultural presence of Westerners within Muslim societies and to the fact that Western money and arms have propped up what are seen as secularizing, even anti-Islamic, regimes such as that of the shah. For all of Khomeini's hyperbolic vitriol against the United States, the core of his reaction is based on what he saw as a simple and unjust lack of symmetry in the American-Iranian relationship during the time of the shah: "American cooks, mechanics, technical and administrative officials together with their families enjoy legal immunity, but the 'ulama of Islam, the preachers and servants of Islam, are banished or imprisoned." In this sense, anti-Westernism among some Muslim activists, although obviously emotionally based, does not necessarily mean that future cooperation, even amity, with Western states is unthinkable, unless, of course, Western decision makers by their own ideological predisposition lock themselves into a self-fulfilling prophecy.

The picture that emerges from these three categories of relationship is mixed. On the one hand, little concrete integration appears to exist among the Muslim states. There is clearly minimal economic integration. On the political level, Islam is either irrelevant, perhaps indirectly relevant--as it is in the relationship of Muslims with non-Muslim states generally--and thereby fails to stimulate greater Islamic cohesion because of the contrast with the non-Muslim world; or, on the other hand, Islam is a tool of individual foreign policymakers who use it to advance their own national interests rather than those of the general Islamic community. This last point is borne out by the national differences of attitude toward the Islamic revolution in Iran, the minority problem in the Philippines and in Thailand, and the role that the OIC was meant to play. With regard to the OIC, Pakistan, for instance, has wanted to develop it further, whereas Indonesia has remained largely aloof. But it must also be said that Pakistani enthusiasm has a great deal to do with its view of the OIC as a convenient foil to India's domination of the Non-Aligned Movement. By playing the Islamic card, a state such as China or the Soviet Union might be more successful than a state such as India in advancing its diplomatic goals. But, in any event, playing the Islamic card adds little to the idea of tangible political cooperation among Muslim states and is scarcely what Muslim visionaries have in mind when they talk of activity consistent with the idea of an Islamic commonwealth.

On the other hand, the picture shows that some substance is being added, almost imperceptibly and certainly gradually, to the idea of the umma (Islamic community). The spiritual longing for unity, not unlike the Welshman's Hiraeth (longing for the Celtic valleys), has always been important to individual Muslims, but in our era it has taken on a measure of institutional coherence. The OIC is certainly not paving the way to a federal or confederal union, but it is no more inept as an interstate institution than any other international organization--all of which, after all, are the instruments of their members. Moreover, it serves as a useful forum for discussion from which an international diplomatic consensus--a contemporary type of ijma--occasionally emerges, such as on Palestine and to some extent on Afghanistan. It may also help to reconcile members at odds with each other, as it did with Pakistan and Bangladesh. To this we must add the contribution it makes through the Islamic Solidarity Fund of supplementing the generosity of individual Arab states and encouraging dakwah activities, such as international Quran recitation competitions, and institutions such as RISEAP. These activities have done much to make Muslims more aware of each other and to familiarize them with the major intellectual currents of Islam today. Sometimes these ideas clash with each other, but even the debates that ensure from such clashes have helped to convince a great many Muslims for the first time in centuries that this is all part of healthy family life.

The picture, then, is a mixed one, and, because of this, there is a danger for the social scientist, the involved Muslim, and the Westerner who are looking at it. The first may be tempted to conclude that Islamic solidarity is more symbolic than real, the second that an Islamic culture is emerging and gradually undermining the culture of nationalism, and the last that the unity that Muslims say is evolving is a challenge to the norms of the interstate system and, in particular, a threat to the West. The situation today seems to require of each a willingness to look at the whole. The social scientist should see the possibility of transnational forces undercutting, or reshaping, the institution of the nation-state. The Muslim should see the possibility that familiarity breeds contempt rather than greater harmony, perhaps leaving hajjis and migrant workers disliking their spiritual brothers when observed at close range; and he should see that existing in each country of the Muslim world is a powerful apparatus of state socialization that has successfully promoted national identities for half a century now or longer. For his part, the Westerner would do well to recognize that there is indeed an enormous reservoir of good will that Muslims can draw upon to increase their cooperation, but that, as this cooperation in fact occurs, there is no reason to assume that it will put them out of bounds of the prevailing interstate system or even that it will automatically mean ill will for the West.

# 13

# Indian Muslim Society

Muslim and non-Muslim, may think that the minority situation can be changed into a majority one by religious conversion, higher birthrates, or immigration, but the chances of this reversal happening in India are highly unlikely. According to the official figures of the Indian census of 1981, which have just been released, the total population of Muslims in India, excluding Assam, is 75.5 million, still only about 11.35 percent of the whole. Estimating Assam at about 4.5 million, the total comes to about 80 million, which makes it the third largest Muslim community in the world, after Indonesia and Pakistan, both Muslim majority countries. Before the partition of British India in 1947, Muslims formed 24 percent of the population. Partition gave the Muslim majority areas, except Kashmir, to Pakistan; since the establishment of Bangladesh in 1971, South Asian Muslims are divided almost equally among the three successor states: India, Pakistan, and Bangladesh. In India, except for the state of Jammu and Kashmir and the Union Territory of Lakshadweep, Muslims do not form a majority in any of the constituent states or territories of the Union.

As for other major states and territories with over 100,000 Muslims, in Punjab and Orissa they form about one to two percent of the population, in Haryana four percent, in Manipur and Tripura seven percent, and in Delhi eight percent.

A country with a Muslim majority can consider a wide range of alternative roles for Islam in public life from the thoroughgoing Islamization of Saudi Arabia or Khomeini 's Iran to the complete secularization of Kemalist Turkey.

**Table 13.1 Muslim Population by State**

| States with Muslim Population over 1 Million | Muslim Population in Millions | % age of Total Population of State | % age of Total Muslim Population of India |
|---|---|---|---|
| Uttar Pradesh | 17.8 | 15.4 | 22.2 |
| West Bengal | 11.7 | 21.5 | 14.7 |
| Bihar | 10.0 | 14.1 | 12.5 |
| Maharashtra | 5.8 | 9.3 | 7.3 |
| Kerala | 5.4 | 21.3 | 6.8 |
| Andhra Pradesh | 4.5 | 8.5 | 5.73 |
| Assam | 4.5 | 24.03 | 5.6 |
| Karnataka | 4.1 | 11.1 | 5.1 |
| Jammu and Kashmir | 3.8 | 64.2 | 4.8 |
| Gujarat | 2.9 | 8.5 | 3.6 |
| Madhya Pradesh | 2.5 | 4.8 | 3.1 |
| Rajasthan | 2.5 | 7.3 | 3.1 |
| Tamil Nadu | 2.5 | 5.2 | 3.1 |
| Lakshadweep | 0.25 | 98.0 | 0.04 |

But a Muslim minority has a narrower range of choice, constrained by the preferences of the dominant, non-Muslim majority. Despite six centuries of Muslim rule in large parts of North India, the realistic alternative in the twentieth century for Muslim minorities is between living as a subordinate group in a country regulated by an alien religion or ideology, for example, the Soviet Union, the People's Republic of China, Israel, or South Africa, on the one hand, or in a constitutionally secular and democratic polity like the Western democracies or India. As Wilfred Cantwell Smith perceptively pointed out in 1957, the Constitution of India offers Muslims for the first time in South Asian history the opportunity to share power as legal equals with non-Muslims rather than simply to be the rulers or the ruled.

With the integrity of the Muslim world threatened since 1800 and Islamic traditions reeling under Western political, economic, and cultural pressure, the reaction was sometimes expressed in the idiom of panIslamic solidarity. Historically, Muslim Indians were involved, perhaps as no other Muslim community outside the Middle East, in the desperate endeavor to save the Ottoman Empire and the khilafat (caliphate) from total disintegration after World War I. Anti-imperialist sentiments were also aroused by the Western effort to create a Jewish homeland in Palestine, by the Italian conquest of Libya, and by the imposition of a French protectorate over North Africa.

After World War II, when the colonial tide receded and Muslim states were reborn one by one, new frontiers arose in the Muslim world, sometimes artificially demarcated along the lines of the division of the spoils of colonialism, but sometimes along historical, geographical and cultural lines of cleavage. Although nursing pan-Islamic sentiments, the Muslim world has been subdivided by following the Western model of nation state. A new ideology of Islamic nationalism, a cross between pan-Islamism and nationalism, appeared on the scene. Although it may provide a blueprint (inadequate nevertheless) for Muslim majority states, it can have no rational application to Muslim minority areas. Beyond the borders of nation-states, Islam has not served to bring together Muslim states to the point of submergence of their national personalities any more than Christianity or communism has done. As for Muslim minorities, they can safeguard their group interests in a non-Muslim environment within the framework of nation-states, provided that the state does not discriminate among citizens on the basis of religion and respects group identity, granting groups enough autonomy to manage their social and cultural institutions. This is where the Indian experiment, howsoever imperfect, is valuable and relevant. Given a plural and segmented society, Indian nationalism must also learn to compromise with the presence of multiple subnationalisms.

Over the years pan-Islamic organizations, like the World Muslim Congress, the Rabita-al-Alam-al-Islami, and even the inter government Organization of Islamic Conferences have made hesitant efforts to enlarge their fields of activity to include Muslim minorities. So far, their involvement has been of a very low order, limited to passing resolutions. Pakistan has often tried to exploit the maltreatment of the Muslim minority in India for its own purposes. India, for its part, has been able to contain Pakistan's efforts in the Arab and Islamic world by taking a pro-Arab position on questions like Palestine. At the First Islamic Conference in Rabat in 1969, Pakistan did succeed in blocking India's participation-even as an observer. But whether out of the inherent weakness of the panIslamic linkage or out of Arabocentric concern in the Middle East, the Muslim world has shown minimal interest in the situation of Indian Muslims, notwithstanding their huge numbers.

What solidarity exists is expressed by occasional charitable contributions for religious purposes, such as establishment of madrasas or construction of mosques. Even on this account, Hindu chauvinist propaganda about Arab support for conversion of Harijans (Untouchables) to Islam apart, the flow of financial aid, whether from Muslim governments or organizations, institutions or individuals, has not been substantial, no more than a small fraction of the flow of funds from Christian countries to Indian Christians or from overseas Hindus to Hindu institutions. Naturally, therefore, even those groups among Indian Muslims who look toward Muslim states for moral or material support are turning their attention from Islamic solidarity more to self-help, despite the emergence of Qaddafi in Libya and Khomeini in Iran.

Tiny fundamentalist groups that exist among Muslim Indians may continue to look beyond the contemporary nation-states and dream of the unification of the Islamic world or the restoration of the khilafat. Yet, objectively speaking, one does not see the possibility of the emergence of a united Muslim state encompassing most, if not all, of the Muslim majority states that would claim to protect Muslims in Muslim minority areas. One does not even sense the advent of an international Islamic movement at the mass level. Such a movement would involve Muslim minority communities so deeply as to divert them from their continuing concern for meeting the demands of adjustment to their national environment or in resolving immediate local problems.

But the world of Islam, as a whole, has become more conscious of the Islamic heritage and the pressures for Islamization are beginning to be felt, strengthening the desire to go back to the roots. Call it fundamentalism, if you like, but in a sense all believers are fundamentalists. For a Muslim minority like India's, this strengthens its resolve to maintain its identity and survive as a distinct community. But assertion of identity need not imply conflict or confrontation or a desire to serve as the avantgarde of an Islamic conquest, physical or spiritual.

## Constitutional Framework

The founding fathers of the Indian Constitution, a nationalist leadership with a liberal and modern outlook, adopted a secular model for the new Indian state. This, to a certain extent, went against the Hindu sentiment that identified Indian nationalism and the national culture of India with Hinduism and considered India to be, in a special sense, the land of the Hindus because they formed almost eighty-one percent of the population. But the Hindu society itself is not homogeneous; it is divided not only among various linguistic groups, but within the same region by caste and sect. Also, Muslims are not the only religious minority for every religious community and every linguistic group faces a minority situation in one or more states of the Indian Union. In addition, the population complexion shows continuous variations as one goes down from the state to the village level, passing through districts, subdivisions, and blocks. In this sense, India is a land of minorities and needs a national norm to deal with minority situations at various levels of administration.

The Constitution, therefore, provides many safeguards for the protection of minorities. Thus, Article 14 grants equality to all citizens without discrimination on the grounds of religion, language, or caste. Under Article 16, all minorities enjoy equality of opportunity in matters of public employment and underrepresented "backward classes" the possibility of reservations in entry. Under Articles 26, 27, and 28, minorities are free to manage their own religious affairs, the state cannot levy taxes for the promotion of any particular religion nor can there be compulsory attendance at religious worship or religious ceremonies in state-supported educational institutions. The state cannot discriminate against minority managed institutions in allocation of resources. Under Article 30, all minorities--religious, linguistic, or cultural--have the right to establish and to administer educational institutions of their choice. Articles 345, 347, 350, 350A, and 350B, which relate to rights of linguistic minorities, are also relevant in this context.

The Constitution of India, on the other hand, has a chapter on "Directive Principles of State Policy" in which two articles are objectionable from the point of view of many in the Muslim community. Under Article 44, the state is to endeavor to secure for the citizens a uniform civil code; and under Article 48, the state is to take steps prohibiting the slaughter of cows and calves and other milch and draught cattle. The possibility of the replacement of the shariah (Muslim personal law) by a common civil code, as demanded by a vocal section of Hindu chauvinists as well as a small fraction of secularist Muslims, is looked on by the bulk of the community as a threat to its religious identity, even though it has been done by a Muslim majority country like Turkey. The anticow slaughter principle is regarded as an attempt to use state power to force the cultural ethos of the Hindu majority upon the minority communities, irrespective of the economic consequences to the nation.

Thus, for the most part, the Indian Constitution provides the formal basis for the full and equal participation of Muslims in the country's public life. Moreover, the state does not support Hinduism as a religion. Although it may be argued that in theory the Constitution provides a model for the protection of the rights and interests of religious, linguistic, and cultural minorities, there has been a noticeable gap between the constitutional safeguards and their actual implementation. Indeed, the very objective of minority politics in India would be summed up by many as the closing of this gap between precept and practice so as to secure for minorities full participation in both polity and economy at every level in equality and dignity and at the same time to maintain the minority's identity against the perceived threat of absorption or assimilation into Hindu society.

## Goals

The possible goals of a minority, however, range all the way from assimilation or integration to autonomy, secession, or domination. In India, the Muslim minority, except for a few individuals, resists absorption, demands cultural autonomy, and does not aim at domination but rejects secession.

It is often asserted that for a Muslim the world is divisible into two mutually exclusive categories of dar-al-Islam (countries where

Islam rules) and dar-al-harb (countries at war with dar-al-Islam). In this view, Islam for its fulfillment requires political power, absolute and unshared, or perpetual confrontation with non-Islam.

During the Indian freedom movement, the ulama (Muslim savants)-who steadfastly espoused the cause of nationalism and, therefore, a united India--conceived of the future in terms of an independent state jointly ruled by Hindus and Muslims. They cited the Holy Prophet Mohammed's pact (ahad) with the Jews of Medina after his hijra (migration) from Mecca as the model and theological justification for sharing power with non-Muslims. In their concept, India was to be dar-al-ahad (land of the pact) ordar-al-aman (Land of peace), which the Muslim jurists and political scientists describe as territory in which the Muslims live peacefully, where their life, honor, and property are safe and where they are free to perform their religious obligations. Logically, the antithesis of dar-al-Islam is dar-al-kufr (land of unbelief) and that of dar-alharb is dar-al-aman.

But Islam also recognizes the concept of watan (homeland) because everyone is presumed to love his land of birth or domicile. In purely theological terms, therefore, from the Islamic view, India is not dar-al-Islam, but neither is it dar-al-kufr nor even dar-al-harb. It is dar-al-ahad, dar-alaman, and watan. In any case, if India were perceived as dar-al-kufr or dar-al-harb, the only alternative to jihad (armed struggle) would be hijra (migration).

In fact, partition in 1947 did lead to an unprecedent emigration of Muslims from India to Pakistan as well as of Sikhs and Hindus in the opposite direction. The exodus was more from North India than from South India, more from urban than from rural areas (except in the Punjab), more from the ranks of the professional classes and intelligentsia than from among workers, peasants, and artisans. This outflow of skilled human resources weakened the economic status of the Muslim community in India, reduced its political role, and disrupted its social structure. Those who remained were looked on with suspicion and distrust by their fellow Indians; the credibility of the leader who remained was at a low ebb. Uncertainty about their future made them wary of investment, and they were subjected in a rather harsh manner to the operation of evacuee and enemy property laws. The former landlords and their retainers could not adjust easily to the abolition of the zamindari and jagirdari (landlord) systems in the north and in native states like Hyderabad. Muslims found the doors of public and private employment virtually closed to them. Even the artisans in the traditional centers languished because of their inability initially to attract state support to replace the loss of aristocratic patronage. Only two classes of Muslims generally remained untouched by partition: the landholding cultivator in the north and the trader in the South. Thus, on the whole, the first two or three decades after partition witnessed the gradual impoverishment of the remaining Muslim community.

Sporadic emigration, spurred by communal riots and better prospects in Pakistan, continued until 1971. Then, with the secession of Bangladesh from Pakistan, disillusionment set in, as Pakistan came to seen not as a source of strength for Indian Muslims but of weakness because it continued to rankle Hindus and discouraged Muslim efforts to improve their situation in India. Thus, emigration virtually ceased until the Arab oil boom opened a new, if temporary, focus for self-improvement for many Indians of all faiths in the Arabian Gulf.

The Muslim minority in India continues to fear enforced assimilation as well as expulsion and extermination, as advocated by various Hindu militants. Genocide against such a large community (in both absolute and relative terms) would seem to be a practical impossibility, whether or not world conscience and Muslim majority states were stirred to do something to prevent it. The Jewish Holocaust in Europe and the Kampuchean case make one hesitant, however, to rule out completely such an attempt. Similarly, expulsion or exodus have their recent precedents in Uganda, Bangladesh, and Afghanistan.

But as between the remaining, less noxious options, assimilation and integration, which do most Indian Muslims want? With the exception of a minuscule but influential segment of secular nationalists who look forward to assimilation of all Indians into a modern, nonreligious composite culture, most Muslims fear that such assimilation and integration mean, instead, absorption into Hinduism, and this they resist. The problem is how to preserve their religious and cultural identity without becoming alienated from the political process or without provoking a massive Hindu reaction that may jeopardize the secular democratic order and also the community's physical security.

Hindu revivalism has been an impediment to Muslim goals since the days of the Arya Samaj and the Hindu Mahasabha before independence and the (RSS) since then. Its most powerful political expression since the 1950s has been the Bharatiya Jana Sangh in the north, reborn in 1980 as the Bharatiya Janata party. It equates Indian with Hindu and aims to Indianize the Muslim minority, that is to assimilate it, as Hinduism has done to other religious minorities in the past. Of late, many new variants, such as Virat Hindu Samaj, the Vishwa Hindu Parishad, and Hindu Maha Sangh have appeared.

## Strategies

Given the difficulty of keeping a balance between autonomy and integration, between a separate identity and national solidarity, how do Muslims seek to obtain their goals through public life in India? They do enter elections and win seats in national and state legislatures as well as local bodies, and they are appointed to cabinets. They also become governors and judges of the Supreme Court and the high courts, though not in proportion to their percentage of the population. Before independence, Muslims had enjoyed disproportionately high representation in the legislatures of British India by means of the systems of communal electorate and reserved seats through proportionate reservation.

**Table 13.2 Muslim Membership in the Lok Sabha (Lower House of Parliament)**

| Year | Number of Muslim Members | Percentage of Total Members |
|---|---|---|
| 1952 | 36 | 7.21 |
| 1957 | 24 | 4.74 |
| 1962 | 32 | 6.27 |
| 1967 | 29 | 5.68 |
| 1972 | 27 | 5.18 |
| 1977 | 32 | 6.03 |
| 1980 | 46 | 8.50 |
| 1985 | 41 | 7.60 |

After independence, these advantages were lost in the framing of the Indian Constitution and Muslims, unlike the Untouchables ("Scheduled Castes") and tribals, had to win representation in legislatures by contesting common constituencies. With rare exceptions in the Muslim majority districts of Kashmir, West Bengal, and Kerala could a Muslim win on the strength of Muslim votes alone or as the nominee of a Muslim political party. The new system was designed, in fact, to assure that only "acceptable" Muslim candidates, those with wide appeal to non Muslims, could win.

Muslim representation is also said to have been reduced by under numeration in the census, gerrymandering in the delimitation of constituencies, and exclusion of Muslims from the electoral rolls on flimsy grounds

**Table 13.3 Districts by State with More than Ten Percent Muslims**

| Districts: States | More than 50% | 20-50% | 10-20% | |
|---|---|---|---|---|
| Andhra Pradesh | -- | 1 | 6 | |
| Assam | -- | 4 | 1 | |
| Bihar | -- | 1 | 11 | |
| Gujarat | -- | -- | 4 | |
| Haryana | -- | -- | 1 | |
| Jammu and Kashmir | 6 | 2 | 1 | |
| Kerala | 1 | 3 | 4 | |
| Madhya Pradesh | -- | -- | 7 | |
| Maharashtra | -- | -- | 9 | |
| Karnataka | -- | -- | 10 | |
| Rajasthan | -- | 1 | 2 | |
| Uttar Pradesh | -- | 11 | 23 | |
| West Bengal | 1 | 6 | 4 | |
| **Total** | **8** | **29** | **84** | **121** |

Burdened with a guilt complex over partition, Muslim participation in the political process began haltingly but has increased with the passage of time. Today, no Muslim group stands, as some did immediately after independence, for nonparticipation in the political process. Even the revivalists Jamaat-i-Islami had to change its line on this in 1967. Most political parties, including those that advocate a Hindu state, project themselves as secular. In order to appear so, they enroll a few Muslim members and include a few even in their leadership.

However, there is widespread dissatisfaction among Muslims with the present political system and the kind of representation it affords them. Generally speaking, Muslim political workers who join a national party receive their party's nomination to contest elections at the municipal, state, or national level are seen as symbols of tokenism among the Muslim electorate, not as legitimate representatives of the Muslim community. They become so dependent on the system that neither within the councils of their party nor in the legislatures do they serve to ventilate effectively the grievances of their fellow Muslims. No wonder that most of those elected are reluctant to identify themselves publicly with the hopes, aspirations, and demands of their Muslim constituents lest they be dubbed communal and be refused party nomination in the future. This is, indeed, ironical, because the fact remains that, with few exceptions, such persons are given party posts and tickets primarily to ensure that the party attract Muslim votes. Rarely has a Muslim candidate won from a constituency with less than twenty percent Muslim votes. Even a stalwart of the National Movement like Maulana Abul Kalam Azad had to seek a safe Muslim constituency. Thus, although the ruling party and the establishment, in their anxiety to buttress their secular credentials, always managed to include some Muslim names, Muslims, in effect, remained underrepresented in the democratic institutions. And so, a communication gap developed between the state and much of the Muslim community, a gap that still remains to be fully bridged. This leads to both the isolation of Muslims from the political mainstream and their alienation from the political system.

For a generation after independence, then, Muslim Indians were too hard-pressed by their circumstances to evolve a strategy for their survival. Many of the Muslim Leaguers had emigrated to Pakistan. And the rank and file were made to feel guilty for their support of partition and their continuing links, both physical and emotional, with Pakistan. Congress Muslims lacked both self-confidence and mass appeal, as they had failed to prevent partition and were likely to be distrusted by ordinary Muslims as agents of the establishment. Thus the generation passed, wallowing in self-pity, lamenting its fate, and leading a double life in which it cursed the power structure for its communalism and partiality when inside its home, yet aligned itself with the same structure when outside, hoping to receive some crumbs and find a place at court. With a few honorable exceptions, Muslim leadership adopted the politics of sycophancy. The Muslim masses were generally advised to keep a low profile and place their trust in the Congress party, which enjoyed a virtual monopoly of power in Indian until 1967.

When the era of Congress-party dominance in politics began to end in that year, Muslims found to their dismay that their identification with one party for so long meant they were taken for granted by that party, ignored, and even distrusted by the others. The Indian Union Muslim League, which survived in Kerala because of a communal balance peculiar to that state, pioneered the strategy of bargaining between two closely matched coalitions, centering on the Congress party and the Communists. So successful was this method that the Muslim League was eventually able to place its leader, the late C. H. Mohammed Koya, in the chief ministership for a time.

In the north, a third strategy was attempted by the Muslim Majlis-eMushawarat (Muslim Consultative Committee), founded in 1965. The Majlis brought together a broad spectrum of Muslim leaders: orthodox members of the Jamiat-ul-Ulema, the revivalist Jamaat-i-Islami, and some modernist Muslims both inside and outside the Congress. It proposed to endorse candidates of various parties who agreed with its positions. This strategy failed because it was not seriously applied in the big states of Uttar Pradesh and Bihar and, therefore, did not overcome party loyalty. After the election, the few victorious candidates it had supported backed out under pressure from Hindu majorities within their own parties.

A fourth possible strategy is one of nonparticipation in the political process. This is a measure of desperation and has been largely rejected by the Muslim community, especially where Muslims have been the rulers and have a long tradition of participation in, if not domination of, public life (e.g., North India and Hyderabad). But it has been pursued successfully by various minuscule but prosperous Muslim business communities, like the Bohras, Khojas, Memons, and Navayats on the west coast. They have few demands on government or the political system except to be left alone. In any case, they have too few votes to sway elections.

Political mobilization of the first three types is tempting for a large minority like Indian Muslims living in a democracy where numbers count. The immense influence wielded by the much smaller Jewish minority in the United States on American policy toward the Middle East is often cited without recognizing that the very existence and continuing confrontation between India and Pakistan engenders a hostile Hindu reaction for which there is no analogy in the United States. Besides, the Jews as a minority are much better organized, more affluent, and more intellectually advanced.

## Issues

Four of the principal issues that Muslim politicians, press, parties, and pressure groups have agitated for in the public life of India since independence not surprisingly reflect the interests and aspirations of the community's largely North Indian elite who live in the Hindi heartland: share of government employment, control of Aligarh Muslim University, preservation of the Urdu language, and preservation of the Muslim Personal Law. A fifth demand, the prevention of communal (i.e., anti-Muslim) violence ought objectively to be of greater concern to the Muslim masses, who suffer the most from it, than to the elite. Subjectively, however, the uneducated and tradition-bound masses are still more readily mobilizable as Muslims by their elite on emotionally charged symbolic issues than on bread-and-butter questions of economic development, health, and education. Only if one believes that the major problem facing the Muslim community in India is to preserve its identity against the assimilative pressure of Hindu chauvinism can these boundary-maintenance issues be regarded as more important than the physical and economic survival of Muslims as individuals. Muslim assertiveness, which the Hindu majority regards with scant patience and tends to dub as antinational, no doubt contributes to the tense atmosphere in which frequent bloody clashes between the two communities have erupted. So, too, does the demand for sharing the economic pie. Issues relating to identity are typically North Indian in origin and flourish in the milieu of the former Muslim imperium. In coastal South India, the relatively prosperous Muslim communities (referred to earlier), with a history of peaceful conversion by Arab merchants, do not speak Urdu, nor send their children to Aligarh, nor compete for the civil service--

they merge culturally with the majority despite their religious orthodoxy.

In West Bengal, the Bengali-speaking Muslims have tended increasingly to support the Marxist parties, primarily because of their relative security from communal riots and minimal restrictions on cow slaughter. Nevertheless, they remain a deprived and backward group. It is part of the rhetoric of Muslim politics in India that Muslims fell behind Hindus in the adoption of modern education and, therefore, in government employment and in the modern economic occupations. Anil Seal and Paul R. Brass have demonstrated conclusively that this was true for neither education nor civil service at the elite level in North India in the late nineteenth and early twentieth centuries. It is often said, therefore, that the Muslim elite has exploited the real backwardness of the Muslim masses and mobilized their religious sentiments in the game of politics in order to increase their own share of the cake. Playing their own game of divide and rule, the British had accorded to this Muslim elite reservations in civil service as in legislatures.

But these were lost after partition and many of the Muslim beneficiaries opted for Pakistan. Since, then, it is charged that Muslims have been discriminated against in India in both public and private employment. As regards the former, Professor Ghanshyam Shah has concluded that during the last thirty years Muslims have not obtained government jobs in proportion to their percentage of the population.

Opinions differ about the causes of this continuing under-representation, whether it is because of their relative backwardness in modern education and their consequent inability to field sufficient eligible candidates, or because of prejudice by Hindu decision-makers against Muslim applicants. To quote Shah again, "There is a widespread complaint, not without foundation, that other things being equal, caste Hindu decision-makers give preference to Hindus or to their own castes over Muslims." Given the anomymity of civil service recruitment procedures except for the oral interview, one suspects that at the higher level the problem is more a lack of qualified Muslim applicants than of discrimination which then becomes a self-fulfilling prophecy as young, educated Muslims become discouraged at the low acceptance rate and cease to apply or to take the examinations. The fact of Muslim under representation at the lower levels, clerical and menial, where there is no organized system of recruitment nor is the standard very high testifies to systematic discrimination more clearly.

Job discrimination against Muslims is much easier and more persistent in the private sector, especially by large industrial and commercial enterprises where the Muslim presence is very low indeed except in a few owned by Muslims themselves, like Jeep Batteries, or in sectors where Muslims are still entrenched such as the hides and skins trade in South India.

**Table 13.4 Muslim Share of Public Employment**

| Name of Service | Years/Number of Establishments | Total | Muslims | %age |
|---|---|---|---|---|
| *A: All India and Central Services* | | | | |
| Indian Administrative Service | Total in 1981 | 3,883 | 116 | 2.99 |
| Indian Public Service | Total in 1981 | 1,753 | 50 | 2.85 |
| Income Tax I | Intake during 1971-80 | 881 | 27 | 3.06 |
| Railway Traffic and Accounts Services | Intake during 1971-80 | 415 | 11 | 2.65 |
| *B: Random Survey of Public Employment* | | | | |
| Central Government Offices | 105 offices in 13 states | 75,951 | 3,346 | 4.41 |
| State Government Offices | 876 offices in 13 states | 826,669 | 49,718 | 6.01 |
| Nationalized Banks | 1,317 branches | 113,772 | 2,479 | 2.18 |
| Public Sector Undertakings (Both Central and State) | 168 undertakings in 13 states | 476,972 | 51,755 | 10.85 |
| Total | | 1,581,296 | 107,492 | 6.60 |

Muslim entrepreneurs have also been handicapped by the prevailing anti-Muslim bias in securing government loans and permits, available on paper, but subject to bureaucratic discretion tempered by bribery. For instance, Muslim industrialists and businessmen are starved of bank credit; their applications for licenses, permits, and quotas, which are the key to success in a government-controlled economy, are said to be more likely to gather dust than to be granted. Discrimination in allotment of housing sites or residences in newly developed government colonies is rampant.

Wherever Muslims--because of their traditional concentration and crafts--have achieved a measure of economic progress, such as in Moradabad (brass), Firozabad (glass), Meerut and Aligarh (locks), Mirzapur and Bhadoi (carpets), Bhiwandi (power looms), and Jamshedpur, Ranchi, and Varanasi, their properties, including their stock-in-trade, have been subjected to looting and destruction in frequent communal riots. This dampens both their desire to go out of Muslim slums and to invest in modernization of production units with imports of high technology.

**Table 13.5 Muslims Share of Private Sector Employment**

| Name of Corporation | Executive Cadre (%) | Supervisory Cadre (%) | Worker Cadre (%) |
|---|---|---|---|
| TISCO | 4.1 | 5.60 | 10.30 |
| Texmaco | nil | 0.30 | 4.40 |
| Mafatlal | nil | 1.72 | 3.53 |
| Calico | 0.68 | na | 10.20 |
| Mahindra and Mahindra | 1.48 | 2.25 | 5.02 |
| Orkay | 3.30 | 3.00 | 11.90 |
| J. K. Industries | 2.63 | 2.28 | 5.41 |
| Indian Explosives | nil | 2.73 | 7.09 |

On the economic scene, one should, however, take note also of the recent signs of affluence in some parts of the country, particularly in Kerala, Karnataka, Andhra Pradesh, Gujarat, and Maharashtra, because of the remittances from Indian workers in the Arabian Gulf states. With the exception of Saudi Arabia, none of these states apply any religious preference in hiring, but, although exact figures are not available, it may be fair to say that the proportion of Muslims among the expatriate Indians there may be considerably higher than their proportion in the population of India. So Muslim Indians as a community may be receiving somewhat higher benefits from the job opportunities in the Gulf than non-Muslims are. Remittances have helped their families repair or acquire property, provide education, renovate mosques and run Muslim institutions. Some surplus is now beginning to be invested in business. It can be assumed that the Gulf job market, at least for the unskilled, will dry up soon and that its lasting impact will depend very much on whether the amounts sent home are wisely invested or frittered away in wasteful and conspicuous consumption.

Parenthetically, it should be noted that Kerala is the only state where (through the bargaining skills of the Muslim League discussed earlier) the entire Muslim community has been classified as "backward" and, therefore, entitled to reservations in education and employment under Article 16 (4) of the Constitution to the extent of fifty percent of their share of the population. Because Kerala Muslims are also conspicuous beneficiaries of Gulf employment, it cannot be mere coincidence that communal riots spread to Kerala in the late 1970s. In a scarcity economy, competition and envy quickly spill over into violence.

Many Hindus see yet another connection between Gulf money and the rising profile of Muslim resurgence in India, symbolized by the recent phenomenon of conversions of some Harijans (Untouchables) to Islam in South India. This, it is believed, was largely motivated by the latter's quest for social equality through escape from the Hindu caste system, but it has led to demands by Hindu organizations for a ban on conversion to non-Indian religions and to widespread propaganda that the conversions were part of an international conspiracy to turn India's Hindu majority into a minority. Hindu resentment at polygamy (permitted but rarely practiced by Muslims in India), at the Muslim's allegedly low acceptance rates of family planning, and at illegal infiltration into Assam stem from the same unreasonable fears.

To return to the educational issue, there is no doubt that Muslim enrollment at every level of education (primary, secondary and higher) is lower than their proportion of the population would indicate. This is even true in the areas of relative Muslim concentration. Generally speaking, too, the dropout rate is higher and the educational performance is poorer, which, in turn, limits their access to higher and professional education. From that stems the community's above-mentioned inability to field an adequate number of candidates for those government jobs that are filled by competitive examination. Thus, since independence, the number of Muslims, whether academics, professionals, business executives, or civil servants, has fallen much below their proportion of the population. This has reduced their presence at the decision-making level in government and out, whatever the level of job discrimination that may exist. Certainly educational backwardness is, therefore, a basic reason why such a sizable minority as the Muslim Indians is unable to make a mark in the economic field or in public life. The community has been caught in a vicious circle of poverty and educational backwardness.

But there are other factors as well behind the relative educational backwardness of the Muslim community: the non availability of schools in Muslim neighborhoods; the neglect of Urdu, the mother tongue of most Muslims particularly in the Hindi-speaking states; the imposition of Sanskrit, the sacred language of Hinduism, as the second language; the prescription of non secular textbooks, which Muslims find offensive; and the celebration of Hindu religious rites in schools. Finally, Muslims of modest means, especially artisans, are relucant to deprive themselves of the fruits of their children's labor or to invest in their education lengthily when they are convinced that with the doors of government employment barred to them, any more than an elementary education is a waste. Female education particularly is neglected by Muslim parents; they tend to withdraw their daughters from school at puberty. Religiously minded parents often send their children to religious schools to receive religious instruction. Hence, large numbers of maktabs and madrasas have been opened to provide pre- or extra school religious instruction. When not supplemented with modern education, this leaves the children unable to compete in the modern world.

In the light of all this, the apparent emphasis on establishing Muslim degree colleges would seem to be a misplaced priority. There is a growing consciousness that the limited resources of the community should have been directed to the creation of more facilities: first at the primary, then at the secondary or vocational level so that Muslim performance at the high school level could be better both in quality and quantity. This would then have led to better admissions rates to colleges and professional institutions run by the state. For lack of that, government-aided institutions of higher education established and administered by Muslims have often been swamped by non-Muslim students.

Education leads directly to the language issue. Over the years, as a consequence of politicization and communalization of the problem, Urdu has come to be identified with the Muslim community, yet neither are all persons who speak Urdu Muslims nor do all Indian Muslims speak Urdu. In fact, even if for purposes of argument all 23 million people who declared Urdu as their mother tongue in 1971 were Muslims, that would mean that only about forty-five percent of Muslims in India use it as their principal language. The Urdu speakers reside chiefly in the Hindi-majority region of Uttar Pradesh and Bihar as well as in pockets in the states of Andhra Pradesh, Maharashtra, and Karnataka where the majority languages are Telugu, Marathi, and Kannada, respectively.

Some states with large Muslim concentrations, such as Assam, Bengal, and Kerala, have very low numbers of Urdu speakers. There, the common language, be it Assamese, Bengali, or Malayalam, bridges the religious divide. Among students of linguistics, there is even a question whether Hindi and Urdu are separate languages or only two forms of the same language, written in two different scripts, Devanagari and Persian. Yet, because of a slow but steady Urduization of the Muslims outside the Hindi belt, the emergence of Urdu as the medium of Islamization, and the deliberate attempt to banish Urdu from its birthplace, the language has become the lingua franca of the Muslim Indian community and a salient issue even for Muslims for whom it is not the mother tongue.

**Table 13.6 Linguistic Diversity of Muslim Indians**

| | Total Muslim Population (million) | Total Urdu-Speaking Population (million) | Coefficient of Urduization (%) | Main Language |
|---|---|---|---|---|
| INDIA | 61.42 | 28.61 | 48 | Urdu |
| Urdu States in Hindi Region | | | | |
| Bihar | 7.59 | 4.99 | 65 | Urdu |
| Madhya Pradesh | 1.81 | 0.99 | 55 | Urdu |
| Rajasthan | 1.78 | 0.65 | 37 | Hindi |
| Uttar Pradesh | 13.68 | 9.27 | 67 | Urdu |
| Urdu States in non-Hindi Region | | | | |
| Andhra Pradesh | 3.68 | 3.30 | 91 | Urdu |
| Karnataka | 3.11 | 2.64 | 85 | Urdu |
| Maharashtra | 4.23 | 3.66 | 87 | Urdu |

| | Total Muslim Population (million) | Total Urdu-Speaking Population (million) | Coefficient of Urduization (%) | Main Language |
|---|---|---|---|---|
| Other States with Muslim Population over 1 Million | | | | |
| Assam | 3.60 | -- | -- | Assamese |
| Gujarat | 2.25 | 0.53 | 26 | Gujarati |
| Jammu and Kashmir | 3.04 | 0.01 | 3 | Kashmiri |
| Kerala | 4.16 | -- | -- | Malayalam |
| Tamil Nadu | 2.10 | 0.76 | 36 | Tamil |
| West Bengal | 9.06 | 0.95 | 10 | Bengali |

A major problem for Urdu is that it is the only constitutionally recognized language of India, with the exception of Sindhi, that does not have a homeland--there is no state or Union territory in which it is the language of the majority. Even in Jammu and Kashmir, where Urdu is the official state language, it has been declared as mother tongue by a minuscule proportion of the people; this is bound, in due course, to come into conflict with the legitimate aspirations of Kashmiri and Dogri.

Thus, whereas Urdu has the status of a minority language in all states of the Union, all other national languages outside their home states also have minority status in one or more other states. Theoretically, it should be possible to work out, in a federal union, a national scheme determining the scope for the use of minority languages in education, administration, or the mass media that would apply equally to all languages in minority situations. The Constitution itself lays down, in articles 345, 347, 350, 350A, and 350B, certain norms for fulfilling the aspirations of linguistic minorities, in order to secure the preservation of their cultures. Yet Urdu with no home base of its own and with the burden of political hostility has not been accorded its due place either in education, administration, or the media. So, it has become a major grievance of the Muslim community and repeatedly a major political issue. Implementation of the Gujral Committee Report of 1976 has become a rallying cry for the Urdu-speaking minority.

Slowly, a national consensus is emerging that in addition to the majority language, minority languages should be used for specified official purposes, not only at the state, but also at the district and block levels, which are the effective levels for development and administration if that linguistic minority forms at least ten percent of the population. Second, in education the basic right of every child to be imparted primary education through the medium of his or her mother tongue must be implemented. Third, at the secondary stage, the mother tongue should have primacy and be taught even where it is not the medium of instruction. The choice of a second language should be limited, then, to modern, not classical languages like Sanskrit.

The lack of job prospects for children educated through the medium of Urdu poses a dilemma for the Muslim community. To preserve their cultural identity, their children must learn Urdu; yet, from the point of view of participation in the economy, it is dysfunctional. Comparative study of the ability of other minorities to survive culturally despite loss of their language (e.g., the Irish) might afford a more optimistic prognosis for Muslim Indians.

The fourth Muslim demand is noninterference by the state in the Muslim personal law (marriage, divorce, inheritance) through introduction of a common civil code. This tends to produce a direct confrontation with the modern secular state. Ever since the French Revolution, the secular ideal has been the same set of laws for all citizens. Many Hindus who have sacrificed important aspects of their own religious customs and practices to this legal reform resent the politically expedient exemption of the Muslim minority from, for instance, the prohibition on polygamy or unilateral divorce. Hindu militants charge, unscientifically, that polygamy causes a higher Muslim birthrate. Muslim modernists argue, more persuasively, that polygamy and purdah (seclusion of women) inhibit the modernization and progress of the community and that instant divorce destabilizes social life. Orthodox Muslims argue that the divinely ordained shariah is an intrinsic part of Islam and that to tamper with the personal law is a violation of freedom of religion. The fact that Turkey abolished shariah and that other Muslim majority countries, like Tunisia and even Pakistan, have introduced procedural changes shows that the resistance to social reform originates in the minority situation of Muslim Indians. It is the prospect of assimilation as well as the fear of Parliament with a non-Muslim majority legislating on Islam that makes even many otherwise progressive Indian Muslims hesitant about the fulfillment of this directive of the Constitution.

Here, too, comparison with Muslim minorities in other countries might be more fruitful than with Muslim majority polities. One may question whether a common civil code in a multicultural and diverse country like India is a condition precedent either for democracy or secularism.

Finally, security of life and property is the fifth Muslim demand, one of much import to the Muslim masses who suffer most from communal riots. Communal, principally Hindu versus Muslim, riots began in the late nineteenth century under British rule. Social tensions are a symptom, ironically, of modernization and have been accentuated by education, economic development, and political consciousness. Communities in traditional society that were separated by functional and hereditary division of labor come into conflict when modernization and democratization open up competition to all. In a fluid and mobile society, the results of competition, for good or ill, are explained in terms of individuals. But in a transitional or segmented society where individuals are still largely subordinate to, and identify strongly with, family, clan, caste, or religious community, the results of competition are apt to be interpreted in terms of relative group standing. Add to this an economy of scarcity unable to meet soaring ambitions and expectations and the scene is set for group rivalry, unfair competition, and discriminatory practices, which, unmitigated by cross pressures, easily spill over into violence.

India and Pakistan were born amid some of the worst mutual slaughter of modern history. The number of riots and casualties declined in the 1950s during Jawaharlal Nehru's rule but have intermittently risen since his death in 1964, except for an apparent dip during the brief period of the "emergency" in 1975-77.

Communal riots, unless government instigated, as in czarist Russia or Nazi Germany, are a phenomenon of democracies in which government is constrained from dealing with them with a strong hand because of electoral considerations. Political parties have been suspected, despite their secular stance, of fomenting communal riots for political gains, for creating or sustaining a fear psychosis in the Muslim community in order to demonstrate to Muslim voters that only a particular individual or party can protect them, or to "punish" the Muslims for not voting for a party's candidates in the preceding election.

**Table 13.7 Communal Riots, 1960-83**

| Year | Number of Communal Incidents | Number of Persons Killed | Number of Persons Injured |
|---|---|---|---|
| 1960 | 26 | na | na |
| 1961 | 92 | | |
| 1962 | 60 | | |
| 1963 | 61 | | |
| 1964 | 1170 | | |
| 1965 | 676 (173)* | | |
| 1966 | 133 | 45 | |
| 1967 | 220 | 251 | |
| 1968 | 346 | 183 | |
| 1969 | 519 | 674 | |
| 1970 | 521 | 298 | |
| 1971 | 321 | 103 | |
| 1972 | 240 | 70 | 1,207 |
| 1973 | 242 | 72 | 1,000 |
| 1974 | 248 | 87 | 1,206 |
| 1975 | 205 | 33 | 962 |
| 1976 | 169 | 39 | 794 |
| 1977 | 188 | 36 | 1,122 |
| 1978 | 230 | 110 | 1,853 |
| 1979 | 304 | 261 | 2,876 |
| 1980 | 427 | 375 | 2,838 |
| 1981 | 319 | 196 | 2,613 |
| 1982 | 474 | 238 | 3,025 |
| 1983* | 404 | 202 | 3,478 |

The immediate trigger for a riot may be trivial or any one of a number of "historic" reasons: cow slaughter by a Muslim, a Hindu religious procession playing music before a mosque at prayer time, defamation of religious leaders, or abduction of women. The proximate cause is not as important as the underlying suspicion and distrust worsened by economic competition. The fact that communal riots have been concentrated in the cities and towns of North India and the Deccan where Muslims once ruled and have until recently been almost absent from South India and the eastern fringe of the country where there was little or no Muslim rule would seem to indicate that there is some causal relationship in these riot-prone areas. Muslims there retain (to an extent) the former ruling-elite mentality, whereas the Hindus have the chip-on-the-shoulder mentality of former subjects. In these areas, the Muslim minority also often tends to be assertive of its rights; this brings about the retaliatory punishment and the Hindu desire to put them in their place.

Also more and more noticeable is the inability of the national leadership of India to control the local police and the state and party functionaries who, apparently, largely share the communal bias of the Hindu majority. This explains why the Indian army and central paramilitary forces have to be called in to control the riots. The longtime exclusion of Muslims from the police force after Partition makes for direct confrontation between the two communities. The police do not generally concern themselves with the safety of the weaker sections and are seen as a partisan force. Also the communication gap between the various communities, caused by residential segregation and lack of social intercourse, allows negative stereotyping and easy acceptance of rumors.

Many commissions of inquiry about major riots, like those at Ranchi, Ahmedabad, Bhiwandi, and Jamshedpur, have made thorough studies and suggested appropriate steps to prevent or at least curb communal violence. The National Integration Council as well as the National Police Commission have gone into the question and government has issued many guidelines based on their recommendations, yet the graph of communal riots shows a sickening rise during much of the last decade.

Recommendations have included a special multi community antiriot force to replace the communally infected state-armed constabularies, imposition of collective fines on disturbed areas, statutory compensation for victims, and special courts. Some of these have even been adopted by government at various levels but not fully or expeditiously enough and therefore have proven ineffective. What seems to be lacking is the political will, such as the finally stopped lynchings of blacks in the southern part of the United States in the 1960s.

Although not among the five demands articulated by Muslim spokesmen, the inadequate and often distorted image of Muslims in the media must contribute to the negative stereotyping referred to. In a democracy, despite the relatively low literacy of the Indian population, the media play an important role in molding public opinion. Muslims are conspicuously underrepresented in the ranks of the national media, both English and Hindi. The Urdu press, with some well-known exceptions (particularly in the Punjab and Delhi), is identified with the Muslim community. On the whole, the Urdu press is anemic and ineffective and serves only the purposes of self-congratulation or lamentation. Moreover, some Urdu papers are closely associated with political parties or ideological groups and therefore have limited appeal. In any case, the Muslim segment of the Urdu press has virtually no readership beyond the Muslim community, and there is no Urdu paper with a nationwide circulation, two or three weeklies apart. In the other regional languages, even when its speakers are largely Muslims, the Muslim point of view is not adequately reflected. Thus the media fail to provide a link between the community and the power structure to bridge the communication gap between the community and the nation as a whole.

Indeed, to a large extent, the media plays the negative role of enlarging the gap through manipulation of news, distortion of facts, and misinterpretation of events. Sometimes, offensive and defamatory writings against Islam, the Holy Prophet, or Islamic history appear. As the government is unable to suppress or punish such malicious writings, these give further impetus to the sense of isolation and alienation in the community and add to the prejudice and distrust of the minority by the majority. The government-controlled radio and television are not free from prejudice and bias and often project Muslims as negative stereotypes. The same is true of films, particularly historical or social ones. To a large extent, the mass media, with the freedom it enjoys in a democratic polity, should be held to share responsibility for maintaining or aggravating intergroup tension and, therefore, impeding reconciliation and harmony. It is not enough and often counterproductive that the press does not refer to Hindus and Muslims by name in reporting riots.

Can this situation be overcome? Can the Muslim community acquire a capacity to project its point of view and to influence the course of events through a press of its own? It is obvious that the Urdu press will not do it because its audience is limited to Urdu-speaking people; nor can newspapers or periodicals in English alone fill the gap. What is needed is Muslim-controlled newspapers and periodicals in English and Hindi as well as in the major national languages: Bengali, Gujerati, Marathi, Telugu, Kannada, Malayalam, and Assamese. In order to make an impact, these papers must have standards matching the best available in those languages. Second, organized efforts must be made for briefing journalists and columnists on the Muslim point of view so that the media as a whole can represent faithfully the Muslim side of the story, even if it leaves the reader free to judge and draw his own conclusions. Third, Muslim youth must be encouraged to take up journalism as a profession.

## Conclusions

What emerges chiefly from a study of Islam and public life in India are a number of important distinctions that limit the applicability of any generalizations to other cases, especially to countries in which Muslims are a majority.

First, the Muslim community in India is, and is likely to remain for the foreseeable future, a minority group. Despite a five percent higher rate of increase than the Hindu community and despite the recent conversion to Islam of some Harijans, the reasonable prediction is that Muslims will remain a large community but will represent a relatively small percentage (11 to 12 percent) of the Indian population. Neither is there any possibility for that minority to reclaim its one-time political dominance over the subcontinent. To the contrary, what is less unlikely is that India, Pakistan, and Bangladesh might willingly or unwillingly be reunited; in which case, Muslims would still be no more than a quarter to a third of the population. Or, if the Indian Republic were to fragment (which could happen to Pakistan too), it seems unlikely that any of the components, except Kashmir, would separate or otherwise come under Muslim rule.

Consequently, the public role of Islam as a body of doctrine, beliefs, and rituals is bound to be more restricted in India than it is, or potentially can be, in a Muslim-majority country like Pakistan or Iran. That is to say, nizam-i-Islam (regulation of polity according to Islam) cannot be achieved in present circumstances in India. Muslim personal law may continue indefinitely as a separate code-

-despite the explicit injunction of the Indian Constitution--owing to Muslim political pressure. Muslims as voters, Muslim politicians, and Muslim lobbyists will certainly affect this and other policies as long as India remains a professedly secular democracy. One has only to look at Soviet Central Asia to see how little impact a Muslim minority may have on the public life of a totalitarian, non-Muslim state.

Some orthodox ulama and revivalist leaders in India may be willing to settle for, or even favor, the transformation of India into a Hindu state-which they claim (incorrectly) it already is in practice--on condition that they should then be allowed, with the sanction of the state, to regulate the affairs of minority Muslims according to the shariah. But that bargain, comparable to the dhimmi status accorded to non-Muslims in traditional Muslim-ruled states, does not even seem to be the intent of the Hindu groups that are bent on Indianizing the Muslim minority.

The second distinction, a diminishing but still relevant one, is between North India and the coastal south. It is visible in different origins (peaceful conversion vs. conquest), sectarian distribution (more Ismailis), languages (not Urdu but regional languages), occupations (business more than professional), political issues (not civil service entry), party organizations (the Muslim League), state of Hindu-Muslim relations and, consequently, in a lower incidence of communal riots. Unfortunately, the nationalization (and Urduization) of Muslim politics in recent decades has tended to narrow these regional differences in the direction of a spread of northern tension into South India rather than of southern harmony into North India.

A third distinction is among Muslims themselves. Just as there are great variations in condition and outlook between elite and mass, so there are significant differences in viewpoints toward Islam--orthodox, revivalist, modernist, and secularist--that, in part, cut across class and regional lines but that put articulate Muslim leaders on opposite sides of various public issues (e.g., the question of reform of the Muslim personal law). The modernists and secularists may be relatively few in number, but they wield influence disproportionate to their number because of their superior access to the media and their buildup by the national parties and leadership. It is true that, like most minorities, Indian Muslims tend to coalesce in times of crisis when a state of siege mentality develops. But there may be some advantages in diversity of elite viewpoints as well as party affiliations for a minority as it can modify sterotypes and help refute fears and accusations on the part of the majority that the minority is a homogeneous fifth column.

Implicit in much of the foregoing is the difference between Islam and Public Life and Muslims and Public Life. Although Muslims get their identity, both self and other, from a core of common Islamic beliefs and practices, they also share to a greater or lesser extent some attitudes and behavior that are secular rather than Islamic and yet affect the public life of the countries in which they live. For example, one might agree with the modernists that purdah (seclusion of women) has no explicit Quranic sanction and, in fact, was borrowed from the Byzantine Greeks or Sassanid Persians. Yet, it is more widespread among Muslims than among other peoples, and it does affect such diverse policy areas as education, family planning, and employment.

Since independence, much of the political energy of the Muslim community in India has been dissipated in dealing with minor but persistent irritations--the ever-simmering threat to physical security or of personal humiliation; offensive articles in periodicals and books; curtailment of religious rites, like Qurbani (ritual slaughter of animals) and Azan (the call to prayers): constraints on construction of mosques and on allotment of land for graveyards; forcible occupation of wakf (waqf) properties; motivated criticism of Muslim personal law; persistent discrimination in employment; imposition of Hindu culture and the denial of facilities for learning Urdu or studying through Urdu in government schools; under enumeration in the census and disenfranchisement in elections; police and administrative harassment, and the government's demand of loyalty. The main remedial approach has been political, that is case-by-case amelioration through political contacts and the building up of pressure through representations and memoranda. This has given rise to a class of powerbrokers, but it has failed to provide a permanent solution, a stable modus vivendi, or an institutional framework.

The political approach is not likely to be abandoned, for the simple reason that there is no viable alternative, but the coming decade may witness an increasing agitational input. Also, the main thrust is shifting from minor irritants to major problems of educational and economic development, from the immediate to the long-term, from the tactical to the strategic. Both these methods for successful handling call for self-reliance as well as a sympathetic milieu. The trouble is that gains always generate pressures for a "due" (proportionate) share of the fruits of development and of public employment. To achieve these goals, Muslims may realize their own political impotence and seek new political alliances with the other relatively deprived sections of the national community. They may demand statutory protection through quota or reservation.

Both the alliance and the demands may, in turn, further exacerbate intercommunal relations unless a national consensus emerges on the rights of minorities and/or demarcates acceptable limits thereto.

In the final analysis, the Muslim community's political goal in India is neither dominance nor separatism. Neither does it look outward for inspiration or support. Its goal is preservation of identity and achievement of equality in a plural society. To the extent that religion continues to define identity, Islam will be a factor in Indian society; and so long as there is de facto discrimination on the basis of religion, Islam shall remain a rallying cry--both for the Hindu and the Muslim communities--and thus a potent factor in the public life of India.

# 14

# Future of Islamic Movement

## Introduction

The connections of al-Palimbani and his group with earlier scholars were more than simply student-teacher relations; throughout their writings they showed their intellectual lineage to earlier major scholars by giving their works as major sources of their thought. It is no surprise to find that they developed equally reformist teachings. Al-Palimbani and his fellow Malay-Indonesian scholars also played an important role in preserving the morale of their fellow Muslims in facing the continuing encroachment of European colonial powers. This period marked a painful transition in the history of Malay-Indonesian Muslims: one after another, the Malay Muslim kingdoms fell into the hands of foreign powers.

These encounters with European powers added a new dimension to the development of Islam in the archipelago. We should not, of course, overemphasise the European factor, but there is little doubt that it contributed to the growing concern among our Malay-Indonesian scholars about the future of Islam in this region. This concern is, in turn, reflected in their writings. We will first attempt to discuss their teachings, particularly in relation to the intellectual currents in the wider networks. Then we will assess their impact on Islamic development in the archipelago. Lastly we will examine their response to the intensification of the European attempts to incorporate the Malay-Indonesian world ino their realm.

## Shari'ah and Tasawwuf: Reconciling Al-ghazali with Ibn 'Arabi

In previous chapters we have examined the central theme of al-Ramri, al-Sinkili and al-Maqassari, which was the harmony between the legal and mystical aspects of Islam. This harmony also became the central theme in the writings of al-Palimbani and his group. Throughout their writings, they were eager to reconcile Ibn 'Arabi'Arabi philosophical mysticism and al-Ghazali's tasawwuf. At the same time, the importance of the shari'ah was repeatedly emphasised.

This tendency in the development of Islamic thought is best seen in Palembang. As Drewes has shown, local religious literature in this region at the end of the eighteenth and beginning of the nineteenth century did not include works of Hamzah al-Fansuri or Shams al-Din al-Samatram, nor any writings that had been considered 'unorthodox' or that even contained some 'heterodox' teachings. On the other hand, works of al-Raniri and al-Sinkili circulated widely. Prominent Palembang scholars such as Shihab al-Din b. 'Abd Allah Muhammad preached neo-SUfism as taught by alJunayd, al-Qushayrl and al-Ghazall. Shihab al-Din even went so far as to condemn the reading of works on the martabat tujuh (seven grades of being). He opposed this doctrine, it appears, simply because he feared that it would lead his fellow Muslims astray. He assumed they would misunderstand it because of their lack of solid grounding in Islamic knowledge, particularly of the shari'ah. As we will see, most MalayIndonesian scholars in the period, from al-Palimbani to al-Fatam, in fact adopted the very same concept of the seven grades of being.

Of all the Malay-Indonesian scholars in the eighteenth century, it was Muhammad Arshad al-Banjarl and Dawud al-Fatam who fostered the entrenchment of the shari'ah in the archipelago. We have seen how Muhammad Arshad played a crucial role in the establishment in the Banjar Sultanate of the administration of justice in accordance with Islamic law. His role in the spread of Islamic legal doctrines in the archipelago, however, was far greater through his works on fiqh, which were widely circulated in the archipelago.

Muhammad Arshad'Arshad principal work was the Sabll al-Muhtadln li al-Tafaqquh fl Amr al-Dln. Without doubt it is one of the major works on fiqh in Malay after the completion of the Sirat al-Mustaqlm of al-Raniri and the Mir 'at al-Tullab of al-Sinkili. As Muhammad Arshad states in his introductory notes, he began to write the Sabll al-Muhtadln in 1193/1779 at the request of Sultan Tahmld Allah. It was completed in 1195/1781. The work is in two volumes, consisting of some 500 pages. It deals with detailed rules of the 'i badah (ritual) aspect of fiqh. It is basically an elaboration, or to some extent a revision, of al-Ranin' s Sirat al-Mustaqlm, which used many Acehnese words hardly understood by Malay-Indonesians in other areas of the archipelago.

The Sabll al-Muhtadln, printed several times in Mecca, Cairo, Istanbul and various places in the archipelago, was highly popular in the MalayIndonesian world, and is still used in many parts of the region. Later, descendants of Muhammad Arshad composed a collection of his teachings on the fundamentals of belief ('aqa'aqa) and fiqh, entitled Perukunan Besar al-Banjarl or Perukunan Melayu. The work enjoyed similar success and was subsequently translated into other languages of the archipelago, such as Javanese and Sundanese. The popularity of Muhammad Arshad'Arshad writings indicates that works explicating Islamic legal precepts were needed by Malay-Indonesian Muslims as practical guides in their daily life. It attests to the fact that Muslims in the archipelago also exhibited a deep interest in the legal aspect of Islam. They were not solely interested in Islamic mysticism, as had been supposed by some scholars.

The main sources of the Sabll al-Muhtadm are Zakariyya al-Ansan'Ansan Shark Minhaj al-Tullab, Shams al-Din al-Ramli's Nihayat al-MuhTaj [ild Sharh al-Minhdj of al-Nawawl], Ibn Hajar al-Haytami'Haytami Tuhfat [al-MuhTaj li Sharh al-Minhaj], and Khatib al-Sharbaym'Sharbaym Mughnl al-MuhTaj Both al-Raniri and al-Sinkili also made extensive use of these sources. al-Raniri's Sirat al-Mustaqlm, which was printed in the margin of Sabll al-Muhtadln, was Muhammad Arshad'Arshad starting point; he then made the works of the scholars mentioned above his major references. Muhammad Arshad thereby strengthened his intellectual connections with some important scholars in the networks. Because of its popularity, the Sabll al-Muhtadln played an important role in establishing the dominance of the above works as standard references of the Shafi'I school of law in the archipelago.

A substantial contribution to the further spread of Islamic legal doctrines was made by Dawud al-Fatam, the most prolific among the MalayIndonesian scholars in the eighteenth century. He is the best example of a scholar successful in his attempts to reconcile the legal and mystical aspects of Islam. We discuss Dawud al-Fatam'Fatam main works on tasawwuf later, focusing our attention now on those works dealing with various aspects of the shari'ah or fiqh. The most important among them are the Bughyat al-Tullab li Murld MaL rifat al-Ahkam bi al-Sawab, which discusses religious observances (fiqh al-'i badah), and Furu' al-Masa'Masa I wa Usul al-Wasa'Wasa l, which deals with rules and guidelines in daily life. Smaller epistles then follow, such as the Jam' al-Fawa'id, on various obligations of a Muslim towards his fellows and others; Hidayat al-MuTa'MuTa wa 'Umdat al-Mu'Mu, on fiqh in general; Munyat al-Musalll, on prayer (salaf)' Nahj al-Raghibln fl Sabll al-Muttaqln, on commercial transactions; Ghayat al-Taqrlb, on inheritance (fara'fara), Idah al-Bab li Murld al-Nikah hi al-Sawab, on matters relating to marriage and divorce; and a number of other shorter writings on particular sections of fiqh.

The Furu' al-Masa'Masa I is another ample work onfiqh' a reprinted Meccan edition (1257/1841), based on an earlier edition published in Cairo (n.d.), consists of two volumes of 275 and 394 pages. The work is an adaptation of both Shams al-Din al-Ramli's al-Fatawa and Husayn b. Muhammad alMahalli'Mahalli Kashf al-Litham, and was written in the form of questions and answers. By adopting this style of writing, al-Fatam introduced a new method of delineating the intricacies of fiqh in what he considered an attractive and effective vehicle for teaching fiqh to his Malay-Indonesian audience.

Al-Fatam, through his works listed above, played a major role in the history of fiqh in the archipelago. Although the works bore Arabic titles, they were in fact written in Malay. This reflects al-Fatam'Fatam concern that his Malay-Indonesian co-religionists should be able to understand the precepts of the shari'ah. He underlines the importance of the shari'ah at fiqh for Muslims by citing a hadith of the Prophet, which states that a goodfaqih can better defend himself against evils than a thousand Muslims who perform religious obligations without sufficient knowledge of fiqh. It must be kept in mind, however, that al-Fatani was not simply a great faqlh or an expert on the shari'ah; he was also a sufi par excellence, devoting a number of writings to tasawwuf and kalam.

So far as the eighteenth century is concerned, al-PALIMBANI was the scholar most responsible for the further spread of neo-SUfism in the archipelago. He was particularly an expert on the Ghazalian tasawwuf. As Al-Baytar informs us, al-PALIMBANI was renowned among his fellow scholars in the Haramayn for his outstanding expertise on al-Ghazali's Ihya' 'Ulum al-Dln. He not only taught his students the tasawwuf of al-Ghazali, appealing to them to study and practise it seriously, but he also wrote several works about it, including the Fadd'Fadd l al-lhya' li al-Ghazali. It is known that al-Raniri, al-Sinkili and al-Maqassari referred to al-Ghazali in their works, but al-Palimbani more than all of them made the Ihyd' 'Ulum al-Dln the basis for his works. Therefore, he can appropriately be considered the most prominent 'translator' of al-Ghazall among MalayIndonesian scholars. The immense popularity of the Ghazalian tasawwuf'tasawwuf the archipelago can to a great extent be attributed to al-Palimbani.

Al-Palimbani's masterpieces, widely circulated in the archipelago, were two works that have been closely associated with al-Ghazali's writings, the Hiddyat al-Sdliklnfl Suluk Maslak al-Muttaqln and Sayr al-Sdlikln ild 'I bddah Rabb al- 'AlAmln. Both works were written in Malay and were thus intended to be read by the wider Malay-Indonesian audience. The Hiddyat al-Sdlikln, completed in Mecca in 1192/1778, was printed at various times in Mecca (1287/1870 and 1303/1885), Bombay (1311/1895), Cairo (1341/1922), Surabaya (1352/1933) and Singapore (n.d.). The Sayr alSdlikln, consisting of four parts, was written in Mecca and Ta'Ta f between 1193/1780 and 1203/1788. Like the Hiddyat al-Sdlikln, the Sayr al-Sdlikln was printed in Mecca (1306/1888) and Cairo (1309/1893 and 1372/1953), and later also reprinted in Singapore, Malaysia and Indonesia.

The Hiddyat al-Sdlikln deals mostly with rules of the shari'ah interpreted in a mystical way. As al-Palimbani himself points out, it is a translation of al-Ghazali's Biddy at al-Hiddyah. But this work can more appropriately be termed an adaptation of the Biddyat al-

Hiddyah, as, according to al-Palimbani, 'it renders several topics found in al-Ghazali's [Biddyat al-Hiddyah] into the Jdwl language, while at the same time it introduces a number of appropriate additional [topics which] are not addressed in it'.

Al-Palimbani, of course, depends heavily on the Biddyat al-Hiddyah, but at the same time he takes material from other works of al-Ghazall, such as the Ihyd' 'Ulum al-Dln, Minhdj al-'Abidln and al-Arba'lnfl Usul al-Dln. Of particular importance, he makes numerous references to works by several prominent scholars in the networks, such as the Yawdqlt al-Jawdhir of al-Sha'Sha, al-Durr al-Thamln of 'Abd Allah al-'Aydarus, al-Bustdn al- 'Arifln of al-Qushashi and Nafhat al-Ildhiyyah of al-Sammani.

In many respects al-PALIMBANI's Sayr al-Sdlikln is a further elaboration of the teachings contained in the Hiddyat al-Sdlikln. According to al-Palimbani, the Sayr al-Sdlikln is a rendering of the Lubdb Ihyd' 'Ulum al-Dln, an abridged version of the Ihyd' 'Ulum al-Dln, written by al-Ghazali's brother, Ahmad b. Muhammad. But the Sayr al-Sdlikln is not just a translation of the Lubdb Ihyd'. As in the Hiddyat al-Sdlikln, alPalimbam in the Sayr al-Sdlikln takes additional material from works of such scholars as Ibn 'Arabi, al-Jili, Ibn 'Ata' Allah, al-Sha'Sha, al-Burhanpurl, al-Shinnawi, al-Qushashi, al-Kurani, al-NAbulusi, al-Bakri and al-Sammani. al-Palimbani also makes references to works of his Malay-Indonesian predecessors, such as al-Sinkili and even Shams al-Dln al-Samatranl, who had been considered by many an unorthodox scholar.

All this again underlines the fact that al-Palimbani possessed not only teacher-disciple connections but also intellectual links to many important scholars in the networks. We are not going to dwell on the detailed contents of the Hidayat al-Salikln and Sayr al-Salikln. It suffices to say that both works elucidate the principles of Islamic faith and religious duties to which every aspirant of the mystical way should commit himself. Like many scholars in the networks, al-Palimbani believes that the grace of God can be attained only through correct faith in the absolute Unity of God and total obedience to the shari'ah precepts. Although he accepts certain notions of Ibn 'Arab! or al-JHi, particularly concerning the doctrine of the Universal Man, al-Palimbani interprets them in light of al-Ghazali's teachings. He puts emphasis in his tasawwufraore on purification of mind and moral conduct than on the exploration of speculative and philosophical mysticism.

With such an emphasis, al-Palimbani adopted the central teaching of other scholars in the networks. He maintained that the fulfilment of the doctrines of the shari'ah concerning rituals and good deeds was the surest way to achieve spiritual progress. At a higher level, further progress would be attained through the intensification of the dhikr. al-Palimbani outlines seven kinds of dhikr, each of which is designed to uplift the nafs (human soul), which has seven corresponding stages. He then goes on to describe in detail various requirements of the dhikr that will enable the person who performs it to achieve the intended aims.

As far as his dhikr is concerned, although al-Palimbani was mostly known as a Sammaniyyah shaykh, he followed the teachings of the Khalwatiyyah tariqah. This is not surprising, as he received this order from al-Sammani. In fact, al-Palimbani's teaching of seven kinds of dhikr and seven stages of the soul was originally developed among the circle of the Khalwatis, and later incorporated by al-Sammani in the body of Sammaniyyah teachings.

However, in contrast to the tendency among the Khalwatiyyah shaykhs to encourage a certain degree of individualism and freedom among their disciples, al-Palimbani subscribes to the older teachings, which emphasise the absolute position of masters vis-a-vis their disciples. al-Palimbani, in accord with al-Maqassari, also a Khalwatiyyah shaykh, requires total obedience of disciples to their master. In order for disciples to succeed, they must pledge their allegiance (bay'bay) to their master and obey him totally, for he is an heir or representative of the Prophet. 25 In the final analysis, the disciples must submit themselves to the master like 'a dead body in the hands of its washers'.

From these teachings one may gain the impression that al-Palimbani encourages some kind of passivity, at least in the realm of mysticism, but it would be unfair to view him only from those teachings. alPALIMBANI, like al-Maqassan, who was an exemplary activist against Dutch colonialism, encouraged activism among his fellow Muslims, such as the jihad against the Dutch. It appears that it was al-Palimbani's concern for disciples who might be led astray if they embarked on the mystical path on their own that inspired him to adopt these teachings. Therefore, he insisted that disciples be guided by trusted masters, who would shield them from confusion about the mystical doctrines.

Al-Palimbani categorises the travellers on the mystical path into three groups: the beginners (al-mubtadT), the intermediates (al-mutawassif), and the advanced (al-muntahl). For each group, al-Palimbani recommends a number of readings. His list of readings is interesting indeed. For the beginnners he lists no fewer than 56 works: among others, six works of al-Ghazall, two works of al-Ansari, seven works of al-Sha'rani, three works of 'Abd al-Qadir al-'Aydarusi, one work each of al-Qushashi, al-Kurani, Taj al-Din al-Hindl and al-Sinkili, some 13 works of al-Bakrl and al-Sammani or their students concerning doctrines and practices of the Khalwatiyyah and al-Sammaniyyah orders, and several works by other scholars. Most of these works were simple elucidations of the fulfilment of the shari'ah in connection with the aim of achieving spiritual progress in the mystical way. With his selection of such works by these scholars, al-Palimbani clearly intends to show to every aspirant of the mystical way that the shari'ah constitutes the fundamental basis of Islamic mysticism.

At the intermediate level, al-Palimbani brings the seekers after truth to a deeper exploration of SUfism. He lists no fewer than 26 works, most of which are more philosophical and theological. He includes the Hikam of Ibn 'Ata' Allah, which must be read along with commentaries by Muhammad b. Ibrahim b. al-'I bad, al-Qushashi and Ahmad b. 'AlAn. He then lists the Hikam of Raslan al-Dimashqi. This work is most probably the same work as the RIsalah ft al-Tawhla, for al-Palimbani mentions its commentary entitled Path al-Rahman by al-Ansari. al-Palimbani points out that he read the Hikam and the RIsalah ft al-Tawhld together with the latter'latter commentaries by al-NAbulusi and al-Sammani. al-Palimbani also includes theological works such as al-Yawaqlt al-Jawahir of al-Sha'rani, Miftah al-Ma'Ma yyahfi al-Tarlqat al-Naqshbandiyyah of al-NAbulusi, and several works of al-Bakrl and al-Sammani.

At the advanced level, the travellers in God'God path are exposed to more complicated and, therefore, somewhat more controversial works. At the top of the list are the works of Ibn 'Arabi, including the Fusiis al-Hikam, Futuhat al-Makkiyyah and Mawaqi' al-Nujum. Then follows the al-Insan al-Kamil of al-Jili, the Ihya'

'Ulum al-Dln of al-Ghazall, the Tuhfat al-Mursalah of al-Burhanpuri together with its commentaries written by al-Kurani and al-NAbulusi, the Lawaqih al-Anwar al-Qudsiyyah of al-Sha'rani, the Mir'Mir al Haqa'Haqa q of al-Shinnawi and the Maslak al-Mukhtar of al-Kurani. Finally he includes works by Malay-Indonesian scholars: theJawahir al-Haqa'Haqa q and Tanblh al-TullabfiMaL rifat al-Malik al-Wahhab of Shams al-Din al-Samatram, the TA'TA al-Bayan Hashiyyah Idah al-Bayanfi Tahqlq Masa 'il al-A 'yan [sic] of al-Sinkili, and finally alPalimbam'Palimbam own work, Zad al-Muttaqln fi Tawhld Rabb al-'AlAmln al-Palimbani states that Zad al-Muttaqln was written as an exposition of the doctrine of wahdat al-Wujud as he received it from al-Sainmam and his student Siddiq b. 'Umar al-Khan.

Al-Palimbani, undoubtedly, was fully aware of the possibility that such works might lead to intellectual and religious confusion. Therefore, the above works were reserved for advanced disciples only. Those who did not totally comprehend and practise the shan'shan and its proper relations with the haqiqah might be led astray or even to heresy by such works.

With regard to the works he recommends, al-Palimbani again demonstrates his intellectual linkage to the tendencies in earlier networks. Following the lead of al-Sha'rani, al-Qushashi, al-Kurani, al-Sinkili and al-Maqassan, who took great care not to sever their intellectual and spiritual links with the philosophical-mystical doctrines of Ibn 'Arabi, alPalimbam made his own attempts to reconcile Ibn 'Arabi'Arabi teachings with those of al-Ghazall, emphasising the importance of the purification of mind and of the fulfilment of religious obligations in the mystical way. alPalimbam was opposed to the uncontrollable speculative notion of mysticism; he denounced the doctrines of the so-called Wujudiyyah mulhid (lit. atheistic unity of being) as well as the practice of religious offerings to the ancestors' spirits. These religious beliefs and practices appear to have had some followers in South Sumatra during the times of al-Palimbani, which inspired him to try to end them.

In the same way as al-Ranin, al-Palimbani divides the doctrines of Wujudiyyah into two kinds: the Wujudiyyah mulhid (atheistic unity of being), and the Wujudiyyah muwahhid (unitarianism of unity of being). alPALIMBANI points out that according to the followers of the doctrine of Wujudiyyah mulhid, the first article of belief that is, la ilah ilia Allah (there is no god but God) means that 'there is no such thing as our being, but only God'God Being, that is, we are God'God Being'. al-Palimbani moreover explains:

> *They further said inna al-haq subhanahu wa Ta'Taa laysa hi mawjud illafl dimn Wujud al-ka'ka nat [sic], that is, the Reality of God does not exist but in the beings of all created things. Thus they insist that the Unity of God exists only in the beings of creation. They, in addition, say that 'we are of the similar nature (sebangsa) and similar being (seWujud) with God and that the Essence of God is knowable, for He exists in the external world (kharij) in time and place'. Such a belief is infidelity (kufr).*

Al-Palimbani apparently did not cite al-Ranin for his denunciation of the followers of Wujudiyyah mulhid. But both scholars share the same teaching. Al-Ranin, for instance, states that:

> *Now I would like to explicate and make you all aware of the falsity of the belief of Wujudiyyah mulhid and zindlq. They maintain that our beings and that of the universe are God'God Being, and [conversely] God'God Being is the being of us and the universe. Let it be known if such a belief of Wujudiyyah [mulhid] is correct, then every thing is God. And if we kill a man and cut him into pieces, then what [we] kill and cut is God.*

Again reminding us of al-Ramri, al-Palimbani includes the followers of Wujudiyyah mulhid among the group of people whom he calls pseudo'sufis (kaum yang bersufi-sufian dirinya). Another group of pseudo-SM/Js, according to al-Palimbani, were the followers of hululiyyah (the doctrine of God'God incarnation). He maintains that their error was their belief that God incarnates Himself into the beings of man and other creations.

Muhammad Arshad al-Banjari is known to have written only one work on SUfism. But because he studied together with al-Palimbani in the same social and intellectual milieu, there is little doubt that he shared alPalimbam'Palimbam views on the subject. Muhammad Arshad opposed the doctrine of Wujudiyyah mulhid. According to local tradition, several years after his return a scholar named Hajl 'Abd al-Hamld Abulung came to South Kalimantan. Despite the obscurity surrounding his life, what is clear is that he introduced to the local Muslims the kind of teachings that have been categorised by both al-Palimbani and al-Raniri as Wujudiyyah mulhid. 'Abd al-Hamld reportedly taught people that 'there is no being but God. There is no 'Abd al-Hamld but God; He is I and I am Him'.

As a result, religious confusion spread among the population and 'Abd al-Hamld was summoned to the royal court. But he fiercely held fast to his belief. This led Muhammad Arshad to issue a fatwa declaring 'Abd alHamld'Hamld teachings heretical and led Sultan Tahmld Allah to order his execution. This is reminiscent of the heresy hunting and killing of Wujudiyyah followers in Aceh during the time of al-Ranm.

In al-Palimbani's opinion, the true sufis were followers of the doctrine of Wujudiyyah muwahhid. These sufis affirmed the absolute Unity of God in Himself. They were called the Wujudiyyah because 'their belief and intellectual disposition centre on the absolute Unity of God'. al-Palimbani does not elaborate his teachings about true SM/JS. However, it is clear from al-Palimbani's short statement that true sufis put more stress on the transcendence of God than on His immanence. Although they accept the notion that God is immanent in creation, it is anathema for them to hear any statement saying that God is identical with creation.

Al-Palimbani shares the view of many scholars in the networks that God and the universe are two different entities: each possesses distinct realities. At this stage, al-Palimbanl and many scholars in the networks accept the view of Ibn 'Arabi that the universe is the exterior expression (al-A'A al-kharijiyyah) of God. As such, the exterior expression of God is not God Himself; it is simply a shadow of God'God Being.

In such a view, the doctrine of Wujudiyyah muwahhid is basically similar to that of wahdat al-Wujud of Ibn 'Arabi, according to which all created beings come into existence only when God reveals Himself. Men and other creatures, in essence, are separate from the Self of God, and it is only through revelation, as a way opened up by God Himself, that they are able to reunite with God. This reunion requires purification and total conformity to the Divine norm on the part of men. All this finally leads to a stage where men fully realize the Unity of Being. This stage of wahdat al-Wujud is also called by al-Palimbani the stage of tawhld al-Siddlqln that is, the stage of the tawhld of the truthful whose spiritual progress makes them occupied solely with God; they come to realise that there is no other being but God. As al-Palimbani points out:

At the fourth stage of tawhld, he [who seeks after truth] sees nothing in the existence of the universe but Dhat (Essence) of the One Supreme God, who is the Necessary Being (al-wdjib al-Wujud) this is the vision of those Siddlqln (who fully believe), those 'arifin (who are adept); the sufi master calls them people who experience fand' (perish) in the tawhld they then will not realize themselves, for their spirit is occupied with the shuhud (vision) of God, the Real Being.

At this point al-Palimbani apparently succeeds in his attempt to reconcile the tradition of Ibn 'Arabi with that of al-Ghazali. The concept of the fourth stage of tawhid of the Siddlqln, taken from al-Ghazali, is equated by alPalimbam with Ibn 'Arabi'Arabi wahdat al-Wujud. But this does not mean they are identical.

To explicate the revelation of God in accordance with the concept of wahdat al-Wujud or to achieve fana' in the fourth stage of tawhld, al-Palimbani adopts the doctrine of the seven stages of revelation or seven grades of being (martabat tujuh). This doctrine was originally developed by Ibn 'Arabi but was later reinterpreted in a more orthodox sense by al-Burhanpun. According to al-Burhanpun, God reveals (ta'ta or Tajalll) Himself through seven stages of being. The creation of man is the last stage of God'God revelation. While al-Burhanpun believes that nobody will be able to grasp the essence of the Real Being, al-Palimbani maintains that it can be known through MaL rifah (gnostic knowledge), centred in the qalb (lit. heart = intuition). Emphasising the teachings of al-Ghazali, al-Palimbani considers that MaL rifah can be attained through spiritual purification and concentration, all of which will result in, as al-Ghazali puts it, 'the vision of the Essence of God'.

An attempt to reconcile the tradition of al-Ghazali's shari'ah-oriented tasawwuf with that of Ibn 'Arab!'s philosophical SUfism was also made by Muhammad Nafls in his Durr al-Nafls. This work, completed in Mecca in 1200/1785, apparently enjoyed wide circulation. Printed several times in various places in the Middle East and the archipelago, it is still used in many places in the Malay-Indonesian world. The Durr al-Nafis was written in the 'JAWI language, so that it can be read by those who do not read Arabic.'

A glance at the Durr al-Nafis attests to the fact that Muhammad Nafis made a conscious attempt to reconcile the tradition of al-Ghazali and that of Ibn 'Arabi. In preparing this work, aside from using the oral teachings of his masters in the Haramayn he makes extensive use of the Futuhat al-Makkiyyah and Fusus al-Hikam of Ibn 'Arabi, the Hikam of Ibn 'Ata' Allah, the al-Insan al-Kamil of al-Jili, the Ihya' 'Ulum al-Dln and Minhaj al- 'Abidln of al-Ghazali, the RIsalat al-Qmhayriyyah of al-Qushayn, the Jawahir wa al-Durar of al-Sha'rani, the Mukhtasar al-Tuhfat al-Mursalah of 'Abd Allah b. Ibrahim al-Mirgham and the Manhat al-MuhammaDiyah of al-Sammani.

According to Muhammad Nafis, the Unity of God (tawhld) falls into four stages: the tawhld al-Af'Af (Unity of the Acts of God), tawhld al-Sifat (Unity of God'God Attributes), tawhld al-AsMaL (Unity of God'God Names), and tawhld al-Dhat (Unity of God'God Essence). At the highest stage, the tawhld al-Dhat, seekers after truth will experienceyana' during which they will be able to have a vision (muShahadah) of God. Like al-Palimbani, Muhammad Nafis believes that the Essence of God cannot be known through the five senses and reason: only with kashf (direct intuition) will one be able to grasp the Essence of God.

Muhammad Nafis stresses the importance of the fulfilment of the shari'ah both outwardly and inwardly in order to attain the stage of kashf. It is impossible for anybody to reach that stage without intensifying his spiritual power through performing the religious rituals and obligations laid down by the shari'ah. A comprehensive study of Dawud al-Fatam'Fatam mystical teachings is not yet available, but it is clear that he was a great proponent of al-Ghazali's tasawwuf as well as a prominent defender among Malay-Indonesian scholars of Ibn 'Arabi'Arabi tradition. Al-Fatam is known to have written several works along the same lines as the doctrines of al-Ghazali, bearing such titles as the Tar jamah Bidayat al-Hidayah and Minhaj al- 'Abidln. For al-Fatam, al-Ghazali was the greatest sufi. As he puts it: 'Imam al-Ghazali is like a very deep sea, containing precious pearls which cannot be found in other seas'.

In al-Fatam'Fatam view, the greatest sufi next to al-Ghazali was al-Sha'rani. He points out in the introductory notes to his Malay translation of al-Sha'rani'rani Kashf al-Ghummah that al-Sha'rani was his 'penghulu' (master), who guided him in the path of God. It is no surprise, therefore, that al-Fatam, like al-Sha'rani, staunchly defends the doctrine of Ibn 'Arab!'s wahdat al-Wujud and the seven grades of being in a little-known but important work entitled Manhal al-Saflfl Bayan Zumar Ahl al-SUFI.

Al-Fatam was very critical of people who styled themselves as sufis while in fact being simply pseudo-, 5M/£s (berlagak seperti sufi) and ignorant of the true teachings of SUfism. According to al-Fatam, among the groups of pseudo-sufi were people who claimed to have complete union (ittihad) with God. He bitterly denounces them:

> *The people of ittihad believe that their essence (dhat) becomes the Essence of God. This is a gross infidelity (kufr). Those who worship idols are much better than they are, they think that they gain the true vision, [in contrast] they have come to the presence of iblls (devil).*

In connection with this view, al-Fatam conceives the Manhal al-Safi as an answer and explanation of various concepts and terms in tasawwuf. In addition to discussing such concepts as wahdat al-Wujud, martabat tujuh and other mystico-theological matters, al-Fatam complements the work with a list of some key terms in sufi vocAbularies and their meanings. In the introductory notes to the Manhal al-Safi, the author again criticises pseudosufis who misunderstood the concept of, for instance, wahdat al-Wujud because they simply embraced its literal meaning. For that reason, he reminds the Muslims that books dealing with such topics should be read only by experts or by those who have solid grounding in the 'tariqah Muhammadiyyah'.

The fact that the Malay-Indonesian scholars in the eighteenth century continued to cling to the central doctrine of Ibn 'Arabi is hardly surprising. Despite criticism of the concept of wahdat al-Wujud, it is in fact the fundamental and central doctrine of all kinds of SUfism. Criticism of this doctrine by such scholars as Ibn Taymiyyah, al-Subkl (d. 745/1344) and Ibn Khaldun (d. 780/1378) is essentially based on the fact that it can be easily misunderstood. It may lead to the belief that there is a continuity, or a total unity, between the creation and God. In other words, it could bring one to a pantheistic belief, which is anathema to legal scholars (ahl al-shar'shar).

It is important to note that the doctrine of wahdat al-Wujud, quite surprisingly, was defended by several eminent legal and hadith scholars, including Muhy al-Din al-Nawawi (d. 676/1278), Jalal al-Din al-Suyuti and Zakariyya al-Ansari. We have shown how al-Ansari, for example, possessed hadith isnad which can be traced to Ibn 'Arabi. The staunchest defender of Ibn 'Arabi among neo-sufis was, of course, al-Sha'Sha, to whom many scholars in the networks traced their mystical teachings.

It is of particular importance to keep in mind that many scholars in the networks, from al-Qushashi, al-Kurani, 'Uthman b. Fudi, al-Sinkili, al-Maqassan, al-PALIMBANI and Muhammad Nafls to al-Fatam, responded in a similar fashion to controversy surrounding Ibn 'Arabi'Arabi doctrines. Much like al-Sha'rani, they insisted that Ibn 'Arabi'Arabi doctrines should not be taken at face value: they must be understood in connection with other mystical concepts.

In order to avoid misinterpretation of Ibn 'Arabi'Arabi doctrines, these scholars unanimously urged disciples in the mystical path to read Ibn 'Arabi'Arabi books only after they had achieved the degree of the 'khass' (elite). Disciples must have firm grounding in all aspects of mysticophilosophical doctrines and understand fully their relations with the legal teachings of Islam before they can understand the teachings of Ibn 'Arab! in their proper contexts. It is equally important to note that these scholars took great care not to associate themselves entirely with Ibn 'Arabi; they cited other authorities, unanimously known as 'orthodox' scholars, such as al-Ghazali, as their central sources.

## Jihad and the Radical Course of Reformism

Sufism, particularly among modernist Muslims, has been regarded as one of the main causes of regression of the Muslim world. Religiously it has been accused of being the source of bid'bid (unwarranted innovation) and takhayyul (delusion) or khurafat (superstitions). Socially, SUfism has been blamed for pulling the Muslim masses into 'passivity' and withdrawal ('uzlah) from worldly affairs. It allegedly promoted escapism from the socioeconomic and political ills of their societies. As a result, so the accusation goes, Muslim societies failed to cope with the advanced but hostile Western world, which from the early seventeenth century increasingly penetrated the Dar al-Islam.

Most of the accusations are ill-founded. There is no need to repeat the arguments and evidence presented throughout this book: that the central teaching of the reformed SUfism or neo-SUfism was puritanical in its nature. It called for the total obedience, both outwardly and inwardly, of Muslims to orthodoxy, or more precisely to the shari'ah. The scholars in the networks agreed that it was simply impossible for the sufis to achieve their spiritual goal without committing themselves fully to the orthodox doctrine of Islam. There were, of course, deviant manifestations of SUfism, particularly at the level of the masses, but these were generated mostly by a lack of understanding of the correct teachings of SUfism. Therefore, SUfism as such could not be held responsible for all bid'bid and khurdfats found in Muslim societies.

Similarly, the modernists' accusation that SUfism encouraged passivity and withdrawal from worldly affairs was based mostly on ignorance or misunderstanding of the whole teachings of SUfism. We have shown throughout this discussion that none of the scholars in the networks taught passivity and withdrawal. On the contrary, they appealed to Muslim activism; for them, the fulfilment of Muslims' worldly duties was an integral part of their spiritual progress in the mystical journey.

In the case of Malay-Indonesian scholars in the seventeenth century, we have seen that al-Sinkili and al-Maqassari presented themselves as exemplary sufis, who were absorbed not only with their own spiritual journeys but also with worldly affairs, holding the office of Mufti in their respective Sultanates. Al-Maqassarl went so far as to become one of the most important leaders and heroes of the Bantenese war against the Dutch.

This was also true of Malay-Indonesian scholars in the eighteenth century. We have already mentioned Muhammad Arshad'Arshad reformism and activism; he was the pioneer of the establishment of the office of Mufti and of Islamic educational institutions in the Sultanate of Banjar. Even though the Sultanate was, from 1021/1612 onwards, continually harassed by the Dutch before they finally subdued it in 1237/1860, it is surprising to find how little Muhammad Arshad had to say about the struggle against the Dutch; neither his own works nor other sources indicate that he ever preached the doctrine of jihad (holy war) against the Dutch.

Appeals for jihad, strangely enough, came from al-Palimbani and al-Fatam, who spent most of their lives and died in the Haramayn. This is strong evidence of their very close attachment to and concern for Islam in their homelands. It indicates that they were not the sufis pictured by modernist Muslims merely occupied with their spiritual journeys and alienated from their societies. This also suggests that contacts and communications between the Malay-Indonesian world and the Haramayn were well maintained, so that the Jawl scholars were well informed about the development of Islam in the archipelago, particularly in connection with the continued encroachment by unbelievers.

On more than one occasion al-Palimbani urged his Malay-Indonesian fellows to wage jihad against European colonialists. Voorhoeve and Drewes even argue that jihad was one of al-Palimbani's specialties. This seems to be an exaggeration, which has led to a misunderstanding and distortion of al-Palimbani's teachings as a whole.

The major work of al-Palimbani on jihad is Nasihat al-Muslimin wa Tadhkirat al-Mu'Mu FadA'i l al-Jihad fi Sabil Allah wa Karamat alMujahidinfi Sabil Allah. The work is unquestionably the first of this type known widely in the archipelago. However, the FadA'i l al-Jihad was apparently intended to be read not only by a Malay-Indonesian audience, but by a much wider one, for it was written in Arabic. He appears to have deliberately not written it in Malay, so that, he might have assumed, the Dutch would not understand it. The work, consisting of seven chapters delineating the virtues of the holy war according to the Qur'an and the hadith, was a concise but substantial writing on the subject. After explaining that it was obligatory for Muslims to wage holy war against hostile unbelievers, al-Palimbani concludes the FadA'i l al-Jihad with a short supplication (du'du'), which would make the mujahidin (those who carry out jihad) invulnerable.

Snouck Hurgronje has maintained that al-Palimbani's FadA'i l al-Jihad was the main source of various works on jihad in the long Acehnese wars against the Dutch. It became the model of the Acehnese version of admonition to Muslims to fight the unbelievers. Known collectively as the Hikayat Prang Sabi, such works played an important role in sustaining the fighting spirit of the Acehnese throughout the protracted wars fought between 1873 and the early twentieth century. Roff rightly points out that the Acehnese resistance to Dutch aggression from the early stages assumed the character of jihad led by the independent 'Ulama' who were best fitted to organise and prosecute a holy war.

Al-Palimbani's appeal to Malay-Indonesian Muslims for jihad was not confined to writing the FadA'i l al-Jihad. He is said to have written letters, three of which were intercepted by the Dutch. They contained exhortations to Javanese rulers and princes to wage holy wars against the infidels. The letters were written in Arabic and later translated into Javanese and then into Dutch. The writer of the letter called himself Muhammad, but in the text of the Javanese translation he is referred to as 'Abd al-Rahman, a Palembang scholar in Mecca. Drewes has established that the writer was 'Abd al-Samad al-Palimbani; according to Arabic sources, al-Palimbani was also called Ibn 'Abd al-Rahman.

The first letter, translated into Dutch in Semarang, Central Java, on 22 May 1772, was addressed to the Sultan of Mataram, Hamangkubuwana I, previously known as Pangeran Mangkubumi. After a quite lengthy doxology in praise of God, al-Palimbani writes:

> *A sample of God'God goodness is that He has moved the heart of the writer [al-Palimbanl] to despatch a letter from Mecca, the Lord has assured that those Sultans shall enter it [paradise] whose magnanimity, virtue and prowess against enemies of other religion [sic] are without equal. Among these is the king of Java, who maintains the religion of Islam and is triumphant over all potentates, and furthermore excels in good works in the war against those of other religion [sic]. The Lord reassures those who act in this way by saying 'Do not think that those who fell in the holy war are dead; certainly not, they are still alive' [Qur'an 2:154, 3:169]. The Prophet Muhammad says: 'I was ordered to kill anyone but those who know God and me, His Prophet' [sic]. Those who are killed in the holy war are in odour of sanctity beyond praise; so this is a warning to all followers of Muhammad.*

The conclusion of the letter then follows, which recommends two hajjis for religious positions in the Mataram and mentions that the writer has sent with them a small quantity of Zemzem (Zamzam) water (from Mecca) for the Sultan.

While the contents and addressee of the second letter were almost identical to the first letter, the third one was sent to Pangeran (Prince) Paku Nagara, or Mangkunagara, together with a banner reading al-Rahman al-Rahim, Muhammad Rasul Allah 'Abd Allah, meaning 'the Merciful and Compassionate [God], His apostle and servant Muhammad'. After praising God and the Prophet in the opening, the letter runs as follows:

*God will forgive the sins of the most pious people like Pangeran Mangkunagara, whom He has created to win such repute in the world, and also because Your Highness is a scion of the House of Mataram, upon whom God has bestowed Abundant mercy beside Muhammad the Prophet, considering that Your Highness' justice is a matter of common knowledge. Furthermore, Your Highness should bear in mind the words of the Qur'an, to the effect that a small host is capable of gaining the victory over a mighty force.*

Will it please Your Highness to also keep in mind that it says in the Qur'an: 'Do not say that those who fell in the holy war are dead'. God has said that the soul of such a one enters into a big pigeon and ascends straight up to the heaven. This is a thing all devout people surely know in their hearts, and more particularly this will be the case with Your Highness, who is compArabie to a flower which gives forth its fragrance from sunrise to sunset, nay all Mecca and Medina and the Malay countries are wondering at this fragrance, and pray to God that Your Highness may triumph over all his enemies. Please think of the word of Muhammad, who has said: 'Kill those who are not of the Islamic faith, one and all, unless they go over to your religion'.

Be confident of permanent good fortune and exert yourself in the fear of the Lord; do not fear misfortune and eschew all evil. One doing so will see the sky without cloud and the earth without squalor. Derive comfort from the following words of the Qur'an: 'Those who have believed and worked the works of righteousness, shall obtain the grace of the Lord [in the paradise]' for the Prophet Muhammad has said: 'If a man can live forever in this world, he will also live forever and enjoy eternal bliss in the hereafter'.

This is to notify Your Highness that I am directed, to deliver to Your Highness the accompanying jimat [amulet, in the form of banner], the potency of which is such that when it is used by Your Highness, when campaigning against your enemies, [with God'God blessing Your Highness] will always be victorious, which will lead to the protection of the Muslim faith and the extermination of all its malevolent adversaries.

The reason why this banner has been sent to you is that we in Mecca have heard that Your Highness, being a truly princely leader, is much feared in battle. Value it and make use of it, please God, in exterminating your enemies and all unbelievers. Good wishes and greetings are conveyed to Your Highness on behalf of the old

Godfearing people of Mecca and Medina: Ibrahim, Imam Shafi'I, Imam Hanafi, Imam Maliki and Imam Hanball, and furthermore on behalf of all the other people here, whose unanimous wish is that the blessings of the Prophet and his four great companions Abu Bakr, 'Umar, 'Uthman and 'AlA, may abide with Your Highness'Highness.

Ricklefs concludes that these letters were a significant historical landmark in the history of the struggles of Malay-Indonesian Muslims against the Dutch. In his opinion, they are the first evidence to come to light of an attempt from the world of international Islam to foment holy war in Java in the second half of the eighteenth century. On the other hand, Drewes argues that the letters had only modest purposes: recommending two scholars for religious posts in the Mataram Sultanate, and sending a banner to a Javanese prince. Even though Drewes recognises that jihad was one of al-Palimbani's concerns, he suspects that the letters were simply a display of the writer'writer learning in religious matters, particularly in the holy war, not really exhortations to wage the jihad.

Even though ido not subscribe to Rickiefs' view that the letters contained the spirit of pan-Islamism, I accept the notion that the main purpose of the letters was indeed to encourage the adressees to lead the jihad. al-Palimbani evidently devoted the larger part of the letters to the virtues of jihad against the unbelievers to incite the Javanese rulers to take the lead in holy wars. The letters, as Ricklefs believes, reinforced potential indigenous antagonism towards the Dutch.

It is worth noting that al-Palimbani did not criticise the Javanese ruling house for division and quarrels among themselves, nor did he question their attachment to Islam. For that reason, it is clear that he did not wish to exacerbate their conflicts by criticising any one among them. Instead, he recalled the greatness of the Mataram Sultanate and, therefore, appealed to its rulers to once again revive it by way of jihad. Although al-Palimbani made no explicit mention of the Dutch in the letters, what he calls unbelievers or infidels were undoubtedly the Dutch, who had intensified their attempts to subdue the Mataram Sultanate: it is the Dutch who were to be the target of the jihad.

Al-Palimbani failed in his attempts to instigate Javanese rulers to wage the jihad, for the Dutch intercepted the letters before they reached their destination. The original letters were subsequently destroyed by order of the Dutch authorities in Batavia. But it is not impossible that the central message of the letters was conveyed orally to the addressees by scholars recommended by al-Palimbani. If so, as Ricklefs argues, the oral communication of the contents of the letters did not immediately affect the course of events in Java. The 1770s marked the beginning of major steps towards political stability on the part of the Javanese monarchs. The incendiary message from al-Palimbani in Mecca did not impede this progress.

Another leading proponent of the jihad among Malay-Indonesian scholars in the eighteenth century was Shaykh Dawud ibn 'Abd Allah al-Fatam. In his case, his period saw the increasing attempts of the Thais to tighten their grip over the Muslim region of Patani. It is hardly surprising, therefore, that this sorry political situation in his homeland also became a main concern for al-Fatam. Abdullah even asserts that al-Fatam returned home to lead jihad himself against the Thais before he finally returned and settled permanently in the Haramayn. We cannot support this assertion, as there is no evidence to corroborate it. Al-Fatam never returned to Patani from the time he left it in search of knowledge: he spent the rest of his life teaching and writing in the Haramayn.

Al-Fatam appeals to Muslims, especially those in Patani, through his writings. However, he did not write a special work on the jihad, nor did he send letters to the Muslim rulers of Patani. He delineated his ideas on the jihad in his various works. It is known, for example, that his work on prayer (salai), entitled Munyat al-Musalli in Malay, completed in Mecca in 1242/1827, has some political overtones. Matheson and Hooker suggest that the work was written particularly for the Muslims in Patani in order to support them in their struggles against the Thais.

Al-Fatam'Fatam teachings on jihad appear to bear some relation to his idea of the Islamic state. In his opinion, an Islamic state (dar al-Islam) should be based on the Qur'an and the hadith; otherwise it would be called a state of unbelievers (dar al-kufr). We have no details on his notion of the Islamic state, particularly with regard to its system and administration. However, an Islamic state must function to protect Islam and the Muslims. Therefore, apostasy (murtadd) from Islam is not allowed, and those who so deviate should be killed.

In connection with the protection of Islạm and the Muslims, according to al-Fatam, it is an essential obligation (fard al- 'ayri) for every Muslim to wage jihad against hostile unbelievers (kafir al-harb). If an Islamic state is attacked and annexed by unbelievers, the Muslims are obliged to fight them until they regain their freedom. As for the jihad to expand the realm of Islam, which involves the subduing of the unbelievers, it is only a fard al-kifayah, an obligation which is acquitted in the name of all as long as it is performed by some. In both cases of the obligation of jihad, al-Fatam stresses the need for Muslims to have fighting strategies; they must not wags jihad if they are ill-prepared militarily.

Having seen such teachings of Malay-Indonesian scholars, known as sufi scholars, it is no surprise that the Dutch in particular considered these teachings and tariqah highly dangerous to their rule. Snouck Hurgronje, the most prominent adviser on Islamic affairs to the Dutch authorities, points out that sufi shaykhs were the most dangerous enemies of Dutch rule in the archipelago. He claims that the menace of Malay-Indonesian sufi scholars to the Dutch was no less than that of the Sanusiyyah to the French in Algeria. For the Dutch, sufi scholars, whom they also called 'independent teachers' were very difficult to control. It is thus not hard to understand why the Dutch did whatever they possibly could to contain their influence, including the banning of their books and interception of their letters.

One of the best-known examples of Islamic renewal and reformism originating among sufi and tariqah circles, which resulted in long wars between the Dutch and the native population, was the Padri Movement in Minangkabau or West Sumatra. We have discussed in Chapter 4 how al-Sinklli'Sinklli renewalist teachings and tariqah, mainly by way of his student Burhan al-Din, spread to this region. Burhan al-Din in turn, through his famous surau of Ulakan, established himself as the most important Minangkabau scholar towards the end of the seventeenth century, with whom most of the next generation of Minangkabau scholars studied. After his death, the tomb of Burhan al-Din became a centre of religious visitation, where pilgrims performed what Hamka calls some strange religious practices but which were in fact the rituals of the tariqah people, such as dhikr followed by dancing or singing.

Despite such practices, Shattariyyah writings, such as those of al-Sinkili and the teachings of Burhan al-Din himself, again and again emphasised the need for the tasawwuf followers to commit themselves totally to the precepts of the shari'ah It appears that tariqah practices in Ulakan, particularly at the popular level, had become uncontrolled and tended to be excessive and extravagant; this in turn invited criticism among ex-students of the Ulakan surau. From this it is evident that the embers of reformism did not die out.

In the late years of the eighteenth century, clearer signs of religious reform came to the forefront in Minangkabau society. For instance, among the Shattariyyah suraus, mainly located in the Minangkabau inner highland (darek), there were conscious attempts to revive al-Sinklli'Sinklli teachings, particularly on the importance of the shari'ah in the practice of tasawwuf. Furthermore, as Jalal al-Din, a contemporary Minangkabau who also took part in this new wave of renewal and reform, tells us, there were constant arrivals in Minangkabau of scholars from Mecca, Medina and Aceh, who contributed to reformism. Jalal al-Din makes no mention of their names, but he does state that scholars from the Haramayn were experts in mantiq (logic) and MaL am (ideal realities), both sciences being crucial to understanding shari'ah as well as tasawwuf. Meanwhile, an Acehnese scholar came to teach such sciences as hadith, tafsir andfara'andfara (inheritance).

The leading scholar in Minangkabau in this period was Tuanku Nan Tuo, the principal teacher of Jalal al-Din. The latter tells us that Tuanku Nan Tuo (1136-1246/1723-1830) of Ampat Angkat was a student of Tuanku Mansiangan Nan Tuo, who was in turn a student of Burhan al-Din. Tuanku Nan Tuo was also reported to have studied in the Ulakan surau with other students of Burhan al-Dln. Later he established his own surau in Cangking, Ampat Angkat, and gained fame as a scholar of both shari'ah and tasawwuf. For his expertise in these two aspects of Islam, Tuanku Nan Tuo earned the title of 'Sultan 'Alim Awliya' Allah' who was the 'leader of all Minangkabau 'Ulama' of the Ahl al-Sunnah wa al-JaMaL ah ('people of the approved way and community').

The surau of Tuanku Nan Tuo accordingly became the best-known centre for the study of fiqh and tasawwuf in Minangkabau. Similarly, the students of Tuanku Nan Tuo, when they later returned to their own villages and devoted themselves to teaching in the suraus or in society in general, stressed the importance of the shari'ah. Jalal al-Dln, the foremost disciple of Tuanku Nan Tuo, for instance, established his surau in Kota Lawas, which was already the home of another, older, Shattariyyah surau. The aim of Jalal al-Dln in establishing his surau was to create a genuine Muslim community in Minangkabau by way of total commitment to the implementation of the Islamic way of life as prescribed by the shan'shan. For that purpose, Jalal al-Din taught his students the various aspects of Islamic law.

Tuanku Nan Tuo committed himself to the cause of the reform of Minangkabau society. He made clear to the people the differences between good and evil, as well as between the conduct of Muslims and kafirs. He impressed on his students the need for the Minangkabaus to follow the path of the Ahl al-Sunnah wa al-JaMaL ah, who based their lives on the Qur'an and the hadith. At the same time, he warned them that failure to do so would only lead to social insecurity and disruption.

Tuanku Nan Tuo was not content with simply lecturing his students in his surau on the importance of the shan'shan' he himself, together with his students, led the way to the field where un-Islamic practices such as robbery, arrack drinking and slavery held sway. According to Jalal alDm, Tuanku Nan Tuo visited places where robbery occurred and people were held captive to be sold as slaves, or where the precepts of the shan'shan were violated. He appealed to those who were involved in such things to rid themselves of those wrongdoings; otherwise they would be attacked and punished. As a result, peace returned to the region and trade once again revived in the region; Tuanku Nan Tuo, himself a well-to-do merchant, was renowned as a 'tempat pernaungan' (protector) of the traders.

The Shattariyyah tariqah was not the only sufi order in Minangkabau. It is known that the Naqshbandiyyah tariqah was introduced to the region in the first half of the seventeenth century by Jamal al-Din, a Minangkabau who initially studied in Pasai before he proceeded to Bayt al-FaqIH, Aden, the Haramayn, Egypt and India. On his way home he stopped in Aceh before finally reaching his homeland in West Sumatra, where he was active in teaching and preaching the Naqshbandiyyah tariqah. Jamal al-Din'n travels remind us of al-Sinkili's earlier. Even though Jamal al-Din provides lively accounts of his travels to these places, unlike al-Sinkili, he makes no mention of his teachers, so we are not able to trace his scholarly connections. Both Van Ronkel and Johns have suggested that Jamal al-Din was the author of a Naqshbandi fiqh text entitled Lubab al-Hidayah, which was based on the teachings of Ahmad Ibn 'AlAn al-Siddiqi al-Naqshbandi. By the late eighteenth century, the Naqshbandiyyah and the Qadiriyyah tariqahs, had made substantial inroads on Minangkabau. Both tariqahs, like the Shattariyyah, contributed significantly to Islamic renewal in the period.

The renewalism of the Shattariyyah, Naqshbandiyyah and Qadiriyyah, best represented by Tuanku Nan Tuo and Jalal al-Din, met strong opposition from the penghulus (adat, custom chiefs) as well as from the followers of the extravagant type of SUfism. More importantly, some disciples of Tuanku Nan Tuo himself considered his reform simply a piecemeal one. The most prominent among such students was Tuanku Nan Renceh, who envIsaged a more thorough and radical reform.

Having failed to persuade Tuanku Nan Tuo to change his evolutionary and peaceful approach to Islamic renewal, Tuanku Nan Renceh found strong supporters in the famous three hajjis who returned from Mecca in 1218/1803: Haji Miskin, Haji Sumanik, and Haji Piobang. Their pilgrimage coincided with the capture of Mecca by the Wahhabis. Therefore, they are considered to have been influenced by the Wahhabi teachings, such as opposition to bid'bid, the use of tobacco and silk clothing, which they attempted to spread by force in the Minangkabau region.

Tuanku Nan Renceh, together with the three hajjis, now known as the Padris, declared jihad against those Muslims who declined to follow their teachings. As a result, civil war erupted among the Minangkabau; the suraus, considered the bastion of bid'bid, were attacked and burned to the ground, including those of Tuanku Nan Tuo and Jalal al-Din. The royal family and the penghulus, who also became a major target, soon asked the help of the Dutch. With the intervention of the Dutch, the Minangkabau struggles for reform led to the famous Padri wars, which ended at the close of the 1830s.

It is beyond the scope of this book to discuss the teachings of the Padris and the course of events surrounding the Padri wars. Important for our purpose here is that Islamic renewal and reform in the Minangkabau region, whether initiated by Tuanku Nan Tuo and the tariqah cirles or launched by Tuanku Nan Renceh and the Padris, found their origins in the scholarly networks. The differences in their approach to renewal and reform, peaceful or evolutionary on the one hand and radical on the other, reveal that the course of reform was not a simple one.

Muhammad Ibn 'Abd al-Wahhab (1115-1201/1703-87), the pioneer of the radical wahhabi movement, despite his connection with the networks, was also influenced by other factors that substantially determined his approach to renewal and reform. Similarly, although most of the leading proponents of the Padris in Minangkabau derived their inspiration for renewal and reform from the tariqah circles, at a later stage they were influenced by a string of other factors, such as the 'success' of the Wahhabis in Arabia and the local conditions in Minangkabau that led them to adopt radicalism.

Despite its excesses, the Padri Movement was a major landmark in the history of Islamic renewal and reform in the archipelago. Its impact on the development of Malay-Indonesian Islam was tremendous. The Padri Movement, in restrospect, not only questioned the degree of renewalism among the tariqah circles but more importantly challenged the established formulation of relations between the 'great tradition' of Islam in the centres and an Islamic 'little tradition' that mixed with the 'adat (customs) at the local level. The transmission of reformist ideas and teachings through all Malay-Indonesian scholars, as we have shown throughout our discussion, constituted a conscious attempt to bring the great tradition of Islam to supremacy in the archipelago. This also becomes one of the most distinctive features of Islamic development in the Malay-Indonesian world in later periods.

## Legacy of the Seventeenth and Eighteenth Century

Some preliminary comment on transmission is, however, apposite at this stage. 'Transmission' means to hand on through time, and we thus need some basic understanding of time in Islam and in Indonesian Islam.

## Time: the Seventeenth and Eighteenth Century

From the linear view, time gives us a past, a present and a future; for Islam the Torah was revealed, as was the Injil, and Islam has completed revelation. Similarly, the networks of transmission are completed transmissions, datable in historical time. This last phrase is clearly referring to linear time, but it also creates two difficulties.

First, from the internal point of view, the Arab biographies are in the present. By this I mean they are a continuing and present authority in the pesantren (traditional Muslim boarding schools) and circles of Muslim scholarship in the fifteenth/twenty-first century in Indonesia. They exist now and have meaning and authority now because they are how we know original Islam. Their time is present. This can be seen for instance in the case of Shaykh Muhammad Yasin al-Padam, who had a number of students that are now kiyais of the pesantrens and 'ulama' at the same time. His students proudly maintain the chain of authority (isnad) from al-Padam, who was regarded as one of the most important authorities of the hadith in the contemporary times. Al-Padam himself produced a manuscript entitled Tarajim 'UlamA' al-Jawl, in which he gave an account of the isnad he and his students possessed.

Second, the truths of Islam, which is transmitted, are timeless. This is not to propose that they are ahistorical, alhough this was the view of much nineteenth century European historiography. Such a view is to comprehensively misunderstand revelation. Unfortunately, remnants of this position persist in occasional social science accounts of Indonesian Islam, which fail to realise that time is historical but that networks are both in the historical past and in the present.

Transmission through time is achieved by isnad and silsilah (chains of transmission). Indeed, Islam may be described (up to a point) as a religion and law formulated by chains of transmission. Accuracy of linkage is thus fundamental. Here time must be historically demonstrable. However, linkages are not solely linear as the Arab biographies show; historical links are equally important. They indicate sometimes a variability in the material being transmitted. There are many examples of these, not only in the isnad 'ilmiyyah (chain of transmission of Islamic learning) but also in the tariqah silsilah (chain of transmission of esoteric sciences of tasawwuf). Among the isnads both isnad 'ilmiyyah and isnad tasawwuf there exist what are called as the isnad 'all (supreme isnads), which indicate that the sources of authority occupied a higher or even highest position, but also that the sciences they had transmitted were of the highest values. This can clearly be seen in some of the isnads of al-Sinklll (seventeenth century), al-Palimbam (eighteenth century), Muhammad Nawawl al-Bantanl (nineteenth century) and Muhammad Yasin al-Padanl (twentieth century).

## New Times, New Authorities: The Nineteenth and Twentieth Centuries

By 1800, the Malay-Indonesian world or, more correctly, the various parts of what later became Indonesia and Malaysia, no longer drew authority, sovereignty or legitimacy primarily from Islam. While it is true that some areas, such as Aceh, maintained an ethic of Muslim authority (and still do, though in a different form) until the end of the nineteenth century, Islam itself began to be redefined in European (Dutch and English) terms. The colonial period saw the introduction of a new sort of authority, which essentially reduced Islam to a private and personal religion and justified itself in secular terms (treaties, the colonial state). This was the context for nineteenth and twentieth century Islam. That was a real context, as it remains today, but this does not mean that seventeenth and eighteenth century isnads and silsilahs became irrelevant; of course they did not, and they persist. What it does mean is that we have to recognise two streams of authority: the traditional isnad and silsilah, and the new 'reform' isnad and silsilah of the nineteenth and twentieth centuries.

## Traditional Isnad and Silsilah

The time is the nineteenth century and the material is the Malay scholarship of this period. That scholarship is extensive, and there is space here only for some illustrative examples, all from the northeast Malayan Peninsula (Kelantan-Patani), a somewhat neglected area.

There are 15 or so major authors, plus a number of others in the mid to late nineteenth century. In terms of time, the context is important. These scholars were writing in the timelessness of revealed Islam, but the context was the time of European triumphalism. The lines of transmission could no longer be taken for granted. The zaman Islam, while timeless and true, was also in European zaman, which imposed its own time. Intellectual SUFIsm was not self-contained, as in the past: it had to cope with a new and apparently superior way of thinking the so-called scientific rationalism, which is even more apparent in the Islamic modernism that began to take roots. This challenge comes through in the writing of the period. The 'ulama' had to look over one shoulder at the past and, at the same time, to a new future in a new world.

The Patani 'ulama' were no exception. By the early to mid-nineteenth century, the scholarship coming from this area was overwhelmingly concerned withfiqh and usul al-dln; tasawwuf\s> poorly represented in the surviving material. In part, this may be explained as a consequence of what was happening in Mecca where, as Snouck describes, the chief branches of learning had been reduced to these two. However, there is also the local factor to take into account. Patani in the nineteenth century was a mere pawn in the power struggle between Britain and France for political control in Southeast Asia. Siam itself was desperately trying to retain its status as an independent state, and part of its success lay in convincing European powers (in this case Britain) of its actual exercise of sovereignty over its southern, and Malay-populated, possessions. The 'ulama' were well aware of this, and their priority became the protection of Malay Muslim identity. In this effort, tasawwufhad little obvious practicality to offer. This is not to say that it was neglected it was not but that the prior emphasis was elsewhere.

An excellent example is Shaykh Dawud ibn 'Abd Allah al-Fatanl discussed above. But we can also give an illustration in the life and work of Shaykh Ahmad Muhammad Zain (1856-1906), one of the greatest Patani 'ulama' in post-Dawud ibn 'Abd Allah period. His grandfather, two of his three uncles and two cousins were all well-known scholars. In Mecca, Shaykh Ahmad studied medicine and later became supervisor of the Malay (JawT) printing press, which published many of Shaykh Dawud'Dawud works. He was also a noted teacher and his students went on to fill high positions in politics, as Mufti in various parts of Malaya, Kalimantan and

Cambodia and as teachers and founders of pondok. His influence has extended into the twentieth century. One of the most prominent of his students was Che Muhammad Yusuf, better known as Tok Kenali (1868-1933), who established the Majlis Ugama Islam in Kelantan and was a leading commentator and teacher of religion in the Malay world. Shaykh Ahmad'Ahmad own writing is distinguished, in particular his al-Fatawa alFataniyyah. This is a complex collection of fatawa and may be compared with those of Ahmad Hassan in the Persis collections one generation later in Indonesia. The pressures of time were clearly beginning to transform isnad and silsilah from those delivered in person to include also those transmitted from a distance through new print media.

However, this transformation has never been linear, as can be shown in the works of Muhammad al-Nawawi al-Bantanl (1813-97). Born in Tanara, Banten, West Java, al-Nawawi settled in Mecca permanently in 1855, where he became one of the most important Jawl 'ulama' in the Haramayn. Prior to his becoming an 'alim, he had studied with a number of prominent 'ulama' in the Haramayn, among whom were Shaykh Ahmad al-Nahrawi, Shaykh Sayyid Ahmad al-Dimyap, Shaykh Sayyid Ahmad Dahlan, and Shaykh Muhammad Khapb al-Hanball. Many Malay-Indonesian flocked to him, and many of them later became kiyais of many pesantrens in Java. They carried with them the isnads and silsilah?, of religious learning and tradition in the time of translation from Islamic traditionalism to modernism. Among al-Nawawi'Nawawi prominent students were Kiyai Haji (KH) Hasyim Asy'Asy (founder of Tebu Ireng pesantren and the Nahdlatul UlamA organisation); KH Khalil of Bangkalan, Madura; and KH Asnawi of Caringin, West Java. He produced 26 works, some of which are still used in many pesantren?, in Indonesia. His most important work is the Tafsir alNur Marah Labid, which, according to Riddell, represents an exegetical approach in harmony with the new reformist spirit of the time.

## The New Isnad and Silsilah

The new isnad and silsilah could just as well be named the 'reform' isnad and silsilah, and we conventionally date them from about 1900, with the works of Egyptian reformers (Muhammad 'Abduh and Rashld Rida) plus the explosion of journals such as al-

Imam and al-Manar. Internally within the Muslim reform groups (Kaum Muda, Sarekat Islam and others), there began the long debate on how to renew Islam in the face of modern challenges, chief among which was the successful Western imperialism and, even more fundamentally, secularism. In addition, from within Muslim thought arose views that were critical of sufi scholars such as al-Bantam and his fellow in Mecca, Shaykh Ahmad Khatib al-Minangkabawi, which were widely disseminated in the later nineteenth century. These 'ulama' on the surface would seem staunchly anti-SUFIsm; but careful examination of their works reveals that what they opposed was the excessive and escapist SUFIsm as practised by certain tariqahs,. On the other hand they accepted a more puritan SUFIsm, which was strongly oriented to the socio-moral reconstruction of Muslim society.

The twentieth century was a time of great intellectual turmoil, and this is represented in a number of authors. Hamka (1908-81) is a good example. He grew up in a religious household and was educated in religious schools. By his mid-20s he had published widely on both religious and secular subjects as well as working as a journalist, including as an editor. He was also a novelist, often using religious themes, and a teacher in religious institutions. His own personal isnad and silsilah, therefore, were formed from a number of different sources which, in typical nineteenth and twentieth century fashion, included new media forms, new educational methods and new intellectual derivations. Taken together, these are perhaps a definition of modernism. His Pelajaran Agama Islam (1984) and Tasawuf Moderen (1987) are good examples, because in them he attempted to show that orthodox sufi belief and practice were consonant with modernity, provided that the individual'individual response to the latter did not lead to syncretism, especially with reference to local customs. He was himself well aware of the dangers of mixing elements of different philosophical traditions.

The same is true of Harun Nasution (1919-98), although the contradictions in his isnad and silsilah are much more marked. He was educated in both Western and Islamic traditions and is now remembered primarily for his reforms of the IAIN curricula in the 1960s-70s. His contribution to Islamic education was notable. But this is not the whole sum of his achievement. Nasution was a bold and constructive thinker on the place of revelation in the contemporary state, Indonesia, which was avowedly secular but populated by Muslims whose intellectual isnad and silsilah went back many centuries. While he did not dismiss that heritage, he was concerned to contextualise it in the new circumstances of the time. This took several forms.

First, he held very strongly to the view that no one of the revealed religions can be held to be prior to any other; time, as such, is not a determinant because any completion of how one knows and experiences God is impossible. All that is possible is the individual effort, the will to approach God, and each of the three monotheisms accepts this premise as fundamental. The logical consequence therefore, for Indonesia, is not an 'Islamic state'. To hold otherwise is to deny that the revealed message is outside time: that is, social, cultural, language and geographic circumstances are the determining factors in how one 'knows'.

Second, and following from this, it is true that these factors cannot either be ignored or diminished at any stage of history. Indonesia is not the Arabic Middle East, though it shares the Prophethood of Muhammad. The temporal factors, therefore, are 'natural' and this itself is God-willed. This allows different temporal expressions of truth but it is the same truth. To insist on a common or general form for truth is (a) not necessary and (b), given the diversity of Muslim cultures and societies, actually quite perverse. Harun is presenting here a form of Mu'Mu argument, which allows even for ascetism. In his view there is no necessity to force oppositions between reason, revelation and/or SUFIsm. Reason, for Nasution, is a God-given capacity, but the ways in which it is exercised are various. However, variety is always limited by revelation, which imposes its own intellectual and spiritual constraints. The laws of science are an example: there is no value-free science, although science does tell us about the 'nature of things'. Scientific truths certainly do describe possible behaviour and do not deny choice.

This rationalist trend also makes the values of Islam relatively compatible with political ideologies, and Nasution himself was not unsympathetic to the ideology of Pancasila. He read it as a possible intellectual justification for modernisation and development, which also allowed space for religion. But to hold this position is to come close to a 'rational' Islam, and the danger here is that revelation itself can be made into an ideology or, worse, reduced to one ideology among others. Pancasila, in fact, becomes a manifestation of Islam for the nation-state.

There is a serious implication here: are the new isnad and silsilah in time, are they conditioned in the modern world by the state and by science? The discussion in the seventeenth and eighteenth centuries was conducted from within Islam. This is not now a possibility, because with the best will in the world it is now hard to avoid the objedification of religion. The new isnad and silsilah are responsive to secularism to the extent that they may now even be conditioned by it. Time, and hence transmission through time, is now linear, so that timeless truths in Islam are now debatable in a place and in the circumstances of that place at a given time. This is the real challenge for Islam in contemporary Indonesia. The lessons of the historical seventeenth and eighteenth century transmissions are thus still with us.

# Bibliography


Ahmad Aijaz. "400 Year War—Moro Struggle in the Philippines", *Southeast Asia Chronicle,* No. 182 ( February 1982).

Ahmad Aziz. *Islamic Modernism in India and Pakistan, 1857-1964.* Oxford: Oxford University Press, 1967.

Ahmad, S. Maqbul. "Ibn Madjid," *The Encyclopedia of Islam*, 2nd edn. Leiden: E. J. Brill, 1960-.

Ajami Fouad. *The Arab Predicament.* New York: Cambridge University Press, 1982.

Akhavi Sharough, *Religion and Politics in Contemporary Iran.* Albany: SUNY Press, 1980.

Akiner Shirin. *Islamic Peoples of the Soviet Union.* London: Kegan Paul, 1983.

Azari Farah, ed. *Women of Iran.* London: Ithaca Press, 1983.

Bakhash Shaul. *The Reign of the Ayatollahs.* New York: Basic Books, 1984.

Banuazizi Ali, and Weiner Myron, eds. *The State, Religion, and Ethnic Politics: Afghanistan, Iran and Pakistan.* Syracuse: Syracuse University Press, 1986.

Behbehani Hashim S. H. *China's Foreign Policy in the Arab World, 1955-75.* London and Boston: Kegan Paul International, 1981.

Benard Cheryl, and Khalilzad Zalmay. *The Government of God": Iran's Islamic Republic.* New York: Columbia University Press, 1984.

Benda Harry J. *Continuity and Change in Southeast Asia.* New Haven: Yale University Southeast Asian Studies, 1972.

Bennigsen Alexandre, and Lemercier-Quelquejay Chantal. *Islam in the Soviet Union*. London: Pall Mall Press, 1967.

Bentley, Jerry H. *Old World Encounters: Cross-Cultural Contacts and Exchanges in Pre-Modern Times*. New York: Oxford University Press, 1993.

Bhacker, M. Reda. *Trade and Empire in Muscat and Zanzibar: Roots of British Domination*. London and New York: Routledge, 1992.

Bhattacharya, S. "The Indian Ocean in the Nineteenth and Early Twentieth Centuries," Satish Chandra, ed., *The Indian Ocean: Explorations in History, Commerce and Politics*. New Delhi: Sage Publications, 1987.

Carrere Helene d'Encausse. *Decline of an Empire: The Soviet Socialist Republics in Revolt*. Trans. Martin Sokolinsky and Henry A. LaFarge. New York: Harper & Row, 1981.

Chelkowski Peter J., ed. *Taziyeh: Ritual and Drama in Iran*. New York: New York University Press, 1979.

Crossette, Barbara. "Sultan Died a Hero, but His Name Is Now Sullied in a Religious Dispute," *The New York Times*. Feb. 1, 1990, p. A4.

Curtin, Philip D. *Cross-Cultural Trade in World History*. Cambridge: Cambridge University Press, 1984.

Dale, Stephen Frederic. *Islamic Society on the South Asian Frontier: The Mappilas of Malabar, 1498-1922*. Oxford: Clarendon Press, 1980.

Davis, David Brion. *Slavery and Human Progress*. New York: Oxford University Press, 1984.

Dawisha Adeed, ed. *Islam in Foreign Policy*. Cambridge and New York: Cambridge University Press, 1983.

Denny, Frederick Mathewson. *An Introduction to Islam*, 2nd edn. New York: Macmillan Publishing Company, 1994.

Donohue John J., and Esposito John L., eds. *Islam in Transition: Muslim Perspectives*. New York: Oxford University Press, 1982.

Dreyer June Teufel. *China's Forty Millions: Minority Nationalities and National Integration in the People's Republic of China*. Cambridge: Harvard University Press, 1976.

Eberhard Wolfram. *China's Minorities: Yesterday and Today*. Belmont, Calif.: Wadsworth, 1982.

Enayat Hamid. *Modern Islamic Political Thought*. Austin: University of Texas Press, 1982.

Endicott K. *An Analysis of Malay Magic*. Oxford: Clarendon Press, 1970.

Esposito John L., ed. *Islam and Development*. Syracuse: Syracuse University Press, 1982.

Fischer Michael M. J. *Iran: From Religious Discourse to Revolution*. Cambridge: Harvard University Press, 1980.

Gellner Ernest. *Muslim Society*. New York: Cambridge University Press, 1981.

George T. J. S. *Revolt in Mindanao: The Rise of Islam in Philippine Politics*. Kuala Lumpur: Oxford University Press, 1980.

Gowing Peter Gordon, and McAmis Robert, eds. *The Muslim Filipinos*. Manila: Solidaridad Publishing House, 1974.

Gowing Peter Gordon. *Muslim Filipinos – Heritage and Horizon*. Quezon City: New Day Publishers, 1979.

Hassan Mohammad Kamal. *Contemporary Muslim Religio-Political Thought in Indonesia: The Response to "New Order Modernization."* Kuala Lumpur: Dewan Bahasa dan Pustaka, 1980.

Hodgson, Marshall G. S. *The Venture of Islam*. 3 vols. Chicago: University of Chicago Press, 1974.

Hooker M. B., ed. *Islam in South-East Asia*. Leiden: E. J. Brill, 1983.

Hooker, M. B., ed. *Islam in South-East Asia*. Leiden: E. J. Brill, 1983.

Hourani, George. *Arab Seafaring in the Indian Ocean in Ancient and Medieval Times*. Princeton: Princeton University Press, 1951.

Ibrahim Ahmad, ed. *Readings on Islam in Southeast Asia*. Institute for Southeast Asian Studies. Forthcoming.

Israeli R. *The Crescent in the East Islam in Asia Minor*. London and Dublin: Curzon Press Ltd.; and Atlantic Highlands, N.J.: Humanities Press Inc., 1982.

Israeli Raphael, and Johns Anthony H., eds. *Islam in Asia*, Vol. 3, Southeast and East Asia. Jerusalem: Magnes Press, Hebrew University, 1984.

Itzkowitz, Norman, *Ottoman Empire and Islamic Tradition*. Chicago: University of Chicago Press, Phoenix Edition, 1980.

Jafri, Husain M. *Origins and Early Development of Shi'a Islam*. London: Longman Group Ltd., 1979.

Johns A. H. "Islam in Southeast Asia, Reflections and New Directions", *Indonesia* (Cornell) No. 19, 21-52.

Keddie Nikki R. *Iran: Religion, Politics and Society*. London: Frank Cass, 1980.

Keddie Nikki R., and Beck Lois, eds. *Women in the Muslim World*. Cambridge: Harvard University Press, 1978.

Keddie Nikki R., and Bovine M., eds. *Modern Iran*. Albany: SUNY Press, 1981.

Keddie Nikki R., and Cole Juan R. I. *Shiism and Social Protest*. New Haven, Yale University Press, 1986.

Khachikian, Lvon. "The Ledger of the Merchant Hovannes Joughayetsi," *Journal of the Asiatic Society*, vol. 8, no. 3. (1966).

Khalidi, Tarif. *Islamic Historiography: The Histories of Mas'udi*. Albany: State University of New York Press, 1975.

Kirkpatrick, William, ed. and trans. *Select Letters of Tippoo Sultan*. London, 1811.

Lambton Ann K. S. *State and Government in Medieval Islam*. Oxford: Oxford University Press, 1981.

Lubin Nancy. *Labour and Nationality in Soviet Central Asia: An Uneasy Compromise*. Princeton: Princeton University Press, 1985.

Ma Huan. *Ying-Yai Sheng-Lan, "The Overall Survey of the Ocean's Shores" (1433)*, trans. and introduced by J. V. G. Mills. Cambridge: The Hakluyt Society, 1970.

MacLean, Derryl. *Religion and Society in Arab Sind*. Leiden: E. J. Brill, 1989.

Madelung, W. "Khodja," *The Encyclopedia of Islam*, 2nd edn. Leiden: E. J. Brill, 1960-.

Majul Cesar A. *Muslims in the Philippines*. Quezon City: University of the Philippines Press for the Asian Center, 1973.

Makdisi, George. "The Sunni Revival," D. S. Richards, ed., *Islamic Civilisation, 950-1150*. Oxford: Bruno Cassirer Ltd., 1973.

Mastura Michael O. *Muslim Filipino Experience: A Collection of Essays*. Manila: Ministry of Muslim Affairs, 1984.

Means G. Malaysia: "Islam in a Plural Society," in C. Caldarela, ed., *Religion and Societies: Asia and the Middle East*. Boston: Mouton, 1982.

Milne R., and Mauzy D. *Politics and the Government of Malaysia*. Vancouver: University of British Columbia Press, 1980.

Momen Moojan. *Shi'ite Islam*. New Haven: Yale University Press, 1985.

Mortimer Edward. *Faith and Power*. New York: Random House, 1982.

Mottahedeh Roy. *The Mantle of the Prophet*. New York: Simon & Schuster, 1985.

Nagata J. *From Peasant Roots to Religious Values: The Reflowering of Malaysian Islam*. Vancouver: University of British Columbia Press, 1985.

Nashat Guity, ed. "Women and Revolution in Iran". Boulder, Col.: Westview Press, 1983.

Nightingale, Pamela. *Trade and Empire in Western India, 1784-1806*. Cambridge: Cambridge University Press, 1970.

Noble Lela Garner, and Suhkre Astri, "Muslims in the Philippines and Thailand," in Suhkre and Noble, eds., *Ethnic Conflict in International Relations*. New York: Praeger, 1977.

Noble Lela Garner. "Ethnicity and Philippine-Malaysian Relations," *Asian Survey*, 15/S ( May 1975), 453-72.

Noer Deliar. "The Modernist Muslim Movement in Indonesia". Singapore: Oxford University Press, 1973.

O'Brien, Patrick. "European Economic Development: The Contribution of the Periphery," *The Economic History Review*, vol. 35, no. 1 (Feb., 1982).

Olschki, Leonardo. *Marco Polo's Asia: An Introduction to His "Description of the World" called "Il Milione."* Berkeley: University of California Press, 1960.

Palat, Ravi, Kenneth Barr, James Matson, Vinay Bahl, and Nesar Ahmad. "The Incorporation and Peripheralization of South Asia, 1600-1950," *Review*, A Journal of the Fernand Braudel Center for the Study of Economics, Historical Systems, and Civilizations, vol. 10, no. 1 (Summer, 1986).

Piscatori James, ed. "Islam in the Political Process". Cambridge and New York: Cambridge University Press, 1983; reprinted 1984.

Poole Fred, and Vanzi Max. *Revolution in the Philippines*: "The United States in a Hall of Cracked Mirrors". New York: McGraw-Hill, 1984.

Rahman Fazlur. *Islam*, 2nd ed. Chicago: University of Chicago Press, 1979.

Ratnam K. J. *Communalism and the Political Process in Malaya*. Kuala Lumpur: University of Malaya, 1965.

Ray, Harapsad. "China and the 'Western Ocean' in the Fifteenth Century," Satish Chandra, ed., *The Indian Ocean: Explorations in History, Commerce and Politics*. New Delhi: Sage Publications, 1987.

Raychaudhuri, Tapan, and Irfan Habib. *The Cambridge History of India*, 2 vols, vol. 1, c. 1200-1750. Cambridge: Cambridge University Press, 1982.

Smith Jane, ed. *Women in Contemporary Muslim Societies*. Lewisburg, Pa.: Bucknell University Press, 1980.

Snodgrass D. *Inequality and Economic Development in Malaysia*. Kuala Lumpur: Oxford, 1980.

Steinberg David Joel. *The Philippines: A Singular and Plural Place*. Boulder, Col.: Westview Press, 1982.

Tabataba'i Muhammad H. *Shi'ite Islam*, 2nd ed. Albany: SUNY Press, 1979.

Tan Samuel K. *The Filipino Muslim Armed Struggle*, 1900- 1972. Manila: Filipinas Foundation, Inc., 1977.

Voll John Obert. *Islam, Continuity and Change in the Modern World*. Boulder, Col.: Westview Press, 1982.

von der F. Mehden "Islamic Resurgence in Malaysia," in J. Esposito, *Islam and Development*. Syracuse: Syracuse University Press, 1980.

Wang C. *Malaysia*. New York: Praeger, 1964.

Weiss Anita, ed. "Islamic Reassertion in Pakistan". Syracuse: Syracuse University Press, 1986.

Winzeler R. "Modern Religion, Society and Politics in Kelantan." Ph.D. dissertation. Chicago: University of Chicago, 1970.

Wright Robin. *Sacred Rage*. New York: Simon & Schuster, 1985.

# Index